CAMBRIDGE LIBRAR
Books of enduring sch

History

The books reissued in this series include accounts of historical events and movements by eye-witnesses and contemporaries, as well as landmark studies that assembled significant source materials or developed new historiographical methods. The series includes work in social, political and military history on a wide range of periods and regions, giving modern scholars ready access to influential publications of the past.

History of the United States of America

Henry Adams (1838–1918), journalist, novelist, and historian, was the great-grandson of John Adams and grandson of John Quincy Adams, both presidents of the United States. A professor of medieval history at Harvard whose areas of research were wide-ranging, he was deeply interested in the evolution of democracy in the United States. While Adams is best remembered for his autobiography *The Education of Henry Adams* (1907), for which he was posthumously awarded a Pulitzer prize, his nine-volume history of the United States during the presidencies of Jefferson and Madison (1801–17), which was published 1889–91, has been hailed as one of the greatest historical works in English. Adams was an advocate of scientific history, and this monumental work adheres to its principles, considering social trends and circumstances rather than focusing on particular events. Volume 9, on Madison's second administration (1813–17), also includes an index to all volumes.

Cambridge University Press has long been a pioneer in the reissuing of out-of-print titles from its own backlist, producing digital reprints of books that are still sought after by scholars and students but could not be reprinted economically using traditional technology. The Cambridge Library Collection extends this activity to a wider range of books which are still of importance to researchers and professionals, either for the source material they contain, or as landmarks in the history of their academic discipline.

Drawing from the world-renowned collections in the Cambridge University Library, and guided by the advice of experts in each subject area, Cambridge University Press is using state-of-the-art scanning machines in its own Printing House to capture the content of each book selected for inclusion. The files are processed to give a consistently clear, crisp image, and the books finished to the high quality standard for which the Press is recognised around the world. The latest print-on-demand technology ensures that the books will remain available indefinitely, and that orders for single or multiple copies can quickly be supplied.

The Cambridge Library Collection will bring back to life books of enduring scholarly value (including out-of-copyright works originally issued by other publishers) across a wide range of disciplines in the humanities and social sciences and in science and technology.

History of the United States of America

During the Second Administration of James Madison 3

VOLUME 9

HENRY ADAMS

CAMBRIDGE
UNIVERSITY PRESS

CAMBRIDGE UNIVERSITY PRESS

Cambridge, New York, Melbourne, Madrid, Cape Town,
Singapore, São Paolo, Delhi, Tokyo, Mexico City

Published in the United States of America by Cambridge University Press, New York

www.cambridge.org
Information on this title: www.cambridge.org/9781108033107

© in this compilation Cambridge University Press 2011

This edition first published 1892
This digitally printed version 2011

ISBN 978-1-108-03310-7 Paperback

This book reproduces the text of the original edition. The content and language reflect
the beliefs, practices and terminology of their time, and have not been updated.

Cambridge University Press wishes to make clear that the book, unless originally published
by Cambridge, is not being republished by, in association or collaboration with, or
with the endorsement or approval of, the original publisher or its successors in title.

THE

SECOND ADMINISTRATION

OF

JAMES MADISON

1813—1817

HISTORY OF THE UNITED STATES.
BY
HENRY ADAMS.

Vols. I. and II.—The First Administration of Jefferson. 1801-1805.

Vols. III. and IV.—The Second Administration of Jefferson. 1805-1809.

Vols. V. and VI.—The First Administration of Madison. 1809-1813.

Vols. VII., VIII., and IX.—The Second Administration of Madison. 1813-1817. With an Index to the Entire Work.

HISTORY

OF THE

UNITED STATES OF AMERICA

DURING THE SECOND ADMINISTRATION OF

JAMES MADISON

By HENRY ADAMS

Vol. IX.

LONDON: G. P. PUTNAM'S SONS
NEW YORK: CHARLES SCRIBNER'S SONS
1892

Copyright, 1890, by Charles Scribner's Sons,
for the United States of America.

Printed by John Wilson and Son,
Cambridge, Mass., U.S.A.

CONTENTS OF VOL. IX.

CHAPTER		PAGE
I.	THE MEETING AT GHENT	1
II.	THE TREATY OF GHENT	24
III.	CLOSE OF HOSTILITIES	54
IV.	DECLINE OF MASSACHUSETTS	80
V.	PEACE LEGISLATION	104
VI.	RETIREMENT OF MADISON	126
VII.	ECONOMICAL RESULTS	154
VIII.	RELIGIOUS AND POLITICAL THOUGHT	175
IX.	LITERATURE AND ART	198
X.	AMERICAN CHARACTER	219

LIST OF MAPS AND PLANS	243
GENERAL INDEX	245

HISTORY OF THE UNITED STATES.

CHAPTER I.

DURING the spring and summer of 1814 the task of diplomacy was less hopeful than that of arms. Brown and Izard with extreme difficulty defended the frontier; but Gallatin and Bayard could find no starting-point for negotiation. Allowed by Castlereagh's courtesy to visit England, they crossed the Channel in April, and established themselves in London. There Gallatin remained until June 21, waiting for the British government to act, and striving with tact, caution, and persistency to bring both governments on common ground; but the attempt was hopeless. England was beside herself with the intoxication of European success.

Although the English newspapers expressed a false idea of the general will, and were even at cross purposes with the Ministry in American matters, their tone was in some respects an indifferent barometer for measuring the elation or depression of the public temper, and exercised some influence, rather apparent than real, on the momentary attitudes of government. Had Castlereagh and his colleagues been really controlled by the press, no American peace could have been made. Whatever spirit of friendship for America might exist was necessarily silent, and only extravagant enmity found expression either in the press or in society.

Perhaps because ministers were believed to wish for peace with the United States, the London "Times," which was not a ministerial journal, made itself conspicuous in demanding war. The "Times" had not previously shown a vindictive spirit, but it represented the Wellesley and Canning interest, which could discover no better course than that of being more English than England, and more patriotic than the Government. The "Times" was always ably written and well edited, but its language toward the United States showed too strong a connection with that of the Federalists, from whose public and private expressions the press of England formed its estimate of American character.

The "Times" indulged to excess in the pleasure of its antipathy. Next to Napoleon, the chief victim of English hatred was Madison. For so mild a man Madison possessed a remarkable faculty of exciting invective. The English press surpassed the American Federalists in their allusions to him, and the "Times" was second to no English newspaper in the energy of its vituperation. "The lunatic ravings of the philosophic statesman of Washington" were in its political category of a piece with "his spaniel-like fawning on the Emperor of Russia.[1] . . . The most abject of the tools of the deposed tyrant; . . . doubtless he expected to be named Prince of the Potomack or Grand Duke of Virginia."[2] The "Sun" somewhat less abusively spoke of "that contemptible wretch Madison, and his gang;"[3] but the "Times" habitually called him liar and impostor.

"Having disposed of all our enemies in Europe," the "Times" in the middle of April turned its attention to the United States. "Let us have no cant of moderation," was its starting-point. "There is no public feeling in the country stronger than that of indignation against the Americans; . . . conduct so base, so loathsome, so hateful. . . . As we urged the principle, No peace with Bonaparte! so we must maintain the doctrine of, No peace with James Madison!"[4] To this rule the "Times" steadily adhered with a degree of ill-temper not easily to be described, and with practical objects freely expressed. "Mr. Madison's dirty, swindling manœuvres in respect to Louisiana and the Floridas remain to be punished," it declared April 27; and May 17 it pursued the idea: "He must fall a victim to the just vengeance of the Federalists. Let us persevere. Let us unmask the impostor. . . . Who cares about the impudence

---

[1] The Times, Feb. 4 and 10, 1814.
[2] The Times, April 23, 1814.
[3] The Sun, Aug. 4, 1814.
[4] The Times, April 15, 1814.

which they call a doctrine? . . . We shall demand indemnity. . . . We shall insist on security for Canada. . . . We shall inquire a little into the American title to Louisiana; and we shall not permit the base attack on Florida to go unpunished." May 18 it declared that Madison had put himself on record as a liar in the cause of his Corsican master. "He has lived an impostor, and he deserves to meet the fate of a traitor. That fate now stares him in the face." May 24 the "Times" resumed the topic: "They are struck to the heart with terror for their impending punishment; and oh may no false liberality, no mistaken lenity, no weak and cowardly policy, interpose to save them from the blow! Strike! chastise the savages, for such they are! . . . With Madison and his perjured set no treaty can be made, for no oath can bind them." When British commissioners were at last announced as ready to depart for Ghent to negotiate for peace with the United States, June 2, the "Times" gave them instructions: "Our demands may be couched in a single word, — Submission!"

The "Morning Post," a newspaper then carrying higher authority than the "Times," used language if possible more abusive, and even discovered, Jan. 18, 1814, "a new trait in the character of the American government. Enjoying the reputation of being the most unprincipled and the most contemptible on the face of the earth, they were already known to be impervious to any noble sentiment; but it is only of late that we find them insensible of the shame of defeat, destitute even of the brutish quality of being beaten into a sense of their unworthiness and their incapacity." Of Madison the "Morning Post" held the lowest opinion. He was "a despot in disguise ; a miniature imitation" and miserable tool of Bonaparte, who wrote his Annual Message : a senseless betrayer of his country.[1]

The "Times" and "Morning Post" were independent newspapers, and spoke only for themselves; but the "Courier" was supposed to draw inspiration from the Government, and commonly received the first knowledge of ministers' intentions. In temper the "Courier" seemed obliged to vie with its less favored rivals. The President's Annual Message of 1813 resembled in its opinion "all the productions of that vain and vulgar Cabinet;" it was "a compound of canting and hypocrisy, of exaggeration and falsehood, of coarseness without strength, of assertions without proof, of the meanest prejudices, and of the most malignant passions; of undisguised hatred of Great Britain, and of ill-concealed partiality and servility toward France."[2] "We know of no man for whom we feel greater contempt than for Mr. Madison," said the "Courier" of May 24. These illustrations of what the "Courier" called "exaggeration and falsehood, of coarseness without strength, of assertions without proof, of the meanest prejudices, and of the most malignant passions" were probably

---

[1] The Morning Post, Jan. 27 and Feb. 1, 1814.
[2] The Courier, Jan. 27, 1814.

in some degree a form as used by the "Courier," which would at a hint from the Ministry adopt a different tone; but announcements of official acts and intentions were more serious, and claimed more careful attention.

Immediately after the capitulation of Paris, March 31, the Ministry turned its attention to the United States, and the "Courier" announced, April 15, that twenty thousand men were to go from the Garonne to America. Mr. Madison, the "Courier" added, had "made a pretty kettle of fish of it." Twenty thousand men were about two thirds of Wellington's English force, and their arrival in America would, as every Englishman believed, insure the success of the campaign. Not until these troops were embarked would the Ministry begin to negotiate; but in the middle of May the military measures were complete, and then the "Courier" began to prepare the public mind for terms of peace.

These terms were the same as those announced by the "Times," except that the "Courier" did not object to treating with Madison. The United States were to be interdicted the fisheries; Spain was to be supported in recovering Louisiana; the right of impressment must be expressly conceded, — anything short of this would be unwise and a disappointment. "There are points which must be conceded by America before we can put an end to the contest."[1] Such language offered no apparent hope of peace; yet what-

[1] The Courier, May 19 and 24, 1814.

ever hope existed lay in Castlereagh, who inspired it. Extravagant as the demands were, they fell short of the common expectation. The "Courier" admitted the propriety of negotiation; it insisted neither on Madison's retirement nor on a division of the Union, and it refrained from asserting the whole British demand, or making it an ultimatum.

The chief pressure on the Ministry came from Canada, and could not be ignored. The Canadian government returned to its old complaint that Canadian interests had been ignorantly and wantonly sacrificed by the treaty of 1783, and that the opportunity to correct the wrong should not be lost. The Canadian official "Gazette" insisted that the United States should be required to surrender the northern part of the State of New York, and that both banks of the St. Lawrence should be Canadian property.[1] A line from Plattsburg to Sackett's Harbor would satisfy this necessity; but to secure Canadian interests, the British government should further insist on acquiring the east bank of the Niagara River, and on a guaranty of the Indian Territory from Sandusky to Kaskaskias, with the withdrawal of American military posts in the Northwest. A pamphlet was published in May to explain the subject for the use of the British negotiators, and the required territorial cessions were marked on a map.[2] The control of

[1] Niles, vi. 322.
[2] Compressed view of the Points to be discussed in treating with America. London, 1814.

the Lakes, the Ohio River as the Indian boundary, and the restitution of Louisiana were the chief sacrifices wished from the United States. The cession of a part of Maine was rather assumed than claimed, and the fisheries were to be treated as wholly English. A memorial from Newfoundland, dated Nov. 8, 1813,[1] pointed out the advantages which the war had already brought to British trade and fisheries by the exclusion of American competition, to the result of doubling the number of men employed on the Labrador shores; and the memorialists added, —

"They cannot too often urge the important policy . . . of wholly excluding foreigners from sharing again in the advantages of a fishery from which a large proportion of our best national defence will be derived."

British confidence was at its highest point when the Emperor of Russia and the King of Prussia visited London, June 7, and received an enthusiastic welcome. Gallatin obtained an interview with the Czar, June 17, and hoped that Russian influence might moderate British demands; but the Czar could give him no encouragement.[2] Gallatin wrote home an often-quoted despatch, dated June 13, warning the President that fifteen or twenty thousand men were on their way to America, and that the United States could expect no assistance from Europe.

"I have also the most perfect conviction," Gallatin continued, "that under the existing unpropitious circumstances of the world, America cannot by a continuance

[1] Niles, vi. 238.   [2] Adams's Gallatin, p. 514.

of the war compel Great Britain to yield any of the maritime points in dispute, and particularly to agree to any satisfactory arrangement on the subject of impressment; and that the most favorable terms of peace that can be expected are the *status ante bellum.*"

Even these terms, Gallatin added, depended on American success in withstanding the shock of the campaign. He did not say that at the time he wrote, the *status ante bellum* would be scouted by public opinion in England as favorable to the United States; but his estimate of the situation was more nearly exact than though he had consulted only the apparent passions of the British press.

"Lord Castlereagh," wrote Gallatin to Clay,[1] "is, according to the best information I can collect, the best disposed man in the Cabinet." Yet Castlereagh did not venture at that stage to show a disposition for peace. He delayed the negotiation, perhaps wisely, six weeks after the American negotiators had assembled at Ghent; and his instructions[2] to the British commissioners, dated July 28, reflected the demands of the press. They offered, not the *status ante bellum*, but the *uti possidetis*, as the starting-point of negotiation. "The state of possession must be considered as the territorial arrangement which would revive upon a peace, except so far as the same may be modified by any new treaty." The state of possession, in view of the orders that had then been

[1] Gallatin to Clay, April 22, 1814; Adams's Gallatin, p. 506.
[2] Castlereagh Correspondence, x. 67.

given, or were to be given, for the invasion of the United States, was likely to cost the Americans half of Maine, between the Penobscot and the Passamaquoddy; Plattsburg, and the northern part of New York, Vermont, and New Hampshire; Fort Niagara, Mackinaw, and possibly New Orleans and Mobile. Besides this concession of the *uti possidetis*, or military occupation at the date of peace, the Americans were required at the outset to admit as a *sine qua non*, or condition precedent to any negotiation, that England's Indian allies, the tribes of the Northwestern Territory, should be included in the pacification, and that a definite boundary should be assigned to them under a mutual guaranty of both Powers. Eastport, or Moose Island, and the fishing privileges were to be regarded as British. With these instructions of July 28, the British commissioners, early in August, started for Ghent.

Between Castlereagh's ideas and those of Madison no relation existed. Gallatin and his colleagues at Ghent were provided with two sets of instructions. The first set had been written in 1813, for the expected negotiation at Petersburg. The second set was written in January, 1814, and was brought to Europe by Clay. Neither authorized the American commissioners to discuss such conditions as Castlereagh proposed. The President gave his negotiators authority to deal with questions of maritime law; but even there they were allowed to exercise no discretion on the chief issue in dispute. Monroe's latest letter, dated January 28, was emphatic. "On impressment, as to the right of the United States to be exempted from it, I have nothing to add," said the secretary;[1] "the sentiments of the President have undergone no change on that important subject. This degrading practice must cease; our flag must protect the crew, or the United States cannot consider themselves an independent nation." The President would consent to exclude all British seamen, except those already naturalized, from American vessels, and to stipulate the surrender of British deserters; but the express abandonment of impressment was a *sine qua non* of treaty. "If this encroachment of Great Britain is not provided against," said Monroe, "the United States have appealed to arms in vain. If your efforts to accomplish it should fail, all further negotiations will cease, and you will return home without delay."

On territorial questions the two governments were equally wide apart. So far from authorizing a cession of territorial rights, Monroe instructed the American commissioners, both at St. Petersburg and at Ghent, "to bring to view the advantage to both countries which is promised by a transfer of the upper parts and even the whole of Canada to the United States."[2] The instructions of January 1

[1] Instructions of Jan. 28, 1814; State Papers, Foreign Affairs, iii. 701.
[2] Monroe's Instructions of June 23, 1813; MSS. State Department Records.

and January 28, 1814, reiterated the reasoning which should decide England voluntarily to cede Canada. "Experience has shown that Great Britain cannot participate in the dominion and navigation of the Lakes without incurring the danger of an early renewal of the war." [1]

These instructions were subsequently omitted from the published documents, probably because the Ghent commissioners decided not to act upon them; [2] but when the American negotiators met their British antagonists at Ghent, each party was under orders to exclude the other, if possible, from the Lakes, and the same divergence of opinion in regard to the results of two years' war extended over the whole field of negotiation. The British were ordered to begin by a *sine qua non* in regard to the Indians, which the Americans had no authority to consider. The Americans were ordered to impose a *sine qua non* in regard to impressments, which the British were forbidden to concede. The British were obliged to claim the basis of possession; the Americans were not even authorized to admit the status existing before the war. The Americans were required to negotiate about blockades, contraband and maritime rights of neutrals; the British could not admit such subjects into dispute. The British regarded their concessions of fishing-rights as terminated by

---

[1] Instructions of Jan. 1 and Jan. 28, 1814; MSS. State Department Records.

[2] Diary of J. Q. Adams, iii. 51.

the war; the Americans could not entertain the idea.

The diplomacy that should produce a treaty from such discordant material must show no ordinary excellence; yet even from that point of view the prospect was not encouraging. The British government made a peculiar choice of negotiators. The chief British commissioner, Lord Gambier, was unknown in diplomacy, or indeed in foreign affairs. A writer in the London "Morning Chronicle" of August 9 expressed the general surprise that Government could make no better selection for the chief of its commission than Lord Gambier, "who was a post-captain in 1794, and happened to fight the 'Defence' decently in Lord Howe's action; who slumbered for some time as a Junior Lord of the Admiralty; who sung psalms, said prayers, and assisted in the burning of Copenhagen, for which he was made a lord."

Gambier showed no greater fitness for his difficult task than was to be expected from his training; and the second member of the commission, Henry Goulburn, could not supply Gambier's deficiencies. Goulburn was Under-Secretary of State to Lord Bathurst; he was a very young man, but a typical under-secretary, combining some of Francis James Jackson's temper with the fixed opinions of the elder Rose, and he had as little idea of diplomacy as was to be expected from an Under-Secretary of State for the colonies. The third and last member was William Adams, Doctor of Civil Law, whose professional knowledge was doubtless supposed to be valuable to the commission, but who was an unknown man, and remained one.

Experience had not convinced the British government that in dealing with the United States it required the best ability it could command. The mistake made by Lord Shelburne in 1783 was repeated by Lord Castlereagh in 1814. The miscalculation of relative ability which led the Foreign Office to assume that Gambier, Goulburn, and William Adams were competent to deal with Gallatin, J. Q. Adams, J. A. Bayard, Clay, and Russell was not reasonable. Probably the whole British public service, including Lords and Commons, could not at that day have produced four men competent to meet Gallatin, J. Q. Adams, Bayard, and Clay on the ground of American interests; and when Castlereagh opposed to them Gambier, Goulburn, and Dr. Adams, he sacrificed whatever advantage diplomacy offered; for in diplomacy as in generalship, the individual commanded success.

The only serious difficulty in the American commission was its excess of strength. By a natural reaction against the attempt to abolish diplomatic offices, the United States government sent into diplomacy its most vigorous men. Under favorable conditions, four minds and wills of so decided a character could not easily work together; but in the Ghent commission an additional difficulty was created by the unfortunate interference of the Senate. Originally Gallatin, as was due to his age, services, and ability, had been the head of the St. Petersburg commission; but the Senate refused to confirm the appointment. The President at last removed Gallatin from the Treasury, and renominated him as a member of the Ghent commission after the other members had been nominated and confirmed. The Senate then gave its approval, — thus making Gallatin the last member of the commission instead of the first, and placing J. Q. Adams above them all.

Gallatin was peculiarly fitted to moderate a discordant body like the negotiators, while Adams was by temperament little suited to the post of moderator, and by circumstances ill-qualified to appear as a proper representative of the commission in the eyes of its other members. Unless Gallatin were one of the loftiest characters and most loyal natures ever seen in American politics, Adams's chance of success in controlling the board was not within reasonable hope. Gallatin was six years the senior, and represented the President, with the authority of close and continuous personal friendship. The board, including Adams himself, instinctively bowed to Gallatin's authority; but they were deferential to no one else, least of all to their nominal head. Bayard, whose age was the same as that of Adams, was still in name a Federalist; and although his party trusted him little more than it trusted Adams or William Pinkney, who had avowedly become Republicans, he was not the more disposed to follow Adams's leadership. Clay, though ten years their junior, was the most difficult of all to control; and Jonathan Russell, though a New Englander, preferred Clay's social charm, and perhaps also his political prospects, to the somewhat repellent temper and more than doubtful popularity of Adams.

Personal rivalry and jealousies counted for much in such a group; but these were not the only obstacles to Adams's influence. By a misfortune commonly reserved for men of the strongest wills, he represented no one but himself and a powerless minority. His State repudiated and, in a manner, ostracized him. Massachusetts gave him no support, even in defending her own rights; by every means in her power she deprived him of influence, and loaded him with the burden of her own unpopularity. Adams represented a community not only hostile to the war, but avowedly laboring to produce peace by means opposed to those employed at Ghent. If the Ghent commission should succeed in making a treaty, it could do so only by some sacrifice of Massachusetts which would ruin Adams at home. If the Ghent commission should fail, Adams must be equally ruined by any peace produced through the treasonable intrigues or overt rebellion of his State.

Such a head to a commission so constituted needed all the force of character which Adams had, and some qualities he did not possess, in order to retain enough influence to shape any project into a treaty that he could consent to sign; while Gallatin's singular tact and nobility of character were never more likely to fail than in the effort to make allowance for the difficulties of his chief's position. Had Castlereagh improved the opportunity by sending to Ghent one competent diplomatist, or even a well-informed and intelligent man of business, like Alexander Baring, he might probably have succeeded in isolating Adams, and in negotiating with the other four commissioners a treaty sacrificing Massachusetts.

The five American commissioners were ready to negotiate in June; but Castlereagh, for obvious reasons, wished delay, and deferred action until August, doubtless intending to prevent the signature of a treaty on the basis of *uti possidetis* until after September, when Sherbrooke and Prevost should have occupied the territory intended to be held. In May and June no one in England, unless it were Cobbett, entertained more than a passing doubt of British success on land and water; least of all did the three British commissioners expect to yield British demands. They came to impose terms, or to break negotiation. They were not sent to yield any point in dispute, or to seek a cessation of arms.

At one o'clock on the afternoon of August 8, the first conference took place in the Hotel des Pays Bas at Ghent. After the usual civilities and forms had passed, Goulburn took the lead, and presented the points which he and his colleagues were authorized to discuss, — (1) Impressment and allegiance; (2)

the Indians and their boundary, a *sine qua non;* (3) the Canadian boundary; (4) the privilege of landing and drying fish within British jurisdiction. Goulburn declared that it was not intended to contest the right of the United States to the fisheries, by which he probably meant the deep-sea fisheries; and he was understood to disavow the intention of acquiring territory by the revision of the Canada boundary; but he urged an immediate answer upon the question whether the Americans were instructed on the point made a *sine qua non* by the British government.

The Americans, seeing as yet only a small part of the British demands, were not so much surprised at Goulburn's points as unable to answer them. The next day they replied in conference that they had no authority to admit either Indian boundary or fisheries into question, being without instructions on these points; and in their turn presented subjects of discussion, — Blockades and Indemnities; but professed themselves willing to discuss everything.

In the conversation following this reply, the British commissioners, with some apparent unwillingness, avowed the intention of erecting the Indian Territory into a barrier between the British possessions and the United States; and the American commissioners declined even to retire for consultation on the possibility of agreeing to such an article. The British commissioners then proposed to suspend conferences until they could receive further instructions, and their wish was followed. Both parties sent despatches to their Governments.

Lord Castlereagh was prompt. As soon as was reasonably possible he sent more precise instructions. Dated August 14,[1] these supplementary instructions gave to those of July 28 a distinct outline. They proposed the Indian boundary fixed by the Treaty of Greenville for the permanent barrier between British and American dominion, beyond which neither government should acquire land. They claimed also a "rectification" of the Canadian frontier, and the cession of Fort Niagara and Sackett's Harbor, besides a permanent prohibition on the United States from keeping either naval forces or land fortifications on the Lakes. Beyond these demands the British commissioners were not for the present to go, nor were they to ask for a direct cession of territory for Canada "with any view to an acquisition of territory as such, but for the purpose of securing her possessions and preventing future disputes;"[2] yet a small cession of land in Maine was necessary for a road from Halifax to Quebec, and an arrangement of the Northwestern boundary was required to coincide with the free navigation of the Mississippi.

As soon as the new instructions reached Ghent the British commissioners summoned the Americans to another conference, August 19; and Goulburn, read-

[1] Castlereagh Correspondence, x. 86.
[2] Note of British Commissioners, Aug. 19, 1814; State Papers, Foreign Affairs, iii. 710.

ing from Castlereagh's despatch, gave to the Americans a clear version of its contents.[1] When he had finished, Gallatin asked what was to be done with the American citizens — perhaps one hundred thousand in number — already settled beyond the Greenville line, in Ohio, Indiana, Illinois, and Michigan? Goulburn and Dr. Adams replied that these people must shift for themselves. They added also that Moose Island and Eastport belonged to Great Britain as indisputably as the county of Northamptonshire, and were not a subject for discussion; but they would not then make a *sine qua non* of the proposition regarding the Lakes. The conference ended, leaving the Americans convinced that their answer to these demands would close the negotiation. Clay alone, whose knowledge of the Western game of brag stood him in good stead, insisted that the British would recede.[2]

The British commissioners the next day, August 20, sent an official note containing their demands, and the Americans before sending their reply forwarded the note to America, with despatches dated August 19 and 20, announcing that they intended to return "a unanimous and decided negative."[3] They then undertook the task of drawing up their reply. Upon Adams as head of the commission fell

[1] Diary of J. Q. Adams, iii. 17, 18.
[2] Diary of J. Q. Adams, iii. 20, 101.
[3] Despatch of Aug. 19, 1814; State Papers, Foreign Affairs, iii. 708.

the duty of drafting formal papers, — a duty which, without common consent, no other member could assume. His draft met with little mercy, and the five gentlemen sat until eleven o'clock of August 24, " sifting, erasing, patching, and amending until we were all wearied, though none of us was yet satiated with amendment." At the moment when they gave final shape to the note which they believed would render peace impossible, the army of General Ross was setting fire to the Capitol at Washington, and President Madison was seeking safety in the Virginia woods.

Only to persons acquainted with the difficulties of its composition did the American note of August 24 show signs of its diverse origin.[1] In dignified temper, with reasoning creditable to its authors and decisive on its issues, it assured the British negotiators that any such arrangement as they required for the Indians was contrary to precedent in public law, was not founded on reciprocity, and was unnecessary for its professed object in regard to the Indians. The other demands were equally inadmissible : —

"They are founded neither on reciprocity, nor on any of the usual bases of negotiation, neither on that of *uti possidetis* nor of *status ante bellum*. They are above all dishonorable to the United States in demanding from them to abandon territory and a portion of their citizens; to admit a foreign interference in their domestic concerns, and to cease to exercise their natural rights

[1] Note of Aug. 24, 1814; State Papers, Foreign Affairs, iii. 711.

on their own shores and in their own waters. A treaty concluded on such terms would be but an armistice."

The negotiators were ready to terminate the war, both parties restoring whatever territory might have been taken, and reserving their rights over their respective seamen; but such demands as were made by the British government could not be admitted even for reference.

The American reply was sent to the British commissioners August 25, " and will bring the negotiation," remarked J. Q. Adams, " very shortly to a close."[1] The American commissioners prepared to quit Ghent and return to their several posts, while the British commissioners waited for instructions from London. Even Gallatin, who had clung to the hope that he could effect an arrangement, abandoned the idea, and believing that the British government had adopted a system of conquest, prepared for an immediate return to America.[2] Goulburn also notified his Government that the negotiation was not likely to continue, and reported some confidential warnings from Bayard that such conditions of peace would not only insure war, but would sacrifice the Federalist party. "It has not made the least impression upon me or upon my colleagues," reported Goulburn to Bathurst.[3]

[1] Diary of J. Q. Adams, Aug. 25, 1814, iii. 23.
[2] Adams's Gallatin, p. 524.
[3] Goulburn to Bathurst, Aug. 23, 1814; Wellington, Supplementary Despatches, ix. 189.

At that point the negotiation remained stationary for two months, kept alive by Liverpool, Castlereagh, and Bathurst, while they waited for the result of their American campaign. The despatch of August 20 crossed the Atlantic, and was communicated to Congress October 10, together with all other papers connected with the negotiation; but not until October 25 did the American commissioners write again to their Government.

CHAPTER II.

THE British note of August 19 and the American rejoinder of August 24, brought about a situation where Lord Castlereagh's influence could make itself felt. Castlereagh had signed the British instructions of July 28 and August 14,[1] and himself brought the latter to Ghent, where he passed August 19, before going to Paris on his way to the Congress at Vienna. He was at Ghent when Goulburn and his colleagues held their conference and wrote their note of August 19;[2] and he could not be supposed ignorant of their language or acts. Yet when he received at Paris letters from Goulburn, dated August 24 and 26,[3] he expressed annoyance that the American commissioners should have been allowed to place England in the attitude of continuing the war for purposes of conquest, and still more that the British commissioners should be willing to accept that issue and break off negotiation upon it. In a letter

[1] Castlereagh Correspondence, x. 67, 86.
[2] Diary of J. Q. Adams, Aug. 19 and 20, 1814, iii. 19, 21.
[3] Goulburn to Bathurst, Aug. 24, 1814; Wellington Supplementary Despatches, ix. 190. Goulburn to Castlereagh, Aug. 26, 1814; Wellington Supplementary Despatches, ix. 193.

to Lord Bathurst, who took charge of the negotiation in his absence, Castlereagh suggested ideas altogether different from those till then advanced in England.[1]

"The substance of the question is," said Castlereagh, "Are we prepared to continue the war for territorial arrangements? And if not, is this the best time to make our peace, saving all our rights, and claiming the fisheries, which they do not appear to question? In which case the territorial questions might be reserved for ulterior discussion. Or is it desirable to take the chance of the campaign, and then to be governed by circumstances? . . . If we thought an immediate peace desirable, as they are ready to waive all the abstract questions, perhaps they might be prepared to sign a provisional article of Indian peace as distinct from limits, and relinquish their pretensions to the islands in Passamaquoddy Bay, and possibly to admit minor adjustments of frontier, including a right of communication from Quebec to Halifax across their territory. But while I state this, I feel the difficulty of so much letting down the question under present circumstances."

At the same time Castlereagh wrote to Goulburn, directing him to wait at Ghent for new instructions from London.[2] Lord Liverpool shared his disapproval of the manner in which the British commissioners had managed the case, and replied to Castlereagh,

[1] Castlereagh to Bathurst, Aug. 28. 1814: Castlereagh Correspondence, x. 100.
[2] Castlereagh to Goulburn, Aug. 28, 1814; Castlereagh Correspondence, x. 102.

September 2, that the Cabinet had already acted in the sense he wished:[1] —

"Our commissioners had certainly taken a very erroneous view of our policy. If the negotiation had been allowed to break off upon the two notes already presented, or upon such an answer as they were disposed to return, I am satisfied that the war would have become quite popular in America."

The idea that the war might become popular in America was founded chiefly on the impossibility of an Englishman's conceiving the contrary; but in truth the Ministry most feared that the war might become unpopular in England.

"It is very material to throw the rupture of the negotiation, if it is to take place, upon the Americans," wrote Liverpool, the same day, to the Duke of Wellington;[2] "and not to allow them to say that we have brought forward points as ultimata which were only brought forward for discussion, and at the desire of the American commissioners themselves. The American note is a most impudent one, and, as to all its reasoning, capable of an irresistible answer."

New instructions were accordingly approved in Cabinet.[3] Drawn by Bathurst, and dated September 1, they contained what Liverpool considered an "irresistible answer" to the American note of August 24;

[1] Liverpool to Castlereagh, Sept. 2, 1814; Wellington Supplementary Despatches, ix. 214.

[2] Liverpool to Wellington, Sept. 2, 1814; Wellington Supplementary Despatches, ix. 212.

[3] Draft of note, etc., Sept. 1, 1814; Wellington Supplementary Despatches, ix. 245.

but their force of logic was weakened by the admission that the previous British demands, though certainly stated as a *sine qua non*, were in reality not to be regarded as such. In private this retreat was covered by the pretext that it was intended only to keep the negotiation alive until better terms could be exacted.

"We cannot expect that the negotiation will proceed at present," continued Liverpool's letter to Castlereagh; "but I think it not unlikely, after our note has been delivered in, that the American commissioners will propose to refer the subject to their Government. In that case the negotiation may be adjourned till the answer is received, and we shall know the result of the campaign before it can be resumed. If our commander does his duty, I am persuaded we shall have acquired by our arms every point on the Canadian frontier which we ought to insist on keeping."

Lord Gambier and his colleagues communicated their new instructions to the American negotiators in a long note dated September 4, and were answered by a still longer note dated September 9, which was also sent to London, and considered in Cabinet. Bathurst felt no anxiety about the negotiation in its actual stage. Goulburn wrote to him that "as long as we answer their notes, I believe that they will be ready to give us replies," and urged only that Sir George Prevost should hasten his reluctant movements in Canada.[1]

[1] Goulburn to Bathurst, Sept. 5 and 16, 1814; Wellington Supplementary Despatches, ix. 221, 265.

Bathurst wrote more instructions, dated September 16, directing his commissioners to abandon the demands for Indian territory and exclusive control of the Lakes, and to ask only that the Indians should be included in the peace.[1] The British commissioners sent their note with these concessions to the Americans September 19; and then for the first time the Americans began to suspect the possibility of serious negotiation. For six weeks they had dealt only with the question whether they should negotiate at all.

The demand that the Indians should be included in the treaty was one that under favorable circumstances the Americans would have rejected; but none of them seriously thought of rejecting it as their affairs then stood. When the American commissioners discussed the subject among themselves, September 20, Adams proposed to break off the negotiation on that issue; but Gallatin good-naturedly overruled him, and Adams would not himself, on cool reflection, have ventured to take such responsibility. Indeed, he suggested an article for an Indian amnesty, practically accepting the British demand.[2] He also yielded to Gallatin the ungrateful task of drafting the answers to the British notes; and thus Gallatin became in effect the head of the commission.

All Gallatin's abilities were needed to fill the place. In his entire public life he had never been required to

[1] Draft of note, etc., Sept. 16, 1814; Wellington Supplementary Despatches, ix. 263.
[2] Diary of J. Q. Adams, Sept. 20, 1814, iii. 38.

manage so unruly a set of men. The British commissioners were trying, and especially Goulburn was aggressive in temper and domineering in tone; but with them Gallatin had little trouble. Adams and Clay were persons of a different type, as far removed from British heaviness as they were from the Virginian ease of temper which marked the Cabinet of Jefferson, or the incompetence which characterized that of Madison. Gallatin was obliged to exert all his faculties to control his colleagues; but whenever he succeeded, he enjoyed the satisfaction of feeling that he had colleagues worth controlling. They were bent on combat, if not with the British, at all events with each other; and Gallatin was partly amused and partly annoyed by the unnecessary energy of their attitude.

The first divergence occurred in framing the reply to the British note of September 19, which while yielding essentials made a series of complaints against the United States, — and among the rest reproached them for their attempt to conquer Canada, and their actual seizure of Florida. Adams, who knew little about the secrets of Jefferson's and Madison's Administrations, insisted on resenting the British charges, and especially on justifying the United States government in its attacks upon Florida. Bayard protested that he could not support such a view, because he had himself publicly in Congress denounced the Government on the subject of Florida; and Gallatin was almost equally committed, for, as he frankly said, he had opposed in Cabinet for a whole year what had been done in Florida before he could succeed in stopping it.[1] Clay said nothing, but he had strong reasons for wishing that the British negotiators should not be challenged to quote his notorious speeches on the conquest of Canada. Adams produced Monroe's instructions, and in the end compelled his colleagues to yield. His mistake in pressing such an issue was obvious to every one but himself, and would have been evident to him had he not been blinded by irritation at the British note. His colleagues retaliated by summarily rejecting as cant his argument that moral and religious duty required the Americans to take and settle the land of the Indians.[2]

After much discussion their note was completed and sent, September 26, to the British commissioners,[3] who forwarded it as usual to London, with a letter from Goulburn of the same date, written in the worst possible temper, and charging the American commissioners with making a variety of false and fraudulent statements.[4] While the British Cabinet detained it longer than usual for consideration, the Americans at Ghent felt their position grow weaker day by day.

[1] Diary of J. Q. Adams, Sept. 25, 1814, iii. 41.
[2] Diary of J. Q. Adams, Sept. 25, 1814, iii. 42.
[3] American note of Sept. 26, 1814; State Papers, Foreign Affairs, iii. 719.
[4] Goulburn to Bathurst, Sept. 26, 1814; Wellington Supplementary Despatches, ix. 287.

Nothing warranted a serious hope of peace. Goulburn and his colleagues showed no thought of yielding acceptable conditions. The London "Courier" of September 29 announced what might be taken for a semi-official expression of the Ministry: —

"Peace they [the Americans] may make, but it must be on condition that America has not a foot of land on the waters of the St. Lawrence, . . . no settlement on the Lakes, . . . no renewal of the treaties of 1783 and 1794; . . . and they must explicitly abandon their newfangled principles of the law of nations."

Liverpool, writing to Castlereagh September 23,[1] said that in his opinion the Cabinet had "now gone to the utmost justifiable point in concession, and if they [the Americans] are so unreasonable as to reject our proposals, we have nothing to do but to fight it out. The military accounts from America are on the whole satisfactory." The news of the cruel humiliation at Bladensburg and the burning of Washington arrived at Ghent October 1, and caused British and Americans alike to expect a long series of British triumphs, especially on Lake Champlain, where they knew the British force to be overwhelming.

Goulburn exerted himself to produce a rupture. His letter of September 26 to Bathurst treated the American offer of an Indian amnesty as a rejection of the British ultimatum. Again Lord Bathurst set him right by sending him, October 5, the draft of a recip-

[1] Liverpool to Castlereagh, Sept. 23, 1814; Wellington Supplementary Despatches, ix. 278.

rocal article replacing the Indians in their situation before the war; and the British commissioners in a note dated October 8, 1814, communicated this article once more as an ultimatum.[1] Harrison's treaty of July 22 with the Wyandots, Delawares, Shawanees, and other tribes, binding them to take up arms against the British, had then arrived, and this news lessened the interest of both parties in the Indian question. None of the American negotiators were prepared to break off negotiations on that point at such a time, and Clay was so earnest to settle the matter that he took from Gallatin and Adams the task of writing the necessary acceptance of the British ultimatum. Gallatin and Clay decided to receive the British article as according entirely with the American offer of amnesty, and the note was so written.[2]

With this cordial admission of the British ultimatum the Americans coupled an intimation that the time had come when an exchange of general projects for the proposed treaty should be made. More than two months of discussion had then resulted only in eliminating the Indians from the dispute, and in agreeing to maintain silence in regard to the Lakes. Another great difficulty which had been insuperable was voluntarily removed by President Madison and his Cabinet, who after long and obstinate resistance at

[1] British note of Oct. 8, 1814; State Papers, Foreign Affairs, iii. 721.
[2] American note of Oct. 13, 1814; State Papers, Foreign Affairs, iii. 723.

last authorized the commissioners, by instructions dated June 27, to omit impressment from the treaty. Considering the frequent positive declarations of the United States government, besides the rejection of Monroe's treaty in 1807 and of Admiral Warren's and Sir George Prevost's armistice of 1812 for want of an explicit concession on that point, Monroe's letter of June 27 was only to be excused as an act of common-sense or of necessity. The President preferred to represent it as an act of common-sense, warranted by the peace in Europe, which promised to offer no further occasion for the claim or the denial of the British right. On the same principle the subject of blockades was withdrawn from discussion; and these concessions, balanced by the British withdrawal from the Indian ultimatum and the Lake armaments, relieved the American commissioners of all their insuperable difficulties.

The British commissioners were not so easily rescued from their untenable positions. The American note of October 13, sent as usual to London, was answered by Bathurst October 18 and 20,[1] in instructions revealing the true British terms more completely than had yet been ventured. Bathurst at length came to the cardinal point of the negotiation. As the American commissioners had said in their note of August 24, the British government must choose between the two ordinary bases of treaties of peace, — the state before the war, or *status*

[1] Castlereagh Correspondence, x. 168-173.

ante bellum; and the state of possession, or *uti possidetis*. Until the middle of October, 1814, the *uti possidetis*, as a basis of negotiation, included whatever country might have been occupied by Sir George Prevost in his September campaign. Bathurst from the first intended to insist on the state of possession, but had not thought proper to avow it. His instructions of October 18 and 20 directed the British commissioners to come to the point, and to claim the basis of *uti possidetis* from the American negotiators: —

"On their admitting this to be the basis on which they are ready to negotiate, but not before they have admitted it, you will proceed to state the mutual accommodations which may be entered into in conformity with this basis. The British occupy Fort Michillimackinaw, Fort Niagara, and all the country east of the Penobscot. On the other hand the forces of the United States occupy Fort Erie and Fort Amherstburg [Malden]. On the government of the United States consenting to restore these two forts, Great Britain is ready to restore the forts of Castine and Machias, retaining Fort Niagara and Fort Michillimackinaw."

Thus the British demand, which had till then been intended to include half of Maine and the whole south bank of the St. Lawrence River from Plattsburg to Sackett's Harbor, suddenly fell to a demand for Moose Island, a right of way across the northern angle of Maine, Fort Niagara with five miles circuit, and the Island of Mackinaw. The reason for the new spirit of moderation was not far to seek. On the afternoon of October 17, while the British Cabinet was still deliberating on the basis of *uti possidetis*, news reached London that the British invasion of northern New York, from which so much had been expected, had totally failed, and that Prevost's large army had precipitately retreated into Canada. The London "Times" of October 19 was frank in its expressions of disappointment: —

"This is a lamentable event to the civilized world. . . . The subversion of that system of fraud and malignity which constitutes the whole policy of the Jeffersonian school . . . was an event to which we should have bent and yet must bend all our energies. The present American government must be displaced, or it will sooner or later plant its poisoned dagger in the heart of the parent State."

The failure of the attempt on Baltimore and Drummond's bloody repulse at Fort Erie became known at the same time, and coming together at a critical moment threw confusion into the Ministry and their agents in the press and the diplomatic service throughout Europe. The "Courier" of October 25 declared that "peace with America is neither practicable nor desirable till we have wiped away this late disaster;" but the "Morning Chronicle" of October 21–24 openly intimated that the game of war was at an end. October 31, the Paris correspondent of the London "Times" told of the cheers that rose from the crowds in the Palais Royal gardens at each recital of the Plattsburg defeat; and October 21 Goulburn wrote from Ghent to Bathurst,[1] —

"The news from America is very far from satisfactory. Even our brilliant success at Baltimore, as it did not terminate in the capture of the town, will be considered by the Americans as a victory and not as an escape. . . . If it were not for the want of fuel in Boston, I should be quite in despair."

In truth the blockade was the single advantage held by England; and even in that advantage the Americans had a share as long as their cruisers surrounded the British Islands.

Liverpool wrote to Castlereagh, October 21,[2] commenting severely on Prevost's failure, and finding consolation only in the thought that the Americans showed themselves even less patriotic than he had supposed them to be: —

"The capture and destruction of Washington has not united the Americans: quite the contrary. We have gained more credit with them by saving private property than we have lost by the destruction of their public works and buildings. Madison clings to office, and I am strongly inclined to think that the best thing for us is that he should remain there."

Castlereagh at Vienna found himself unable to make the full influence of England felt, so long as

[1] Goulburn to Bathurst; Wellington Supplementary Despatches, ix. 366.
[2] Liverpool to Castlereagh, Oct. 21, 1814; Wellington Supplementary Despatches, ix. 367.

such mortifying disasters by land and sea proved her inability to deal with an enemy she persisted in calling contemptible.

On the American commissioners the news came, October 21, with the effect of a reprieve from execution. Gallatin was deeply moved; Adams could not believe the magnitude of the success; but as far as regarded their joint action, the overthrow of England's scheme produced no change. Their tone had always been high, and they saw no advantage to be gained by altering it. The British commissioners sent to them, October 21, the substance of the new instructions, offering the basis of *uti possidetis*, subject to modifications for mutual convenience.[1] The Americans by common consent, October 23, declined to treat on that basis, or on any other than the mutual restoration of territory.[2] They thought that the British government was still playing with them, when in truth Lord Bathurst had yielded the chief part of the original British demand, and had come to what the whole British empire regarded as essentials, — the right of way to Quebec, and the exclusion of American fishermen from British shores and waters.

The American note of October 24, bluntly rejecting the basis of *uti possidetis*, created a feeling akin to

[1] British note of Oct. 21, 1814; State Papers, Foreign Affairs, iii. 724.
[2] American note of Oct. 24, 1814; State Papers, Foreign Affairs, iii. 725.

consternation in the British Cabinet. At first, ministers assumed that the war must go on, and deliberated only on the point to be preferred for a rupture. "We still think it desirable to gain a little more time before the negotiation is brought to a close," wrote Liverpool to the Duke of Wellington,[1] October 28; and on the same day he wrote to Castlereagh at Vienna to warn him that the American war "will probably now be of some duration," and treating of its embarrassments without disguise.[2] The Czar's conduct at Vienna had annoyed and alarmed all the great Powers, and the American war gave him a decisive advantage over England; but even without the Russian complication, the prospect for ministers was not cheering.

"Looking to a continuance of the American war, our financial state is far from satisfactory," wrote Lord Liverpool; ". . . the American war will not cost us less than £10,000,000, in addition to our peace establishment and other expenses. We must expect, therefore, to hear it said that the property tax is continued for the purpose of securing a better frontier for Canada."

A week passed without bringing encouragement to the British Cabinet. On the contrary the Ministry learned that a vigorous prosecution of hostilities would cost much more than ten million pounds, and

[1] Liverpool to Wellington, Oct. 28, 1814; Wellington Supplementary Despatches, ix. 384.
[2] Liverpool to Castlereagh, Oct. 28, 1814; Wellington Supplementary Despatches, ix. 382.

when Liverpool next wrote to Castlereagh, November 2,[1] although he could still see "little prospect for our negotiations at Ghent ending in peace," he added that "the continuance of the American war will entail upon us a prodigious expense, much more than we had any idea of." A Cabinet meeting was to be held the next day, November 3, to review the whole course of policy as to America.

Throughout the American difficulties, from first to last, the most striking quality shown by the British government was the want of intelligence which caused the war, and marked the conduct of both the war and the negotiations. If the foreign relations of every government were marked by the same character, politics could be no more than rivalry in the race to blunder; but in October, 1814, another quality almost equally striking became evident. The weakness of British councils was as remarkable as their want of intelligence. The government of England had exasperated the Americans to an animosity that could not forget or forgive, and every dictate of self-interest required that it should carry out its policy to the end. Even domestic politics in Parliament might have been more easily managed by drawing public criticism to America, while in no event could taxes be reduced to satisfy the public demand.[2] Another year

[1] Liverpool to Castlereagh, Nov. 2, 1814; Wellington Supplementary Despatches, ix. 382.
[2] Liverpool to Castlereagh, Jan. 16, 1815; Castlereagh Correspondence, x. 240.

of war was the consistent and natural course for ministers to prefer.

So the Cabinet evidently thought; but instead of making a decision, the Cabinet council of November 3 resorted to the expedient of shifting responsibility upon the Duke of Wellington. The Duke was then Ambassador at Paris. His life had been threatened by angry officers of Napoleon, who could not forgive his victories at Vittoria and Toulouse. For his own security he might be sent to Canada, and if he went, he should go with full powers to close the war as he pleased.

The next day, November 4, Liverpool wrote to Wellington, explaining the wishes of the Cabinet, and inviting him to take the entire command in Canada, in order to bring the war to an honorable conclusion.[1] Wellington replied November 9, — and his words were the more interesting because, after inviting and receiving so decided an opinion from so high an authority, the Government could not easily reject it. Wellington began by reviewing the military situation, and closed by expressing his opinion on the diplomatic contest:[2] —

"I have already told you and Lord Bathurst that I feel no objection to going to America, though I don't

[1] Liverpool to Wellington, Nov. 4, 1814; Liverpool to Castlereagh, Nov. 4, 1814; Wellington Supplementary Despatches, ix. 404, 405.

[2] Wellington to Castlereagh, Nov. 9, 1814; Wellington Supplementary Despatches, i. 426.

promise to myself much success there. I believe there are troops enough there for the defence of Canada forever, and even for the accomplishment of any reasonable offensive plan that could be formed from the Canadian frontier. I am quite sure that all the American armies of which I have ever read would not beat out of a field of battle the troops that went from Bordeaux last summer, if common precautions and care were taken of them. That which appears to me to be wanting in America is not a general, or a general officer and troops, but a naval superiority on the Lakes."

These views did not altogether accord with those of Americans, who could not see that the British generals made use of the Lakes even when controlling them, but who saw the troops of Wellington retire from one field of battle after another, — at Plattsburg, Baltimore, and New Orleans, — while taking more than common precautions Wellington's military comments showed little interest in American affairs, and evidently he saw nothing to be gained by going to Canada. His diplomatic ideas betrayed the same bias : —

" In regard to your present negotiations, I confess that I think you have no right, from the state of the war, to demand any concession of territory from America.
You have not been able to carry it into the enemy's territory, notwithstanding your military success and now undoubted military superiority, and have not even cleared your own territory on the point of attack. You cannot on any principle of equality in negotiation claim a cession of territory excepting in exchange for other advan-

tages which you have in your power. . . . Then if this reasoning be true, why stipulate for the *uti possidetis?* You can get no territory; indeed, the state of your military operations, however creditable, does not entitle you to demand any."

After such an opinion from the first military authority of England, the British Ministry had no choice but to abandon its claim for territory Wellington's letter reached London about November 13, and was duly considered in the Cabinet. Liverpool wrote to Castlereagh, November 18, that the Ministry had made its decision; the claim for territory was to be abandoned. For this retreat he alleged various excuses, — such as the unsatisfactory state of the negotiations at Vienna, and the alarming condition of France; the finances, the depression of rents, and the temper of Parliament.[1] Such reasoning would have counted for nothing in the previous month of May, but six months wrought a change in public feeling. The war had lost public favor. Even the colonial and shipping interests and the navy were weary of it, while the army had little to expect from it but hard service and no increase of credit. Every Englishman who came in contact with Americans seemed to suffer. Broke, the only victor by sea, was a lifelong invalid; and Brock and Ross, the only victors on land, had paid for their success with their lives. Incessant disappointment made the war an unpleasant

[1] Liverpool to Castlereagh, Nov. 18, 1814; Wellington Supplementary Despatches, ix. 438.

thought with Englishmen. The burning of Washington was an exploit of which they could not boast. The rate of marine insurance was a daily and intolerable annoyance So rapidly did the war decline in favor, that in the first half of December it was declared to be decidedly unpopular by one of the most judicious English liberals, Francis Horner; although Horner held that the Americans, as the dispute then stood, were the aggressors.[1] The tone of the press showed the same popular tendency, for while the "Times" grumbled loudly over the Canada campaign, the "Morning Chronicle" no longer concealed its hostility to the war, and ventured to sneer at it, talking of "the entire defeat and destruction of the last British fleet but one; for it has become necessary to particularize them now."[2]

While the Cabinet still waited, the first instalment of Ghent correspondence to August 20, published in America October 10, returned to England November 18, and received no flattering attention. "We cannot compliment our negotiators," remarked the "Morning Chronicle;" and the "Times" was still less pleased. "The British government has been tricked into bringing forward demands which it had not the power to enforce. . . . Why treat at all with Mr. Madison?" In Parliament, November 19, the liberal opposition attacked the Government

[1] Horner to J. A. Murray, Dec. 10, 1814; Horner's Memoirs, ii. 213.
[2] The Morning Chronicle, Nov. 19, 1814.

for setting up novel pretensions. Ministers needed no more urging, and Bathurst thenceforward could not be charged with waste of time.

During this interval of more than three weeks the negotiators at Ghent were left to follow their own devices. In order to provide the Americans with occupation, the British commissioners sent them a note dated October 31 calling for a counter-project, since the basis of *uti possidetis* was refused.[1] This note, with all the others since August 20, was sent by the Americans to Washington on the same day, October 31; and then Gallatin and Adams began the task of drafting the formal project of a treaty. Immediately the internal discords of the commission broke into earnest dispute. A struggle began between the East and the West over the fisheries and the Mississippi.

The treaty of 1783 coupled the American right of fishing in British waters and curing fish on British shores with the British right of navigating the Mississippi River. For that arrangement the elder Adams was responsible. The fisheries were a Massachusetts interest. At Paris in 1783 John Adams, in season and out of season, with his colleagues and with the British negotiators, insisted, with the intensity of conviction, that the fishing rights which the New England people held while subjects of the British crown were theirs by no grant or treaty, but as

[1] British note of Oct. 31, 1814; State Papers, Foreign Relations, iii. 726.

a natural right, which could not be extinguished by war; and that where British subjects had a right to fish, whether on coasts or shores, in bays, inlets, creeks, or harbors, Americans had the same right, to be exercised wherever and whenever they pleased. John Adams's persistence secured the article of the definitive treaty, which, without expressly admitting a natural right, coupled the in-shore fisheries and the navigation of the Mississippi with the recognition of independence. In 1814 as in 1783 John Adams clung to his trophies, and his son would have waged indefinite war rather than break his father's heart by sacrificing what he had won; but at Ghent the son stood in isolation which the father in the worst times had never known. Massachusetts left him to struggle alone for a principle that needed not only argument but force to make it victorious. Governor Strong did not even write to him as he did to Pickering, that Massachusetts would give an equivalent in territory for the fisheries. As far as the State could influence the result, the fisheries were to be lost by default.

Had Adams encountered only British opposition he might have overborne it as his father had done; but since 1783 the West had become a political power, and Louisiana had been brought into the Union. If the fisheries were recognized as an indefeasible right by the treaty of 1783, the British liberty of navigating the Mississippi was another indefeasible right, which must revive with peace. The Western people naturally objected to such a proposition. Neither they nor the Canadians could be blamed for unwillingness to impose a mischievous servitude forever upon their shores, and Clay believed his popularity to depend on preventing an express recognition of the British right to navigate the Mississippi. Either Clay or Adams was sure to refuse signing any treaty which expressly sacrificed the local interests of either.

In this delicate situation only the authority and skill of Gallatin saved the treaty. At the outset of the discussion, October 30, Gallatin quietly took the lead from Adams's hands, and assumed the championship of the fisheries by proposing to renew both privileges, making the one an equivalent for the other. Clay resisted obstinately, while Gallatin gently and patiently overbore him. When Gallatin's proposal was put to the vote November 5, Clay and Russell alone opposed it, — and the support then given by Russell to Clay was never forgotten by Adams. Clay still refusing to sign the offer, Gallatin continued his pressure, until at last, November 10, Clay consented to insert, not in the project of treaty, but in the note which accompanied it, a paragraph declaring that the commissioners were not authorized to bring into discussion any of the rights hitherto enjoyed in the fisheries: " From their nature, and from the peculiar character of the treaty of 1783 by which they were recognized, no further stipulation has been deemed necessary by the Government of the United

States to entitle them to the full enjoyment of all of them "

Clay signed the note,[1] though unwillingly; and it was sent, November 10, with the treaty project, to the British commissioners, who forwarded it to London, where it arrived at the time when the British Cabinet had at last decided on peace. Bathurst sent his reply in due course; and Goulburn's disgust was great to find that instead of breaking negotiation on the point of the fisheries as he wished,[2] he was required once more to give way. "You know that I was never much inclined to give way to the Americans," he wrote, November 25.[3] "I am still less inclined to do so after the statement of our demands with which the negotiation opened, and which has in every point of view proved most unfortunate."

The British reply, dated November 26,[4] took no notice of the American reservation as to the fisheries, but inserted in the project the old right of navigating the Mississippi. Both Bathurst and Goulburn thought that their silence, after the American declaration, practically conceded the American right to the fisheries, though Gambier and Dr. Adams thought

[1] American note of Nov. 10, 1814; State Papers, Foreign Relations, iii. 733.

[2] Goulburn to Bathurst, Nov. 10, 1814; Wellington Supplementary Despatches, ix. 427.

[3] Goulburn to Bathurst, Nov. 10, 1814; Wellington Supplementary Despatches, ix. 452.

[4] British note of Nov. 26, 1814; State Papers, Foreign Relations, iii. 740.

differently.¹ In either case the British note of November 26, though satisfactory to Adams, was far from agreeable to Clay, who was obliged to endanger the peace in order to save the Mississippi. Adams strongly inclined to take the British project precisely as it was offered,² but Gallatin overruled him, and Clay would certainly have refused to sign. In discussing the subject, November 28, Gallatin proposed to accept the article on the navigation of the Mississippi if the British would add a provision recognizing the fishing rights. Clay lost his temper, and intimated something more than willingness to let Massachusetts pay for the pleasure of peace;³ but during the whole day of November 28, and with the same patience November 29, Gallatin continued urging Clay and restraining Adams, until at last on the third day he brought the matter to the point he wished.

The result of this long struggle saved not indeed the fisheries, but the peace. Clay made no further protest when, in conference with the British commissioners December 1, the Americans offered to renew both the disputed rights.⁴ Their proposal was sent to London, and was answered by Bathurst December 6, in a letter offering to set aside for future negotiation

[1] Goulburn to Bathurst, Nov. 25, 1814; Wellington Supplementary Despatches, ix. 452.
[2] Diary of J. Q. Adams, Nov. 27, 1814, iii. 70.
[3] Diary of J. Q. Adams, iii. 72.
[4] Protocol of Dec. 1, 1814; State Papers, Foreign Relations, iii. 742.

the terms under which the old fishing liberty and the navigation of the Mississippi should be continued for fair equivalents.[1] The British commissioners communicated this suggestion in conference December 10, and threw new dissension among the Americans.

The British offer to reserve both disputed rights for future negotiation implied that both rights were forfeited, or subject to forfeit, by war, — an admission which Adams could not make, but which the other commissioners could not reject. At that point Adams found himself alone. Even Gallatin admitted that the claim to the natural right of catching and curing fish on British shores was untenable, and could never be supported. Adams's difficulties were the greater because the question of peace and war was reduced to two points, — the fisheries and Moose Island, — both interesting to Massachusetts alone. Yet the Americans were unwilling to yield without another struggle, and decided still to resist the British claim as inconsistent with the admitted basis of the *status ante bellum*.

The struggle with the British commissioners then became warm. A long conference, December 12, brought no conclusion. The treaty of 1783 could neither be followed nor ignored, and perplexed the Englishmen as much as the Americans. During December 13 and December 14, Adams continued to

[1] Bathurst to the Commissioners, Dec. 6, 1814; Castlereagh Correspondence, x. 214.

press his colleagues to assert the natural right to the fisheries, and to insist on the permanent character of the treaty of 1783; but Gallatin would not consent to make that point an ultimatum. All the commissioners except Adams resigned themselves to the sacrifice of the fisheries; but Gallatin decided to make one more effort before abandoning the struggle, and with that object drew up a note rejecting the British stipulation because it implied the abandonment of a right, but offering either to be silent as to both the fisheries and the Mississippi, or to admit a general reference to further negotiation of all subjects in dispute, so expressed as to imply no abandonment of right.

The note was signed and sent December 14,[1] and the Americans waited another week for the answer. Successful as they had been in driving their British antagonists from one position after another, they were not satisfied. Adams still feared that he might not be able to sign, and Clay was little better pleased. "He said we should make a damned bad treaty, and he did not know whether he would sign it or not."[2] Whatever Adams thought of the treaty, his respect for at least two of his colleagues was expressed in terms of praise rarely used by him. Writing to his wife, September 27,[3] Adams said: "Mr. Gallatin

[1] American note of Dec. 14, 1814; State Papers, Foreign Relations, iii. 743.
[2] Diary of J. Q. Adams, Dec. 14, 1814, iii. 118.
[3] J. Q. Adams to his wife, Sept. 27, 1814; Adams MSS.

keeps and increases his influence over us all. It would have been an irreparable loss if our country had been deprived of the benefit of his talents in this negotiation." At the moment of final suspense he wrote again, December 16: —

"Of the five members of the American mission, the Chevalier [Bayard] has the most perfect control of his temper, the most deliberate coolness; and it is the more meritorious because it is real self-command. His feelings are as quick and his spirits as high as those of any one among us, but he certainly has them more under government. I can scarcely express to you how much both he and Mr. Gallatin have risen in my esteem since we have been here living together. Gallatin has not quite so constant a supremacy over his own emotions; yet he seldom yields to an ebullition of temper, and recovers from it immediately. He has a faculty, when discussion grows too warm, of turning off its edge by a joke, which I envy him more than all his other talents; and he has in his character one of the most extraordinary combinations of stubbornness and of flexibility that I ever met with in man. His greatest fault I think to be an ingenuity sometimes trenching upon ingenuousness."

Gallatin's opinion of Adams was not so enthusiastic as Adams's admiration for him. He thought Adams's chief fault to be that he lacked judgment "to a deplorable degree."[1] Of Clay, whether in his merits or his faults, only one opinion was possible. Clay's character belonged to the simple Southern or Virginia type, somewhat affected, but

[1] Adams's Gallatin, p. 599.

not rendered more complex, by Western influence, — and transparent beyond need of description or criticism.

The extraordinary patience and judgment of Gallatin, aided by the steady support of Bayard, carried all the American points without sacrificing either Adams or Clay, and with no quarrel of serious importance on any side. When Lord Bathurst received the American note of December 14, he replied December 19, yielding the last advantage he possessed:[1] "The Prince Regent regrets to find that there does not appear any prospect of being able to arrive at such an arrangement with regard to the fisheries as would have the effect of coming to a full and satisfactory explanation on that subject;" but since this was the case, the disputed article might be altogether omitted.

Thus the treaty became simply a cessation of hostilities, leaving every claim on either side open for future settlement. The formality of signature was completed December 24, and closed an era of American history. In substance, the treaty sacrificed much on both sides for peace. The Americans lost their claims for British spoliations, and were obliged to admit question of their right to Eastport and their fisheries in British waters; the British failed to establish their principles of impressment and blockade, and admitted question of their right to navigate the Mississippi and trade with the Indians.

[1] Castlereagh Correspondence, x. 221.

Perhaps at the moment the Americans were the chief losers; but they gained their greatest triumph in referring all their disputes to be settled by time, the final negotiator, whose decision they could safely trust.

CHAPTER III.

ENGLAND received the Treaty of Ghent with feelings of mixed anger and satisfaction. The "Morning Chronicle" seemed surprised at the extreme interest which the news excited. As early as November 24, when ministers made their decision to concede the American terms, the "Morning Chronicle" announced that " a most extraordinary sensation was produced yesterday" by news from Ghent, and by reports that ministers had abandoned their ground. When the treaty arrived, December 26, the same Whig newspaper, the next morning, while asserting that ministers had " humbled themselves in the dust and thereby brought discredit on the country," heartily approved what they had done; and added that "the city was in a complete state of hurricane during the whole of yesterday, but the storm did not attain its utmost height until toward the evening. . . . Purchases were made to the extent of many hundred thousand pounds." The importance of the United States to England was made more apparent by the act of peace than by the pressure of war. "At Birmingham," said the "Courier," "an immense assemblage witnessed the arrival of the mail, and immediately took the horses out, and drew the mail to the post-office with the loudest acclamations," — acclamations over a treaty universally regarded as discreditable.

The "Times" admitted the general joy, and denied only that it was universal. If the "Times" in any degree represented public opinion, the popular satisfaction at the peace was an extraordinary political symptom, for in its opinion the Government had accepted terms such as "might have been expected from an indulgent and liberal conqueror. . . . We have retired from the combat," it said, December 30, "with the stripes yet bleeding on our back, — with the recent defeats at Plattsburg and on Lake Champlain unavenged." During several succeeding weeks the "Times" continued its extravagant complaints, which served only to give the Americans a new idea of the triumph they had won.

In truth, no one familiar with English opinion during the past ten years attempted to deny that the government of England must admit one or the other of two conclusions, — either it had ruinously mismanaged its American policy before the war, or it had disgraced itself by the peace. The "Morning Chronicle," while approving the treaty, declared that the Tories were on this point at odds with their own leaders: [1] "Their attachment to the ministers, though strong, cannot reconcile them to this one step, though surely if they would look back with an impartial eye

[1] The Morning Chronicle, Dec. 30, 1814.

on the imbecility and error with which their idols conducted the war, they must acknowledge their prudence in putting an end to it. One of them very honestly said, two days ago, that if they had not put an end to the war, the war would have put an end to their Ministry." Whatever doubts existed about the temper of England before that time, no one doubted after the peace of Ghent that war with the United States was an unpopular measure with the British people.

Nevertheless the "Times" and the Tories continued their complaints until March 9, when two simultaneous pieces of news silenced criticism of the American treaty. The severe defeat at New Orleans became known at the moment when Napoleon, having quitted Elba, began his triumphal return to Paris. These news, coming in the midst of Corn Riots, silenced further discussion of American relations, and left ministers free to redeem at Waterloo the failures they had experienced in America.

In the United States news of peace was slow to arrive. The British sloop-of-war "Favorite" bore the despatches, and was still at sea when the month of February began. The commissioners from Massachusetts and Connecticut, bearing the demands of the Hartford Convention, started for Washington. Every one was intent on the situation of New Orleans, where a disaster was feared. Congress seemed to have abandoned the attempt to provide means of defence, although it began another effort to create a bank on Dallas's plan. A large number of the most intelligent citizens believed that two announcements would soon be made, — one, that New Orleans was lost; the other, that the negotiation at Ghent had ended in rupture. Under this double shock, the collapse of the national government seemed to its enemies inevitable.

In this moment of suspense, the first news arrived from New Orleans. To the extreme relief of the Government and the Republican majority in Congress, they learned, February 4, that the British invasion was defeated and New Orleans saved. The victory was welcomed by illuminations, votes of thanks, and rejoicings greater than had followed the more important success at Plattsburg, or the more brilliant battles at Niagara; for the success won at New Orleans relieved the Government from a load of anxiety, and postponed a crisis supposed to be immediately at hand. Half the influence of the Hartford Convention was destroyed by it; and the commissioners, who were starting for the capital, had reason to expect a reception less favorable by far than they would have met had the British been announced as masters of Louisiana. Yet the immediate effect of the news was not to lend new vigor to Congress, but rather to increase its inertness, and to encourage its dependence on militia, Treasury notes, and good fortune.

A week afterward, on the afternoon of Saturday, February 11, the British sloop-of-war " Favorite " sailed up New York harbor, and the city quickly heard rumors of peace. At eight o'clock that evening the American special messenger landed, bringing the official documents intrusted to his care; and when the news could no longer be doubted, the city burst into an uproar of joy. The messenger was slow in reaching Washington, where he arrived only on the evening of Tuesday, February 13, and delivered his despatches to the Secretary of State.

Had the treaty been less satisfactory than it was, the President would have hesitated long before advising its rejection, and the Senate could hardly have gained courage to reject it. In spite of rumors from London and significant speculations on the London Exchange, known in America in the middle of January, no one had seriously counted on a satisfactory peace, as was proved by the steady depression of government credit and of the prices of American staples. The reaction after the arrival of the news was natural, and so violent that few persons stopped to scrutinize the terms. Contrary to Clay's forebodings, the treaty, mere armistice though it seemed to be, was probably the most popular treaty ever negotiated by the United States. The President sent it to the Senate February 15; and the next day, without suggestion of amendment, and apparently without a criticism, unless from Federalists, the Senate unanimously confirmed it, thirty-five senators uniting in approval.

Yet the treaty was not what the Government had

expected in declaring the war, or such as it had a right to demand. The Republicans admitted it in private, and the Federalists proclaimed it in the press. Senator Gore wrote to Governor Strong:[1] "The treaty must be deemed disgraceful to the Government who made the war and the peace, and will be so adjudged by all, after the first effusions of joy at relief have subsided." Opinions differed widely on the question where the disgrace belonged, — whether to the Government who made the war, or to the people who refused to support it; but no one pretended that the terms of peace, as far as they were expressed in the treaty, were so good as those repeatedly offered by England more than two years before. Yet the treaty was universally welcomed, and not a thought of continued war found expression.

In New England the peace was received with extravagant delight. While the government messenger who carried the official news to Washington made no haste, a special messenger started from New York at ten o'clock Saturday night, immediately on the landing of the government messenger, and in thirty-two hours arrived in Boston. Probably the distance had rarely been travelled in less time, for the Boston "Centinel" announced the expense to be two hundred and twenty-five dollars; and such an outlay was seldom made for rapidity of travel or news. As the messenger passed from town to town he announced

[1] Gore to Strong, Feb. 18, 1815; Lodge's Cabot, p. 563.

the tidings to the delighted people.[1] Reaching the "Centinel" office, at Boston, early Monday morning, he delivered his bulletin, and a few minutes after it was published all the bells were set ringing; schools and shops were closed, and a general holiday taken; flags were hoisted, the British with the American; the militia paraded, and in the evening the city was illuminated. Yet the terms of peace were wholly unknown, and the people of Massachusetts had every reason to fear that their interests were sacrificed for the safety of the Union. Their rejoicing over the peace was as unreasoning as their hatred of the war.

Only along the Canadian frontier where the farmers had for three years made large profits by supplying both armies, the peace was received without rejoicing.[2] South of New York, although less public delight was expressed, the relief was probably greater than in New England. Virginia had suffered most, and had felt the blockade with peculiar severity. A few weeks before the treaty was signed, Jefferson wrote : [3] —

"By the total annihilation in value of the produce which was to give me sustenance and independence, I shall be like Tantalus, — up to the shoulders in water, yet dying with thirst. We can make indeed enough to eat, drink, and clothe ourselves, but nothing for our salt,

[1] Goodrich's Recollections, i. 503-505.
[2] Montreal Herald, March 18, 1815; Niles, viii. 132.
[3] Jefferson to W. Short, Nov. 28, 1814; Works, vi. 398.

iron, groceries, and taxes which must be paid in money. For what can we raise for the market? Wheat?—we only give it to our horses, as we have been doing ever since harvest. Tobacco?—it is not worth the pipe it is smoked in."

While all Virginia planters were in this situation February 13, they awoke February 14 to find flour worth ten dollars a barrel, and groceries fallen fifty per cent. They were once more rich beyond their wants.

So violent and sudden a change in values had never been known in the United States. The New York market saw fortunes disappear and other fortunes created in the utterance of a single word. All imported articles dropped to low prices. Sugar which sold Saturday at twenty-six dollars a hundred-weight, sold Monday at twelve dollars and a half. Tea sank from two dollars and a quarter to one dollar a pound; tin fell from eighty to twenty-five dollars a box; cotton fabrics declined about fifty per cent. On the other hand flour, cotton, and the other chief staples of American produce rose in the same proportion. Nominally flour was worth seven and a half dollars on Saturday, though no large amounts could have been sold; on Monday the price was ten dollars, and all the wheat in the country was soon sold at that rate.

Owing to the derangement of currency, these prices expressed no precise specie value. The effect of the peace on the currency was for a moment to restore an apparent equilibrium. In New York the specie premium of twenty-two per cent was imagined for a time to have vanished. In truth, United States six-per-cents rose in New York from seventy-six to eighty-eight in paper; Treasury-notes from ninety-two to ninety-eight. In Philadelphia, on Saturday, six-per-cents sold at seventy-five; on Monday, at ninety-three. The paper depreciation remained about twenty per cent in New York, about twenty-four per cent in Philadelphia, and about thirty per cent in Baltimore. The true value of six-per-cents was about sixty-eight; of Treasury notes about seventy-eight, after the announcement of peace.

As rapidly as possible the blockade was raised, and ships were hurried to sea with the harvests of three seasons for cargo; but some weeks still passed before all the operations of war were closed. The news of peace reached the British squadron below Mobile in time to prevent further advance on that place; but on the ocean a long time elapsed before fighting wholly ceased.

Some of the worst disasters as well as the greatest triumphs of the war occurred after the treaty of peace had been signed. The battle of New Orleans was followed by the loss of Fort Bowyer. At about the same time a British force occupied Cumberland Island on the southern edge of the Georgia coast, and January 13 attacked the fort at the entrance of the St. Mary's, and having captured it without loss, ascended the river the next day to the town of

St. Mary's, which they seized, together with its merchandise and valuable ships in the river. Cockburn established his headquarters on Cumberland Island January 22, and threw the whole State of Georgia into agitation, while he waited the arrival of a brigade with which an attack was to be made on Savannah.

The worst disaster of the naval war occurred January 15, when the frigate "President" — one of the three American forty-fours, under Stephen Decatur, the favorite ocean hero of the American service — suffered defeat and capture within fifty miles of Sandy Hook. No naval battle of the war was more disputed in its merits, although its occurrence in the darkest moments of national depression was almost immediately forgotten in the elation of the peace a few days later.

Secretary Jones retired from the Navy Department Dec. 19, 1814, yielding the direction to B. W. Crowninshield of Massachusetts, but leaving a squadron ready for sea at New York under orders for distant service. The "Peacock" and "Hornet," commanded by Warrington and Biddle, were to sail with a storeship on a long cruise in Indian waters, where they were expected to ravage British shipping from the Cape of Good Hope to the China seas. With them Decatur was to go in the "President," and at the beginning of the new year he waited only an opportunity to slip to sea past the blockading squadron. January 14 a strong westerly wind drove the British fleet out of sight. The "President" set sail, but in crossing the bar at night grounded, and continued for an hour or more to strike heavily, until the tide and strong wind forced her across. Decatur then ran along the Long Island coast some fifty miles, when he changed his course to the southeast, hoping that he had evaded the blockading squadron. This course was precisely that which Captain Hayes, commanding the squadron, expected;[1] and an hour before daylight the four British ships, standing to the northward and eastward, sighted the "President," standing to the southward and eastward, not more than two miles on the weather-bow of the "Majestic," — the fifty-six-gun razee commanded by Captain Hayes.

The British ships promptly made chase. Captain Hayes's squadron, besides the "Majestic," consisted of the "Endymion," a fifty-gun frigate, with the "Pomone" and "Tenedos," frigates like the "Guerriere," "Macedonian," and "Java," armed with eighteen-pound guns. Only from the "Endymion" had Decatur much to fear, for the "Majestic" was slow and the other ships were weak; but the "Endymion" was a fast sailer, and especially adapted to meet the American frigates. The "Endymion," according to British authority, was about one hundred and fifty-nine feet in length on the lower deck, and nearly forty-three feet in extreme breadth; the

[1] Report of Captain Hayes, Jan. 17, 1815; James, Appendix, p. clxxx; Niles, viii. 175.

"President," on the same authority, was about one hundred and seventy-three feet in length, and forty-four feet in breadth. The "Endymion" carried twenty-six long twenty-four-pounders on the main deck; the "President" carried thirty. The "Endymion" mounted twenty-two thirty-two pound carronades on the spar deck; the "President" mounted twenty. The "Endymion" had also a long brass eighteen-pounder as a bow-chaser; the "President" a long twenty-four-pounder as a bow-chaser, and another as a stern-chaser. The "Endymion" was short-handed after her losses in action with the "Prince de Neufchatel," and carried only three hundred and forty-six men; the "President" carried four hundred and fifty. The "Endymion" was the weaker ship, probably in the proportion of four to five; but for her immediate purpose she possessed a decisive advantage in superior speed, especially in light winds.

At two o'clock in the afternoon, the "Endymion" had gained so much on the "President" as to begin exchanging shots between the stern and bow-chasers.[1] Soon after five o'clock, as the wind fell, the "Endymion" crept up on the "President's" starboard quarter, and "commenced close action."[2] After bearing the enemy's fire for half an hour without reply, Decatur was obliged to alter his course and accept

[1] Log of the "Pomone;" Niles, viii. 133. Log of the "Endymion;" James, p. 427.
[2] Report of Captain Hayes; Niles, viii. 175.

battle, or suffer himself to be crippled.[1] The battle lasted two hours and a half, until eight o'clock, when firing ceased; but at half-past nine, according to the "Pomone's" log, the "Endymion" fired two guns, which the "President" returned with one.[2] According to Decatur's account the "Endymion" lay for half an hour under his stern, without firing, while the "President" was trying to escape. In truth the "Endymion" had no need to fire; she was busy bending new sails, while Decatur's ship, according to his official report, was crippled, and in the want of wind could not escape.

In a letter written by Decatur to his wife immediately after the battle, he gave an account of what followed, as he understood it.[3]

"The 'Endymion,'" he began, . . . "was the leading ship of the enemy. She got close under my quarters and was cutting my rigging without my being able to bring a gun to bear upon her. To suffer this was making my capture certain, and that too without injury to the enemy. I therefore bore up for the 'Endymion' and engaged her for two hours, when we silenced and beat her off. At this time the rest of the ships had got within two miles of us. We made all the sail we could from them, but it was in vain. In three hours the 'Pomone' and 'Tenedos' were alongside, and the 'Majestic' and 'Endymion' close to us. All that was now left for me to do was to receive the fire of the nearest ship and surrender."

[1] Decatur's Report of Jan. 18, 1815; Niles, viii. 8.
[2] Log of the "Pomone;" Niles, viii. 133.
[3] Niles, vii. 364.

The "Pomone's" account of the surrender completed the story:[1]—

"At eleven, being within gunshot of the 'President' who was still steering to the eastward under a press of sail, with royal, top-gallant, topmast, and lower studding-sails set, finding how much we outsailed her our studding-sails were taken in, and immediately afterward we luffed to port and fired our starboard broadside. The enemy then also luffed to port, bringing his larboard broadside to bear, which was momentarily expected, as a few minutes previous to our closing her she hoisted a light abaft, which in night actions constitutes the ensign. Our second broadside was fired, and the 'President' still luffing up as if intent to lay us on board, we hauled close to port, bracing the yards up, and setting the mainsail; the broadside was again to be fired into his bows, raking, when she hauled down the light, and we hailed demanding if she had surrendered. The reply was in the affirmative, and the firing immediately ceased. The 'Tenedos,' who was not more than three miles off, soon afterward came up, and assisted the 'Pomone' in securing the prize and removing the prisoners. At three quarters past twelve the 'Endymion' came up, and the 'Majestic' at three in the morning."

Between the account given by Decatur and that of the "Pomone's" log were some discrepancies. In the darkness many mistakes were inevitable; but if each party were taken as the best authority on its own side, the connected story seemed to show that Decatur, after beating off the "Endymion," made

[1] Niles, viii. 133.

every effort to escape, but was impressed by the conviction that if overtaken by the squadron, nothing was left but to receive the fire of the nearest ship, and surrender. The night was calm, and the "President" made little headway. At eleven o'clock one of the pursuing squadron came up, and fired two broadsides. "Thus situated," reported Decatur, "with about one fifth of my crew killed and wounded, my ship crippled, and a more than fourfold force opposed to me, without a chance of escape left, I deemed it my duty to surrender."

The official Court of Inquiry on the loss of the "President" reported, a few months afterward, a warm approval of Decatur's conduct:[1] —

"We fear that we cannot express in a manner that will do justice to our feelings our admiration of the conduct of Commodore Decatur and his officers and crew.... As well during the chase as through his contest with the enemy [he] evinced great judgment and skill, perfect coolness, the most determined resolution, and heroic courage."

The high praise thus bestowed was doubtless deserved, since the Court of Inquiry was composed of persons well qualified to judge; but Decatur's battle with the "Endymion" was far from repeating the success of his triumph over the "Macedonian." Anxious to escape rather than to fight, Decatur in consequence failed either to escape or resist with effect. The action with the "Endymion" lasted three

[1] Niles, viii. 147.

hours from the time when the British frigate gained the "President's" quarter. For the first half hour the "President" received the "Endymion's" broadsides without reply. During the last half hour the firing slackened and became intermittent. Yet for two hours the ships were engaged at close range, a part of the time within half musket-shot, in a calm sea, and in a parallel line of sailing.[1] At all times of the battle, the ships were well within point-blank range,[2] which for long twenty-four-pounders and thirty-two-pound carronades was about two hundred and fifty yards.[3] Decatur had needed but an hour and a half to disable and capture the "Macedonian," although a heavy swell disturbed his fire, and at no time were the ships within easy range for grape, which was about one hundred and fifty yards. The "Endymion" was a larger and better ship than the "Macedonian," but the "President" was decidedly less efficient than the "United States."

According to Captain Hope's report, the "Endymion" lost eleven men killed and fourteen wounded. The "President" reported twenty-five killed and sixty wounded. Of the two ships the "President" was probably the most severely injured.[4] The masts of both were damaged, and two days afterward both

[1] Log of the "Endymion;" James, p. 428.
[2] Cooper's Naval History, ii. 466.
[3] Adye's Bombardier, p. 197. Douglas's Naval Gunnery (Fourth edition), p. 103.
[4] Report of Injuries received by the "President;" James, Appendix, p. cxciv, no. 107.

were dismasted in a gale; but while the "President" lost all her masts by the board, the "Endymion" lost only her fore and main masts considerably above deck. On the whole, the injury inflicted by the "President" on the "Endymion" was less than in proportion to her relative strength, or to the length of time occupied in the action. Even on the supposition that the "President's" fire was directed chiefly against the "Endymion's" rigging, the injury done was not proportional to the time occupied in doing it. According to the "Pomone's" log, the "Endymion" was able to rejoin the squadron at quarter before one o'clock in the night. According to the "Endymion's" log, she repaired damages in an hour, and resumed the chase at nine o'clock.[1]

The British ships were surprised that Decatur should have surrendered to the "Pomone" without firing a shot. Apparently the "Pomone's" broadside did little injury, and the "Tenedos" was not yet in range when the "Pomone" opened fire. The question of the proper time to surrender was to be judged by professional rules; and if resistance was hopeless, Decatur was doubtless justified in striking when he did; but his apparent readiness to do so hardly accorded with the popular conception of his character.

As usual the sloops were more fortunate than the frigate, and got to sea successfully, January 22, in a gale of wind which enabled them to run the

[1] James's Naval Occurrences, p. 429.

blockade. Their appointed rendezvous was Tristan d'Acunha. There the "Hornet" arrived on the morning of March 23, and before she had time to anchor sighted the British sloop-of-war "Penguin," — a new brig then cruising in search of the American privateer "Young Wasp."

Captain Biddle of the "Hornet" instantly made chase, and Captain Dickinson of the "Penguin" bore up and stood for the enemy. According to British authority the vessels differed only by a "trifling disparity of force."[1] In truth the American was somewhat superior in size, metal, and crew, although not so decisively as in most of the sloop battles. The "Hornet" carried eighteen thirty-two-pound carronades and two long twelve-pounders; the "Penguin" carried sixteen thirty-two-pound carronades, two long guns differently reported as twelve-pounders and six-pounders, and a twelve-pound carronade. The crews were apparently the same in number, — about one hundred and thirty-two men. Captain Dickinson had equipped his vessel especially for the purpose of capturing heavy privateers, and was then looking for the "Young Wasp," — a vessel decidedly superior to the "Hornet."[2] Although he had reason to doubt his ability to capture the "Young Wasp," he did not fear a combat with the "Hornet," and showed his confidence by brushing up close alongside and

[1] James, p. 498.
[2] Admiral Tyler to Captain Dickinson, Jan. 31, 1815; Niles, viii. 345.

firing a gun, while the "Hornet," all aback, waited for him.

The result was very different from that of Decatur's two-hour battle with the "Endymion." In little more than twenty minutes of close action the "Penguin's" foremast and bowsprit were gone, her captain killed, and thirty-eight men killed or wounded, or more than one fourth the crew. The brig was "a perfect wreck," according to the British official report, when the senior surviving officer hailed and surrendered.[1] The "Hornet" was not struck in the hull, but was very much cut up in rigging and spars. She had two killed, and nine wounded. "It was evident," said Captain Biddle's report, "that our fire was greatly superior both in quickness and effect."

The "Penguin" was destroyed, and the "Hornet" and "Peacock" continued their cruise until April 27, when they chased for twenty-four hours a strange sail, which proved to be the British seventy-four "Cornwallis." On discovering the character of the chase Biddle made off to windward, but found that the enemy "sailed remarkably fast and was very weatherly." At daylight of the 29th, the "Cornwallis" was within gunshot on the "Hornet's" lee-quarter. Her shot did not take effect, and Biddle, by lightening his ship, drew out of fire; but a few hours later the enemy again came up within

[1] Report of Lieutenant McDonald, April 6, 1815; James, Appendix, p. cc, no. 111.

three quarters of a mile, in a calm sea, and opened once more. Three shot struck the "Hornet," but without crippling her. Biddle threw over everything that could be spared, except one long gun; and a fortunate change of wind enabled him a second time to creep out of fire. He escaped; but the loss of his guns, anchors, cables, and boats obliged him to make for San Salvador, where he heard the news of peace.[1]

Captain Warrington in the "Peacock" continued his cruise to the Indian Ocean, and captured four Indiamen. In the Straits of Sunda, June 30, he encountered a small East India Company's cruiser, whose commander hailed and announced peace. Warrington replied, "directing him at the same time to haul his colors down if it were the case, in token of it, — adding that if he did not, I should fire into him." The brig refused to strike its colors, and Warrington nearly destroyed her by a broadside.[2] For this violence little excuse could be offered, for the "Nautilus" was not half the "Peacock's" strength, and could not have escaped. Warrington, like most officers of the American navy, remembered the "Chesapeake" too well.

The cruise of the "President," "Peacock," and "Hornet" ended in the loss of the "President," the disabling of the "Hornet," and the arrival of the "Peacock" alone at the point intended for their

[1] Biddle's Report of June 10, 1815; Niles, viii. 438.
[2] Warrington's Letter of Nov. 11, 1815; Niles, x. 58.

common cruising-ground. No other national vessels were at sea after peace was signed, except the "Constitution," which late in December sailed from Boston under the command of Captain Charles Stewart, — a Philadelphian of Irish descent, not thirty-nine years old, but since 1806 a captain in the United States service.

Cruising between Gibraltar and Madeira, at about one o'clock on the afternoon of February 20 Captain Stewart discovered two sail ahead, which he chased and overtook at six o'clock. Both were ship-rigged sloops-of-war. The larger of the two was the "Cyane." Americans preferred to call her a frigate, but that designation, though vague at best, could hardly be applied to such a vessel. The "Cyane" was a frigate-built sloop-of-war, or corvette, like the "Little Belt," carrying a regular complement of one hundred and eighty-five men. Her length on the lower deck was one hundred and eighteen feet; her breadth was thirty-two feet. She carried thirty-three guns, all carronades except two long-nines or twelves. Her companion, the "Levant," was also a sloop-of-war of the larger sort, though smaller than the "Cyane." She mounted twenty-one guns, all carronades except two long nine-pounders. Her regular crew was one hundred and thirty-five men and boys.

Either separately or together the British ships were decidedly unequal to the "Constitution," which could, by remaining at long range, sink them both without receiving a shot in return. The "Constitution" carried thirty-two long twenty-four-pounders; while the two sloops could reply to these guns only by four long nine-pounders. The "Constitution" carried four hundred and fifty men; the two sloops at the time of the encounter carried three hundred and thirty-six seamen, marines, and officers.[1] The "Constitution" was built of great strength; the two sloops had only the frames of their class. The utmost that the British captains could hope was that one of the two vessels might escape by the sacrifice of the other.

Instead of escaping, the senior officer, Captain George Douglass of the "Levant," resolved to engage the frigate, "in the hopes, by disabling her, to prevent her intercepting two valuable convoys that sailed from Gibraltar about the same time as the 'Levant' and 'Cyane.'"[2] Captain Douglass knew his relative strength, for he had heard that the American frigate was on his course.[3] Yet he seriously expected to disable her, and made a courageous attempt to do so.

The two ships, close together, tried first for the weather-gauge, but the "Constitution" outsailed them also on that point. They then bore up in hope of delaying the engagement till night, but the "Constitution" overhauled them too rapidly for the success

[1] Statement of the actual force, etc., Stewart's Report; Niles, viii. 219.
[2] James, Naval Occurrences, p. 458.
[3] James, Naval Occurrences, p. 458.

of that plan. They then stood on the starboard tack, the "Cyane" astern, the "Levant" a half-cable length ahead, while the "Constitution" came up to windward and opened fire. Commodore Stewart's report described the result:[1] —

"At five minutes past six ranged up on the starboard side of the sternmost ship [the 'Cyane'], about three hundred yards distant, and commenced the action by broadsides, — both ships returning our fire with great spirit for about fifteen minutes. Then the fire of the enemy beginning to slacken, and the great column of smoke collected under our lee, induced us to cease our fire to ascertain their positions and conditions. In about three minutes the smoke clearing away, we found ourselves abreast of the headmost ship [the 'Levant'], the sternmost ship luffing up for our larboard quarter."

Three hundred yards was a long range for carronades, especially in British sloops whose marksmanship was indifferent at best. According to the British court-martial on the officers of the "Cyane" and "Levant," their carronades had little effect.[2] If Stewart managed his ship as his duty required, the two sloops until that moment should have been allowed to make little effective return of the "Constitution's" broadside of sixteen twenty-four-pounders except by two nine-pounders. They were in the position of the "Essex" at Valparaiso. The "Cyane" naturally luffed up, in order to bring her carronades

[1] Minutes of the Action; Niles, viii. 219.
[2] Niles, viii. 363. Cf. Letter of Lieutenant Shubrick; Niles, viii. 383.

to bear, but she was already cut to pieces, and made the matter worse by closing.

"We poured a broadside into the headmost ship," continued the American account, "and then braced aback our main and mizzen topsails and backed astern under cover of the smoke abreast the sternmost ship, when the action was continued with spirit and considerable effect until thirty-five minutes past six, when the enemy's fire again slackened."

The "Levant," after receiving two stern-raking fires, bore up at forty minutes past six and began to repair damages two miles to leeward. The "Cyane," having become unmanageable, struck at ten minutes before seven. The most remarkable incident of the battle occurred after the "Cyane" struck, when the "Constitution" went after the "Levant" which was in sight to leeward. The little "Levant," instead of running away, stood directly for the huge American frigate, more than three times her size, and ranging close alongside fired a broadside into her as the two ships passed on opposite tacks. Although the sloop received the "Constitution's" broadside in return, she was only captured at last after an hour's chase, at ten o'clock, much cut up in spars and rigging, but still sea-worthy, and with seven men killed and sixteen wounded, or only one casualty to six of her crew.

In truth, the injury inflicted by the "Constitution's" fire was not so great as might have been expected. The "Cyane" lost twelve killed and twenty-six wounded, if the American report was correct. Neither ship was dismasted or in a sinking condition. Both arrived safely, March 10, at Porto Praya. On the other hand, the "Constitution" was struck eleven times in the hull, and lost three men killed and twelve wounded, three of the latter mortally. She suffered more than in her battle with the "Guerriere," — a result creditable to the British ships, considering that in each case the "Constitution" could choose her own range.

Stewart took his prizes to the Cape de Verde Islands. At noon, March 11, while lying in port at Porto Praya, three British frigates appeared off the harbor, and Stewart instantly stood to sea, passing the enemy's squadron to windward within gunshot. The three frigates made chase, and at one o'clock, as the "Cyane" was dropping astern, Stewart signalled to her to tack ship, and either escape, if not pursued, or return to Porto Praya. The squadron paid no attention to the "Cyane," but followed the "Constitution" and "Levant." At three o'clock, the "Levant" falling behind, Stewart signalled her also to tack. Immediately the whole British squadron abandoned pursuit of the "Constitution" and followed the "Levant" to Porto Praya, where they seized her under the guns of the Portuguese batteries. Meanwhile the "Constitution" and "Cyane" escaped, and reached the United States without further accident. The extraordinary blunders of the British squadron were never satisfactorily explained.

These combats and cruises, with the last ravages of the privateers, closed the war on the ocean as it had long ceased on land; and meanwhile the people of the United States had turned their energies to undertakings of a wholly different character.

CHAPTER IV.

THE long, exciting, and splendid panorama of revolution and war, which for twenty-five years absorbed the world's attention and dwarfed all other interests, vanished more quickly in America than in Europe, and left fewer elements of disturbance. The transformation scene of a pantomime was hardly more sudden or complete than the change that came over the United States at the announcement of peace. In a single day, almost in a single instant, the public turned from interests and passions that had supplied its thought for a generation, and took up a class of ideas that had been unknown or but vaguely defined before.

At Washington the effect of the news was so extraordinary as to shake faith in the seriousness of party politics. Although the peace affected in no way party doctrine or social distinctions, a new epoch for the Union began from the evening of February 13, when the messenger from Ghent arrived with the treaty. No one stopped to ask why a government, which was discredited and falling to pieces at one moment, should appear as a successful and even a glorious national representative a moment afterward.

Politicians dismissed the war from their thoughts, as they dismissed the treaty, with the single phrase: "Not an inch ceded or lost!"[1] The commissioners from Massachusetts and Connecticut who appeared at Washington with the recommendations of the Hartford Convention, returned home as quietly as possible, pursued by the gibes of the press. The war was no more popular then than it had been before, as the subsequent elections proved; but the danger was passed, and passion instantly subsided.

Only by slow degrees the country learned to appreciate the extraordinary feat which had been performed, not so much by the people as by a relatively small number of individuals. Had a village rustic, with one hand tied behind his back, challenged the champion of the prize-ring, and in three or four rounds obliged him to draw the stakes, the result would have been little more surprising than the result of the American campaign of 1814. The most intelligent and best educated part of society both in the United States and in Great Britain could not believe it, and the true causes of British defeat remained a subject of conjecture and angry dispute. The enemies of the war admitted only that peace had saved Madison; but this single concession, which included many far-reaching consequences, was granted instantly, and from that moment the national government triumphed over all its immediate dangers.

[1] Ingersoll, ii. 311.

While the Senate unanimously ratified the treaty February 16, the House set to work with much more alacrity than was its habit to dispose of the business before it. Haste was necessary. Barely fourteen days remained before the Thirteenth Congress should expire, and in that interval some system of peace legislation must be adopted. The struggle over the proposed Bank charter was still raging, for the Senate had passed another bill of incorporation February 11, over which the House was occupied the whole day of February 13 in a sharp and close contest. The first effect of the peace was to stop this struggle. By a majority of one vote, seventy-four to seventy-three, February 17, the House laid the subject aside.

Three days afterward, February 20, the President sent to Congress a Message transmitting the treaty with its ratifications, and congratulating the country on the close of a war "waged with the success which is the natural result of the wisdom of the legislative councils, of the patriotism of the people, of the public spirit of the militia, and of the valor of the military and naval forces of the country." After recommending to Congress the interests of the soldiers and sailors, the Message passed to the reduction of expenditures, which required immediate attention:

"There are, however," continued Madison, "important considerations which forbid a sudden and general revocation of the measures that have been produced by the war. Experience has taught us that neither the pacific dispositions of the American people, nor the pacific character of their political institutions, can altogether exempt them from that strife which appears, beyond the ordinary lot of nations, to be incident to the actual period of the world; and the same faithful monitor demonstrates that a certain degree of preparation for war is not only indispensable to avert disasters in the onset, but affords also the best security for the continuance of peace."

The avowal that experience had shown the error of the principle adopted by the nation in 1801 was not confined to President Madison. Monroe spoke even more plainly. In a letter to the military committee, February 24, Monroe urged that an army of twenty thousand men should be retained on the peace establishment. Each soldier of the rank-and-file was supposed to cost in peace about two hundred dollars a year, and Monroe's proposal involved an annual expense of more than five million dollars.

As far as concerned Madison and Monroe the repudiation of old Republican principles seemed complete; but the people had moved less rapidly than their leaders. Had Congress, while debating the subject February 25, known that Napoleon was then quitting Elba to seize once more the control of France, and to rouse another European convulsion with all its possible perils to neutrals, the President's views might have been adopted without serious dispute; but in the absence of evident danger, an army of twenty thousand men seemed unnecessary. The finances warranted no such extravagance. Dallas wrote to

Eppes, the chairman of the Ways and Means Committee, a letter [1] dated February 20, sketching a temporary financial scheme for the coming year. He proposed to fund at seven per cent the outstanding Treasury notes, amounting to $18,637,000; and even after thus sweeping the field clear of pressing claims, he still required the extravagant war-taxes in order to meet expenses, and depended on a further issue of Treasury notes, or a loan, to support the peace establishments of the army and navy. The state of the currency was desperate, and the revenue for the year 1815 was estimated at $18,200,000 in the notes of State banks, — a sum little in excess of the estimated civil necessities.

The military committee of the House showed no sympathy with the new principles urged upon Congress by the Executive. Troup of Georgia reported a bill, February 22, fixing the peace establishment at ten thousand men, with two major-generals and four brigadiers. In submitting this proposal, Troup urged the House, February 25, to accept the reduction to ten thousand as the lowest possible standard, requiring only the expense of two and a half millions; but no sooner did he take his seat than Desha of Kentucky moved to substitute "six" for "ten," and a vigorous debate followed, ending in the adoption of Desha's amendment in committee by a majority of nineteen votes. The war leaders were greatly annoyed by this new triumph of the peace party. As a

[1] Annals of Congress, 1814–1815; iii. 1178.

matter of principle, the vote on Desha's amendment affirmed Jefferson's pacific system and condemned the Federalist heresies of Madison and Monroe. The war leaders could not acquiesce in such a decision, and rallying for another effort, February 27, they remonstrated hotly. Forsyth of Georgia was particularly emphatic in defining the issue : [1] —

"He had hoped that the spirit of calculation falsely styled economy, whose contracted view was fixed upon present expense, and was incapable of enlarging it to permanent and eventual advantage, had been laid forever by the powerful exorcisms of reason and experience. It would seem however that it had been only lulled by the presence of a more powerful demon. Since the potent spell of necessity had been broken, the troubled spirit of petty calculation was again awakened to vex the counsels and destroy the best hopes of the country."

For three years the friends of strong government, under the pressure of war, had been able to drive Congress more or less in their own direction; but at the announcement of peace their power was greatly lessened, and their unwilling associates were no longer disposed to follow their lead or to tolerate their assumptions of superiority. Desha retaliated in the tone of 1798 : —

"Do they suppose that the House do not understand the subject; or do they suppose that by this great flow of eloquence they can make the substantial part of the House change their opinions in so short a time? When I speak of the substantial part of the House, I mean

[1] Annals of Congress, 1814–1815, pp. 1213, 1250.

those who think much and speak but little; who make common-sense their guide, and not theoretical or visionary projects. . . . Some gentlemen advocate ten thousand and others twenty thousand of a standing army. The policy is easy to be seen through. The advocates of a perpetual system of taxation discover that if they cannot retain a considerable standing army, they will have no good plea for riveting the present taxes on the people."

In the process of national growth, public opinion had advanced since 1801 several stages in its development; but the speeches of Forsyth, Calhoun, and Lowndes on one side, like that of Desha on the other, left still in doubt the amount of change. While Forsyth admitted that he had under-estimated the strength of the economical spirit, Desha certainly over-estimated the force of the men "who think much and speak but little." With Federalist assistance, Desha's friends passed the bill for an army of six thousand men by a vote of seventy-five to sixty-five; but the Senate, by a more decided vote of eighteen to ten, substituted "fifteen" for "six." With this amendment the bill was returned to the House March 2, which by an almost unanimous vote refused to concur. The bill was sent to a conference committee, which reported the original plan of ten thousand men; and in the last hours of the session, March 3, the House yielded. By a vote of seventy to thirty-eight the peace establishment was fixed at ten thousand men.

The movement of public opinion was more evident in regard to the navy. Instead of repeating the experiments of 1801, Congress maintained the whole war establishment, and appropriated four million dollars chiefly for the support of frigates and ships-of-the-line. The vessels on the Lakes were dismantled and laid up; the gunboats, by an Act approved February 27, were ordered to be sold; but the sum of two hundred thousand dollars was appropriated for the annual purchase of ship-timber during the next three years, and the whole navy thenceforward consisted of cruisers, which were to be kept as far as possible in active service. As the first task of the new ships, an Act, approved March 3, authorized hostilities against the Dey of Algiers, who had indulged in the plunder of American commerce.

These hasty arrangements for the two services, coupled with an equally hasty financial makeshift, completed the career of the Thirteenth Congress, which expired March 4, as little admired or regretted as the least popular of its predecessors. Not upon Congress but upon the Executive Departments fell the burden of peace as of war, and on the Executive the new situation brought many embarrassments.

The first and most delicate task of the Government was the reduction of the army. No one could greatly blame Monroe for shrinking from the invidious duty of dismissing two thirds of the small force which had sustained so well and with so little support the character of the country; but the haste which he showed in leaving the War Department suggested also how keenly he must have suffered under its burdens. His name was sent to the Senate, February 27, as Secretary of State; no Secretary of War was nominated, but Dallas, with the courage that marked his character, undertook to manage the War Department as well as the Treasury until the necessary arrangements for the new army should be made.

April 8 Dallas wrote to six generals, — Brown, Jackson, Scott, Gaines, Macomb, and Ripley, — requesting their attendance at Washington to report a plan for the new army. Jackson and Gaines were unable to attend. The rest of the board reported a scheme dividing the country into two military districts, north and south; and into nine departments, five in the northern, four in the southern division, — allotting to each the troops needed for its service. May 17 the new arrangements were announced. Brown was ordered to command the northern district, with Ripley and Macomb as brigadiers. Jackson took the southern district, with Scott and Gaines as brigadiers. Eight regiments of infantry, one of riflemen, and one of light artillery were retained, together with the corps of artillery and engineers. As far as possible, all the officers whose names became famous for a generation received rank and reward.

No such operation was necessary for the navy, where no reduction was required. In the civil service, Madison enjoyed the satisfaction of rewarding the friends who had stood by him in his trials. February 27 he sent to the Senate, with the nomination of Monroe as Secretary of State, the name of J. Q. Adams as Minister to England. At the same time Bayard was appointed to St. Petersburg, and Gallatin to Paris. The nomination of Bayard proved to be an empty compliment, for he arrived, August 1, in the Delaware River, in the last stages of illness, and was carried ashore the next day only to die.

These appointments were well received and readily confirmed by the Senate; but Madison carried favoritism too far for the Senate's approval when, March 1, he nominated Major-General Dearborn to be Secretary of War. Dearborn had few or no enemies, but the distinction thus shown him roused such strong remonstrance that Madison hastened to recall the nomination, and substituted Crawford in Dearborn's place. The Senate had already rejected Dearborn, but consented to erase the record from their journal,[1] and Crawford became Secretary of War.

Thus the government in all its branches glided into the new conditions, hampered only by the confusion of the currency, which could not be overcome. The people were even more quick than the government to adapt themselves to peace. In New Orleans alone a few weeks of alarm were caused by extraordinary acts of arbitrary power on the part of General Jackson during the interval before the peace became officially known; but public order was not seriously dis-

[1] Madison to Dearborn, March 4, 1815; Madison's Works, ii. 598.

turbed, and the civil authority was restored March 13. Elsewhere the country scarcely stopped to notice the cost or the consequences of the war.

In truth the cost was moderate. Measured by loss of life in battle, it was less than that reported in many single battles fought by Napoleon. An army which never exceeded thirty thousand effectives, or placed more than four thousand regular rank-and-file in a single action, could not sacrifice many lives. According to the received estimates the number of men killed in battle on land did not much exceed fifteen hundred, including militia, while the total of killed and wounded little exceeded five thousand.[1] Sickness was more fatal than wounds, but a population of eight millions felt camp-diseases hardly more than its periodical malarial fevers.

The precise financial cost of the war, measured only by increase of debt, was equally moderate. During three years,— from February, 1812, until February, 1815,— the government sold six per cent bonds at various rates of discount, to the amount of fifty million dollars, and this sum was the limit of its loans, except for a few bank discounts of Treasury notes not exceeding a million in all. By forcing Treasury notes on its creditors the Treasury obtained the use of twenty millions more. After the peace it issued bonds and new Treasury notes, which raised the aggregate amount of war debt, as far as could be ascertained, to about eighty million five hundred

[1] Niles, x. 154.

thousand dollars, which was the war-addition to the old nominal capital of debt, and increased the total indebtedness to one hundred and twenty-seven millions at the close of the year 1815.[1]

The debt had exceeded eighty millions twenty years before, and in the interval the country had greatly increased its resources. The war debt was a trifling load, and would not have been felt except for the confusion of the currency and the unnecessary taxation imposed at the last moments of the war. That the currency and the war taxes were severe trials was not to be denied, but of other trials the people had little to complain.

Considering the dangers to which the United States were exposed, they escaped with surprising impunity. The shores of Chesapeake Bay and of Georgia were plundered; but the British government paid for the slaves carried away, and no town of importance except Washington was occupied by an enemy. Contrary to the usual experience of war, the richest parts of the country suffered least. Only the Niagara frontier was systematically ravaged. When the blockade of the coast was raised, every seaboard city was able instantly to resume its commercial habits without having greatly suffered from the interruption. The harvests of two seasons were ready for immediate export, and the markets of Europe were waiting to receive them. Every man found occupation, and capital instantly returned to its old channels. From the

[1] Dallas's Report of Dec. 6, 1815; State Papers, Finance, iii. 8.

moment of peace the exports of domestic produce began to exceed five million dollars a month, while four millions was the highest average for any previous twelvemonth, and the average for the seven years of embargo and blockade since 1807 fell much short of two and a half millions. The returns of commerce and navigation showed that during the seven months from March 1 to October 1, 1815, domestic produce valued at forty-six million dollars was exported, and American shipping to the amount of eight hundred and fifty-four thousand tons was employed in the business of export.[1]

The ease and rapidity of this revolution not only caused the war to be quickly forgotten, but also silenced political passions. For the first time in their history as a nation, the people of the United States ceased to disturb themselves about politics or patronage. Every political principle was still open to dispute, and was disputed; but prosperity put an end to faction. No evidence could be given to prove that the number or weight of persons who held the opinions commonly known as Federalist, diminished either then or afterward. Massachusetts showed no regret for the attitude she had taken. At the April election, six weeks after the proclamation of peace, although Samuel Dexter was the Republican candidate, the State still gave to Governor Strong a majority of about seven thousand in a total vote of ninety-five thousand. The Federalists reasonably

[1] State Papers, Commerce and Navigation, ii. 647.

regarded this vote as an express approval of the Hartford Convention and its proposed measures, and asked what would have been their majority had peace not intervened to save the Government from odium. They believed not only that their popular support would have been greater, but that it would also have shown a temper beyond control; yet the Federalist majority in April was no longer hostile to the Government.

The other elections bore the same general character. Even in New York the popular reaction seemed rather against the war than in its favor. New York city in April returned Federalist members to the State legislature, causing a tie in the Assembly, each party controlling sixty-three votes.[1] In Virginia the peace produced no change so decided as to warrant a belief that the war had become popular. In April John Randolph defeated Eppes and recovered control of his district. The State which had chosen sixteen Republicans and seven opposition congressmen in 1813, elected in 1815 seventeen Republicans and six opposition members. The stability of parties was the more remarkable in New York and Virginia, because those States were first to feel the effects of renewed prosperity.

After the excitement of peace was past, as the summer drew toward a close, economical interests dwarfed the old political distinctions and gave a new character to parties. A flood of wealth poured into

[1] Hammond, i. 401.

the Union at a steady rate of six or seven million dollars a month, and the distribution of so large a sum could not fail to show interesting results. The returns soon proved that the larger portion belonged to the Southern States. Cotton, at a valuation of twenty cents a pound, brought seventeen and a half millions to the planters; tobacco brought eight and a quarter millions; rice produced nearly two million eight hundred thousand dollars. Of fifty millions received from abroad in payment for domestic produce within seven or eight months after the peace, the slave States probably took nearly two thirds, though the white population of the States south of the Potomac was less than half the white population of the Union. The stimulus thus given to the slave system was violent, and was most plainly shown in the cotton States, where at least twenty million dollars were distributed in the year 1815 among a white population hardly exceeding half a million in all, while the larger portion fell to the share of a few slave-owners.[1]

Had the Northern States shared equally in the effects of this stimulus, the situation would have remained relatively as before; but the prosperity of the North was only moderate. The chief export of the Northern States was wheat and Indian corn. Even of these staples, Maryland and Virginia furnished a share; yet the total value of the wheat and corn exported from the Union was but eight million

[1] State Papers, Commerce and Navigation, ii. 23.

three hundred and fifty thousand dollars, while that of tobacco alone was eight and a quarter millions. While flour sold at nine or ten dollars a barrel, and Napoleon's armies were vying with the Russians and Austrians in creating an artificial demand, the Middle States made a fair profit from their crops, although much less than was made by the tobacco and cotton planters; but New England produced little for export, and there the peace brought only ruin.

Ordinarily shipping was the source of New England's profits. For twenty-five years the wars in Europe had given to New England shipping advantages which ceased with the return of peace. At first the change of condition was not felt, for every ship was promptly employed; but the reappearance of foreign vessels in American harbors showed that competition must soon begin, and that the old rates of profit were at an end.

Had this been all, Massachusetts could have borne it; but the shipping on the whole suffered least among New England interests. The new manufactures, in which large amounts of capital had been invested, were ruined by the peace. If the United States poured domestic produce valued at fifty million dollars into the markets of Great Britain, Great Britain and her dependencies poured in return not less than forty million dollars' worth of imports into the United States, and inundated the Union with manufactured goods which were sold at any sacrifice to relieve the

British markets. Although the imported manufactures paid duties of twenty-five per cent or more, they were sold at rates that made American competition impossible.

The cotton manufacturers of Rhode Island, in a memorial to Congress, dated October 20, 1815, declared that their one hundred and forty manufactories, operating one hundred and thirty thousand spindles, could no longer be worked with profit, and were threatened with speedy destruction.[1] New England could foresee with some degree of certainty the ultimate loss of the great amount of capital invested in these undertakings; but whether such fears for the future were just or not, the loss of present profits was not a matter of speculation, but of instant and evident notoriety. Before the close of the year 1815 little profit was left to the new industries. The cotton manufacture, chiefly a New England interest, was supposed to employ a capital of forty million dollars, and to expend about fifteen millions a year in wages.[2] The woollen manufacture, largely in Connecticut, was believed to employ a capital of twelve million dollars.[3] Most of the large factories for these staples were altogether stopped.

From every quarter the peace brought distress upon New England. During the war most of the

[1] Annals of Congress, 1815–1816, p. 1651.
[2] Report on Manufactures, Feb. 13, 1816; Niles ix. 447.
[3] Report on Woollen Manufactures, March 6, 1816; Niles, x. 82.

richer prizes had been sent to New England ports, and the sale of their cargoes brought money and buyers into the country; but this monopoly ceased at the same moment with the monopoly of manufactures. The lumber trade was almost the last surviving interest of considerable value, but in November Parliament imposed duties on American lumber which nearly destroyed the New England trade. The fisheries alone seemed to remain as a permanent resource.

The effect of these changes from prosperity to adversity was shown in the usual forms. Emigration became active. Thousands of native New Englanders transferred themselves to the valley of the Mohawk and Western New York. All the cities of the coast had suffered a check from the war; but while New York and Philadelphia began to recover their lost ground, Boston was slow to feel the impulse. The financial reason could be partly seen in the bank returns of Massachusetts. In January, 1814, the Massachusetts banks held about $7,300,000 in specie.[1] In January and February, 1815, when peace was declared, the same banks probably held still more specie, as the causes which led to the influx were not removed. In June, about three months later, they held only $3,464,000 in specie, and the drain steadily continued, until in June, 1816, the specie in their vaults was reduced to $1,260,000, while their

[1] Niles's Articles on the New England Convention, Dec. 8, 1814; Niles, vii. 196.

discounts were not increased and their circulation was diminished.[1]

The state of the currency and the policy pursued by the Treasury added to the burden carried by New England. There alone the banks maintained specie payments. In the autumn of 1815, while the notes of the Boston banks were equivalent to gold, Treasury notes were at eleven per cent discount in Boston; New York bank-notes were at eleven and a half per cent discount; Philadelphia at sixteen; Baltimore at seventeen and eighteen; and United States six-percent bonds sold at eighty-six. In New England the Government exacted payments either in Treasury notes or in the notes of local banks equivalent to specie. Elsewhere it accepted the notes of local banks at a rate of depreciation much greater than that of Treasury notes. This injustice in exacting taxes was doubled by an equivalent injustice in paying debts. In New England the Treasury compelled creditors to take payment in whatever medium it had at hand, or to go unpaid. Elsewhere the Treasury paid its debts in the currency it received for its taxes.

Dallas admitted the wrong, but made no serious attempt to correct it. So complicated was the currency that the Treasury was obliged to keep four accounts with each of its ninety four banks of deposit, — (1) in the currency of the bank itself; (2) in

[1] Schedule etc.; Massachusetts Senate Document, No. 38, Jan. 17, 1838.

special deposits of other bank currency; (3) in special deposits of Treasury notes bearing interest; (4) in small Treasury notes not bearing interest. In New England, and also in the cities of New York and Philadelphia, for some months after the peace the taxes were paid in Treasury notes. So little local currency was collected at these chief centres of business that the Treasury did not attempt to discharge its warrants there in currency. As the Treasury notes gradually appreciated in value above the local bank-notes of the Middle States, tax-payers ceased to make payments in them, and paid in their local bank-notes. Little by little the accumulation of local currency in the Treasury deposits at Philadelphia and New York increased, until the Treasury was able to draw on them in payment of its warrants; but even at those points this degree of credit was not attained in 1815, and in New England the Treasury still made no payments except in Treasury notes, or the notes of distant banks at a discount still greater than that of Treasury notes. This exceptional severity toward New England was admitted by Dallas, and excused only for the reason that if he were just to New England he must be severe to the rest of the country. Every holder of a Treasury warrant would have demanded payment at the place where the local medium was of the highest value, which was Boston; and as the Treasury could not pay specie at Boston without exacting specie elsewhere, Dallas paid no attention to Constitutional scruples or legal objections, but arbitrarily excluded Boston from the number of points where warrants were paid in local currency.[1]

The people of Boston criticised, with much severity and with apparent justice, Dallas's management of the finances, which seemed to require some explanation not furnished in his reports. By an Act approved March 3, Congress authorized a loan of $18,452,800 to absorb the outstanding Treasury notes. At that time, under the momentary reaction of peace excitement, Treasury notes were supposed to be worth about ninety-four cents in the dollar, and Dallas expected to convert them nearly dollar for dollar into six-per-cent bonds. His proposals were issued March 10, inviting bids for twelve millions, and requiring only "that the terms of the proposals should bear some relation to the actual fair price of stock in the market of Philadelphia or New York." When the bids were received, Dallas rejected them all, because in his opinion they were below the market rates. "In point of fact," he afterward said, "no direct offer was made to subscribe at a higher rate than eighty-nine per cent, while some of the offers were made at a rate even lower than seventy-five per cent." Although the old six-per-cents were then selling at eighty-nine, eighty-eight, and eighty-seven in Boston and New York, Dallas held that "the real condition of the public credit" required him to insist upon ninety-five as the value of the new stock.

[1] Dallas's Report of Dec. 3, 1816; State Papers, Finance, iii. 130.

After failing to obtain ninety-five or even ninety as the price of his bonds, Dallas resorted to expedients best described in his own words. As he could not fund the Treasury notes at the rate he wished, he abandoned the attempt, and used the loan only to supply the local wants of the Treasury : —

"The objects of the loan being to absorb a portion of the Treasury-note debt, and to acquire a sufficiency of local currency for local purposes, the price of the stock at the Treasury was of course independent of the daily up-and-down prices of the various stock markets in the Union, and could only be affected by the progress toward the attainment of those objects. Thus while the wants of the Treasury were insufficiently supplied, offers to subscribe were freely accepted, and the parties were sometimes authorized and invited to increase the amount of their offers; but where the local funds had so accumulated as to approach the probable amount of the local demands, the price of the stock was raised at the Treasury, and when the accumulation was deemed adequate to the whole amount of the local demands the loan was closed." [1]

Governments which insisted upon borrowing at rates higher than the money market allowed, could do so only by helping to debase the currency. Dallas's course offered encouragement to the suspended banks alone. The schedule of his loans proved that he paid a premium to insolvency. Of all places where he most needed " a sufficiency of local cur-

[1] Report of the Secretary of the Treasury, Dec. 6, 1815 ; State Papers, Finance, iii. 11.

rency for local purposes," Boston stood first; but he borrowed in Boston less than one hundred thousand dollars, and this only in Treasury notes. Next to Boston stood New York; but in New York Dallas borrowed only $658,000, also in Treasury notes. In Philadelphia he obtained more than three millions, and took $1,845,000 in the depreciated local currency. In Baltimore he took nearly two millions in local currency; and in the bank paper of the District of Columbia, which was the most depreciated of all, he accepted $2,282,000 in local currency.[1] Thus the loan which he had asked Congress to authorize for the purpose of absorbing the excess of Treasury notes, brought into the Treasury only about three millions in these securities, while it relieved the banks of Philadelphia, Baltimore, and Washington of six millions of their depreciated paper, worth about eighty cents in the dollar, and provided nothing to redeem the government's overdue bills at Boston and New York.

Had Dallas pursued a different course and funded all the overdue Treasury notes at the market rate, he might not have relieved New England, but he would have placed the government in a position to deal effectually with the suspended banks elsewhere. The immediate result of his refusal to redeem the dishonored Treasury notes was to depress their market value, and to discredit the government. Treasury notes fell to eighty-eight and eighty-seven, while the

[1] Report of Dec. 6, 1815; State Papers, Finance, iii. 11.

six-per-cents fell as low as eighty-one. In Washington, Baltimore, and Philadelphia Dallas obtained enough local currency to meet local obligations, and doubtless saved to the government a small percentage by thus trafficking in its own discredit; but in gaining this advantage he offered encouragement to the over-issues of the suspended banks, and he helped to embarrass the solvent banks in the chief commercial centres as well as those in New England.[1]

At the close of the year 1815 the general effect of the peace was already well defined. The Southern States were in the full enjoyment of extraordinary prosperity. The Middle States were also prosperous and actively engaged in opening new sources of wealth. Only the Eastern States suffered under depression; but there it was so severe as to warrant a doubt whether New England could recover from the shock. The new epoch of American history began by the sudden decline of Massachusetts to the lowest point of relative prosperity and influence she had ever known, and by an equally sudden stimulus to the South and West. So discredited was Massachusetts that she scarcely ventured to complain, for every complaint uttered by her press was answered by the ironical advice that she should call another Hartford Convention.

[1] Gallatin to Jefferson, Nov. 27, 1815; Gallatin's writings, i. 666. Gallatin to Macon, April 23, 1816; Gallatin's writings, i. 697.

CHAPTER V.

BETWEEN 1801 and 1815, great changes in the American people struck the most superficial observer. The Rights of Man occupied public thoughts less, and the price of cotton more, in the later than in the earlier time. Although in 1815 Europe was suffering under a violent reaction against free government, Americans showed little interest and no alarm, compared with their emotions of twenty years before. Napoleon resumed his empire, and was overthrown at Waterloo, without causing the people of the United States to express a sign of concern in his fate; and France was occupied by foreign armies without rousing among Americans a fear of England. Foreign affairs seemed reduced to the question whether England would consent to negotiate a treaty of commerce.

After excluding most of the American demands, Lord Castlereagh consented to a commercial convention abolishing discriminating duties, and admitting American commerce with the East Indies. This treaty, signed July 3, seemed to satisfy American demands, and the British Ministry showed no wish to challenge new disputes. With France, the disturbed condition of government permitted no diplomatic arrangement. The only foreign country that required serious attention was Algiers; and Decatur, with a strong squadron of the new American cruisers, speedily compelled the Dey to sign a treaty more favorable to the United States than he had yet signed with any other nation. Tunis and Tripoli showed a similar disposition, and Decatur returned home in the autumn, having settled to his satisfaction all the matters intrusted to his care.

Under such circumstances, without an anxiety in regard to foreign or domestic affairs, President Madison sent his Annual Message to Congress December 5, 1815. It told a pleasant story of successful administration and of rapidly growing income; but its chief historical interest lay in the lines of future party politics that Madison more or less unconsciously sketched. The Message proved, or seemed to prove, that Madison's views and wishes lay in the direction of strong government. He advised "liberal provision" for defence; more military academies; an improved and enlarged navy; effectual protection to manufactures; new national roads and canals; a national university; and such an organization of the militia as would place it promptly and effectually under control of the national government. Madison seemed to take his stand, beyond further possibility of change, on the system of President Washington.

Dallas's report echoed the tone of Alexander Hamilton. Very long, chiefly historical, and interesting beyond the common, this Treasury Report of 1815 recommended a scale of annual expenditure exceeding twenty-seven millions, in place of the old scale of ten millions. The expenditure was to be but a part of the system. A protective tariff of customs duties was assumed to be intended by Congress, and a national bank was urged as the only efficient means by which the government could recover control over the currency.

Although the President was less emphatic than the secretary in holding a national bank to be the only cure for the disorders of the currency, he was prepared to go a step further by issuing government paper as a national currency, and suggested that alternative in his Message. A national bank or a national currency was an equally energetic exercise of supreme central powers not expressly granted by the Constitution and much disputed by theorists. Dallas's objection to the national currency did not relate to its inefficiency, but to the practical difficulty of issuing paper and keeping it in issue. Either course of action implied a recurrence to the principles of President Washington. The Executive proposed to start afresh in 1816 from its point of departure in 1790.

The Fourteenth Congress was well disposed to support the attempt. Under the stress of war the people had selected as their representatives the ablest and most vigorous men of their generation. The war leaders were mostly returned, — Calhoun, Clay, Lowndes, Richard M. Johnson, Peter B. Porter, and John Forsyth, — while the old peace party was strongly represented by Timothy Pickering, Daniel Webster, John Randolph, Grosvenor of New York, and Stanford of North Carolina; but perhaps the most distinguished member of all was William Pinkney of Maryland. A swarm of younger men, far above the average, reinforced both sides of the House. Philip P. Barbour sat again for Virginia. John McLean sat again for Ohio. Henry St. George Tucker came for the first time into the House. Joseph Hopkinson, Samuel D. Ingham, and John Sergeant raised the character of the Pennsylvania delegation; and Samuel Smith, at last ejected from the Senate by a Federalist legislature in Maryland, reappeared in the House for the first time since 1803.

The Senate was also improved. The disappearance of Leib and Samuel Smith was made more suggestive by the resignation of Giles. David Stone of North Carolina, another independent much given to opposition at critical moments, also resigned; and another of the same class, Joseph Anderson of Tennessee, who had been a member of the Senate since 1797, retired to become First Comptroller of the Treasury. These retirements removed the chief abettors of faction, and changed the character of the Senate until it seemed to belong to a different epoch. Jonathan Roberts still sat in the place of Leib. Armistead Mason took the seat of Giles, and with James Barbour gave Madison for the first time the full support of Virginia. Macon took the place of David Stone. George W. Campbell took the place of Joseph Anderson. Robert G. Harper, the old champion of Federalism, succeeded Samuel Smith from Maryland. The Senate scarcely recognized itself as the same body that since 1808 had so persistently thwarted and fretted the President.

In the arrangement of new party divisions the Fourteenth Congress, unlike its recent predecessors, consciously aimed to take a decided share. The House seemed for the first time in many years to pride itself on intellectual superiority. William Pinkney, Calhoun, Lowndes, Clay, Daniel Webster, John Randolph, and their associates were not men who bowed to authority, even of the people, but rather looked on the task of government as a function of superior intellect. They proposed to correct what they considered mistaken popular tendencies. Each expressed his ideas with sufficient clearness in the form natural to him. Calhoun generalized before descending to particulars.[1]

"In the policy of nations," reasoned Calhoun, "there are two extremes: one extreme, in which justice and moderation may sink in feebleness; another, in which that lofty spirit which ought to animate all nations, particularly free ones, may mount up to military violence. These extremes ought to be equally avoided; but of the two, I consider the first far the most dangerous. . . . I

[1] Speech of Jan. 31, 1816; Annals of Congress, 1815–1816, p. 830.

consider the extreme of weakness not only the most dangerous of itself, but as that extreme to which the people of this country are peculiarly liable."

Clay, aiming at the same objects, dwelt chiefly on foreign dangers as the motive of the strong government he wished to establish. "That man must be blind to the indications of the future," he declared,[1] "who cannot see that we are destined to have war after war with Great Britain, until, if one of the two nations be not crushed, all grounds of collision shall have ceased between us." He wished to create a government that should control the destinies of both American continents by a display of armed force. "He confessed with infinite regret that he saw a supineness throughout the country which left him almost without hope that what he believed the correct policy would be pursued," toward aiding the Spanish colonies against their mother country. Both Calhoun and Clay admitted that they wished to govern in a sense not approved by an apparent majority of the nation; and the sympathies of the House were openly or secretly with them.

Of the contrary sentiment, John Randolph was the champion. Although his early career had ended in the most conspicuous failure yet known in American politics, he returned to the House, with intelligence morbidly sharpened, to begin a second epoch of his life with powers and materials that gave him

[1] Speech of Jan. 29, 1816; Annals of Congress, 1815-1816, p. 787.

the position of equal among men like Calhoun, Pinkney, and Webster. Randolph held a decisive advantage in wishing only to obstruct. He had no legislation to propose, and his political philosophy suited that extreme " to which," according to Calhoun, " the people of this country are peculiarly liable." Early in the session Randolph showed that he understood even better than Calhoun and Clay the division between himself and them. " If the warning voice of Patrick Henry," he said in the debate of January 31, 1816,[1] " had not apprised me long ago, the events of this day would have taught me that this Constitution does not comprise one people, but that there are two distinct characters in the people of this nation." In every growing people two or more distinct characters were likely to rise, else the people would not grow; but the primal character, which Randolph meant to represent, enjoyed the political advantage of passive resistance to impulse from every direction.

In reply to Calhoun, Randolph defined the issue with his usual skill of words : [2] —

" As the gentleman from South Carolina has presented the question to the House, they and the nation cannot have the slightest difficulty in deciding whether they will give up the States or not; whether they will, in fact, make this an elective monarchy. The question is whether or not we are willing to become one great consolidated

[1] Annals of Congress, 1815–1816, p. 841.
[2] Annals of Congress. 1815–1816, p. 844.

nation; or whether we have still respect enough for those old, respectable institutions to regard their integrity and preservation as a part of our policy."

Randolph's eccentricities, which amounted to insanity, prevented him from exercising in the House the influence to which his experience and abilities entitled him, but did not prevent him from reflecting the opinions of a large part of the nation, particularly in the South. Between these two impulses the Fourteenth Congress was to choose a path, subject to the future judgment of their constituents.

The Executive urged them on. Dallas began by sending to Calhoun, the chairman of the Committee on Currency, a plan for a national bank with a capital of thirty-five millions and power to increase it to fifty millions; with twenty-five directors, five of whom were to be appointed by the government to represent its share in the bank stock, of which the government was to subscribe one fifth.[1]

In another report, dated Feb. 12, 1816, Dallas recommended a protective tariff and sketched its details. Upon cotton fabrics he proposed a duty of thirty-three and one half per cent on their value; on woollens, twenty-eight per cent; on linen, hemp, and silk, twenty per cent; on paper, leather, etc., thirty-five per cent; on earthenware, glassware, etc., thirty per cent; on bar-iron, seventy-five cents per hundred weight; on rolled iron, a dollar and a half; and

[1] Dallas to Calhoun, Dec. 24, 1815; Annals of Congress, 1815–1816, p. 505.

on unenumerated articles, fifteen per cent. These duties were avowedly protective, intended to serve as the foundation of a system, and to perpetuate the policy to which the Government stood pledged by its legislation for the last six years. In connection with a proposed reduction of internal taxes, the Bank and the Tariff covered the financial field.

The House first grappled with the subject of revenue. The Committee of Ways and Means, through William Lowndes, reported, Jan. 9, 1816, a scheme embodied in twelve Resolutions intended to serve as the guide to definite legislation. Lowndes assumed a net annual revenue of $25,369,000; and to obtain this sum he proposed to shift the burden of about seven million dollars from internal taxation to the customs, by an addition of forty-two per cent to the rates of permanent duty.[1] The direct tax was to be retained to the amount of three million dollars, and an annual fund of $13,500,000 was to be set aside for the interest and principal of the national debt.

Hardly had the debate begun when Randolph, January 16, dragged the question of a protective system into the prominence it was thenceforward to maintain. Two years of repose had singularly improved his skill in the choice of language and in the instigation of class against class.

"The manufacturer," said he,[2] "is the citizen of no place or any place; the agriculturist has his property, his

[1] Report of Committee; Annals of Congress, 1815–1816, p. 516.
[2] Annals of Congress, 1815–1816, p. 687.

lands, his all, his household Gods to defend, — and like that meek drudge the ox, who does the labor and ploughs the ground, then for his reward takes the refuse of the farm-yard, the blighted blades and the mouldy straw, and the mildewed shocks of corn for his support. . . . Alert, vigilant, enterprising, and active, the manufacturing interest are collected in masses, and ready to associate at a moment's warning for any purpose of general interest to their body. Do but ring the fire-bell, and you can assemble all the manufacturing interest of Philadelphia in fifteen minutes. Nay, for the matter of that they are always assembled; they are always on the Rialto, and Shylock and Antonio meet there every day as friends, and compare notes, and possess in trick and intelligence what, in the goodness of God to them, the others can never possess."

Randolph's political sagacity was nowhere better shown than in replying, Jan. 31, 1816, to a speech of Calhoun: "On whom do your impost duties bear?" he asked.[1] "Upon whom bears the duty on coarse woollens and linens and blankets, upon salt, and all the necessaries of life? On poor men, and on slaveholders." With a perception abnormally keen, Randolph fixed on the tariff and the slaveholders as the necessary combination to oppose the nationalizing efforts of Calhoun and Clay.

No leader of note supported Randolph. He stood alone, or with only the support of Stanford, as far as concerned debate; but he led nearly half the House. Upon Benjamin Hardin's motion, February 3, to re-

[1] Annals of Congress, 1815-1816, p. 842.

peal the direct tax immediately and altogether, a motion which struck at the root of Dallas's scheme, the House decided by eighty-one votes against seventy-three to sustain the secretary. On the passage of the bill to continue the direct tax of three million dollars for one year, the minority lacked but a change of three votes to defeat it. The bill passed, March 4, by a vote of sixty-seven to sixty-three.

On the tariff the House was more closely divided. The Committee of Ways and Means consisted of seven members. Lowndes was chairman. Three other members were from the South, one of whom, Robertson of Louisiana, wished protection for sugar. Three members were from the North, one of whom, Ingham of Pennsylvania, represented Dallas's views. The chief question concerned the duty on cottons and woollens. So close was the division that Ingham, to use his own words, was struck dumb with astonishment when the committee, after adopting a duty of fifty-six per cent for the protection of sugar, voted to impose a duty of only twenty per cent on cottons and woollens. "It was, however, too glaringly inconsistent and palpably wrong to be persisted in, and therefore it was that the Committee of Ways and Means, upon reconsideration, substituted the twenty-five per cent which was reported in the bill."[1]

When the bill came before the House, Clay moved, March 21, to substitute the rate of thirty-three and

[1] Annals of Congress, 1815–1816, p. 1245.

one third per cent for that of twenty-five per cent on cottons, for the express purpose of testing the sense of the House. Clay and the Northern protectionists held that the committee's bill did not afford protection enough. The committee, also admitting the propriety of protection, maintained that twenty-five per cent was sufficient. On both sides some temper was shown, and charges of sectionalism were made. By a vote of sixty-eight to sixty-one, the House in committee voted, March 22, to impose a duty of thirty per cent. Daniel Webster then moved to limit this rate to two years, after which the duty should be twenty-five per cent for two years more, when it should be reduced to twenty per cent. Finally the House adopted a duty of twenty-five per cent for three years. Webster also carried, March 27, a motion to reduce the proposed duty on bar-iron from seventy-five to forty-five cents a hundred weight.

All the members of note, except Randolph, professed to favor protection. Calhoun was as decided as Ingham. "He believed the policy of the country required protection to our manufacturing establishments."[1] The bill was assumed to offer protection enough, and the House disputed only whether the adopted duties were or were not sufficient. The actual free-trade sentiment was shown, April 8, when Randolph made a final motion to postpone, and was beaten by a vote of ninety-five to forty-seven.

[1] Annals of Congress, 1815–1816, p. 1272.

The bill promptly passed the Senate, and was approved by the President April 27; but the true issue was undecided. No one could deny that if the duty of twenty-five per cent on cottons and woollens should prove to be insufficient, the House was pledged to increase it. The bill was avowedly protective. In regard to the coarser Indian cottons, it was practically prohibitive, since it valued them all, for tariff purposes, at twenty-five cents a yard, — a rate which on the cheaper fabrics raised the duty above one hundred per cent. Yet when the tariff of 1816 proved to be little protective, in after years it was commonly represented as a revenue and not a protective tariff. In substance, Randolph's opinions controlled the House.

Dallas was more fortunate in regard to the Bank. Randolph's hostility to State banks was greater than to the Bank of the United States. Calhoun reported, January 8, the bill to incorporate for twenty years a new National Bank with a capital of thirty-five million dollars, and supported it, February 26, by a speech showing that the Bank was a proper means for attaining the Constitutional object of restoring the money of the country to its true medium. Active opposition came chiefly from the Federalists. Even Samuel Smith seemed to plead rather that the State banks should be gently treated than that the National Bank should be opposed. Randolph, while professing hostility to the new Bank on any and every ground suggested by others, concluded by pledging himself to support any adequate means for reducing the overpowering influence of the State banks. Clay thought himself obliged to leave the Speaker's chair in order to recant in the most public manner his errors of 1811. Forsyth, one of Calhoun's ablest allies, went so far in his support of the measure as to assert without reserve that the power to suspend specie payments — a power expressly reserved to the government by Calhoun's bill — belonged undoubtedly to Congress, an opinion which the House did not share. In the Republican ranks open opposition to the Bank seemed almost silenced; and the member who made himself most conspicuous in hostility to the bill was Daniel Webster, — the last of all in whom such a course was natural.

Webster's criticism on Calhoun's Constitutional argument was made in his loftiest manner. The currency, he said, needed no reform, for it was, by the Constitution and the law, gold and silver; nor had Congress the right to make any other medium current. The true remedy was for Congress to interdict the bills of the suspended banks.[1] Had he been content to rest his opposition on that ground alone, Webster could not have been answered, although he might have been regarded as an impracticable politician; but as the bill came toward its passage, and as several Federalists declared in its favor, he pressed his hostility so far, and with so much dogmatism, that several of his own party revolted, and Grosvenor of

[1] Annals of Congress, 1815–1816, p. 1091.

New York replied sharply that he did not propose to be drilled to vote on whatever any one might choose to call a principle.

In spite of determined opposition from Webster, Pitkin, John Sergeant, and other Federalists, the House passed the bill, March 14, by a vote of eighty to seventy-one. The majority was small, but of the minority not less than thirty-eight were Federalists; and, omitting Randolph and Stanford, only thirty-one Republicans voted against the bill. The House contained one hundred and seventeen Republicans. In the Senate the opposition was almost wholly confined to Federalists, and the bill passed by a majority much larger than that in the House. Twenty-two senators voted in its favor; only twelve voted against it, and of the twelve only four were Republicans. The President approved it April 10; and thus, after five years of financial disorder, the Republican party reverted to the system of Washington, and resumed powers it had found indispensable to government.

The Federalists of New England were in a situation too alarming to bear even the little delay required to organize the Bank. For them a general return to specie payments was the only escape from imminent ruin; and acting on this conviction, Webster moved, April 26, a joint Resolution ordering that all taxes should be collected after Feb. 1, 1817, in some medium equivalent to specie, thus allowing but nine months for the work of resumption. The same day the House passed the Resolution by the decisive majority of seventy-one to thirty-four. The Senate substituted February 20 as the day of resumption, and passed the Resolution April 29, which was approved by the President the next day.

In contrast with the imbecility of many previous Congresses, the vigor of the Fourteenth Congress in thus settling the new scale of government was remarkable; but other measures of importance were not wanting. An Act approved April 29 appropriated one million dollars annually for three years to build ships of war; an Act approved April 19 authorized the people of Indiana to form a State government. A bill, which passed the House but was postponed by the Senate and became law at the next session, provided for the admission of Mississippi. In still another direction the House showed its self-confidence in a manner that caused unusual popular excitement. It undertook to increase the pay of its own members and of senators.

The scale of salary for public officials was low. The President, relatively highly paid, received twenty-five thousand dollars. The Secretaries of State and Treasury received five thousand; those of War and Navy, four thousand; the Attorney-General, three thousand; Chief-Justice Marshall was paid four thousand, and the six associate justices received thirty-five hundred dollars each.

While the Executive and Judiciary were paid regular salaries, Congress stood on a different footing. Legislators had never been paid what was considered an equivalent for their time and services. They were supposed to be unpaid; but such a rule excluded poor men from the public service, and therefore the colonial legislatures adopted a practice, which Congress continued, of allowing what were supposed to be the reasonable expenses of members. The First Congress fixed upon six dollars a day, and six dollars for every twenty miles of estimated journey, as a suitable scale of expense both for senators and representatives;[1] and the same rate had been continued for twenty-five years. No one supposed it sufficient to support a household, but poor men could live upon it. Desha of Kentucky averred that it was a fair allowance for the average representative. According to him, board was twelve or thirteen dollars a week, and the total cost of a session of one hundred and fifty days amounted to five hundred and seventy or eighty dollars; so that the western and southwestern members, with whose habits he was familiar, carried home, with their mileage, about four hundred and fifty dollars in savings.[2]

In the pride of conscious superiority the Fourteenth Congress undertook to change the system; and Richard M. Johnson, probably the most popular member of the House, assumed the risk of popular displeasure. In moving for a committee, March 4, Johnson repudiated the idea of increasing the pay; and his committee, including Webster, Pitkin, Jackson, the

[1] Act of Sept. 22, 1789. Act of March 10, 1796.
[2] Annals of Congress; 1816–1817, p. 492.

President's brother-in-law, Grosvenor, and McLean of Ohio, reported through him that fifteen hundred dollars a year was the correct equivalent of six dollars a day.

The bill known as the Compensation Bill was reported March 6, and was debated for two days with some animation. Among its supporters John Randolph was prominent, and gave offence to the opponents of the measure by his usual tactics. Most of the friends of the bill stoutly insisted that it did not increase the pay; most of its opponents averred that it more than doubled the amount. Calhoun admitted the increase of pay, and favored it, in order to retain "young men of genius without property" in the public service. The bill was hurried through the House.

"The Compensation Bill," said Forsyth at the next session,[1] "was the only one of any interest pushed through the Committee of the whole House and ordered to a third reading in a single day. All motions to amend were rejected; for the committee to rise and report progress and ask leave to sit again, met with a similar fate. . . . The House refused repeated propositions to adjourn, and continued its sittings until the bill was ordered to be engrossed."

No time was lost. Johnson moved for a committee March 4; the committee reported the bill March 6; the House in committee took it up March 7, and reported it the same day. The House passed it March

[1] Annals of Congress; 1816–1817, p. 559.

8, by a vote of eighty-one to sixty-seven. In the Senate the bill was read for a second time March 12. In the course of the debate one of the New Jersey senators, commenting on the haste shown by the House to pass the bill, added that also "in the Senate postponement, commitment, and amendment are all refused, and it is to be pushed through by main strength with a haste altogether unusual." The Senate passed it March 14, by a vote of twenty-one to eleven; and it received the President's signature March 19, barely a fortnight after Johnson's request for a committee.

At the time when the bill was still under consideration by the President, and the House had just passed the Bank Act, the Republican members of both Houses met to nominate a candidate to succeed Madison as President. Three candidates were in the field,— Daniel D. Tompkins, William H. Crawford, and James Monroe.

The choice was a matter of small consequence, for any candidate of the Republican party was sure of almost unanimous election, and all were respectable men; but Tompkins could expect little support at a time when Congress selected the candidate, for only men well known in the national service were likely to satisfy the standard of Congressmen. The true contest lay between Crawford and Monroe, and was complicated, as far as the candidates themselves understood it, by personal intrigues on both sides. Perhaps Crawford's strength was the greater, for four fifths of the New York members favored him rather than the Virginian.[1] In cases where no strong feeling fixed results, dexterity in management might overcome a preference between persons; and by some means never explained, the preference of the New York members for Crawford was overcome. One of these members — a competent observer — believed that Martin Van Buren and Peter B. Porter, for reasons of their own, prevented New York from declaring for Crawford when such a declaration would have decided the result.[2] Crawford himself at the last professed to withdraw from the contest,[3] and several of his warm friends did not attend the caucus. On the evening of March 15, one hundred and nineteen senators and representatives appeared in the hall of the House of Representatives in obedience to an anonymous notice addressed to one hundred and forty-three Republican members. Sixty-five, or less than half the Republican representation, voted for Monroe; fifty-four voted for Crawford; and eighty-five then united in nominating Governor Tompkins as Vice-President.

Monroe's character was well known, and his elevation to the Presidency was a result neither of great popularity nor of exceptional force, but was rather due to the sudden peace which left him the residuum of Madison's many Cabinets. A long list of resig-

[1] Hammond's New York, i. 409.
[2] Hammond's New York, i. 409.
[3] Crawford to Gallatin, May 10, 1816; Gallatin's Writings, i. 702.

nations alone remained to recall the memory of his associates. Robert Smith, Cæsar Rodney, William Eustis, Paul Hamilton, Gallatin, G. W. Campbell, William Jones, William Pinkney, and John Armstrong had all resigned in succession, leaving Monroe and Dallas in possession of the government when peace was declared. Dallas was not a popular character, whatever were his abilities or services; and no other man occupied high ground. Under such circumstances the strength shown by Crawford was surprising, and proved that Monroe, notwithstanding his advantages, was regarded with no exclusive favor.

In truth Monroe had no party. His original friends were the old Republicans, — John Taylor of Caroline, Littleton Tazewell, John Randolph, and their associates, from whom he had drawn apart. His new friends were chiefly northern Democrats, whose motives for preferring him to Crawford were selfish. In any case an epoch of personal politics could be foreseen, for men like Crawford, Calhoun, and Clay never submitted long to a superior; and for such an epoch Monroe was probably the best choice.

Shortly after the nomination Dallas gave notice to the President that he meant to retire from the Treasury in order to resume his practice at the bar.[1] Madison immediately wrote to Gallatin, April 12, inviting him to resume charge of the Treasury; but

[1] Life and Writings of A. J. Dallas, p. 139.

Gallatin was weary of domestic politics, and preferred diplomacy. He went as minister to France, while Dallas remained at the Treasury until October, to set the new Bank in motion.

These arrangements closed the first session of the Fourteenth Congress, which adjourned April 30, leaving Madison in unaccustomed peace, harassed by no more enemies or dissensions, to wait the close of his public life.

CHAPTER VI.

THE prosperity that followed the Peace of Ghent suffered no check during the year 1816, or during the remainder of Madison's term. The exports of domestic produce, officially valued at $45,000,000 for the year ending Sept. 30, 1815, were valued at nearly $65,000,000 for the following year, and exceeded $68,000,000 for 1817. The Southern States still supplied two thirds of the exported produce. Cotton to the amount of $24,000,000, tobacco valued at nearly $13,000,000, and rice at $3,500,000, contributed more than forty of the sixty-five millions of domestic exports in 1816. The tables [1] showed that while South Carolina, Georgia, and Louisiana gained with unparalleled rapidity, New England lost ground, and New York only maintained its uniform movement. While the domestic exports of Georgia and Louisiana trebled in value, those of New York increased from eight to fourteen millions.

Notwithstanding the great importations from Europe which under ordinary conditions would have counterbalanced the exports, the exchanges soon turned in favor of the United States. Before the close of 1816

[1] State Papers; Commerce and Navigation, i. 929.

specie in considerable quantities began to flow into the country. Canada, being nearest, felt the drain first, and suffered much inconvenience from it; but during the summer of 1816 and 1817 Europe also shipped much specie to America. Every ship brought some amount, until the export began to affect the Bank of England, which at last found its bullion diminishing with alarming rapidity. The returns showed a drain beginning in July or August, 1817, when the Bank of England held £11,668,000, until August, 1819, when the supply was reduced to £3,595,000; and in the interval a commercial crisis, with a general destruction of credit, occurred. The reaction could not fail in the end to affect America as it affected England, but the first result was stimulating beyond all previous experience. In England the drain of specie embarrassed government in returning to specie payments. In the United States the influx of specie made the return easy, if not necessary.

The recovery of internal exchanges kept pace with the influx of specie. At Boston, July 27, 1816, United States six-per-cent bonds were quoted at eighty-five, and Treasury notes at ninety-four to ninety-four and one-half; at New York six-per-cents stood at ninety, and Treasury notes at par; in Philadelphia six-per-cents were worth ninety-eight, and Treasury notes one hundred and seven; in Baltimore six-per-cents were selling at one hundred and two, and Treasury notes at one hundred and twelve.

During the next five months the recovery was steady and rapid. The banks of New York, September 26, began to cash their one-dollar notes, thus relieving the community from the annoyance of fractional currency. October 26 the six-per-cents stood at ninety-two in Boston, at ninety-three and one-half in New York, at ninety-eight in Philadelphia, and at one hundred and one and one-half in Baltimore. November 28 they sold at ninety-six in Boston; November 30 they sold at ninety-six and one-quarter in New York, at one hundred and one and one-half in Philadelphia, and at one hundred and five in Baltimore. January 1, 1817, the Treasury resumed payments at Boston in Boston money, and no further discredit attached to government securities.

The banks of the Middle States were less disposed than the government to hasten the return of specie payments. In order to do so, they were obliged to contract their circulation and discounts to an extent that would have been unendurable in any time but one of great prosperity; and only the threats of Dallas overcame their reluctance, even under most favorable conditions. Both Dallas and the President were irritated by their slowness.[1] July 22, 1816, the Secretary of the Treasury issued a circular warning them that, at whatever cost, the Treasury must carry into effect the order of Congress to collect the revenue, after Feb. 20, 1817, only in specie or its equivalent. "The banks in the States to the South," he

[1] Madison to Dallas, July 16, 1816; Life of A. J. Dallas, p. 453.

said,[1] "and to the west of Maryland, are ready and willing, it is believed, to co-operate in the same measure. The objection, or the obstacle to the measure, principally rests with the banks of the Middle States." Dallas invited them to assist the Treasury in resuming specie payments with the least possible delay; and accordingly the banks of the Middle States held a convention at Philadelphia, August 6, to consider their course.

This convention, on discussing the possibility of resumption, agreed that the banks needed more time than the government was disposed to allow. Credit had been necessarily expanded by the unusual scale of commerce and enterprise. So sudden and violent a contraction as was required for specie payments could not fail to distress the public, and might cause great suffering. Yet in some degree the new United States Bank could relieve this pressure; and therefore the resumption should not be attempted by the State banks until the National Bank should be fairly opened and ready to begin its discounts. The State banks in convention foresaw, or imagined, that the United States Bank could not begin operations so early as Feb. 20, 1817, and they declined to risk resumption without its aid. Acting on this impression, they met Dallas's urgency by a formal recommendation that their banks should begin to pay specie, not on the 20th of February, but on the first Monday of July, 1817.

[1] Niles, x. 376.

This decision, though unsatisfactory to Dallas and the President, could not be considered unreasonable. Credit was expanded beyond the limit of safety, and the government was largely responsible for the expansion. Many of the State banks were probably unsound from the first, and needed careful management. Between 1810 and 1830, on a total capital of one hundred and forty millions, the bank failures amounted to thirty millions, or more than one fifth of the whole.[1] In Pennsylvania the country banks reduced their issues from $4,756,000 in November, 1816, to $1,318,000 in November, 1819. The latter moment was one of extreme depression, but the former was probably not that of the greatest expansion. When the banks of the Middle States held their convention, Aug. 6, 1816, contraction had already begun, and steadily continued, while specie flowed into the country to supply a foundation for bank paper. Under such circumstances the banks asked no extravagant favor in recommending that eleven months, instead of seven, should be allowed for resumption.

Dallas was not disposed to concede this favor. Having at last the necessary machinery for controlling the State banks, he used it with the same vigor that marked all his acts. No sooner had the convention announced its unwillingness to co-operate with the Treasury in executing the order of Congress, than Dallas issued instructions, August 16,[2]

[1] Gallatin, Banks and Currency; Works, iii. 293.
[2] Niles, x. 423.

hastening the preparations for opening the National Bank as early as Jan. 1, 1817. Soon afterward, September 12, he renewed his notice that the notes of suspended banks would be rejected by the Treasury after Feb. 20, 1817.

The Bank subscription was filled in August, a deficit of three million dollars being taken by Stephen Girard in a single mass.[1] In October the board of directors was chosen by the shareholders, and in November the directors met and elected as President the former Secretary of the Navy, William Jones. One of their first acts was much debated, and was strongly opposed in the board of directors by J. J. Astor. They sent John Sergeant, of Philadelphia, abroad with authority to purchase some millions of bullion; and his mission was calculated to impress on the public the conviction that specie payments were to be resumed as soon as the Bank could open its doors.

Hurried by Dallas, the Bank actually began its operations in January, 1817, and under the double pressure from the Treasury the State banks had no choice but to yield. Another meeting was held at Philadelphia, February 1, consisting of delegates from the banks of New York, Philadelphia, Baltimore, and Richmond. The convention entered into a compact with the Secretary of the Treasury to resume payments, on certain conditions, at the day fixed by Congress. The compact was carried into effect

[1] Dallas to Madison, Aug. 27, 1816; Life of Dallas, p. 471.

February 20, a few days before the close of Madison's Presidency. Its success was magical. In New York, at ten o'clock on the morning of February 20, specie was at two and one half per cent premium. The banks opened their doors, and in half an hour all was once more regular and normal.

Thus the worst financial evil of the war was removed within two years after the proclamation of peace. A debt of about one hundred and thirty millions remained; but the people which only twenty years before had shrunk with fear and disgust from a debt of eighty millions, gave scarcely a thought in 1816 to their funded obligations. The difference between the two periods was not so much economical as political. Population and wealth had increased, but the experience of the people had advanced more rapidly than their numbers or capital. In measuring the political movement shrewd judges might easily err, for the elections of 1816 showed little apparent change in parties; but in truth parties had outgrown their principles, and in politics, as in finance, the close of Madison's Administration obliterated old distinctions.

Neither party admitted the abandonment of its dogmas. The New York election in the spring of 1816 showed no considerable change in votes. In 1810 Governor Tompkins was elected by ten thousand majority; even in the dark days of 1813 he had a majority of thirty-six hundred; in 1816, notwithstanding his popularity and the success of his war administration, his majority was less than seven thousand. In Massachusetts John Brooks, who succeeded Governor Strong as candidate of the Federalist party, received forty-nine thousand five hundred votes, while Samuel Dexter received forty-seven thousand four hundred. Six years before, in 1810, the Republican candidate, Elbridge Gerry, had received more than forty-six thousand five hundred, and Governor Strong had polled only forty-four thousand. Apparently the Republicans had lost ground in Massachusetts since 1810. In Connecticut, where the election turned on church issues, the result was somewhat different. The Anglican church, a small body but rich and influential, strongly Federalist in politics and conservative in character, joined the Democrats to overthrow the reign of the Congregational clergy. Oliver Wolcott, a Federalist who supported the war, was their candidate; and the combination nearly carried the State. Wolcott received about ten thousand two hundred votes ; his Federalist opponent was elected by eleven thousand three hundred and seventy votes. The Federalists also carried Rhode Island, once a strongly Democratic State, and seemed socially as well as politically to be little affected by their many mistakes and misfortunes.

Yet every one felt that real distinctions of party no longer existed. The Anglicans of Connecticut, the Unitarians of Boston, the Universalists and Baptists, looked chiefly to the overthrow of the established New England church ; and the Democrats of New York, like the Republicans of Virginia and North Carolina, labored for a system of internal improvements and for increased energy in national government. Parties, no longer held together by discipline, were liable at any moment to fall into confusion; and, as frequently happened in such stages of public opinion, they were extraordinarily affected by influences seemingly trivial. In 1816 the relaxation of party spirit resulted in a phenomenon never before witnessed. The whole community rose against its own representatives, and showed evident pleasure in condemning them. The occasion for this outbreak of popular temper was the Compensation Bill; but the instinct that could alone account for the public pleasure in punishing public men, could not be explained by a cause so trifling as that Act.

At the next session of Congress, Calhoun, lapsing in the middle of a speech into his usual meditative speculation, remarked, as though he were perplexed to account for his own theory, that in his belief the House of Representatives was not a favorite with the American people.[1] Had he expressed the opinion that freedom of thought or speech was not a favorite with the American people, he would have said nothing more surprising. If the House was not a favorite, what part of the government was popular, and what could be hoped for representative government itself? Of all the machinery created by the Constitution, the House alone directly reflected and

[1] Annals of Congress, 1816–1817, pp. 392, 505, 604.

represented the people; and if the people disliked it, they disliked themselves.

The people best knew whether Calhoun was right. Certainly the House, owing in part to its size, its frequent elections and changes, its lack of responsibility and of social unity, was the least steady and least efficient branch of government. Readers who have followed the history here closed, have been surprised at the frequency with which the word *imbecility* has risen in their minds in reading the proceedings of the House. So strong was the same impression at the time, that in the year 1814, at the close of the war, every earnest patriot in the Union, and many men who were neither earnest nor patriotic, were actively reproaching the House for its final failure, at an apparent crisis of the national existence, to call out or organize any considerable part of the national energies. The people in truth, however jealous of power, would have liked in imagination, though they would not bear in practice, to be represented by something nobler, wiser, and purer than their own average honor, wisdom, and purity. They could not make an ideal of weakness, ignorance, or vice, even their own; and as they required in their religion the idea of an infinitely wise and powerful deity, they revolted in their politics from whatever struck them as sordid or selfish. The House reflected their own weaknesses; and the Compensation Act seemed to them an expression of their own least agreeable traits. They rebelled against a petty appropriation of money, after enduring for years a constant succession of worse offences.

"Who would have believed," asked John Randolph,[1] six months afterward, — "who would have believed," he repeated, "that the people of the United States would have borne all the privations and losses of the late war, and of the measures that led to it; that they would have quietly regarded a national debt, swelled to an amount unknown, — to an amount greater than the whole expense of our seven years' war; that they would have seen the election of President taken out of their hands [by the caucus]; that they would have borne with abuse and peculation through every department of the government, — and that the great Leviathan, which slept under all these grievances, should be roused into action by the Fifteen-Hundred-Dollar Law?"

Only with difficulty could members persuade themselves that the public anger was real. They could not at first conceive that the people should be seriously angry because Congress had thought proper to pay its members a sum not in itself extravagant or adequate to their services. Not until the members returned to their homes did they appreciate the force of public feeling; but they soon felt themselves helpless to resist it. Richard M. Johnson and Henry Clay, the two most popular men in Kentucky, found their entire constituency attacking them. "When I went home," said Clay,[2] "I do not recollect to have

[1] Annals of Congress, 1816–1817, p. 501.
[2] Annals of Congress, 1816–1817, p. 497.

met with one solitary individual of any description of party who was not opposed to the Act, — who did not, on some ground or other, think it an improper and unjust law." Benjamin Hardin,[1] another of the Kentucky victims, said : " If a man came into the county court to be appointed a constable or surveyor of the road, he entered his solemn protest against the Compensation Law. If a petty demagogue wanted to get into the legislature, he must post up, or put in the newspapers, his protest against it."

" There was at first a violent excitement," said Philip P. Barbour of Virginia ;[2] " gentlemen might call it, if they pleased, a storm. But that storm, even when its fury abated, subsided into a fixed and settled discontent at the measure ; it met the disapprobation and excited the discontent of the grave, the reflecting, and the deliberate ; and such he believed to be the case with an immense majority of the American people."

Grand juries denounced it in Vermont and Georgia ; the State legislature denounced it in Massachusetts ; town-meetings protested against it ; county conventions sat upon it ; all classes and parties united in condemning it, and the brunt of this sweeping popular reproval fell upon the House of Representatives. Close as the House stood to the people, its want of popularity was evident, — as Calhoun, with his usual insight, bore witness. The House had as a body few friends and no protection against popular tem-

[1] Annals of Congress, 1816–1817, p. 535.
[2] Annals of Congress, 1816–1817, p. 517.

pests. The first to suffer, it was always the last to escape. One after another the weaker members gave way, and either declined re-election or were not re-elected. The chiefs succeeded for the most part by personal popularity in maintaining their hold on their districts, although several leading members lost their seats.

Even against so feeble and factious a body as the Thirteenth Congress, such condemnation would have seemed exceptional; but the peculiarity that made this popular reproof singular and suggestive was the popular admission that the Fourteenth Congress, for ability, energy, and usefulness, never had a superior, and perhaps, since the First Congress, never an equal. Such abilities were uncommon in any legislative body, American or European. Since Federalist times no Congress had felt such a sense of its own strength, and such pride in its own superiority; none had filled so fully the popular ideal of what the people's representatives should be. That this remarkable body of men should have incurred almost instantly the severest popular rebuke ever visited on a House of Representatives, could not have been mere accident.

The politics of 1816 seemed absorbed in the Compensation Act, and in the union of parties to condemn their representatives. The Senate escaped serious censure; and President Madison, so far from being called to account for errors real or imaginary, seemed to enjoy popularity never before granted to any President at the expiration of his term. The apparent contentment was certainly not due to want of grievances. The internal taxes pressed hard on the people, especially in New England, where the suffering was general and in some places severe; but no popular cry for reduction of taxes disturbed the elections. No portion of the country seemed displeased that a fourth Virginian should be made President by the intrigues of a Congressional caucus. The State legislatures for the most part chose as usual the Presidential electors; and in December the public learned, almost without interest, that James Monroe had received one hundred and eighty-three electoral votes, representing sixteen States, while Rufus King had received thirty-four electoral votes, representing Massachusetts, Connecticut, and Delaware. Daniel D. Tompkins of New York was made Vice-President by the same process. Nothing in the elections, either for President or for Congress, showed that the people were disposed to scrutinize sharply the workings of any part of their government except the House of Representatives.

As the winter approached when Madison was to meet Congress for the last time, the sixteen years of his official service, which had been filled with excitement and violence, were ending in political stagnation. Party divisions had so nearly disappeared that nothing prevented the President elect from selecting as the head of his Cabinet the son of the last Federalist President, who had been the object of more violent attack from the Republican party than had been directed against any other Federalist. Old Republicans, like Macon and John Randolph, were at loss to know whether James Monroe or J. Q. Adams had departed farthest from their original starting-points. At times they charged one, at times the other, with desertion of principle; but on the whole their acts tended to betray a conviction that J. Q. Adams was still a Federalist in essentials, while Monroe had ceased to be an old Republican. In the political situation of 1817, if Jefferson and his contemporaries were right in their estimates, Federalist views of government were tending to prevail over the views of the Jeffersonian party.

With this tendency, the national prosperity and the state of the Treasury had much to do. Dallas carried out his purpose, and in October quitted the Treasury. In retiring, he left with the President a sketch of the condition of the finances such as no previous secretary had been so fortunate as to present. For the year ending Sept. 30, 1816, the receipts amounted to $47,670,000.[1] From the customs, which Dallas had estimated at $21,000,000, duties to the amount of $36,000,000 were received. A surplus of more than $20,000,000 was likely to accumulate in the Treasury before the close of the year.

Old ideas of economy and strict restraints on expenditure could not long maintain themselves in the presence of such an income; but besides the temptation to expand the sphere of government in expen-

[1] Statement, etc.; State Papers, Finances, iii. 487.

ditures, other influences were at work to establish Federalist principles in the system itself. Dallas remained in office chiefly in order to organize the Bank, and to render certain the resumption of specie payments. When he retired, in October, 1816, both objects were practically attained. His administration of the Treasury had then lasted two years. He found the government bankrupt; he left it with a surplus of twenty millions for the year. His measures not only relieved the country from financial disorders equalled only by those of the Revolutionary War, but also fixed the financial system in a firm groove for twenty years. He failed only in his attempt to obtain from Congress a larger degree of protection for domestic industries. Had his scheme of protection been adopted, possibly the violence of subsequent changes in revenue and legislation might have been moderated, and certainly the result could have been no more mischievous than it was.

Dallas retired to private life by his own wish, and the public three months afterward heard with surprise and regret the news of his sudden death. Like most of the men who rendered decisive services during the war, he received no public reward commensurate with his deserts. He fared better than Armstrong, who created the army; but even Gallatin, who shaped the diplomatic result, was content to retire into the comparative obscurity of the mission to Paris; while Perry and Macdonough, whose personal qualities had decided the fortunes of two campaigns and won the military basis on which peace could be negotiated, received no more reward than fell to the lot of third-rate men. In the case of Dallas and Gallatin, the apparent neglect was their own choice. Gallatin might have returned to the Treasury, but declined it; and the President transferred W. H. Crawford from the War Department to the charge of the finances, while Clay was offered the War Department in succession to Crawford.

These arrangements affected Madison but little. He had no longer an object to gain from the disposal of patronage, and he sought to smooth the path of his successor rather than to benefit himself. Few Presidents ever quitted office under circumstances so agreeable as those which surrounded Madison. During the last two years of his Administration almost every month brought some difficulty to an end, or accomplished some long-desired result. The restoration of the finances was perhaps his greatest source of satisfaction; but the steadiness with which the whole country, except New England, recovered prosperity and contentment afforded him a wider and more constant pleasure. The ravages of war left few traces. Even at Washington the new public buildings were pressed forward so rapidly that the effects of fire were no longer seen. The Capitol began to rise from its ruins. The new halls of Congress promised to do honor to Madison's judgment. Benjamin Latrobe was the architect in charge; and his Representative Chamber, without reproducing that which Jefferson had helped to design, was dignified and worthy of its object. The old sandstone columns were replaced by another material. On the shore of the Potomac, near Leesburg, Latrobe noticed a conglomerate rock, containing rounded pebbles of various sizes and colors, and capable of being worked in large masses. His love of novelty led him to employ this conglomerate as an ornamental stone for the columns of the Hall of Representatives; and the effect was not without elegance.

Several years were still to pass before Congress occupied its permanent quarters, and Madison did not return to the White House; but the traces of national disaster disappeared in the process of reconstruction before he quitted the Presidency.

Surrounded by these pleasant conditions, Madison saw Congress assemble for the last time to listen to his requests. The Message which he sent to the legislature December 3 showed the extinction of party issues, and suggested no action that seemed likely to revive party disputes in any new form. The President expressed regret at the depression in shipping and manufactures, the branches of industry unfavorably affected by the peace. He suggested that Congress should consider especially the need of laws counteracting the exclusive navigation system of Great Britain. He recommended once more the time-worn subjects of the Militia and a National University. He asked for legislation against the Slave Trade, and urged a re-modification of the Judiciary.

He requested Congress to create a new Executive department for Home or Interior Affairs, and to place the Attorney-General's office on the footing of a department. He gave a flattering account of the finances; and his Message closed with a panegyric on the people and their government, for seeking "by appeals to reason, and by its liberal examples, to infuse into the law which governs the civilized world a spirit which may diminish the frequency or circumscribe the calamities of war, and meliorate the social and beneficent relations of peace: a government, in a word, whose conduct, within and without, may bespeak the most noble of all ambitions, — that of promoting peace on earth and good-will to man."

For the moment, Congressmen were too much interested in their own quarrel to sympathize strongly with panegyrics on the people or their government. The members of the House returned to Washington mortified, angry, and defiant, disgusted alike with the public and with the public service. No sooner were the standing committees announced, December 4, than Richard M. Johnson moved for a special committee on the repeal of the Compensation Law, and supported his motion in an unusually elaborate speech, filled with argument, complaint, and irritation. The committee was appointed, — Johnson at its head; William Findley of Pennsylvania, second; Daniel Webster, third, with four other members. After twelve days' consideration, December 18, the committee presented a report, written by Webster, defending the Act, but recommending a return to the *per diem* system, in deference to the popular wish. The scale of the new allowance was left for Congress to determine.

Until this personal quarrel was discussed, no other business received attention. The debate — postponed till Jan. 14, 1817, to save the dignity of the House — lasted, to the exclusion of other business, until January 23. As an exhibition of personal and corporate character, it was entertaining; but it contained little of permanent interest or value. Calhoun, always above his subject, spoke with much force against yielding to popular outcry. "This House," he said, "is the foundation of the fabric of our liberty. So happy is its constitution, that in all instances of a general nature its duty and its interests are inseparable. If he understood correctly the structure of our government, the prevailing principle is not so much a balance of power, as a well-connected chain of responsibility. That responsibility commenced here, and this House is the centre of its operation." The idea that the people had "resolved the government into its original elements, and resumed to themselves their primitive power of legislation," was inconsistent with the idea that responsibility commenced and centred in the House. "Are we bound in all cases to do what is popular?" asked Calhoun. Could the House shift responsibility from itself to the people without destroying the foundation of the entire fabric?

Like most of Calhoun's speculations, this question could receive its answer only in some distant future. The Compensation Law lowered permanently the self-respect of the House, which had already declined from the formation of the government. " Of that House," said Richard Henry Wilde of Georgia,[1] " he feared it might be said in the words of Claudian: 'A fronte recedant imperii.' Yes, sir, they were receding, — they had receded from the front of empire. That House, formerly the favorite of the American nation, the first and most important branch of the government, the immediate image of the people, had been losing, and continued to lose, — certainly by no fault of theirs, but by the working of causes not for him to develop, — that rank and power in the government originally belonging to them, and which others at their expense had been secretly acquiring." Yet the House, while repealing the law, refused to admit itself in the wrong. The law was repealed only so far as it applied to subsequent Congresses. Leaving its successors to fix whatever compensation they thought proper for their services, the Fourteenth Congress adhered to its own scale, and took the money it was expected to refund.

Having disposed of this personal affair, the House turned to serious business, and completed its remarkable career by enacting several measures of far-reaching importance.

The first of these measures was a Navigation Act,

[1] Annals of Congress, 1816–1817, p. 604.

approved March 1, 1817, imposing on foreign vessels the same restrictions and prohibitions which were imposed by foreign nations on Americans. The second resembled the first in its object, but related only to the importation of plaster of Paris from Nova Scotia and New Brunswick. These two Acts began a struggle against the foreign navigation systems, which ended in their overthrow.

For the present the House postponed the establishment of an Interior Department, and allowed the Attorney-General to remain without an office or a clerk; but it passed an Act, approved March 3, 1817, concentrating in the Treasury the accounting business of government, and appointing four more auditors and one more comptroller for the purpose.

The fourth and most important measure that became law was a Neutrality Act, approved March 3, 1817, which authorized collectors of customs to seize and detain "any vessel manifestly built for warlike purposes, . . . when the number of men shipped on board, or other circumstances, shall render it probable that such vessel is intended by the owner" to cruise against the commerce of a friendly State. Nearly fifty years were to pass before the people of the United States learned to realize the full importance of this Act, which laid the foundation for all the subsequent measures taken by the United States and Great Britain for preserving neutrality in their relations with warring countries.[1] The Neu-

[1] Dana's Wheaton, pp. 541–542, *note*.

trality Act of 1817 furnished the measure of neutral obligations.

Besides these important laws, the Fourteenth Congress passed another bill, which closed its own activity and that of President Madison. None of the previous measures bore any direct relation to party politics, either past or future; but the bill for internal improvements, which Congress passed and the President vetoed, was an event of no small meaning in party history.

Calhoun moved, December 16, "that a committee be appointed to inquire into the expediency of setting apart . . . a permanent fund for internal improvement." The committee was appointed the same day, — Calhoun, Sheffey of Virginia, Creighton of Ohio, Grosvenor of New York, and Ingham of Pennsylvania. December 23 Calhoun reported a bill [1] setting aside the bonus paid by the Bank, $1,500,000, and the future dividends from Bank stock, "as a fund for constructing roads and canals." February 4 he introduced his bill by a speech, showing that a system of internal improvements was necessary, and could, in certain instances, be created by the national government alone.

"Let it not be forgotten," said Calhoun,[2] with the air of sombre forecast which marked his mind and features, "let it be forever kept in mind, that the extent of our republic exposes us to the greatest of all calamities, next

[1] Annals of Congress, 1816–1817, p. 361.
[2] Annals of Congress, 1816–1817, pp. 853, 854.

to the loss of liberty, and even to that in its consequence, — *disunion*. We are great, and rapidly — I was about to say fearfully — growing. This is our pride and danger, our weakness and our strength. Little does he deserve to be intrusted with the liberties of this people, who does not raise his mind to these truths. We are under the most imperious obligation to counteract every tendency to disunion. . . . If . . . we permit a low, sordid, selfish, and sectional spirit to take possession of this House, this happy scene will vanish. We will divide, and in its consequences will follow misery and despotism."

The Constitutional question Calhoun reserved for the future; he thought it scarcely worth discussion, since the good sense of the States might be relied on to prevent practical evils. Nevertheless he discussed it, and drew sufficient authority from the " general welfare " clause, and from the power to " establish " post-roads. Granting that the Constitution was silent, he saw no restraint on Congress : —

" If we are restricted in the use of our money to the enumerated powers, on what principle can the purchase of Louisiana be justified? . . . If it cannot, then are we compelled either to deny that we had the power to purchase, or to strain some of the enumerated powers to prove our right."

The debate was interesting. Timothy Pickering, with the accumulated experience of seventy years, suggested that the right to regulate commerce among the several States, as in the case of light-houses and beacons, covered the proposed appropriation. Clay supported the bill with his usual energy, avowing that among his strongest motives was the wish to add this new distinction to the Fourteenth Congress, so harshly judged by the people. The chief Constitutional argument against the measure was made by Philip P. Barbour of Virginia; but other members opposed it on different grounds, and chiefly because as long as the internal taxes were still exacted, internal improvements should not be undertaken.

If the final vote was a correct test, Constitutional objections had but little weight with Congress. The bill passed the House, February 8, by the small majority of eighty-six to eighty-four. Of the minority no less than thirty-three were New England Federalists, whose opposition was founded on local and sectional reasons. From the slave States about forty-two votes were given against the bill; but a number of these were Federalist, and others were influenced by peculiar reasons. Two thirds of the Virginians voted against the bill; two thirds of the South Carolinians voted in its favor. Probably not more than twenty-five or thirty members, in the total number of one hundred and seventy, regarded the Constitutional difficulty as fatal to the bill.

In the Senate the bill passed by a vote of twenty to fifteen. Of the minority nine represented New England, and six represented Southern States. Every senator from the Middle States, as well as both senators from Virginia, supported the bill. Both senators from Massachusetts, the Republican Varnum and the Federalist Ashmun, opposed it; while Jeremiah Mason of New Hampshire and Rufus King of New York voted in its favor. The confusion of parties was extreme; but the State-rights school of old Republicans seemed to command not more than five or six votes in thirty-five.

The divisions on this bill seemed to leave no question that Congress by an overwhelming majority regarded the Constitutional point as settled. No one doubted that the Judiciary held the same opinion. The friends of the bill had reason to feel secure in regard to the Constitutional issue if on nothing else, and were the more disappointed when, March 3, President Madison exercised for the last time his official authority by returning the bill with a veto founded on Constitutional objections.

"The power to regulate commerce among the several States," he said, "cannot include a power to construct roads and canals, and to improve the navigation of water-courses in order to facilitate, improve, and secure such a commerce, without a latitude of construction departing from the ordinary import of the terms, strengthened by the known inconveniences which doubtless led to the grant of this remedial power to Congress. To refer the power in question to the clause ' to provide for the common defence and general welfare' would be contrary to the established and consistent rules of interpretation, as rendering the special and careful enumeration of powers which follow the clause nugatory and improper. Such a view of the Constitution would have the effect of giving to Congress a general power of legislation."

Every one who looked at the Constitution as an instrument or machine to be employed for the first time, must have admitted that Madison was right. Interpreted by no other aid than its own terms and the probable intent of a majority of the Convention which framed and the States which adopted it, the Constitution contained, and perhaps had been intended to contain, no power over internal improvements. The wide difference of opinion which so suddenly appeared between the President and Congress could not have been the result so much of different views of the Constitution, as of conclusions reached since the Constitution was framed. Congress held the bill to be Constitutional, not because it agreed with the strict interpretation of the text, but because it agreed with the interpretation which for sixteen years the Republican party, through Congress and Executive, had imposed upon the text.

On that point Calhoun's argument left no doubt; and his question — the last of his speculations pregnant with future history — echoed unanswered: " On what principle can the purchase of Louisiana be justified?" Dismissing all other violations or violence offered to the Constitution by President Madison or his predecessors, — such as the Bank, the Embargo, the Enforcement laws, the laws for the government of Orleans Territory, the seizure of West Florida, — Calhoun's question went to the heart of the issue between President and Congress.

From the Virginia side only one answer was possible. In returning to their early views of resistance to centralization, Madison and Jefferson must have maintained the invalidity of precedents to affect the Constitution. The veto seemed to create a new classification of public acts into such as were Constitutional; such as were unconstitutional, but still valid; and such as were both unconstitutional and invalid. The admitted validity of an act, like the purchase of Louisiana, even though it were acknowledged to be unconstitutional, did not create a precedent which authorized a repetition of a similar act.

Viewed only from a political standpoint, the veto marked the first decided reaction against the centralizing effect of the war. Unfortunately for the old Republican party, whose principles were thus for a second time to be adopted in appearance by a majority of the people, sixteen years had affected national character; and although precedents might not bind Congress or Executive, they marked the movement of society.

The Veto Message of March 3, 1817, was Madison's Farewell Address. The next day he surrendered to Monroe the powers of government, and soon afterward retired to Virginia, to pass, with his friend Jefferson, the remaining years of a long life, watching the results of his labors.

CHAPTER VII.

THE Union, which contained 5,300,000 inhabitants in 1800, numbered 7,240,000 in 1810, and 9,634,000 in 1820. At the close of Madison's Administration, in 1817, the population probably numbered not less than 8,750,000 persons. The average rate of annual increase was about three and five-tenths per cent, causing the population to double within twenty-three years.

The rate of increase was not uniform throughout the country, but the drift of population was well defined. In 1800 the five New England States contained about 1,240,000 persons. Virginia and North Carolina, united, then contained nearly 1,360,000, or ten per cent more than New England. In 1820 the two groups were still nearer equality. New England numbered about 1,665,000; the two Southern States numbered 1,700,000, or about two per cent more than New England. While these two groups, containing nearly half the population of the Union, increased only as one hundred to one hundred and twenty-nine, the middle group, comprising New York, New Jersey, and Pennsylvania, increased in the relation of one hundred to one hundred and ninety-two, — from

1,402,000 in 1800, to 2,696,000 in 1820. Their rate was about the average ratio for the Union; and the three Western States,— Ohio, Kentucky, and Tennessee,— grew proportionally faster. Their population of 370,000 in 1800 became 1,567,000 in 1820, in the ratio of one hundred to four hundred and twenty-three.

Careful study revealed a situation alarming to New England and Virginia. If only Connecticut, Rhode Island, and Massachusetts, without its district of Maine, were considered, a total population numbering 742,000 in 1800 increased only to 881,000 in 1820, or in the ratio of one hundred to one hundred and eighteen in twenty years. If only the white population of Virginia and North Carolina were taken into the estimate, omitting the negroes, 852,000 persons in 1800 increased to 1,022,000 in 1820, or in the ratio of one hundred to one hundred and twenty. Maryland showed much the same result, while Delaware, which rose from 64,270 in 1800 to 72,674 in 1810, remained stationary, numbering only 72,749 in 1820,— a gain of seventy-five persons in ten years. The white population showed a positive decrease, from 55,361 in 1810 to 55,282 in 1820.

Probably a census taken in 1817 would have given results still less favorable to the sea-coast. The war affected population more seriously than could have been reasonably expected, and stopped the growth of the large cities. New York in 1800 contained 60,000 persons; in 1810 it contained 96,400, but a corporation census of 1816 reported a population of only one hundred thousand, although two of the six years were years of peace and prosperity. From that time New York grew rapidly, numbering 124,000 in 1820, — a gain of about twenty-five per cent in four years. Even the interior town of Albany, which should have been stimulated by the war, and which increased four thousand in population between 1800 and 1810, increased only three thousand between 1810 and 1820. Philadelphia fared worse, for its population of 96,000 in 1810 grew only to 108,000 in 1820, and fell rapidly behind New York. Baltimore grew from 26,000 in 1800 to 46,000 in 1810, and numbered less than 63,000 in 1820. Boston suffered more than Baltimore; for its population, which numbered 24,000 in 1800, grew only to 32,000 in 1810, and numbered but 43,000 in 1820. Charleston was still more unfortunate. In 1800 its population numbered about eighteen thousand; in 1810, 24,700; in 1817 a local census reported a decrease to 23,950 inhabitants, and the national census of 1820 reported 24,780, or eighty persons more than in 1810. The town of Charleston and the State of Delaware increased together by the same numbers.

Although the war lasted less than three years, its effect was so great in checking the growth of the cities that during the period from 1810 to 1820 the urban population made no relative increase. During every other decennial period in the national history the city population grew more rapidly than that of the rural districts; but between 1810 and 1820 it remained stationary, at four and nine-tenths per cent of the entire population. While Boston, Philadelphia, and Charleston advanced slowly, and New York only doubled its population in twenty years, Western towns like Pittsburg, Cincinnati, and Louisville grew rapidly and steadily, and even New Orleans, though exposed to capture, more than trebled in size; but the Western towns were still too small to rank as important. Even in 1820 the only cities which contained a white population of more than twenty thousand were New York, Philadelphia, Baltimore, and Boston.

The severest sufferers from this situation were the three southern States of New England, — Connecticut, Rhode Island, and Massachusetts, excluding the district of Maine, which was about to become a separate State. Fortunately the northern part of New England, notwithstanding the war, increased much more rapidly than the southern portion; but this increase was chiefly at the cost of Massachusetts, and returned little in comparison with the loss. The situation of Massachusetts and Connecticut was dark. Had not wealth increased more rapidly than population, Massachusetts would have stood on the verge of ruin; yet even from the economical point of view, the outlook was not wholly cheerful.

Judged by the reports of Massachusetts banks, the increase of wealth was surprising. The official returns of 1803, the first year when such returns were made, reported seven banks in the State, with a capital of $2,225,000 and deposits of $1,500,000. In June, 1816, twenty-five banks returned capital stock amounting nearly to $11,500,000 and deposits of $2,133,000. The deposits were then small, owing to the decline of industry and drain of specie that followed the peace, but the capital invested in banks had more than quintupled in thirteen years.

This multiplication was not a correct measure of the general increase in wealth. Indeed, the banks were in excess of the public wants after the peace, and their capital quickly shrunk from $11,500,000 in June, 1816, to $9,300,000 in June, 1817, a decline of nearly twenty per cent in a year. From that time it began to increase again, and held its improvement even in the disastrous year 1819. Assuming 1803 and 1817 as the true terms of the equation, the banking capital of Massachusetts increased in fourteen years from $2,225,000 to $9,300,000, or more than quadrupled.

Gauged by bank discounts the increase of wealth was not so great. In 1803 the debts due to the banks were returned at $3,850,000; in June, 1817, they were $12,650,000. If the discounts showed the true growth of industry, the business of the State somewhat more than trebled in fourteen years. Probably the chief industries that used the increased banking capital were the new manufactures, for the older sources of Massachusetts wealth showed no equivalent gain. Tested by the imports, the improvement was moderate. In 1800 the gross amount of duties collected in Massachusetts was less than $3,200,000; in 1816 it somewhat exceeded $6,100,000, but had not permanently doubled in sixteen years. Tested by exports of domestic produce, Massachusetts showed no gain. In 1803 the value of such produce amounted to $5,400,000; in 1816, to $5,008,000.[1]

Other methods of calculating the increase of wealth gave equally contradictory results. The registered tonnage of Massachusetts engaged in foreign trade exceeded two hundred and ten thousand tons in 1800; in 1816 it was two hundred and seventy-four thousand tons. In the coasting-trade Massachusetts employed seventy-five thousand tons in 1800, and one hundred and twenty-nine thousand in 1816. The tonnage employed in the fisheries showed no growth. The shipping of Massachusetts seemed to indicate an increase of about forty per cent in sixteen years.

The system of direct taxation furnished another standard of comparison. In 1798 a valuation was made in certain States of houses and lands for direct taxes; another was made in 1813; a third in 1815. That of 1798 amounted to eighty-four million dollars for Massachusetts; that of 1813, to one hundred and forty-nine millions; that of 1815, to one hundred and forty-three millions, — a gain of seventy per cent in sixteen years; but such a valuation in 1817 would probably have shown a considerable loss on that of 1815.

Evidently the chief increase in wealth consisted in

[1] Pitkin, pp. 55-56.

the growth of manufactures, but after the prostration of the manufacturing interest in 1816 no plausible estimate of their true value could be made, unless the bank discounts measured their progress. The result of the whole inquiry, though vague, suggested that wealth had increased in Massachusetts more rapidly than population, and had possibly gained seventy or eighty per cent in sixteen years;[1] but in spite of this increase the State was in a pitiable situation. Neither steamboats, canals, nor roads could help it. Thousands of its citizens migrated to New York and Ohio, beyond the possibility of future advantage to the land they left. Manufactures were prostrate. Shipping was driven from the carrying trade. Taxation weighed far more heavily than ever before. A load of obloquy rested on the State on account of its war policy and the Hartford Convention. The national government treated it with severity, and refused to pay for the Massachusetts militia called into service by the President during the war, because the governor had refused to place them under national officers.

The condition of Massachusetts and Maine was a picture of New England. Democratic Rhode Island suffered equally with Federalist Connecticut. Maine, New Hampshire, and Vermont showed growth, but the chief possibility of replacing lost strength lay in immigration. During the European wars, no considerable number of immigrants were able to reach

[1] Pitkin, p. 373.

the United States; but immediately after the return of peace, emigration from Europe to America began on a scale as alarming to European governments as the movement to western New York and Ohio was alarming to the seaboard States of the Union. During the year 1817 twenty-two thousand immigrants were reported as entering the United States.[1] Twelve or fourteen thousand were probably Irish; four thousand were German. More than two thousand arrived in Boston, while about seven thousand landed in New York and the same number in Philadelphia. The greater part probably remained near where they landed, and in some degree supplied the loss of natives who went west. The rapid growth of the northern cities of the sea-coast began again only with the flood of immigration.

Although the three southern States of New England were the severest sufferers, the Virginia group — comprising Delaware, Maryland, Virginia, and North Carolina — escaped little better. In twenty years their white population increased nineteen and five tenths per cent, while that of Massachusetts, Connecticut, and Rhode Island increased eighteen per cent. The wealth of Southern States consisted largely in slaves; and the negro population of the Virginia group increased about twenty-five per cent in numbers during the sixteen years from 1800 to 1816. The exports of domestic produce increased about forty per cent in value, comparing the average of

[1] Niles, 1817.

1801-1805 with that of 1815-1816. The net revenue collected in Virginia increased nearly seventy per cent, comparing the year 1815 with the average of the five years 1800-1804; while that collected in North Carolina more than doubled.

Measured by these standards, the growth of wealth in the Virginia group of States was not less rapid than in Massachusetts, and the same conclusion was established by other methods. In 1816 Virginia contained two State banks, with branches, which returned for January 1 a capital stock of $4,590,000, with a note circulation of $6,000,000, and deposits approaching $2,500,000. Their discounts amounted to $7,768,000 in January, 1816, and were contracted to $6,128,000 in the following month of November.[1] Although Virginia used only half the banking capital and credits required by Massachusetts, the rate of increase was equally rapid, and the tendency toward banking was decided. In 1817 the legislature created two new banks, one for the valley of Virginia, the other for western Virginia, with a capital stock of $600,000, and branches with capital stock of $100,000 for each. Between 1800 and 1817, banking capital exceeding five million dollars was created in Virginia, where none had existed before.

If the estimates made by Timothy Pitkin, the best statistician of the time, were correct, the returns for direct taxes showed a greater increase of wealth in Virginia than in Massachusetts.[2] The valuation of

[1] Niles, ix. 427; xi. 196.   [2] Pitkin, p. 372.

Virginia for 1799 was $71,000,000; that of 1815 was $165,000,000. The valuation of North Carolina in 1799 was $30,000,000; that of 1815 was $51,000,000. Maryland was estimated at $32,000,000 in 1799, at $106,000,000 in 1815. The average increase for the three States was in the ratio of one hundred to two hundred and forty, while that for Massachusetts, Rhode Island, and Connecticut was nearer one hundred to one hundred and seventy-five. The normal increase for the Union was in the ratio of one hundred to two hundred and sixty-three.

The result obtained from the estimates for direct taxes was affected by a doubt in regard to the correctness of the valuation of 1799, which was believed to have been too low in the Southern States; but the general conclusion could not be doubted that the Virginia group of States increased steadily in wealth. The rapidity of increase was concealed by an equally rapid impoverishment of the old tobacco-planting aristocracy, whose complaints drowned argument. As the lands of the ancient families became exhausted, the families themselves fell into poverty, or emigrated to the richer Ohio valley. Their decline or departure gave rise to many regrets and alarms. With the impressions thus created, the people associated the want of economical machinery as a cause of their backwardness, and became clamorous for roads, canals, and banks. The revolution in their ideas between 1800 and 1816 was complete.

The North Carolinians were first to denounce their

old habits of indifference, and to declare their State in danger of ruin on that account. A committee of the State legislature reported Nov. 30, 1815, that vigorous measures for self-protection could no longer be postponed : [1] —

"With an extent of territory sufficient to maintain more than ten millions of inhabitants, . . . we can only boast of a population something less than six hundred thousand, and it is but too obvious that this population under the present state of things already approaches its maximum. Within twenty-five years past more than two hundred thousand of our inhabitants have removed to the waters of the Ohio, Tennessee, and Mobile ; and it is mortifying to witness the fact that thousands of our wealthy and respectable citizens are annually moving to the West, . . . and that thousands of our poorer citizens follow them, being literally driven away by the prospect of poverty. In this state of things our agriculture is at a stand."

The Virginians showed an equally strong sense of their perils. Twelve months after the North Carolina legislature took the matter in hand, a committee of the Virginia legislature in December, 1816, discussed the same topic and reached the same conclusion.[2] Although something had been done by corporations to open canals on the Potomac, the James River, and to the Dismal Swamp, the State of Virginia had in sixteen years made little advance in material welfare. While New England had built turnpikes wherever a profit could be expected, in

[1] Niles, ix., Supplement, p. 165.
[2] Niles, ix., Supplement, p. 149.

Virginia, said the committee, "the turnpike-roads of the Commonwealth, except a few short passes of particular mountains and a road recently begun from Fredericksburg to the Blue Ridge, are confined principally to the county of Loudon, the adjacent counties of Fairfax, Fauquier, and Frederick, and to the vicinity of the seat of government." In other respects the situation was worse.

"While many other States," said the committee,[1] "have been advancing in wealth and numbers with a rapidity which has astonished themselves, the ancient Dominion and elder sister of the Union has remained stationary. A very large proportion of her western territory is yet unimproved, while a considerable part of her eastern has receded from its former opulence. How many sad spectacles do her low-lands present of wasted and deserted fields, of dwellings abandoned by their proprietors, of churches in ruins! The genius of her ancient hospitality, benumbed by the cold touch of penury, spreads his scanty hoard in naked halls, or seeks a coarser but more plenteous repast in the lonely cabins of the West. The fathers of the land are gone where another outlet to the ocean turns their thoughts from the place of their nativity, and their affections from the haunts of their youth."

Another committee reported to the House of Delegates Jan. 5, 1816, in favor of extending the banking system of the State.[2] The report used language new as an expression of Virginian opinions.

[1] Niles, ix., Supplement, p. 150.
[2] Niles, ix., Supplement, p. 155.

"Your committee believe that a prejudice has gone abroad, which they confidently trust experience will prove to be unfounded even to the satisfaction of those by whom it is entertained, that the policy of Virginia is essentially hostile to commerce and to the rights of commercial men. Upon the removal of this prejudice must depend the future contributions of this Commonwealth toward the prosperity and glory if not the happiness and safety of the United States. Without the confidence of foreigners there can exist no foreign commerce. Without foreign commerce there can exist neither ships, seamen, nor a navy; and a tremendous lesson has taught Virginia that without a navy she can have no security for her repose."

Notwithstanding the gloom of these recitals, the evidence tended to show that while the white population of Virginia increased only about nineteen per cent in sixteen years, its wealth nearly doubled. Comparison with the quicker growth of the Middle States — New York, New Jersey, and Pennsylvania — caused much of the uneasiness felt by New England and Virginia. The banking capital of New York, which probably did not much exceed three million dollars in 1800, amounted in 1816 to nearly $19,000,000; that of Pennsylvania exceeded $16,000,000. The valuation of houses and lands for the direct tax rose in New York from $100,000,000 in 1799 to nearly $270,000,000 in 1815; and in Pennsylvania, from $102,000,000 in 1799 to $346,000,000 in 1815.[1] The net revenue collected in New York

[1] Pitkin, p. 372.

was $2,700,000 in 1800, and $14,500,000 in 1815; that collected in Pennsylvania was $1,350,000 in 1800, and $7,140,000 in 1815. This rate of increase did not extend to exports. The value of the domestic exports from New York in 1803 was about $7,500,000; in 1816 it exceeded $14,000,000; while the value of Pennsylvanian exports increased little, — being $4,021,000 in 1803 and $4,486,000 in 1816. The population of New York doubled while that of Massachusetts and Virginia hardly increased one third. Pennsylvania grew less rapidly in numbers, but still about twice as fast as New England.

Although this rate of progress seemed to leave New England and Virginia far behind the Middle States, it was less striking than the other economical changes already accomplished or foreseen. The movement of population or of wealth was not so important as the methods by which the movement was effected. The invention of the steamboat gave a decisive advantage to New York over every rival. Already in 1816 the system had united New York city so closely with distant places that a traveller could go from New York to Philadelphia by steamboat and stage in thirteen hours; or to Albany in twenty-four hours; and taking stage to Whitehall in twelve hours could reach Montreal in thirty hours, and go on to Quebec in twenty-four hours, — thus consuming about five and a half successive days in the long journey from Philadelphia to Quebec, sleeping comfortably on his way, and all at an expense of fifty dollars. This economy of time and money was a miracle; but New York could already foresee that it led to other advantages of immeasurable value. The steamboat gave impetus to travel, and was a blessing to travellers; but its solid gain for the prosperity of the United States lay not in passenger traffic so much as in freight, and New York was the natural centre of both.

While Pennsylvania, Virginia, and the Carolinas were building roads and canals across a hundred miles of mountains, only to reach at last an interior region which enjoyed an easier outlet for freight, New York had but to people a level and fertile district, nowhere fifty miles from navigable water, in order to reach the great Lake system, which had no natural outlet within the Union except through the city of New York. So obvious was the idea of a canal from the Lakes to the Hudson that it was never out of men's minds, even before the war; and no sooner did peace return than the scheme took large proportions. Active leaders of both political parties pressed the plan, — De Witt Clinton, Gouverneur Morris, and Peter B. Porter were all concerned in it; but the legislature and people then supposed that so vast an undertaking as a canal to connect Lake Erie with the ocean, national in character and military in its probable utility, required national aid. Supposing the Administration to be pledged to the policy outlined by Gallatin and approved by Jefferson in the Annual Message of 1806, the New York commissioners applied to Congress for assistance, and uniting with other local interests procured the passage of Calhoun's bill for internal improvements.

They were met by Madison's veto. This act, although at first it seemed to affect most the interests of New York, was in reality injurious only to the Southern States. Had the government lent its aid to the Erie Canal, it must have assisted similar schemes elsewhere, and in the end could hardly have refused to carry out Gallatin's plan of constructing canals from the Chesapeake to the Ohio, and from the Santee to the Tennessee River. The veto disappointed New York only for the moment, but was fatal to Southern hopes. After the first shock of discouragement, the New York legislature determined to persevere, and began the work without assistance. The legislature of Pennsylvania at the same time appropriated half a million dollars for roads and canals, and for improvements of river navigation, devoting nearly one hundred and fifty thousand dollars to aid the turnpike-road to Pittsburg. The fund established by the State of Ohio, as a condition of its admission to the Union, had in 1816 produced means to construct the National or Cumberland Road to the hundred and thirteenth mile. The indifference to internal improvements which had been so marked a popular trait in 1800, gave place to universal interest and activity in 1816; but the Middle States were far in advance of the Eastern and Southern in opening communications with the West; and New York, owing in no small degree to the veto, could already foresee the time when it would wrest from Pennsylvania the supply of the valley of the Ohio, while expanding new tributary territory to an indefinite extent along the Lakes.

When Madison retired from the Presidency, the limits of civilization, though rapidly advancing, were still marked by the Indian boundary, which extended from the western end of Lake Erie across Indiana, Kentucky, Tennessee, and the Southwestern territory. Only weak and helpless tribes remained east of the Mississippi, waiting until the whites should require the surrender of their lands; but the whites, already occupying land far in advance of their needs, could not yet take the whole. Not until 1826 were the Indian titles generally extinguished throughout Indiana. The military work was done, and the short space of sixteen years had practically accomplished the settlement of the whole country as far as the Mississippi; but another generation was needed in order to take what these sixteen years had won.

As population spread, the postal service struggled after it. Except on the Hudson River, steamboats were still irregular in their trips; and for this reason the mails continued to be carried on horseback through the interior. In 1801 the number of post-offices was 957; in 1817 it was 3,459. In 1801 the length of post-roads was less than 25,000 miles; in 1817 it was 52,689. In 1800 the gross receipts from postage were $280,000; in 1817 they slightly exceeded $1,000,000.

In each case the increase much surpassed the ratio for population, and offered another means for forming some estimate of the increase of wealth. The Fourteenth Congress pressed the extension of post-routes in western New York, Ohio, and Indiana; but none was yet established beyond the Mississippi. Rapidity of motion was also increased on the main routes. From New York to Buffalo, four hundred and seventy-five miles, the traveller went at an average rate of five miles an hour, and, sleeping every night, he arrived in about four days. Between Philadelphia and Pittsburg, where no watercourse shortened the distance, the stage-coach consumed five and a half days, allowing for stoppage at night. These rates of travel were equal to those common on routes of similar length in Europe; but long after 1817 the mail from Washington to New Orleans, by a route 1,380 miles in length, required twenty-four days of travel.

Had the steamboat system been at once perfected, the mail could have been carried with much more rapidity; but the progress of the new invention was slow. After the trial trip of the "Clermont," Aug. 17, 1807, five years elapsed before the declaration of war; yet in 1812 New York possessed no other steam-line than the Albany packets. Steam-ferries plied to Hoboken, Amboy, and other places in the immediate neighborhood; but neither Newport, New London, nor New Haven enjoyed steam communication with New York until after the war. In the spring of 1813 eight or nine steamboats belonged to the city of New

York, but only three, which ran to Albany, were more than ferries. At the same time Philadelphia possessed six such ferry-boats. From Baltimore a steamer ran to the head of Chesapeake Bay; but the southern coast and the town of Charleston saw no steamboat until a year after the war was ended.

The West was more favored. In 1811 a boat of four hundred tons was built at Pittsburg and sent down the river to New Orleans, where it plied between New Orleans and Natchez. Two more were built at the same place in 1813–1814; and one of them, the "Vesuvius," went down the river in the spring of 1814, rousing general interest in the midst of war by making the trip in nine days and a half, or two hundred and twenty-seven hours. The "Vesuvius" remained on the Mississippi for the next two years, but was burned with her cargo in the summer of 1816. By that time the world was thinking much of steamboats, and their use was rapidly extending, though regular trips were still uncommon except in the east.

The result of the sixteen years, considered only in the economical development of the Union, was decisive. Although population increased more rapidly than was usual in human experience, wealth accumulated still faster. From such statistics as the times afforded, a strong probability has been shown that while population doubled within twenty-three years, wealth doubled within twenty. Statistics covering the later period of national growth, warrant the belief that a valuation of $1,742,000,000 in 1800 corresponded to a valuation of $3,734,000,000 in 1820; and that if a valuation of $328 per capita is assumed for 1800, a valuation of $386 per capita may be estimated for 1820.[1]

These sixteen years set at rest the natural doubts that had attended the nation's birth. The rate of increase both in population and wealth was established and permanent, unless indeed it should become even more rapid. Every serious difficulty which seemed alarming to the people of the Union in 1800 had been removed or had sunk from notice in 1816. With the disappearance of every immediate peril, foreign or domestic, society could devote all its energies, intellectual and physical, to its favorite objects. This result was not the only or even the chief proof that economical progress was to be at least as rapid in the future as at the time when the nation had to struggle with political difficulties. Not only had the people during these sixteen years escaped from dangers, they had also found the means of supplying their chief needs. Besides clearing away every obstacle to the occupation and development of their continent as far as the Mississippi River, they created the steamboat, the most efficient instrument yet conceived for developing such a country. The continent lay before them, like an uncovered ore-bed. They could see, and they could even calculate with reasonable accu-

[1] The Wealth of the United States and the Rate of its Increase. By Henry Gannett, International Review, May, 1882.

racy, the wealth it could be made to yield. With almost the certainty of a mathematical formula, knowing the rate of increase of population and of wealth, they could read in advance their economical history for at least a hundred years.

CHAPTER VIII.

THE movement of thought, more interesting than the movement of population or of wealth, was equally well defined. In the midst of political dissension and economical struggles, religion still took precedence; and the religious movement claimed notice not merely for its depth or for its universality, but also and especially for its direction. Religious interest and even excitement were seen almost everywhere, both in the older and in the newer parts of the country; and every such movement offered some means of studying or illustrating the development of national character. For the most part the tendency seemed emotional rather than intellectual; but in New England the old intellectual pre-eminence, which once marked the Congregational clergy, developed a quality both new and distinctive.

The Congregational clergy, battling with the innate vices of human nature, thought themselves obliged to press on their hearers the consequences of God's infinite wrath rather than those of his infinite love. They admitted that in a worldly sense they erred, and they did not deny that their preaching sometimes leaned to severity; but they would have been false to their charge and undeserving of their high character had they lost sight of their radical doctrine that every man was by nature personally depraved, and unless born again could not hope to see the kingdom of God. Many intellectual efforts had been made by many ages of men to escape the logic of this doctrine, but without success. The dogma and its consequences could not be abandoned without abandoning the Church.

From this painful dilemma a group of young Boston clergymen made a new attempt to find a path of escape. Their movement drew its inspiration from Harvard College, and was simultaneous with the sway of Jefferson's political ideas; but the relationship which existed between religious and political innovation was remote and wholly intellectual. Harvard College seemed to entertain no feeling toward Jefferson but antipathy, when in 1805 the corporation appointed Henry Ware, whose Unitarian tendencies were well known, to be Hollis Professor of Theology. The Unitarianism of Henry Ware and his supporters implied at that time no well-defined idea beyond a qualified rejection of the Trinity, and a suggestion of what they thought a more comprehensible view of Christ's divine character; but it still subverted an essential dogma of the Church, and opened the way to heresy. The Calvinists could no longer regard Harvard College as a school proper for the training of clergy; and they were obliged to establish a new theological seminary, which they attached to a previously existing

Academy at Andover, in Essex County, Massachusetts. The two branches of the New England Calvinists — known then as old Calvinism and Hopkinsianism — united in framing for the instructors of the Andover school a creed on the general foundation of the Westminster Assembly's Shorter Catechism, and thus provided for the future education of their clergy in express opposition to Unitarians and Universalists.

Thenceforward the theological school of Harvard College became more and more Unitarian. The Massachusetts parishes, divided between the two schools of theology, selected, as pleased a majority of their church-members, either Orthodox or Unitarian pastors; and while the larger number remained Calvinistic, though commonly preferring ministers who avoided controversy, the Boston parishes followed the Unitarian movement, and gradually filled their pulpits with young men. The Unitarian clergy soon won for themselves and for their city a name beyond proportion with their numbers.

Joseph Stevens Buckminster, the first, and while he lived the most influential, of these preachers, began his career in 1805 by accepting a call from one of the old Boston churches. He died in 1812 at the close of his twenty-eighth year. His influence was rather social and literary than theological or controversial. During his lifetime the Unitarian movement took no definite shape, except as a centre of revived interest in all that was then supposed to be best and purest in religious, literary, and artistic feeling. After his death, Unitarians learned to regard William Ellery Channing as their most promising leader. Channing had accepted the charge of a Boston church as early as 1803, and was about four years older than Buckminster. A third active member of the Boston clergy was Samuel Cooper Thacher, who took charge of a Boston parish in 1811, and was five years younger than Channing. In all, some seven or eight churches were then called Unitarian; but they professed no uniform creed, and probably no two clergymen or parishes agreed in their understanding of the precise difference between them and the Orthodox church. Shades of difference distinguished each Unitarian parish from every other, and the degree of their divergence from the old creed was a subject of constant interest and private discussion, although the whole body of churches, Congregational as well as Unitarian, remained in external repose.

The calm was not broken until the close of the war relieved New England from a political anxiety which for fifteen years had restrained internal dissensions. No sooner did peace restore to New England the natural course of its intellectual movement than the inevitable schism broke out. In June, 1815, the "Panoplist," the mouthpiece of the Congregational clergy, published an article charging the Unitarians with pursuing an unavowed propaganda, and calling upon the Church to refuse them communion. Channing and his friends thought the attack to require reply, and, after consultation, Channing published a "Letter to the Rev. Samuel C. Thacher," which began a discussion and a theological movement of no slight interest to American history.

Channing's theology at that time claimed no merit for originality. His letter to Thacher betrayed more temper than he would afterward have shown; but in no particular was he more earnest than in repelling the idea that he or his brethren were innovators. In whatever points they disagreed, they were most nearly unanimous in repudiating connection with the English Unitarians who denied the divinity of Christ. Channing declared " that a majority of our brethren believe that Jesus Christ is more than man; that he existed before the world ; that he literally came from heaven to save our race; that he sustains other offices than those of a teacher and witness to the truth ; and that he still acts for our benefit, and is our intercessor with the Father." So far was Channing from wishing to preach a new theology that he would gladly have accepted the old had he thought it intelligible :

"It is from deep conviction that I have stated once and again that the differences between Unitarians and Trinitarians lie more in sounds than in ideas ; that a barbarous phraseology is the chief wall of partition between these classes of Christians ; and that could Trinitarians tell us what they mean, their system would generally be found little else than a mystical form of the Unitarian doctrine."

Calvinists could not be blamed for thinking that their venerable creed, the painful outcome of the closest and most strenuous reasoning known in the Christian world, was entitled to more respect than to be called "little else than a mystical form of the Unitarian doctrine." The Unitarians themselves scarcely attempted to make the infinite more intelligible to the finite by any new phraseology. They avowed a dislike for dogma as their merit. During these early years they systematically avoided controversy; in the pulpit they never assailed and seldom mentioned other forms of Christian faith, or even the scheme of Trinity which caused their schism.

"So deeply are we convinced," said Channing's letter, "that the great end of preaching is to promote a spirit of love, a sober, righteous, and godly life, and that every doctrine is to be urged simply and exclusively for this end, that we have sacrificed our ease, and have chosen to be less striking preachers rather than to enter the lists of controversy."

Yet the popular dislike of Calvinistic severity could not wholly make good the want of doctrinal theology. The Unitarian clergy, however unwilling to widen the breach between themselves and the old Church, were ill at ease under the challenges of Orthodox critics, and could not escape the necessity of defining their belief.

"According to your own concession," rejoined Dr. Samuel Worcester to Channing's letter, "the party in whose behalf you plead generally deny the essential divinity of the Saviour, and hold him to be a being entirely 'distinct from God,' entirely 'dependent,'— in other words, a mere creature. . . . You doubtless do not suppose that by any mere creature atonement could be made for the sins of an apostate world of sufficient merit for the pardon, sanctification, and eternal salvation of all who should trust in him; therefore if you hold to atonement in any sense, yet unquestionably not in the sense of a proper propitiatory sacrifice. Upon this denial of atonement must follow of course the denial of pardon procured by the blood of Christ, of justification through faith in him, of redemption from eternal death unto everlasting life by him. Connected, and generally if not invariably concomitant, with the denial of these doctrines is a denial of the Holy Spirit in his personal character and offices, and of the renewal of mankind unto holiness by his sovereign agency, as held by Orthodox Christians. Now, sir, are these small and trivial points of difference between you and us?"

Channing protested against these inferences; but he did not deny — indeed, he affirmed — that Unitarians regarded dogma as unnecessary to salvation. "In our judgment of professed Christians," he replied, "we are guided more by their temper and lives than by any peculiarities of opinion. We lay it down as a great and indisputable opinion, clear as the sun at noonday, that the great end for which Christian truth is revealed is the sanctification of the soul, the formation of the Christian character; and wherever we see the marks of this character displayed in a professed disciple of Jesus, we hope, and rejoice to hope, that he has received all the truth which is necessary to his salvation." The hope might help to soothe anxiety and distress, but it defied conclusions reached by the most anxious and often renewed labors of churchmen for eighteen hundred years. Something more than a hope was necessary as the foundation of a faith.

Not until the year 1819, did Channing quit the cautious attitude he at first assumed. Then, in his "Sermon on the Ordination of Jared Sparks" at Baltimore, he accepted the obligation to define his relation to Christian doctrine, and with the support of Andrews Norton, Henry Ware, and other Unitarian clergymen gave a doctrinal character to the movement. With this phase of his influence the present story has nothing to do. In the intellectual development of the country, the earlier stage of Unitarianism was more interesting than the later, for it marked a general tendency of national thought. At a time when Boston grew little in population and but moderately in wealth, and when it was regarded with antipathy, both political and religious, by a vast majority of the American people, its society had never been so agreeable or so fecund. No such display of fresh and winning genius had yet been seen in America as was offered by the genial outburst of intellectual activity in the early days of the Unitarian schism. No more was heard of the Westminster doctrine that man had lost all ability of will to any spiritual good accompanying salvation, but was dead in sin. So strong was the reaction against old dogmas that for thirty years society seemed less likely to resume the ancient faith in the Christian Trinity than to establish a new Trinity, in which a deified humanity should have place. Under the influence of Channing and his friends, human nature was adorned with virtues hardly suspected before, and with hopes of perfection on earth altogether strange to theology. The Church then charmed. The worth of man became under Channing's teachings a source of pride and joy, with such insistence as to cause his hearers at last to recall, almost with a sense of relief, that the Saviour himself had been content to regard them only as of more value than many sparrows.

The most remarkable quality of Unitarianism was its high social and intellectual character. The other more popular religious movements followed for the most part a less ambitious path, but were marked by the same humanitarian tendency. In contrast with old stringency of thought, the religious activity of the epoch showed warmth of emotion. The elder Buckminster, a consistent Calvinist clergyman, settled at Portsmouth in New Hampshire, while greatly distressed by his son's leanings toward loose theology, was at the same time obliged to witness the success of other opinions, which he thought monstrous, preached by Hosea Ballou, an active minister in the same town. This new doctrine, which took the name of Universalism, held as an article of faith " that there is one God, whose nature is love, revealed in one Lord Jesus Christ, by one Holy Spirit of grace, who will finally restore the whole family of mankind to holiness and happiness."

In former times any one who had publicly professed belief in universal salvation would not have been regarded as a Christian. With equal propriety he might have preached the divinity of Ammon or Diana. To the old theology one god was as strange as the other; and so deeply impressed was Dr. Buckminster with this conviction, that he felt himself constrained in the year 1809 to warn Hosea Ballou of his error, in a letter pathetic for its conscientious self-restraint. Yet the Universalists steadily grew in numbers and respectability, spreading from State to State under Ballou's guidance, until they became as well-established and as respectable a church as that to which Buckminster belonged.

A phenomenon still more curious was seen in the same year, 1809, in western Pennsylvania. Near the banks of the Monongahela, in Washington County, a divergent branch of Scotch Presbyterianism established a small church, and under the guidance of Thomas Campbell, a recent emigrant from Scotland, issued, Sept. 7, 1809, a Declaration:

"Being well aware from sad experience of the heinous nature and pernicious tendency of religious controversy among Christians, tired and sick of the bitter jarrings and janglings of a party spirit, we would desire to be at rest; and were it possible, would also desire to adopt and recommend such measures as would give rest to our brethren throughout all the churches, as would restore unity, peace, and purity to the whole Church of God. This desirable rest, however, we utterly despair either to find for ourselves, or to be able to recommend to our brethren, by continuing amid the diversity and rancor of party contentions the varying uncertainty and clashings of human opinions; nor indeed can we reasonably expect to find it anywhere but in Christ and his simple word, which is the same yesterday, to-day, and forever. Our desire, therefore, for ourselves and our brethren would be that rejecting human opinions and the inventions of men as of any authority, or as having any place in the Church of God, we might forever cease from further contentions about such things, returning to and holding fast by the original standard."

Campbell's Declaration expressed so wide a popular want that his church, in a few years, became one of the largest branches of the great Baptist persuasion. Perhaps in these instances of rapid popular grouping, love of peace was to some extent supplemented by jealousy of learning, and showed as much spirit of social independence as of religious instinct. The growth of vast popular sects in a democratic community might testify to intellectual stagnation as well as to religious or social earnestness; but whatever was the amount of thought involved in such movements, one character was common to them all, as well as to the Unitarians, — they agreed in relaxing the strictness of theological reasoning. Channing united with Campbell in suggesting that the Church should ignore what it could not comprehend. In a popular and voluntary form they proposed self-restraints which should have the same effect as the formal restraints of the hierarchies. "Rejecting," like Campbell, "human opinions and the inventions of men," — preaching, like Channing and Ballou, "that there is one God, whose nature is love," and that doctrine was useless except to promote a spirit of love, — they founded new churches on what seemed to resemble an argument that the intellectual difficulties in their path must be unessential because they were insuperable.

Wide as the impulse was to escape the rigor of bonds and relax the severity of thought, organizations so deeply founded as the old churches were not capable of destruction. They had seen many similar human efforts, and felt certain that sooner or later such experiments must end in a return to the old standards. Even the Congregational Church of New England, though reduced in Boston to a shadow of its old authority, maintained itself at large against its swarm of enemies, — Unitarian, Universalist, Baptist, Methodist, — resisting, with force of character and reasoning, the looseness of doctrine and vagueness of thought which marked the time. Yale College remained true to it. Most of the parishes maintained their old relations. If the congregations in some instances crumbled away or failed to increase, the Church could still stand erect, and might reflect with astonishment on its own strength, which survived so long a series of shocks apparently fatal. For half a century the Congregational clergy had struggled to prevent innovation, while the people emigrated by hundreds of thousands in order to innovate. Obliged to insist on the infinite justice rather than on the infinite mercy of God, they shocked the instincts of the new generation, which wanted to enjoy worldly blessings without fear of future reckoning. Driven to bay by the deistic and utilitarian principles of Jefferson's democracy, they fell into the worldly error of defying the national instinct, pressing their resistance to the war until it amounted to treasonable conspiracy. The sudden peace swept away much that was respectable in the old society of America, but perhaps its noblest victim was the unity of the New England Church.

The Church, whether Catholic or Protestant, Lutheran or Calvinistic, always rested in the conviction that every divergence from the great highways of religious thought must be temporary, and that no permanent church was possible except on foundations already established; but the State stood in a position less self-confident. The old principles of government were less carefully developed, and Democrats in politics were more certain than Unitarians or Universalists in theology that their intellectual conclusions made a stride in the progress of thought. Yet the sixteen years with which the century opened were singularly barren of new political ideas. Apparently the extreme activity which marked the political speculations of the period between 1775 and 1800, both in America and in Europe, had exhausted the energy of society, for Americans showed interest only in the practical working of their experiments, and added nothing to the ideas that underlay them. With such political thought as society produced, these pages have been chiefly filled; the result has been told. The same tendency which in religion led to reaction against dogma, was shown in politics by general acquiescence in practices which left unsettled the disputed principles of government. No one could say with confidence what theory of the Constitution had prevailed. Neither party was satisfied, although both acquiesced. While the Legislative and Executive branches of the government acted on no fixed principle, but established precedents at variance with any consistent theory, the Judiciary rendered so few decisions that Constitutional law stood nearly still. Only at a later time did Chief-Justice Marshall begin his great series of judicial opinions, — McCulloch against the State of Maryland in 1819; Dartmouth College in the same year; Cohens against the State of Virginia in 1821. No sooner were these decisive rulings announced, than they roused the last combative energies of Jefferson against his old enemy the Judiciary: "That body, like gravity, ever acting, with noiseless foot and unalarming advance, gaining ground step by step, and holding what it gains, is engulfing insidiously the special governments."

Marshall had few occasions to decide Constitutional points during the Administrations of Jefferson and Madison, but the opinions he gave were emphatic. When Pennsylvania in 1809 resisted, in the case of Gideon Olmstead, a process of the Supreme Court, the chief-justice, without unnecessary words, declared that "if the legislatures of the several States may at will annul the judgments of the courts of the United States, and destroy the rights acquired under those judgments, the Constitution itself becomes a solemn mockery, and the nation is deprived of the means of enforcing its laws by the instrumentality of its own tribunals." Pennsylvania yielded; and Marshall, in the following year, carried a step further the authority of his court. He overthrew the favorite dogma of John Randolph and the party of State rights, so long and vehemently maintained in the Yazoo dispute.

The Yazoo claims came before the court in the case of Fletcher against Peck, argued first in 1809 by Luther Martin, J. Q. Adams, and Robert G. Harper; and again in 1810 by Martin, Harper, and Joseph Story. March 16, 1810, the chief-justice delivered the opinion. Declining, as "indecent in the extreme," to enter into an inquiry as to the corruption of "the sovereign power of a State," he dealt with the issue whether a legislature could annul rights vested in an individual by a law in its nature a contract.

"It may well be doubted," he argued, "whether the nature of society and government does not prescribe some limits to the legislative power; and if any are to be prescribed, where are they to be found if the property of an individual, fairly and honestly acquired, may be seized without compensation? To the legislature all legislative power is granted; but the question whether the act of transferring the property of an individual to the public be in the nature of the legislative power, is well worthy of serious reflection. It is the peculiar province of the legislature to prescribe general rules for the government of society: the application of those rules to individuals in society would seem to be the duty of other departments. How far the power of giving the law may involve every other power, in cases where the Constitution is silent, never has been and perhaps never can be definitely stated."

In the case under consideration, Marshall held that the Constitution was not silent. The provision that no State could pass any law impairing the obligation of contracts, as well as " the general principles which are common to our free institutions," restrained the State of Georgia from passing a law whereby the previous contract could be rendered void. His decision settled, as far as concerned the Judiciary, a point regarded as vital by the State-rights school. Four years afterward Congress gave the required compensation for the contract broken by Georgia.

The chief-justice rendered no more leading Constitutional decisions during Madison's term of office; but his influence was seen in a celebrated opinion delivered by Justice Story in 1816, in the case of Martin against Hunter's Lessee. There the court came in conflict with the State of Virginia. The Court of Appeals of that State refused to obey a mandate of the Supreme Court, alleging that the proceedings of the Supreme Court were *coram non judice,* or beyond its jurisdiction, being founded on section 25 of the Judiciary Act of 1789, which was unconstitutional in extending the appellate jurisdiction of the Supreme Court over the State courts.

The Court of Appeals was unfortunate in the moment of its resistance to the authority of the national courts. While the case was passing through its last stage peace was declared, and the national authority sprang into vigor unknown before. The chief-justice would not with his own hand humiliate the pride of the Court of Appeals, for which as a Virginian and a lawyer he could feel only deep respect. He devolved the unpleasant duty on young Justice Story, whose own State of Massachusetts was then far from being an object of jealousy to Virginia, and who, a Republican in politics, could not be prejudiced by party feeling against the Virginia doctrine. Much of the opinion bore the stamp of Marshall's mind; much showed the turn of Story's intelligence; yet the same principle lay beneath the whole, and no one could detect a divergence between the Federalism of the Virginia chief-justice and the Democracy of the Massachusetts lawyer.

"It has been argued," said the court, "that such an appellate jurisdiction over State courts is inconsistent with the genius of our governments and the spirit of the Constitution; that the latter was never designed to act upon State sovereignties, but only upon the people; and that if the power exists, it will materially impair the sovereignty of the States and the independence of their courts. We cannot yield to the force of this reasoning; it assumes principles which we cannot admit, and draws conclusions to which we do not yield our assent. It is a mistake that the Constitution was not designed to operate upon States in their corporate capacity. It is crowded with provisions which restrain or annul the sovereignty of the States in some of the highest branches of their prerogatives. . . . When, therefore, the States are stripped of some of the highest attributes of sovereignty, and the same are given to the United States; when the legislatures of the States are in some respects under the control of Congress, and in every case are, under the Constitution, bound by the paramount authority of the United States, — it is certainly difficult to support the argument that the appellate power over the decisions of State courts is contrary to the genius of our institutions."

So far were the political principles of the people from having united in a common understanding, that while the Supreme Court of the United States thus differed from the Virginia Court of Appeals in regard to the genius of the government and the spirit of the Constitution, Jefferson still publicly maintained that the national and state governments were "as independent, in fact, as different nations," and that the function of one was foreign, while that of the other was domestic. Madison still declared that Congress could not build a road or clear a watercourse; while Congress believed itself authorized to do both, and in that belief passed a law which Madison vetoed. In politics as in theology, the practical system which resulted from sixteen years of experience seemed to rest on the agreement not to press principles to a conclusion.

No new idea was brought forward, and the old ideas, though apparently incapable of existing together, continued to exist in rivalry like that of the dogmas which perplexed the theological world; but between the political and religious movement a distinct difference could be seen. The Church showed no tendency to unite in any creed or dogma, — indeed, religious society rather tended to more divisions; but in politics public opinion slowly moved in a fixed direction. The movement could not easily be measured, and was subject to reaction; but its reality was shown by the protests of Jefferson, the veto of Madison, and the decisions of the Supreme Court. No one doubted that a change had occurred since 1798. The favorite State-rights dogma of that time had suffered irreparable injury. For sixteen years the national government in all its branches had acted, without listening to remonstrance, on the rule that it was the rightful interpreter of its own powers. In this assumption the Executive, the Legislature, and the Judiciary had agreed. Massachusetts and Pennsylvania, as well as Virginia and Georgia, yielded. Louisiana had been bought and admitted into the Union; the Embargo had been enforced; one National Bank had been destroyed and another established; every essential function of a sovereignty had been performed, without an instance of failure, though not without question. However unwilling the minority might be to admit in theory the overthrow of their principles, every citizen assented in daily practice to the rule that the national government alone interpreted its own powers in the last resort. From the moment the whole people learned to accept the practice, the dispute over theory lost importance, and the Virginia Resolutions of 1798 marked only a stage in the development of a sovereignty.

The nature of the sovereignty that was to be the result of American political experiment, the amount of originality which could be infused into an idea so old, was a matter for future history to settle. Many years were likely to elapse before the admitted practice of the government and people could be fully adopted into the substance of their law, but the process thus far had been rapid. In the brief space of thirty years, between 1787 and 1817, — a short generation, — the Union had passed through astonishing stages. Probably no great people ever grew more rapidly and became more mature in so short a time. The ideas of 1787 were antiquated in 1815, and lingered only in districts remote from active movement. The subsidence of interest in political theories was a measure of the change, marking the general drift of society toward practical devices for popular use, within popular intelligence. The only work that could be said to represent a school of thought in politics was written by John Taylor of Caroline, and was probably never read, — or if read, certainly never understood, — north of Baltimore by any but curious and somewhat deep students, although to them it had value.

John Taylor of Caroline might without irreverence be described as a *vox clamantis*, — the voice of one crying in the wilderness. Regarded as a political thinker of the first rank by Jefferson, Monroe, John Randolph, and the Virginia school, he admitted, with the geniality of the class to which he belonged, that his disciples invariably deserted in practice the rules they praised in his teaching; but he continued to teach, and the further his scholars drifted from him the more publicly and profusely he wrote. His first large volume, "An Inquiry into the Principles and Policy of the Government of the United States," published in 1814, during the war, was in form an answer to John Adams's "Defence of the Constitutions" published in London twenty-five years before. In 1787 John Adams, like Jefferson, Hamilton, Madison, Jay, and other constitution-makers, might, without losing the interest of readers, indulge in speculations more or less visionary in regard to the future character of a nation yet in its cradle; but in 1814 the character of people and government was formed; the lines of their activity were fixed. A people which had in 1787 been indifferent or hostile to roads, banks, funded debt, and nationality, had become in 1815 habituated to ideas and machinery of the sort on a great scale. Monarchy or aristocracy no longer entered into the public mind as factors in future development. Yet Taylor resumed the discussions of 1787 as though the interval were a blank; and his only conclusion from the experience of thirty years was that both political parties were equally moving in a wrong direction.

"The two parties, called Republican and Federal," he concluded, "have hitherto undergone but one revolution. Yet each when in power preached Filmer's old doctrine of passive obedience in a new form, with considerable success; and each, out of power, strenuously controverted it. The party in power asserted that however absurd or slavish this doctrine was under other forms of the numerical analysis, the people under ours were *identified* (the new term to cog this old doctrine upon the United States) with the government; and that therefore an opposition to the government was an opposition to the nation itself. . . . This identifying doctrine . . . puts an end to the idea of a responsibility of the government to the nation; . . . it renders useless the freedom of speech and of the press; it converts the representative into the principal; it destroys the division of power between the people and the government, as being themselves indivisible; and in short it is inconsistent with every principle by which politicians and philosophers have hitherto defined a free government."

The principle to which Taylor so strenuously objected was nevertheless the chief political result of national experience. Somewhere or another a point was always reached where opposition became treasonable,— as Virginia, like Massachusetts, had learned both when in power and when out. Taylor's speculations ended only in an admission of their own practical sterility, and his suggestions for restraining the growth of authority assumed the possibility of returning to the conditions of 1787. Banks were his horror. Stocks and bonds, or paper evidences of indebtedness in any form, he thought destructive to sound principles of government. The Virginia and Kentucky Resolutions of 1798 were his best resource for the preservation of civil liberty. However well-founded his fears might be, his correctives could no longer be applied. Political philosophers of all ages were fond of devising systems for imaginary Republics, Utopias, and Oceanas, where practical difficulties could not stand in their way. Taylor was a political philosopher of the same school, and his Oceana on the banks of the Rappahannock was a reflection of his own virtues.

CHAPTER IX.

SOCIETY showed great interest in the statesmen or preachers who won its favor, and earnestly discussed the value of political or religious dogmas, without betraying a wish to subject itself ever again to the rigor of a strict creed in politics or religion. In a similar spirit it touched here and there, with a light hand, the wide circuit of what was called *belles lettres*, without showing severity either in taste or temper.

For the first four or five years of the century, Dennie's "Portfolio" contained almost everything that was produced in the United States under the form of light literature. The volumes of the "Portfolio" for that period had the merit of representing the literary efforts of the time, for Philadelphia insisted on no standard of taste so exacting as to exclude merit, or even dulness, in any literary form. Jacobins, as Dennie called Democrats, were not admitted into the circle of the "Portfolio;" but Jacobins rarely troubled themselves with *belles lettres*.

The "Portfolio" reflected a small literary class scattered throughout the country, remarkable chiefly for close adhesion to established English ideas. The English standard was then extravagantly Tory, and the American standard was the same. At first sight the impression was strange. A few years later, no ordinary reader could remember that ideas so illiberal had seriously prevailed among educated Americans. By an effort, elderly men could, in the next generation, recall a time when they had been taught that Oliver Cromwell was a monster of wickedness and hypocrisy; but they could hardly believe that at any period an American critic coldly qualified " Paradise Lost," and " Avenge, O Lord, thy slaughtered saints," as good poetry, though written by a Republican and an enemy of established order. This was the tone of Dennie's criticism, and so little was it confined to him that even young Buckminster, in his Phi Beta Kappa Oration of 1809, which was regarded as making almost an epoch in American literature, spoke of Milton's eyes as " quenched in the service of a vulgar and usurping faction," and of Milton's life as " a memorable instance of the temporary degradation of learning." Buckminster was then remonstrating against the influence of politics upon letters rather than expressing a political sentiment, but his illustration was colored by the general prejudices of British Toryism. Half a century before, Dr. Johnson had taken the tone of Tory patronage toward Milton's genius, and Johnson and Burke were still received in America as final authorities for correct opinion in morals, literature, and politics. The "Portfolio" regarded Johnson not only as a "superlative" moralist and politician, but also as a "sublime" critic and a "transcendent" poet. Burke and Cicero stood on the same level, as masters before whose authority criticism must silently bow.

Yet side by side with these conventional standards, the "Portfolio" showed tendencies which seemed inconsistent with conservatism, — a readiness to welcome literary innovations contradicting every established canon. No one would have supposed that the critic who accepted Johnson and Pope as transcendent poets, should also delight in Burns and Wordsworth; yet Dennie was unstinted in praise of poetry which, as literature, was hardly less revolutionary than the writings of Godwin in politics. Dennie lost no opportunity of praising Coleridge, and reprinted with enthusiasm the simplest ballads of Wordsworth. Moore was his personal friend, and Moore's verses his models. Wherever his political prejudices were untouched, he loved novelty. He seemed to respect classical authority only because it was established, but his literary instincts were broader than those of Jefferson.

The original matter of the "Portfolio" was naturally unequal, and for the most part hardly better than that of a college magazine. Dennie was apt to be commonplace, trivial, and dull. His humor was heavy and commonly coarse; he allowed himself entire freedom, and no little grossness of taste. Of scholarship, or scholarly criticism, his paper showed great want. He tried to instruct as well as to amuse, but society soon passed the stage to which his writing belonged. The circulation of the " Portfolio " probably never exceeded fifteen hundred copies, and Dennie constantly complained that the paper barely supported itself. When the Bostonians, in the year 1805, began to feel the spirit of literary ambition, they took at once a stride beyond Dennie's power, and established a monthly magazine called the "Anthology and Boston Review," which in 1806 numbered four hundred and forty subscribers. The undertaking was doubly remarkable; for the Anthology Society which supported the Review combined with it the collection of a library, limited at first to periodical publications, which expanded slowly into the large and useful library known as the Boston Athenæum. The Review and Library quickly became the centre of literary taste in Boston, and, in the words of Josiah Quincy many years afterward, might be considered as a revival of polite learning in America. The claim was not unreasonable, for the Review far surpassed any literary standards then existing in the United States, and was not inferior to any in England; for neither the Edinburgh nor the Quarterly Review was established until several years later.

The Anthology Society, which accomplished the feat of giving to Boston for the first time the lead of American literary effort, consisted largely of clergymen, and represented, perhaps unintentionally, the coming Unitarian movement. Its president and controlling spirit had no sympathy with either division of the Congregational Church, but was a clergyman of the Church of England. John Sylvester John Gardiner, the rector of Trinity, occupied a peculiar position in Boston. Of American descent, but English birth and education, he was not prevented by the isolation of his clerical character from taking an active part in affairs, and his activity was sometimes greater than his discretion. His political sermons rivalled those of the Congregational ministers Osgood and Parish, in their violence against Jefferson and the national government; his Federalism was that of the Essex Junto, with a more decided leaning to disunion; but he was also an active and useful citizen, ready to take his share in every good work. When he became president of the Anthology Society, he was associated with a clergyman of Unitarian opinions as vice-president, — the Rev. William Emerson, a man of high reputation in his day, but better known in after years as the father of Ralph Waldo Emerson. The first editor was Samuel Cooper Thacher, to whom, ten years afterward, Channing addressed his earliest controversial letter. Young Buckminster and William Tudor, a Boston man, who for the next twenty years was active in the literary life of Massachusetts, were also original members. The staff of the "Anthology" was greatly superior to ordinary editorial resources; and in a short time the Review acquired a reputation for ability and sharpness of temper never wholly forgiven. Its unpopularity was the greater because its aggressiveness took the form of assaults on Calvinism, which earned the ill-will of the Congregational clergy.

Buckminster and Channing were the editor's closest friends, and their liberality of thought was remarkable for the time and place; yet the point from which the liberality of Boston started would have been regarded in most parts of the Union as conservative. Channing's fear of France and attachment to England were superstitious.

"I will not say," began his Fast Day Sermon in 1810, "that the present age is as strongly marked or distinguished from all other ages as that in which Jesus Christ appeared; but with that single exception, perhaps the present age is the most eventful the world has ever known. We live in times which have no parallel in past ages; in times when the human character has almost assumed a new form; in times of peculiar calamity, of thick darkness, and almost of despair. . . . The danger is so vast, so awful, and so obvious, that the blindness, the indifference, which prevail argue infatuation, and give room for apprehension that nothing can rouse us to those efforts by which alone the danger can be averted. Am I asked what there is so peculiar and so tremendous in the times in which we live? . . . I answer: In the very heart of Europe, in the centre of the civilized world, a new power has suddenly arisen on the ruins of old institutions, peculiar in its character, and most ruinous in its influence."

While Channing felt for France the full horror of his Federalist principles, he regarded England with equivalent affection.

"I feel a peculiar interest in England," he explained in a note appended to the Fast Day Sermon; "for I believe that there Christianity is exerting its best influences on the human character; that there the perfections of human nature, wisdom, virtue, and piety are fostered by excellent institutions, and are producing the delightful fruits of domestic happiness, social order, and general prosperity."

The majority of Americans took a different view of the subject; but even those who most strongly agreed with Channing would have been first to avow that their prejudice was inveterate, and its consequences sweeping. Such a conviction admitted little room for liberalism where politics were, directly or remotely, involved. Literature bordered closely on politics, and the liberalism of Unitarian Boston was bounded even in literature by the limits of British sympathies. Buckminster's Phi Beta Kappa Oration of 1809 was as emphatic on this point as Channing's Fast Day Sermon of 1810 was outspoken in its political antipathies.

"It is our lot," said Buckminster, "to have been born in an age of tremendous revolution, and the world is yet covered with the wrecks of its ancient glory, especially of its literary renown. The fury of that storm which rose in France is passed and spent, but its effects have been felt through the whole system of liberal education. The foul spirit of innovation and sophistry has been seen wandering in the very groves of the Lyceum, and is not yet completely exorcised, though the spell is broken."

The liberalism of Boston began in a protest against " the foul spirit of innovation," and could hardly begin at any point more advanced. " Infidelity has had one triumph in our days, and we have seen learning as well as virtue trampled under the hoofs of its infuriated steeds, let loose by the hand of impiety." From this attitude of antipathy to innovation, the Unitarian movement began its attempts to innovate, and with astonishing rapidity passed through phases which might well have required ages of growth. In five years Channing began open attack upon the foundation, or what had hitherto been believed the foundation, of the Church; and from that moment innovation could no longer be regarded as foul.

Of the intellectual movement in all its new directions, Harvard College was the centre. Between 1805 and 1817 the college inspired the worn-out Federalism of Boston with life till then unimagined. Not only did it fill the pulpits with Buckminsters, Channings, and Thachers, whose sermons were an unfailing interest, and whose society was a constant stimulus, but it also maintained a rivalry between the pulpit and the lecture-room. The choice of a new professor was as important and as much discussed as the choice of a new minister. No ordinary political event caused more social interest than the appointment of Henry Ware as Professor of Theology in 1805. In the following year J. Q. Adams was made Professor of Rhetoric, and delivered a course of lectures, which created the school of oratory to which Edward Everett's generation adhered. Four younger men, whose influence was greatly felt in their branches of instruction, received professorships in the next few years, — Jacob Bigelow, who was appointed Professor of Medicine in 1813; Edward Everett, Greek Professor in 1815; John Collins Warren, Professor of Anatomy in the same year; and George Ticknor, Professor of *Belles Lettres* in 1816. In the small society of Boston, a city numbering hardly forty thousand persons, this activity of college and church produced a new era. Where thirty-nine students a year had entered the college before 1800, an average number of sixty-six entered it during the war, and took degrees during the four or five subsequent years. Among them were names familiar to the literature and politics of the next half century. Besides Ticknor and Everett, in 1807 and 1811, Henry Ware graduated in 1812, and his brother William, the author of "Zenobia," in 1816; William Hickling Prescott, in 1814; J. G. Palfrey, in 1815; in 1817, George Bancroft and Caleb Cushing graduated, and Ralph Waldo Emerson entered the college. Boston also drew resources from other quarters, and perhaps showed no stronger proof of its vigor than when, in 1816, it attracted Daniel Webster from New Hampshire to identify himself with the intellect and interests of Massachusetts. Even by reaction the Unitarians stimulated Boston, — as when, a few years afterward, Lyman Beecher accepted the charge of a Boston church in order to resist their encroachments.

The "Anthology," which marked the birth of the new literary school, came in a few years to a natural end, but was revived in 1815 under the name of the "North American Review," by the exertions of William Tudor. The life of the new Review belonged to a later period, and was shaped by other influences than those that surrounded the "Anthology." With the beginning of the next epoch, the provincial stage of the Boston school was closed. More and more its influence tended to become national, and even to affect other countries. Perhaps by a natural consequence rather than by coincidence, the close of the old period was marked by the appearance of a short original poem in the "North American Review" for September, 1817: —

" . . . The hills,
Rock-ribbed and ancient as the sun; the vales
Stretching in pensive quietness between;
The venerable woods; the floods that move
In majesty, and the complaining brooks
That wind among the meads and make them green,
Are but the solemn declarations all,
Of the great tomb of man. The golden sun,
The planets, all the infinite host of heaven
Are glowing on the sad abodes of death
Through the still lapse of ages. All that tread
The globe are but a handful to the tribes
That slumber in its bosom. Take the wings
Of morning, and the Borean desert pierce;
Or lose thyself in the continuous woods
That veil Oregan, where he hears no sound

> Save his own dashings, — yet the dead are there ;
> And millions in these solitudes, since first
> The flight of years began, have laid them down
> In their last sleep : the dead reign there alone.
> So shalt thou rest : and what if thou shalt fall
> Unnoticed by the living, and no friend
> Take note of thy departure ? Thousands more
> Will share thy destiny. The tittering world
> Dance to the grave. The busy brood of care
> Plod on, and each one chases as before
> His favorite phantom. Yet all these shall leave
> Their mirth and their employments, and shall come
> And make their bed with thee."

The appearance of "Thanatopsis" and "Lines to a Waterfowl" in the early numbers of the "North American Review," while leaving no doubt that a new national literature was close at hand, proved also that it was not to be the product of a single source; for Bryant, though greatly tempted to join the Emersons, Channing, Dana, Allston, and Tudor in Boston, turned finally to New York, where influences of a different kind surrounded him. The Unitarian school could not but take a sober cast, and even its humor was sure to be tinged with sadness, sarcasm, or irony, or some serious purpose or passion; but New York contained no atmosphere in which such a society could thrive. Busy with the charge of practical work, — the development of industries continually exceeding their power of control, — the people of New York wanted amusement, and shunned what in Boston was considered as intellectual. Their tastes were gratified by the appearance of a writer whose first book created a school of literature as distinctly marked as the Unitarian school of Boston, and more decidedly original. "The History of New York, by Diedrich Knickerbocker," appeared in 1809, and stood alone. Other books of the time seemed to recognize some literary parentage. Channing and Buckminster were links in a chain of theologians and preachers. "Thanatopsis" evidently drew inspiration from Wordsworth. Diedrich Knickerbocker owed nothing to any living original.

The "History of New York" was worth more than passing notice. In the development of a national character, as well as of the literature that reflected it, humor was a trait of the utmost interest; and Washington Irving was immediately recognized as a humorist whose name, if he fulfilled the promise of his first attempt, would have a chance of passing into the society of Rabelais, Cervantes, Butler, and Sterne. Few literary tasks were more difficult than to burlesque without vulgarizing, and to satirize without malignity; yet Irving in his first effort succeeded in doing both. The old families, and serious students of colonial history, never quite forgave Irving for throwing an atmosphere of ridicule over the subject of their interest; but Diedrich Knickerbocker's History was so much more entertaining than ordinary histories, that even historians could be excused for regretting that it should not be true.

Yet the book reflected the political passions which marked the period of the Embargo. Besides the burlesque, the "History" contained satire; and perhaps its most marked trait was the good-nature which, at a time when bitterness was universal in politics, saved Irving's political satire from malignity. Irving meant that no one should mistake the character of the universal genius, Governor Wilhelmus Kieft, surnamed the Testy, who as a youth had made many curious investigations into the nature and operations of windmills, and who came well-nigh being smothered in a slough of unintelligible learning, — "a fearful peril, from the effects of which he never perfectly recovered."

"No sooner had this bustling little man been blown by a whiff of fortune into the seat of government, than he called together his council and delivered a very animated speech on the affairs of the government; . . . and here he soon worked himself into a fearful rage against the Yankees, whom he compared to the Gauls who desolated Rome, and to the Goths and Vandals who overran the fairest plains of Europe. . . . Having thus artfully wrought up his tale of terror to a climax, he assumed a self-satisfied look, and declared with a nod of knowing import that he had taken measures to put a final stop to these encroachments, — that he had been obliged to have recourse to a dreadful engine of warfare, lately invented, awful in its effects but authorized by direful necessity; in a word, he was resolved to conquer the Yankees — by Proclamation."

Washington Irving's political relations were those commonly known as Burrite, through his brother Peter, who edited in Burr's interest the "Morning

Chronicle." Antipathy to Jefferson was a natural result, and Irving's satire on the President was the more interesting because the subject offered temptations for ill-tempered sarcasm such as spoiled Federalist humor. The Knickerbocker sketch of Jefferson was worth comparing with Federalist modes of expressing the same ideas: —

"The great defect of Wilhelmus Kieft's policy was that though no man could be more ready to stand forth in an hour of emergency, yet he was so intent upon guarding the national pocket that he suffered the enemy to break its head. . . . All this was a remote consequence of his education at the Hague; where, having acquired a smattering of knowledge, he was ever a great conner of indexes, continually dipping into books without ever studying to the bottom of any subject, so that he had the scum of all kinds of authors fermenting in his pericranium. In some of these titlepage researches he unluckily stumbled over a grand political *cabalistic word*, which with his customary facility he immediately incorporated into his great scheme of government, to the irretrievable injury and delusion of the honest province of Nieuw Nederlands, and the eternal misleading of all experimental rulers."

Little was wanting to make such a sketch bitter; but Irving seemed to have the power of deadening venom by a mere trick of hand. Readers of the "History," after a few years had passed, rarely remembered the satire, or supposed that the story contained it. The humor and the style remained to characterize a school.

The originality of the Knickerbocker humor was the more remarkable because it was allowed to stand alone. Irving published nothing else of consequence until 1819, and then, abandoning his early style, inclined to imitate Addison and Steele, although his work was hardly the less original. Irving preceded Walter Scott, whose "Waverley" appeared in 1814, and "Guy Mannering" in 1815; and if either author could be said to influence the other, the influence of Diedrich Knickerbocker on Scott was more evident than that of "Waverley" on Irving.

In the face of the spontaneous burst of genius which at that moment gave to English literature and art a character distinct even in its own experience, Americans might have been excused for making no figure at all. Other periods produced one poet at a time, and measured originality by single poems; or satisfied their ambition by prose or painting of occasional merit. The nineteenth century began in England with genius as plenty as it was usually rare. To Beattie, Cowper, and Burns, succeeded Wordsworth, Coleridge, Scott, Byron, Crabbe, Campbell, Charles Lamb, Moore, Shelley, and Keats. The splendor of this combination threw American and even French talent into the shade, and defied hope of rivalry; but the American mind, as far as it went, showed both freshness and originality. The divergence of American from English standards seemed insignificant to critics who required, as they commonly did, a national literature founded on some new conception, — such as the Shawanee or Aztecs could be supposed to suggest; but to those who expected only a slow variation from European types, the difference was well marked. Channing and Irving were American in literature, as Calhoun and Webster were American in politics. They were the product of influences as peculiar to the country as those which produced Fulton and his steamboat.

While Bryant published "Thanatopsis" and Irving made his studies for the "Sketch-Book," another American of genius perhaps superior to theirs — Washington Allston — was painting in London, before returning to pass the remainder of his life in the neighborhood of Boston and Harvard College. Between thirty and forty years of age, Allston was then in the prime of his powers; and even in a circle of artists which included Turner, Wilkie, Mulready, Constable, Callcott, Crome, Cotman, and a swarm of others equally famous, Allston was distinguished. Other Americans took rank in the same society. Leslie and Stuart Newton were adopted into it, and Copley died only in 1815, while Trumbull painted in London till 1816; but remarkable though they were for the quality of their art, they belonged to a British school, and could be claimed as American only by blood. Allston stood in a relation somewhat different. In part, his apparent Americanism was due to his later return, and to his identification with American society; but the return itself was probably caused by a peculiar bent of character. His mind was not wholly English.

Allston's art and his originality were not such as might have been expected from an American, or such as Americans were likely to admire; and the same might be said of Leslie and Stuart Newton. Perhaps the strongest instance of all was Edward Malbone, whose grace of execution was not more remarkable than his talent for elevating the subject of his exquisite work. So far from sharing the imagination of Shawanee Indians or even of Democrats, these men instinctively reverted to the most refined and elevated schools of art. Not only did Allston show from the beginning of his career a passion for the nobler standards of his profession, but also for technical quality, — a taste less usual. Washington Irving met him in Rome in 1805, when both were unknown; and they became warm friends.

"I do not think I have ever been more captivated on a first acquaintance," wrote Irving long afterward. "He was of a light and graceful form, with large blue eyes and black silken hair. Everything about him bespoke the man of intellect and refinement. . . . He was exquisitely sensitive to the graceful and the beautiful, and took great delight in paintings which excelled in color; yet he was strongly moved and aroused by objects of grandeur. I well recollect the admiration with which he contemplated the sublime statue of Moses, by Michael Angelo."

The same tastes characterized his life, and gave to his work a distinction that might be Italian, but was certainly not English or usual.

"It was Allston," said Leslie, "who first awakened what little sensibility I may possess to the beauties of color. For long time I took the merit of the Venetians on trust, and if left to myself should have preferred works which I now feel to be comparatively worthless. I remember when the picture of 'The Ages' by Titian was first pointed out to me by Allston as an exquisite work, I thought he was laughing at me." Leslie, if not a great colorist, was seldom incorrect; Stuart Newton had a fine eye for color, and Malbone was emphatically a colorist; but Allston's sensibility to color was rare among artists, and the refinement of his mind was as unusual as the delicacy of his eye.

Allston was also singular in the liberality of his sympathies. "I am by nature, as it respects the arts, a wide liker," he said. In Rome he became acquainted with Coleridge; and the remark of Coleridge which seemed to make most impression on him in their walks "under the pines of the Villa Borghese" was evidently agreeable because it expressed his own feelings. "It was there he taught me this golden rule: never to judge of any work of art by its defects." His admiration for the classics did not prevent him from admiring his contemporaries; his journey through Switzerland not only showed him a new world of Nature, but also "the truth of Turner's Swiss scenes, — the poetic truth, — which none before or since have given." For a young American art-student in 1804, such sympathies were remarkable; not so much because they were correct, as because they were neither American nor English. Neither in America nor in Europe at that day could art-schools give to every young man, at the age of twenty-five, eyes to see the color of Titian, or imagination to feel the "poetic truth" of Turner.

Other painters, besides those whose names have been mentioned, were American or worked in America, as other writers besides Bryant and Irving, and other preachers besides Buckminster and Channing, were active in their professions; but for national comparisons, types alone serve. In the course of sixteen years certain Americans became distinguished. Among these, suitable for types, were Calhoun and Clay in Congress, Pinkney and Webster at the bar, Buckminster and Channing in the pulpit, Bryant and Irving in literature, Allston and Malbone in painting. These men varied greatly in character and qualities. Some possessed strength, and some showed more delicacy than vigor; some were humorists, and some were incapable of a thought that was not serious; but all were marked by a keen sense of form and style. So little was this quality expected, that the world inclined to regard them as un-American because of their refinement. Frenchmen and Italians, and even Englishmen who knew nothing of America but its wildness, were disappointed that American oratory should be only a variation from Fox and Burke; that American literature should reproduce Steele and Wordsworth; and that American art should, at its first bound, go back to the ideals of Raphael and Titian. The incongruity was evident. The Americans themselves called persistently for a statesmanship, religion, literature, and art which should be American; and they made a number of experiments to produce what they thought their ideals. In substance they continued to approve nothing which was not marked by style as its chief merit. The oratory of Webster and Calhoun, and even of John Randolph bore the same general and common character of style. The poetry of Bryant, the humor of Irving, the sermons of Channing, and the painting of Allston were the objects of permanent approval to the national mind. Style remained its admiration, even when every newspaper protested against the imitation of outworn forms. Dennie and Jefferson, agreeing in nothing else, agreed in this; the South Carolinian Allston saw color as naturally as the New Englander Bryant heard rhythm; and a people which seemed devoid of sense or standards of beauty, showed more ambition than older societies to acquire both.

Nothing seemed more certain than that the Americans were not artistic, that they had as a people little instinct of beauty; but their intelligence in its higher as in its lower forms was both quick and refined.

Such literature and art as they produced, showed qualities akin to those which produced the swift-sailing schooner, the triumph of naval architecture. If the artistic instinct weakened, the quickness of intelligence increased.

CHAPTER X.

UNTIL 1815 nothing in the future of the American Union was regarded as settled. As late as January, 1815, division into several nationalities was still thought to be possible. Such a destiny, repeating the usual experience of history, was not necessarily more unfortunate than the career of a single nationality wholly American; for if the effects of divided nationality were certain to be unhappy, those of a single society with equal certainty defied experience or sound speculation. One uniform and harmonious system appealed to the imagination as a triumph of human progress, offering prospects of peace and ease, contentment and philanthropy, such as the world had not seen; but it invited dangers, formidable because unusual or altogether unknown. The corruption of such a system might prove to be proportionate with its dimensions, and uniformity might lead to evils as serious as were commonly ascribed to diversity.

The laws of human progress were matter not for dogmatic faith, but for study; and although society instinctively regarded small States, with their clashing interests and incessant wars, as the chief obstacle to improvement, such progress as the world knew had been coupled with those drawbacks. The few examples offered by history of great political societies, relieved from external competition or rivalry, were not commonly thought encouraging. War had been the severest test of political and social character, laying bare whatever was feeble, and calling out whatever was strong; and the effect of removing such a test was an untried problem.

In 1815 for the first time Americans ceased to doubt the path they were to follow. Not only was the unity of their nation established, but its probable divergence from older societies was also well defined. Already in 1817 the difference between Europe and America was decided. In politics the distinction was more evident than in social, religious, literary, or scientific directions; and the result was singular. For a time the aggressions of England and France forced the United States into a path that seemed to lead toward European methods of government; but the popular resistance, or inertia, was so great that the most popular party leaders failed to overcome it, and no sooner did foreign dangers disappear than the system began to revert to American practices; the national government tried to lay aside its assumed powers. When Madison vetoed the bill for internal improvements he could have had no other motive than that of restoring to the government, as far as possible, its original American character.

The result was not easy to understand in theory or to make efficient in practice; but while the drift of public opinion, and still more of practical necessity, drew the government slowly toward the European standard of true political sovereignty, nothing showed that the compromise, which must probably serve the public purpose, was to be European in form or feeling. As far as politics supplied a test, the national character had already diverged from any foreign type. Opinions might differ whether the political movement was progressive or retrograde, but in any case the American, in his political character, was a new variety of man.

The social movement was also decided. The war gave a severe shock to the Anglican sympathies of society, and peace seemed to widen the breach between European and American tastes. Interest in Europe languished after Napoleon's overthrow. France ceased to affect American opinion. England became an object of less alarm. Peace produced in the United States a social and economical revolution which greatly curtailed the influence of New England, and with it the social authority of Great Britain. The invention of the steamboat counterbalanced ocean commerce. The South and West gave to society a character more aggressively American than had been known before. That Europe, within certain limits, might tend toward American ideas was possible, but that America should under any circumstances follow the experiences of European development might thenceforward be reckoned as improbable. American character was formed, if not fixed.

The scientific interest of American history centred in national character, and in the workings of a society destined to become vast, in which individuals were important chiefly as types. Although this kind of interest was different from that of European history, it was at least as important to the world. Should history ever become a true science, it must expect to establish its laws, not from the complicated story of rival European nationalities, but from the methodical evolution of a great democracy. North America was the most favorable field on the globe for the spread of a society so large, uniform, and isolated as to answer the purposes of science. There a single homogeneous society could easily attain proportions of three or four hundred million persons, under conditions of undisturbed growth.

In Europe or Asia, except perhaps in China, undisturbed social evolution had been unknown. Without disturbance, evolution seemed to cease. Wherever disturbance occurred, permanence was impossible. Every people in turn adapted itself to the law of necessity. Such a system as that of the United States could hardly have existed for half a century in Europe except under the protection of another power. In the fierce struggle characteristic of European society, systems were permanent in nothing except in the general law, that, whatever other character they might possess they must always be chiefly military.

The want of permanence was not the only or the

most confusing obstacle to the treatment of European history as a science. The intensity of the struggle gave prominence to the individual, until the hero seemed all, society nothing; and what was worse for scientific purposes, the men interested more than the societies. In the dramatic view of history, the hero deserved more to be studied than the community to which he belonged; in truth, he was the society, which existed only to produce him and to perish with him. Against such a view historians were among the last to protest, and protested but faintly when they did so at all. They felt as strongly as their audiences that the highest achievements were alone worth remembering either in history or in art, and that a reiteration of commonplaces was commonplace. With all the advantages of European movement and color, few historians succeeded in enlivening or dignifying the lack of motive, intelligence, and morality, the helplessness characteristic of many long periods in the face of crushing problems, and the futility of human efforts to escape from difficulties religious, political, and social. In a period extending over four or five thousand years, more or less capable of historical treatment, historians were content to illustrate here and there the most dramatic moments of the most striking communities. The hero was their favorite. War was the chief field of heroic action, and even the history of England was chiefly the story of war.

The history of the United States promised to be

free from such disturbances. War counted for little, the hero for less; on the people alone the eye could permanently rest. The steady growth of a vast population without the social distinctions that confused other histories, — without kings, nobles, or armies; without church, traditions, and prejudices, — seemed a subject for the man of science rather than for dramatists or poets. To scientific treatment only one great obstacle existed. Americans, like Europeans, were not disposed to make of their history a mechanical evolution. They felt that they even more than other nations needed the heroic element, because they breathed an atmosphere of peace and industry where heroism could seldom be displayed; and in unconscious protest against their own social conditions they adorned with imaginary qualities scores of supposed leaders, whose only merit was their faculty of reflecting a popular trait. Instinctively they clung to ancient history as though conscious that of all misfortunes that could befall the national character, the greatest would be the loss of the established ideals which alone ennobled human weakness. Without heroes, the national character of the United States had few charms of imagination even to Americans.

Historians and readers maintained Old-World standards. No historian cared to hasten the coming of an epoch when man should study his own history in the same spirit and by the same methods with which he studied the formation of a crystal. Yet history had its scientific as well as its human side, and in American history the scientific interest was greater than the human. Elsewhere the student could study under better conditions the evolution of the individual, but nowhere could he study so well the evolution of a race. The interest of such a subject exceeded that of any other branch of science, for it brought mankind within sight of its own end.

Travellers in Switzerland who stepped across the Rhine where it flowed from its glacier could follow its course among mediæval towns and feudal ruins, until it became a highway for modern industry, and at last arrived at a permanent equilibrium in the ocean. American history followed the same course. With prehistoric glaciers and mediæval feudalism the story had little to do; but from the moment it came within sight of the ocean it acquired interest almost painful. A child could find his way in a river-valley, and a boy could float on the waters of Holland; but science alone could sound the depths of the ocean, measure its currents, foretell its storms, or fix its relations to the system of Nature. In a democratic ocean science could see something ultimate. Man could go no further. The atom might move, but the general equilibrium could not change.

Whether the scientific or the heroic view were taken, in either case the starting-point was the same, and the chief object of interest was to define national character. Whether the figures of history were treated as heroes or as types, they must be taken to represent the people. American types were especially worth study if they were to represent the greatest democratic evolution the world could know. Readers might judge for themselves what share the individual possessed in creating or shaping the nation; but whether it was small or great, the nation could be understood only by studying the individual. For that reason, in the story of Jefferson and Madison individuals retained their old interest as types of character, if not as sources of power.

In the American character antipathy to war ranked first among political traits. The majority of Americans regarded war in a peculiar light, the consequence of comparative security. No European nation could have conducted a war, as the people of America conducted the War of 1812. The possibility of doing so without destruction explained the existence of the national trait, and assured its continuance. In politics, the divergence of America from Europe perpetuated itself in the popular instinct for peaceable methods. The Union took shape originally on the general lines that divided the civil from the military elements of the British constitution. The party of Jefferson and Gallatin was founded on dislike of every function of government necessary in a military system. Although Jefferson carried his pacific theories to an extreme, and brought about a military reaction, the reactionary movement was neither universal, violent, nor lasting; and society showed no sign of changing its convictions. With greater strength the country might acquire greater familiarity with warlike methods, but in the same degree was less likely to suffer any general change of habits. Nothing but prolonged intestine contests could convert the population of an entire continent into a race of warriors.

A people whose chief trait was antipathy to war, and to any system organized with military energy, could scarcely develop great results in national administration; yet the Americans prided themselves chiefly on their political capacity. Even the war did not undeceive them, although the incapacity brought into evidence by the war was undisputed, and was most remarkable among the communities which believed themselves to be most gifted with political sagacity. Virginia and Massachusetts by turns admitted failure in dealing with issues so simple that the newest societies, like Tennessee and Ohio, understood them by instinct. That incapacity in national politics should appear as a leading trait in American character was unexpected by Americans, but might naturally result from their conditions. The better test of American character was not political but social, and was to be found not in the government but in the people.

The sixteen years of Jefferson's and Madison's rule furnished international tests of popular intelligence upon which Americans could depend. The ocean was the only open field for competition among nations. Americans enjoyed there no natural or artificial advantages over Englishmen, Frenchmen, or Spaniards; indeed, all these countries possessed navies, resources, and experience greater than were to be found in the United States. Yet the Americans developed, in the course of twenty years, a surprising degree of skill in naval affairs. The evidence of their success was to be found nowhere so complete as in the avowals of Englishmen who knew best the history of naval progress. The American invention of the fast-sailing schooner or clipper was the more remarkable because, of all American inventions, this alone sprang from direct competition with Europe. During ten centuries of struggle the nations of Europe had labored to obtain superiority over each other in ship-construction, yet Americans instantly made improvements which gave them superiority, and which Europeans were unable immediately to imitate even after seeing them. Not only were American vessels better in model, faster in sailing, easier and quicker in handling, and more economical in working than the European, but they were also better equipped. The English complained as a grievance that the Americans adopted new and unwarranted devices in naval warfare; that their vessels were heavier and better constructed, and their missiles of unusual shape and improper use. The Americans resorted to expedients that had not been tried before, and excited a mixture of irritation and respect in the English service, until Yankee smartness became a national misdemeanor.

The English admitted themselves to be slow to

change their habits, but the French were both quick and scientific; yet Americans did on the ocean what the French, under stronger inducements, failed to do. The French privateer preyed upon British commerce for twenty years without seriously injuring it; but no sooner did the American privateer sail from French ports, than the rates of insurance doubled in London, and an outcry for protection arose among English shippers which the Admiralty could not calm. The British newspapers were filled with assertions that the American cruiser was the superior of any vessel of its class, and threatened to overthrow England's supremacy on the ocean.

Another test of relative intelligence was furnished by the battles at sea. Instantly after the loss of the "Guerriere" the English discovered and complained that American gunnery was superior to their own. They explained their inferiority by the length of time that had elapsed since their navy had found on the ocean an enemy to fight. Every vestige of hostile fleets had been swept away, until, after the battle of Trafalgar, British frigates ceased practice with their guns. Doubtless the British navy had become somewhat careless in the absence of a dangerous enemy, but Englishmen were themselves aware that some other cause must have affected their losses. Nothing showed that Nelson's line-of-battle ships, frigates, or sloops were as a rule better fought than the "Macedonian" and "Java," the "Avon" and "Reindeer." Sir Howard Douglas, the chief authority on the subject, attempted in vain to explain British reverses by the deterioration of British gunnery. His analysis showed only that American gunnery was extraordinarily good. Of all vessels, the sloop-of-war, — on account of its smallness, its quick motion, and its more accurate armament of thirty-two-pound carronades, — offered the best test of relative gunnery, and Sir Howard Douglas in commenting upon the destruction of the "Peacock" and "Avon" could only say, —

"In these two actions it is clear that the fire of the British vessels was thrown too high, and that the ordnance of their opponents were expressly and carefully aimed at and took effect chiefly in the hull."

The battle of the "Hornet" and "Penguin" as well as those of the "Reindeer" and "Avon," showed that the excellence of American gunnery continued till the close of the war. Whether at point-blank range or at long-distance practice, the Americans used guns as they had never been used at sea before.

None of the reports of former British victories showed that the British fire had been more destructive at any previous time than in 1812, and no report of any commander since the British navy existed showed so much damage inflicted on an opponent in so short a time as was proved to have been inflicted on themselves by the reports of British commanders in the American war. The strongest proof of American superiority was given by the best British officers, like Broke, who strained every nerve to maintain an equality with American gunnery. So instantaneous and energetic was the effort that, according to the British historian of the war, "a British forty-six-gun frigate of 1813 was half as effective again as a British forty-six-gun frigate of 1812;" and, as he justly said, "the slaughtered crews and the shattered hulks" of the captured British ships proved that no want of their old fighting qualities accounted for their repeated and almost habitual mortifications.[1]

Unwilling as the English were to admit the superior skill of Americans on the ocean, they did not hesitate to admit it, in certain respects, on land. The American rifle in American hands was affirmed to have no equal in the world. This admission could scarcely be withheld after the lists of killed and wounded which followed almost every battle; but the admission served to check a wider inquiry. In truth, the rifle played but a small part in the war. Winchester's men at the river Raisin may have owed their over-confidence, as the British Forty-first owed its losses, to that weapon, and at New Orleans five or six hundred of Coffee's men, who were out of range, were armed with the rifle; but the surprising losses of the British were commonly due to artillery and musketry fire. At New Orleans the artillery was chiefly engaged. The artillery battle of January 1, according to British accounts, amply proved the superiority of American gunnery on that occasion, which was probably the fairest test during the war.

[1] James, pp. 525, 528.

The battle of January 8 was also chiefly an artillery battle; the main British column never arrived within fair musket range; Pakenham was killed by a grape-shot, and the main column of his troops halted more than one hundred yards from the parapet.

The best test of British and American military qualities, both for men and weapons, was Scott's battle of Chippawa. Nothing intervened to throw a doubt over the fairness of the trial. Two parallel lines of regular soldiers, practically equal in numbers, armed with similar weapons, moved in close order toward each other, across a wide open plain, without cover or advantage of position, stopping at intervals to load and fire, until one line broke and retired. At the same time two three-gun batteries, the British being the heavier, maintained a steady fire from positions opposite each other. According to the reports, the two infantry lines in the centre never came nearer than eighty yards. Major-General Riall reported that then, owing to severe losses, his troops broke and could not be rallied. Comparison of the official reports showed that the British lost in killed and wounded four hundred and sixty-nine men; the Americans, two hundred and ninety-six. Some doubts always affect the returns of wounded, because the severity of the wound cannot be known; but dead men tell their own tale. Riall reported one hundred and forty-eight killed; Scott reported sixty-one. The severity of the losses showed that the battle was sharply contested, and proved the personal bravery of both armies. Marksmanship decided the result, and the returns proved that the American fire was superior to that of the British in the proportion of more than fifty per cent if estimated by the entire loss, and of two hundred and forty-two to one hundred if estimated by the deaths alone.

The conclusion seemed incredible, but it was supported by the results of the naval battles. The Americans showed superiority amounting in some cases to twice the efficiency of their enemies in the use of weapons. The best French critic of the naval war, Jurien de la Gravière said: "An enormous superiority in the rapidity and precision of their fire can alone explain the difference in the losses sustained by the combatants."[1] So far from denying this conclusion the British press constantly alleged it, and the British officers complained of it. The discovery caused great surprise, and in both British services much attention was at once directed to improvement in artillery and musketry. Nothing could exceed the frankness with which Englishmen avowed their inferiority. According to Sir Francis Head, " gunnery was in naval warfare in the extraordinary state of ignorance we have just described, when our lean children, the American people taught us, rod in hand, our first lesson in the art." The English textbook on Naval Gunnery, written by Major-General Sir Howard Douglas immediately after the peace, devoted more attention to the short American war

[1] Guerres Maritimes, ii. 286, 287.

than to all the battles of Napoleon, and began by admitting that Great Britain had " entered with too great confidence on war with a marine much more expert than that of any of our European enemies." The admission appeared " objectionable " even to the author;[1] but he did not add, what was equally true, that it applied as well to the land as to the sea service.

No one questioned the bravery of the British forces, or the ease with which they often routed larger bodies of militia; but the losses they inflicted were rarely as great as those they suffered. Even at Bladensburg, where they met little resistance, their loss was several times greater than that of the Americans. At Plattsburg, where the intelligence and quickness of Macdonough and his men alone won the victory, his ships were in effect stationary batteries, and enjoyed the same superiority in gunnery. " The ' Saratoga,' " said his official report, " had fifty-five round-shot in her hull; the ' Confiance,' one hundred and five. The enemy's shot passed principally just over our heads, as there were not twenty whole hammocks in the nettings at the close of the action."

The greater skill of the Americans was not due to special training, for the British service was better trained in gunnery, as in everything else, than the motley armies and fleets that fought at New Orleans and on the Lakes. Critics constantly said that every

[1] Naval Gunnery (Second edition), p. 3.

American had learned from his childhood the use of the rifle, but he certainly had not learned to use cannon in shooting birds or hunting deer, and he knew less than the Englishman about the handling of artillery and muskets. The same intelligence that selected the rifle and the long pivot-gun for favorite weapons was shown in handling the carronade, and every other instrument however clumsy.

Another significant result of the war was the sudden development of scientific engineering in the United States. This branch of the military service owed its efficiency and almost its existence to the military school at West Point, established in 1802. The school was at first much neglected by government. The number of graduates before the year 1812 was very small; but at the outbreak of the war the corps of engineers was already efficient. Its chief was Colonel Joseph Gardner Swift, of Massachusetts, the first graduate of the academy: Colonel Swift planned the defences of New York harbor. The lieutenant-colonel in 1812 was Walker Keith Armistead, of Virginia, — the third graduate, who planned the defences of Norfolk. Major William McRee, of North Carolina, became chief engineer to General Brown, and constructed the fortifications at Fort Erie, which cost the British General Gordon Drummond the loss of half his army, besides the mortification of defeat. Captain Eleazer Derby Wood, of New York, constructed Fort Meigs, which enabled Harrison to defeat the attack of Proctor in May,

1813. Captain Joseph Gilbert Totten, of New York, was chief engineer to General Izard at Plattsburg, where he directed the fortifications that stopped the advance of Prevost's great army. None of the works constructed by a graduate of West Point was captured by the enemy; and had an engineer been employed at Washington by Armstrong and Winder, the city would have been easily saved.

Perhaps without exaggeration the West Point Academy might be said to have decided, next to the navy, the result of the war. The works at New Orleans were simple in character, and as far as they were due to engineering skill were directed by Major Latour, a Frenchman; but the war was already ended when the battle of New Orleans was fought. During the critical campaign of 1814, the West Point engineers doubled the capacity of the little American army for resistance, and introduced a new and scientific character into American life.

In the application of science the steamboat was the most striking success; but Fulton's invention, however useful, was neither the most original nor the most ingenious of American efforts, nor did it offer the best example of popular characteristics. Perhaps Fulton's torpedo and Stevens's screw-propeller showed more originality than was proved by the "Clermont." The fast-sailing schooner with its pivot-gun — an invention that grew out of the common stock of nautical intelligence — best illustrated the character of the people.

That the individual should rise to a higher order either of intelligence or morality than had existed in former ages was not to be expected, for the United States offered less field for the development of individuality than had been offered by older and smaller societies. The chief function of the American Union was to raise the average standard of popular intelligence and well-being, and at the close of the War of 1812 the superior average intelligence of Americans was so far admitted that Yankee acuteness, or smartness, became a national reproach; but much doubt remained whether the intelligence belonged to a high order, or proved a high morality. From the earliest ages, shrewdness was associated with unscrupulousness; and Americans were freely charged with wanting honesty. The charge could neither be proved nor disproved. American morality was such as suited a people so endowed, and was high when compared with the morality of many older societies; but, like American intelligence, it discouraged excess. Probably the political morality shown by the government and by public men during the first sixteen years of the century offered a fair gauge of social morality. Like the character of the popular inventions, the character of the morals corresponded to the wants of a growing democratic society; but time alone could decide whether it would result in a high or a low national ideal.

Finer analysis showed other signs of divergence from ordinary standards. If Englishmen took pride in one trait more than in another, it was in the steady uniformity of their progress. The innovating and revolutionary quality of the French mind irritated them. America showed an un-English rapidity in movement. In politics, the American people between 1787 and 1817 accepted greater changes than had been known in England since 1688. In religion, the Unitarian movement of Boston and Harvard College would never have been possible in England, where the defection of Oxford or Cambridge, and the best educated society in the United Kingdom, would have shaken Church and State to their foundations. In literature the American school was chiefly remarkable for the rapidity with which it matured. The first book of Irving was a successful burlesque of his own ancestral history; the first poem of Bryant sang of the earth only as a universal tomb; the first preaching of Channing assumed to overthrow the Trinity; and the first paintings of Allston aspired to recover the ideal perfection of Raphael and Titian. In all these directions the American mind showed tendencies that surprised Englishmen more than they struck Americans. Allston defended himself from the criticism of friends who made complaint of his return to America. He found there, as he maintained, not only a growing taste for art, but "a quicker appreciation" of artistic effort than in any European land. If the highest intelligence of American society were to move with such rapidity, the time could not be far distant when it would pass into regions which England never liked to contemplate.

Another intellectual trait, as has been already noticed, was the disposition to relax severity. Between the theology of Jonathan Edwards and that of William Ellery Channing was an enormous gap, not only in doctrines but also in methods. Whatever might be thought of the conclusions reached by Edwards and Hopkins, the force of their reasoning commanded respect. Not often had a more strenuous effort than theirs been made to ascertain God's will, and to follow it without regard to weaknesses of the flesh. The idea that the nature of God's attributes was to be preached only as subordinate to the improvement of man, agreed little with the spirit of their religion. The Unitarian and Universalist movements marked the beginning of an epoch when ethical and humanitarian ideas took the place of metaphysics, and even New England turned from contemplating the omnipotence of the Deity in order to praise the perfections of his creatures.

The spread of great popular sects like the Universalists and Campbellites, founded on assumptions such as no Orthodox theology could tolerate, showed a growing tendency to relaxation of thought in that direction. The struggle for existence was already mitigated, and the first effect of the change was seen in the increasing cheerfulness of religion. Only when men found their actual world almost a heaven, could they lose overpowering anxiety about the world to come. Life had taken a softer aspect, and as a consequence God was no longer terrible. Even the wicked became less mischievous in an atmosphere where virtue was easier than vice. Punishments seemed mild in a society where every offender could cast off his past, and create a new career. For the first time in history, great bodies of men turned away from their old religion, giving no better reason than that it required them to believe in a cruel Deity, and rejected necessary conclusions of theology because they were inconsistent with human self-esteem.

The same optimism marked the political movement. Society was weary of strife, and settled gladly into a political system which left every disputed point undetermined. The public seemed obstinate only in believing that all was for the best, as far as the United States were concerned, in the affairs of mankind. The contrast was great between this temper of mind and that in which the Constitution had been framed; but it was no greater than the contrast in the religious opinions of the two periods, while the same reaction against severity marked the new literature. The rapid accumulation of wealth and increase in physical comfort told the same story from the standpoint of economy. On every side society showed that ease was for a time to take the place of severity, and enjoyment was to have its full share in the future national existence.

The traits of intelligence, rapidity, and mildness seemed fixed in the national character as early as

1817, and were likely to become more marked as time should pass. A vast amount of conservatism still lingered among the people; but the future spirit of society could hardly fail to be intelligent, rapid in movement, and mild in method. Only in the distant future could serious change occur, and even then no return to European characteristics seemed likely. The American continent was happier in its conditions and easier in its resources than the regions of Europe and Asia, where Nature revelled in diversity and conflict. If at any time American character should change, it might as probably become sluggish as revert to the violence and extravagances of Old-World development. The inertia of several hundred million people, all formed in a similar social mould, was as likely to stifle energy as to stimulate evolution.

With the establishment of these conclusions, a new episode in American history began in 1815. New subjects demanded new treatment, no longer dramatic but steadily tending to become scientific. The traits of American character were fixed; the rate of physical and economical growth was established; and history, certain that at a given distance of time the Union would contain so many millions of people, with wealth valued at so many millions of dollars, became thenceforward chiefly concerned to know what kind of people these millions were to be. They were intelligent, but what paths would their intelligence select? They were quick, but what solution of insoluble problems would quickness hurry? They were scientific, and what control would their science exercise over their destiny? They were mild, but what corruptions would their relaxations bring? They were peaceful, but by what machinery were their corruptions to be purged? What interests were to vivify a society so vast and uniform? What ideals were to ennoble it? What object, besides physical content, must a democratic continent aspire to attain? For the treatment of such questions, history required another century of experience.

GENERAL LIST OF MAPS AND PLANS.

VOLUME I.
	PAGE
THE STATES OF NORTH AFRICA	244

VOLUME II.
THE COAST OF WEST FLORIDA AND LOUISIANA	1

VOLUME VI.
INDIANA TERRITORY	67
SEAT OF WAR ABOUT LAKE ERIE	299
DETROIT RIVER	312
STRAITS OF NIAGARA FROM LAKE ERIE TO LAKE ONTARIO	336

VOLUME VII.
BATTLE OF THE THAMES	137
EAST END OF LAKE ONTARIO AND RIVER ST. LAWRENCE FROM KINGSTON TO FRENCH MILLS	144
EAST END OF LAKE ONTARIO	164
RIVER ST. LAWRENCE FROM WILLIAMSBURG TO MONTREAL	172
SEAT OF WAR AMONG THE CREEKS	217
ATTACK ON CRANEY ISLAND	272

VOLUME VIII.

	PAGE
BATTLE OF CHIPPAWA	40
BATTLE OF LUNDY'S LANE, AT SUNSET	50
BATTLE OF LUNDY'S LANE, AT TEN O'CLOCK	56
ATTACK AND DEFENCE OF FORT ERIE	67
NAVAL BATTLE AT PLATTSBURG	107
POSITION OF BRITISH AND AMERICAN ARMIES AT PLATTSBURG	111
CAMPAIGN OF WASHINGTON AND BALTIMORE	120
BATTLE OF BLADENSBURG	139
ATTACK AND DEFENCE OF BALTIMORE	168
SEAT OF WAR IN LOUISIANA AND WEST FLORIDA	311
ATTACK ON FORT BOWYER	322
LANDING OF BRITISH ARMY AT NEW ORLEANS	337
ATTACK MADE BY MAJOR-GENERAL JACKSON, DEC. 23, 1814	347
BRITISH AND AMERICAN POSITIONS AT NEW ORLEANS	359
ATTACK AND DEFENCE OF THE AMERICAN LINES, JAN. 8, 1815	367
CAPTURE OF FORT BOWYER	383

GENERAL INDEX.

ABBOT, CHARLES, Speaker of the House of Commons, iv. 97.
Abolition Society, an early, i. 128.
Acts of Congress, of Sept. 24, 1789, to establish the Judiciary, i. 259, 260, 275, 276; of June 13, 1798, to suspend intercourse with France, 383; of June 25, 1798, concerning aliens, 140, 141, 206, 207, 259, 286; of July 14, 1798, concerning sedition, 140, 141, 206, 207, 259, 261, 286; vi. 146; of Jan. 30, 1799, called Logan's Act, ii. 259 ; iv. 236; of Feb. 9, 1799, further to suspend intercourse with France, i. 384; of Feb. 13, 1801, to provide for the more convenient organization of the courts, 274–276, 278, 280, 288, 293, 297; of Jan. 14, 1802, for the apportionment of representatives, 301; of March 8, 1802. to repeal the Judiciary Act of 1801, 280, 281, 284–298; of March 16, 1802, fixing the military peace establishment, 301 ; of April 6, 1802, to repeal the internal taxes, 272; of April 29, 1802, for the redemption of the public debt, 272; of April 29, 1802, to amend the judicial system, 298; of April 30, 1802, to enable Ohio to form a State government, 302; of Feb. 28, 1803, for building four sloops-of-war and fifteen gunboats, ii. 77; of Oct. 31, 1803, to take possession of Louisiana, 119, 120; of Feb. 24, 1804, for collecting duties within the territories ceded to the United States, 257, 260-263, 291, 293, 304, 380 (Mobile Act) ; of March 25, 1804, to establish the Mediterranean Fund, 141 ; of March 26, 1804, for the temporary government of Louisiana, 120–129 ; of Jan. 19, 1805, to erect a dam from Mason's island, 209; of March 2, 1805, further providing for the government of Orleans Territory, 401; of March 3, 1805, for the more effectual preservation of peace in the ports and harbors of the United States, 397, 398 ; of March 3, 1805, regulating trade with St. Domingo, iii. 88; of Feb. 13, 1806, called the Two Million Act, 138, 139, 147, 170; of Feb. 28, 1806, prohibiting trade with St. Domingo, 140, 141: of April 18, 1806, prohibiting the importation of certain goods from Great Britain, 175; of March 29, 1806, for laying out the Cumberland Road, 181; of April 21, 1806, for continuing the Mediterranean Fund, 183; of Dec. 19, 1806, for suspending the Non-importation Act of April 18, 1806, 349; of March 3, 1807, repealing the salt-tax and continuing the Mediterranean Fund, 349, 367, 369; of Feb. 10, 1807, establishing a coast survey, 355; of March 2, 1807, prohibiting the importation of slaves, 356-365; of Dec. 18, 1807,

246 GENERAL INDEX.

providing for the building of one hundred and eighty-eight gunboats, iv. 161; of Dec. 22, 1807, for laying an embargo, 168-176; of Jan. 9, 1808, supplementary to the embargo, 200; of March 12, 1808, supplementary to the embargo, 201-204; of April 12, 1808, to raise eight new regiments, 212-218; of April 22, 1808, authorizing the President under certain conditions to suspend the embargo, 223, 306; of Jan. 9, 1809, to enforce the embargo, 398-400; of Jan. 30, 1809, calling an extra session on the fourth Monday in May, 424; of March 1, 1809; to interdict commercial intercourse between the United States and Great Britain and France, 444-453, of June 28, 1809, restoring intercourse with Great Britain, v. 80; of June 28, 1809, suspending the recruiting service, 85; of June 28, 1809, reducing the naval establishment, 85; of March 1, 1810, concerning the commercial intercourse between the United States and Great Britain and France, 194-198 (see Non-intercourse); of Feb. 14, 1810, appropriating sixty thousand dollars for the Cumberland Road, 209; of March 26, 1810, providing for the Third Census, 209; of March 30, 1810, appropriating five thousand dollars for experiments on the submarine torpedo, 209; of Feb. 20, 1811, admitting the State of Louisiana into the Union, 326; of Jan. 15, 1811, authorizing the occupation of East Florida, 327; of March 2, 1811, reviving non-intercourse against Great Britain, 338-354 (see Non-intercourse): of Jan. 11, 1812 to raise an additional military force of twenty-five thousand men, vi. 147, 153; of Feb. 6, 1812, to accept volunteers, 159-161; of March 14, 1812, authorizing a loan for eleven million dollars, 169; of April 4, 1812, laying an embargo for ninety days, 201, 202, 203; of April 8, 1812, admitting the State of Louisiana into the Union, 235; of April 10, 1812, authorizing a call for one hundred thousand militia, 204; of April 14, 1812, to enlarge the limits of the State of Louisiana, 236; of May 14, 1812, to enlarge the boundaries of the Mississippi Territory, 236; of June 18, 1812, declaring war against Great Britain, 228, 229; of July 1, 1812, doubling the duties on imports, 235; of Dec. 12, 1812, increasing the pay of the army, 435; of Jan. 20, 1813, increasing the bounty for recruits, 436; of Jan. 2, 1813, for building four seventy-fours and six frigates, 436; of Jan. 5, 1813, remitting fines, forfeitures, etc., 443; of Jan. 29, 1813, for raising twenty regiments for one year, 449; of Feb. 8, 1813, authorizing loan of sixteen millions, 448; of Feb. 24, 1813, for appointing six major-generals and six brigadiers, 449; of Feb. 25, 1813, authorizing the issue of Treasury notes for five millions, 448; of March 3, 1813, to provide for the supplies of the army, 449; of March 3, 1813, for the better organization of the general staff, 449; of March 3, 1813, for building six sloops-of-war, 449: of March 3, 1813, for the regulation of seamen on board the public and private vessels of the United States, 453-458; of Feb. 24, 1813, for appointing six major-generals and six brigadiers, vii. 36, 37: of March 3, 1813, for the regulation of seamen, etc., 47; of July 22, 1813, for the assessment and collection of direct taxes and internal

GENERAL INDEX. 247

revenue, 55, 71; of July 24, 1813, laying duties on carriages, 55, 71; of July 24, 1813, laying duties on licenses to distillers, 55, 71; of July 24, 1813, laying duties on sales at auction, 71; of July 29, 1813, laying a duty on imported salt, 71; of Aug. 2, 1813, to lay and collect a direct tax, 71; of Aug. 2, 1813, laying duties on licenses to retailers, 71; of Aug. 2, 1813, authorizing a loan for seven million, five hundred thousand dollars, 71; of Aug. 2, 1813, laying stamp duties, 71; of Aug. 2, 1813, to prohibit British licenses of trade, 71; secret, of Feb. 12, 1813, authorizing the President to seize West Florida, 208, 209; of Aug. 2, 1813, reducing duties on prize goods, 336; of Aug. 3, 1813, allowing a bounty for prisoners taken by privateers, 336; of Aug. 2, 1813, extending the pension law to privateers, 337; of Dec. 17, 1813, laying an embargo, 369; of Jan. 25, 1814, relieving Nantucket from the Embargo Act, 369; of Jan. 27, 1814, for filling the ranks of the regular army, 381–384; of March 9, 1814, for building steam-batteries, 385; of March 24, 1814, authorizing a loan for twenty-five millions, 389, 390; of March 4, 1814, authorizing the issue of ten million treasury notes, 389, 390; of March 31, 1814, for the indemnification of Mississippi land claimants (Yazoo Act), 402; of Nov. 15, 1814, for building twenty 16-gun sloops-of-war, viii. 281; of Dec. 10, 1814, making further provision for filling the ranks of the army, 268, 273, 274; of Dec. 21, 1814, laying additional duties on stills, 248, 255; of Dec. 23, 1814, doubling the internal revenue taxes, 248, 255; of Dec. 26, 1814, authorizing the issue of treasury notes to the amount of ten million five hundred thousand dollars, 254; of Jan. 9, 1815, raising the direct tax to six million dollars, 248, 255; of Jan. 18, 1815, increasing the customs duties, 248, 255; of January 18, 1815, increasing the duties on household furniture, etc., 248, 255; of Jan. 27, 1815, authorizing the President to accept the services of State troops, 282–285; of Feb. 7, 1815, creating a board of navy commissioners, 281; of March 2, 1815, fixing the military peace establishment, ix. 84–86; of Feb. 27, 1815, concerning the flotilla service and gunboats, 87; of March 3, 1815, for the support of the navy, 87; of March 3, 1815, for protecting commerce against Algerine cruisers, 87; of March 3, 1815, authorizing a loan for eighteen millions, 100–102; of March 5, 1816, to reduce the amount of direct tax, 112, 114; of April 10, 1816, to incorporate the subscribers to the Bank of the United States, 116–118; of April 27, 1816, to regulate the duties on imports, 114–116; of April 29, 1816, for the gradual increase of the navy, 119; of March 19, 1816, to change the mode of Compensation to the members of the Senate and House of Representatives, 120–122; of April 19, 1816, to admit Indiana into the Union, 119; of Feb. 6, 1817, to repeal the Compensation Act, 144–146; of March 1, 1817, concerning the navigation of the United States, 146, 147; of March 3, 1817, to regulate the trade in plaster of Paris, 147; of March 3, 1817, to provide for the prompt settlement of public accounts, 147; of March 3, 1817, more effectually

248 GENERAL INDEX.

to preserve the neutral relations of the United States, 147.

Act of the territorial legislature of Indiana, permitting the introduction of slaves, vi. 76.

Acts of Parliament, on navigation, ii. 319, 320, 327, 413, 414; of 6th Anne, naturalizing foreign seamen, ii. 338; vii. 21-23; on merchant-shipping, ii. 345; of 13th George II. naturalizing foreign seamen, vii. 21-23.

Adair, John, senator from Kentucky, iii. 127, 139; in Wilkinson's confidence, 220, 223, 241, 255, 274; refuses to testify, 282; accompanies Burr to Nashville, 287; his remarks on Andrew Jackson, 288; starts for New Orleans by land, 291; Burr's despatches to, 295; arrives in New Orleans, and is arrested, 324; discharged from custody, 340; commands Kentucky militia at New Orleans, viii. 368; his dispute with Jackson, 371, 373, 378; his account of the battle on the west bank, 379.

Adams, John, i. 181, 191, 290, 311, 358, 384, 386, 412; ii. 110, 309; iii. 452; iv. 455; his description of Pickering, 402; expenditures of his administration, v. 200, 205, 206; Randolph's allusion to, in 1814, viii. 265; George Ticknor's account of his remarks on the Hartford Convention, 307, 308; his struggle for the fisheries in 1783, ix. 44, 45; his "Defence of the Constitutions," 195.

Adams, John Quincy, senator from Massachusetts, ii. 110, 117, 184, 379; proposes draft of Constitutional amendment, 118, 160, 164; his interviews with Jefferson, iii. 129, 430, 431; his part in the Non-importation Resolutions, 151; his remarks on Yrujo, 188; attends "Chesapeake" meetings in Boston, iv. 29; pledged to support opposition to England, 146; chairman of the committee on the embargo, 171; urges the passage of the Embargo Act, 173; offers a resolution for removing the embargo, 187; votes for Clinton and replies to Pickering's letter, 240 et seq.; resigns his seat in the Senate, 242, 255, 283, 401; nominated as minister to Russia, v. 11; renominated and confirmed, 86; nominated and confirmed Justice of the Supreme Court, 360; sails for Russia, 408; arrives, 409; his negotiations in 1809, 409, 411; his negotiations in 1810, 412-418; his success, 419, 420, 422; receives and forwards the Czar's offer of mediation, vii. 27-29; nominated as joint envoy to treat of peace at St. Petersburg, 59; his appointment confirmed, 61; ignorant of the Czar's motives, 344; informed by Roumanzoff that England refused mediation, 346; designated as minister to London, 347; informed that the Czar would renew offer, 348; surprised by Roumanzoff's contradictions, 349; nominated and confirmed as joint envoy to treat of peace at Ghent, 371; chief of the commission, ix. 15; his difficulties, 16; his account of the American note of August 24, 21; despairs of peace, 22; insists on defending the Florida policy, 29, 30; struggles to preserve the fisheries, 44-50; his opinion of Gallatin and Bayard, 51; appointed minister to England, 89; appointed Secretary of State by Monroe, 139, 140; Professor of Rhetoric at Harvard College, 205.

Adams, William, LL.D. British commissioner at Ghent, ix. 13;

GENERAL INDEX. 249

states British demands, 20; on the fisheries, 47.

"Adams," brig, launched at Detroit, vi. 304; captured and recaptured, 347; destroyed, 347.

"Adams," 28-gun corvette, vi. 364; at Washington, vii. 56, 277, 287, 311; her cruise in 1814, viii. 95; her destruction in the Penobscot, 96.

Addington ministry, ii. 358, 416.

Addington, Henry (Lord Sidmouth), succeeds Pitt, ii. 342, 347; retires from office, 418. (See Sidmouth.)

Addison, Judge, impeached, ii. 195.

Admiralty courts in the West Indies, ii. 340.

"Aeolus," case of, vi. 273.

"Aeolus," British frigate, vi. 368.

"Africa," British frigate, vi. 368.

Alabama Indians, members of the Creek nation, vii. 222; the centre of Creek fanaticism, 222, 223; outbreak among, 226, 227; escape of, 257.

Albany in 1800, i. 3; headquarters of Dearborn, vi. 304, 305, 308, 309, 310; increase in population of, ix. 156.

"Alert," British sloop-of-war, her action with the "Essex," vi. 35, 377.

"Alexander," Salem privateer captured, vii. 329.

Alexander, Czar of Russia, iii. 425; signs treaty of Tilsit, iv. 62; wishes diplomatic relations with Jefferson, 465; with Napoleon at Erfurt, v. 23; his alliance with Napoleon, 134, 257; his approaching rupture with Napoleon, 385, 408-424; interferes for American commerce in Denmark, 410, 411; his reply to Napoleon's demands, 413, 414; gives special orders to release American ships, 415; his attachment to the United States, 415; his ukase on foreign trade, 418; offers mediation, vii. 26-29, 41, 353; continues war in Germany, 339, 345; forced back to Silesia, 340; at Gitschin during armistice, 340; his difficulties and hesitations, 344, 345; orders Nesselrode, July 9, 1813, to acquiesce in British refusal of mediation, 345, 346, 349; orders Roumanzoff, July 20, to renew offer of mediation, 348, 353; acquiesces, August 20, in British refusal of mediation, 350; orders Roumanzoff, September 20, to renew offer of mediation, 352; his motives, 353, 354; takes no notice of American commissioners, 351, 352, 354, 355; Andrew Jackson's report of, viii. 320; visits London, ix. 8; his conduct at Vienna, 38.

Alexandria, town of, capitulates to British fleet, viii. 157, 158.

Alfred, Maine, the town of, protests against the embargo, iv. 415.

Algiers, hostilities against, in 1815, ix. 87. 105.

Allen, John, colonel of Kentucky Rifles, vii. 88, 89; killed at the River Raisin, 96.

Allen, W. H., third lieutenant of the "Chesapeake," iv. 19; commander in U. S. navy, vii. 303; commands "Argus," 304; his action with the "Pelican," 305; killed. 306.

Alien and sedition laws, i. 140, 206, 259. (See Acts of Congress.)

Allston, Joseph, Burr's son-in-law, iii. 220. 240; guarantees Blennerhassett from loss, 260; with Burr in Kentucky, 260, 268; to go with recruits from Charleston, 265, 266; his part in Burr's trial, 463 et seq.

Allston, Mrs. (Theodosia Burr), accompanies Burr on his expedition, iii. 255; at Blennerhassett's island, 257; to be Queen of Mexico, 259;

GENERAL INDEX.

infatuation of Luther Martin for, 444.
Allston, Washington, i. 149, 238; ix. 208; his art, 213-217.
Alquier, French minister at Madrid, i. 363, 368.
Alsop, Richard, i. 102.
Alston, Willis, member of Congress from North Carolina, iii. 354; on war with England, iv. 376.
Amelia Island, v. 165; vii. 206, 208, 210.
Amendment to the Constitution, the twelfth, ii. 132.
Amendments of the Constitution, proposed by the Hartford Convention, viii. 297, 298.
"American Citizen," the, i. 331.
Ames, Fisher, i. 82, 83; iv. 348; his opinion of democracy, i. 84; in conversation, 86; speech of, on the British treaty, 88, 93: his language toward opponents, 119; ii. 164.
Amherst, town-meeting address voted, January, 1814, viii. 5.
Amherst, Jeffery, British major-general, his expedition against Montreal in 1760, vii. 178.
Amiens, peace of, i. 370; ii. 59, 290, 326, 347, 385. (See Treaties.)
Amusements in 1800, in New England, i. 50; in Virginia, 51.
"Anaconda," privateer, captured, vii. 277, 329.
Anderson, Joseph, senator from Tennessee, ii. 157, his remark on the two-million bill, iii. 139; defeats mission to Russia, v. 12; criticises Giles, vi. 150; chairman of committee on declaration of war, 228; chairman of committee on Gallatin's mission, vii. 59, 60; member of committee on Swedish mission, 62; reports bill for seizing Florida, 208; votes against Giles's militia bill, viii. 273; appointed first comptroller, ix. 107.

Anderson, Patton, iii. 287.
Andover, foundation of theological school at, ix. 176, 177.
"Annual Register," on the battle of Plattsburg, viii. 112; on privateers in 1814, 197.
"Anthology and Boston Review," ix. 201-203, 207.
Arbuthnot, James, captain of British sloop-of-war "Avon," viii. 188; his report of action with the "Wasp," 189, 190.
"Argus," sloop-of-war, vi. 363, 364, 378, 381; vii. 303; carries W. H. Crawford to France, 304; captured by the "Pelican," 305-308; number of her prizes, 312, 333, 334.
"Aristides." Pamphlet by W. P. Van Ness, ii. 73, 172; iii. 209.
Armistead, George, major of Artillery Corps, commands Fort McHenry at Baltimore, viii. 166.
Armistead, Walker Keith, captain of U. S. engineers, fortifies Norfolk, vii. 271; ix. 235.
Armistice, between Dearborn and Prevost, vi. 322, 323, 324, 404; known to Brock, 330; disavowed by Madison, 340, 404; ix. 33; an advantage to Dearborn, vi. 343; proposed by Monroe, 403; proposed by Admiral Warren, 416.
Armstrong, John, senator from New York, i. 108, 113, 230, 234, 281; ii. 157; succeeds Livingston as minister at Paris, 291, 308; notifies Monroe of Napoleon's decision on Spanish claims and boundaries, iii. 31, 32; recommends a course toward Texas and Florida, 39; to be employed in the Florida negotiation, 78; receives Talleyrand's conditions for an arrangement with Spain, 104; attacked in the Senate, 153; opposition to his appointment with Bowdoin to conduct the Florida negotiation,

GENERAL INDEX. 251

153, 172; watching Talleyrand in Paris, 370; offers to execute Talleyrand's plan, 376; approaches Napoleon through Duroc, 386; asks Decrès for an explanation of the Berlin Decree, 390; refused passports for Napoleon's headquarters, iv. 105; protests against the "Horizon" judgment, 110; reports Napoleon's order relating to the Berlin Decree, 112; well informed with regard to Napoleon's projects, 113; remonstrates against the Milan Decree, 292; receives from Champagny an offer of the Floridas as the price of an alliance with France, 294; replies to Champagny, 294; refuses to present the case of the burned vessels to the French government, 313; his discontent, v. 28; his relations with Roumanzoff, 29; his complaints in 1809, 39; communicates Non-intercourse Act of March 1, 1809, 135, 235; his comments on the right of search, 145; his interview with King Louis of Holland, 147, 148; his despatch on Fouché and Montalivet, 224; on Napoleon's motives, 225; his minute for a treaty. 228; his recall asked by Napoleon, 228, 229, 252; his remonstrance against the doctrine of retaliation, 233, 234; his report of Jan. 10, 1810, 238; inquires condition of revoking decrees, 251; communicates Non-intercourse Act of May 1, 1810, 252; his reception of Cadore's letter of Aug. 5, 1810, 259, 260; returns to America, 260, 261, 381; declares Napoleon's conditions to be not precedent, 261; silent about indemnity, 260, 296; Virginian jealousy of, 370; on Napoleon's designs on the Baltic, 417; becomes brigadier-general, vi. 427; his attitude toward Monroe and Madison, 426, 427; nominated Secretary of War, 428; his character, 428; a source of discord, vii. 34; Dallas's opinion of, 35; nominates Monroe as major-general, 36; intends to command in chief, 37, 38; alienates Gallatin, 39–41; comments on military diplomacy, 100; changes the plan of campaign in the northwest, 102, 103, 115; comments on Harrison and Proctor, 114; comments on strategy, 144; his plan for attacking Kingston, in April, 1813, 148-150; his plan changed by Dearborn and Chauncey, 153; issues order dividing the Union into military districts, 156; removes Dearborn from command, 171; orders Wilkinson to Sackett's Harbor, 172, 173, 215; orders Hampton to Plattsburg, 174; orders Wilkinson to attack Kingston, 175, 176; goes to Sackett's Harbor, 179; his difficulties with Wilkinson, 180-182; orders Hampton to prepare winter quarters, 183; returns to Washington, 185, 186, 198; his treatment of Hampton, 199, 200; his orders for the defence of Fort George, 201, 202; his responsibility for the loss of Fort Niagara, 203; dismisses Andrew Jackson's corps, 209, 210; orders withdrawal from Amelia Island, 210; orders Wilkinson to seize Mobile, 213, 214; his instructions on capitulation of the Creeks, 259; orders the confinement of hostages for naturalized soldiers, 361, disliked by Virginians, 403, 404; disliked by Madison, 405, 406; feared, 406; introduces new energy into the army, 407–409; his irregular conduct in the appointment of Andrew Jackson, 410, 411; his removal urged by Monroe, 411–414; his share in the court-martial of William Hull, 414, 415; his treatment of Hampton, 416; Wilkinson's remarks on, viii. 25; orders Brown to attack Kingston, 27; his letter to Brown on mistakes, 28; his plan of a campaign at Niagara, 30-33; orders Brown to cross the Niagara River, 33; orders Izard to fortify Rouse's Point, 97; orders Izard to move his army to Sackett's Harbor, 98-101; his severity toward Izard, 114; his neglect of the defences of Washington, 120; his excuses, 121; his attitude toward the defence of Washington, 122; after August 20 alive to the situation, 132; joins Winder on the morning of August 24, 137; on Bladensburg battle-field, 149; his conduct during the British advance, 155; retires to Frederick, 156, 157; militia refuse to serve under, 159; returns to Washington, 160; goes to Baltimore and resigns, 161; cause of his retirement, 162; his provision for the defence of New Orleans, 316, 317; his criticism on Jackson's Pensacola campaign, 330; his criticism on Jackson's first measures at New Orleans, 334; his criticism on Jackson's loss of Fort Bowyer, 384.

Army, Jefferson's chaste reformation of, i. 238; peace establishment in 1801 three thousand men, organized in one regiment of artillery and two of infantry, 242, 261, 272, 301; Jefferson's principle regarding the, iii. 14, 15; its condition in 1806, 334; popular antipathy to, 349, 350-354; increase of, to ten thousand men, in 1808, iv. 195, 198; debate on increase of, 212-218; establishment of 1808, one regiment of artillery, one regiment of light artillery, one regiment of dragoons, one regiment of riflemen, and seven regiments of infantry, 222-224; enlistments stopped in June, 1809, v. 85; its condition in 1809, 164, 169-171, 289; encampment of, at Terre aux Bœufs, 171-175; debate on reduction of, in 1810, 199-207; raised to thirty-five thousand men by Act of Jan. 11. 1812, vi. 147, 148, 151, 153; useless, 165; condition of, 289, 292; recruiting for, in May, 1812, 294; war establishment in 1812, corps of engineers, two regiments of light dragoons, one regiment of light artillery, three regiments of artillerists, one regiment of riflemen, and twenty-five regiments of infantry, — by law thirty-five thousand men, 295; enlistments in, 337, 390, 391, 401; difficulty of filling ranks of, 394; acts of Congress for filling ranks of, 435, 436; war establishment of 1813, corps of engineers, two regiments of light dragoons, one regiment of light artillery, three regiments of artillery one regiment of riflemen, and forty-four regiments of infantry, rangers, and sea-fencibles, — by law fifty-eight thousand men, 449; vii. 148, 381; Monroe's estimate of number of troops required in 1813, vii. 148; actual force, in February, 1813, nineteen thousand men, 148, 149, 380; mode of stating force of, in rank-and-file, 150; aggregate strength of, in February, June, and December, 1813, and January, 1814, 380, 381; Troup's bill for filling ranks of, 381, 382; bounty and pay of, 382; appropriations for, in 1814, 384; organization of, in 1814, 384; condition of, in 1814, viii. 17; aggregate strength of, June and December, 1813, January, July, and September, 1814, 216; weakness of, in the field, 217; bounties for, paid in Massachusetts

GENERAL INDEX. 253

and Virginia, 235; Monroe recommends raising to one hundred thousand men by draft, 264, 265; failure in recruiting service for, 266; Congress unwilling to adopt efficacious measures for, 266, 267; Giles's bill for filling, 268, 273, 280; "a mere handful of men," 279; aggregate strength of, December, 1814, and Feb. 16, 1815, 281; allotment of, to military districts, 316, 317; peace establishment discussed, ix. 83-86; peace establishment fixed at ten thousand men, 86, reduction of, 87-88. (See Artillery, Infantry, Engineers.)

Artillery, one regiment of, on the army establishment of 1801, i. 301; one regiment of light, added in 1808, iv. 223; two regiments of, added in 1812, vi. 295, 345, 347; corps of, vii. 384; Hindman's battalion of, viii. 37; Towson's company at Chippawa, 43, 44; Hindman's battalion at Lundy's Lane, 50-53, 56-59; and at Fort Erie, 71, 72, 75, 76, 83; in military district No. 7, viii. 316; in the night battle at New Orleans, 344, 345, 348; in Jackson's lines, 355, 358, 359, 361; in the battle of Jan. 1, 1815, 361-366; in the battle of Jan. 8, 374, 375. (See Gunnery.)

Ash Island in the Richelieu River, a fortified British post, viii. 97.

Ashe, an English traveller, i. 43, 52, 53, 54.

Ashmun, Eli Porter, senator from Massachusetts, votes against internal improvements, ix. 151.

"Asia," American ship, burned by French squadron, vi. 193, 198.

Aspinwall, Thomas, lieutenant-colonel of the Ninth Infantry, viii. 35; commands Scott's brigade, 71; wounded in the sortie from Fort Erie, 88.

Astor, John Jacob, i. 28; vi. 301; shares loan of 1813, vii. 44, 45; director of United States Bank, ix. 131.

"Atlas," privateer, captured, vii. 277.

Attorney General. (See Levi Lincoln, Robert Smith, John Breckinridge, Cæsar A. Rodney, William Pinkney, Richard Rush.)

Auckland, Lord, iii. 407.

"Aurora" newspaper, i. 118, 121; iii. 119.

Austerlitz, battle of, iii. 163, 370.

Austria, v. 27, 134; fights battles of Essling and Wagram, 106; interferes in Russian war, vii. 340; declares war on Napoleon, 350.

"Avon," British 18-gun sloop-of-war, sunk by the "Wasp," viii. 188-192.

"Avon," privateer, viii. 194.

BACON, EZEKIEL, member of Congress from Massachusetts, determined to overthrow the embargo, iv. 432, 436, 441, 450, 455, 463; chairman of ways and means committee, vi. 156; votes against frigates, 164; moves war taxes, 165, 166.

Baen, William C., captain of Fourth U. S. Infantry, killed at Tippecanoe, vi. 104.

Bailen, capitulation at, iv. 315, 341.

Bailey, Dixon, Creek half-breed, attacks Peter McQueen at Burnt Corn, vii. 228, 229; surprised and killed at Fort Mims, 229-231.

Bailey, Theodorus, i. 231, 266, 296.

Bainbridge, William, captain in U. S. navy, ii. 137, 426; vi. 384; takes command of the "Constitution," 384; captures "Java," 385, 386; blockades the "Bonne Citoyenne," vii. 288.

254 GENERAL INDEX.

Baldwin, Abraham, senator from Georgia, i. 305; iii. 126.
Ball, James V., lieutenant-colonel of Second U. S. Light Dragoons, vii. 128.
Ballou, Hosea, his Universalism, ix. 183, 184.
Ballston Spa, i. 92.
Baltimore in 1800, i. 29, 131; population in 1810, v. 289; threatened by Cockburn, vii. 269; chief object of British attack, viii. 121, 127; defences of, 166, 167; British attack on, 168-172; banks suspend payment, 213; saved by engineers and sailors, 219; inhabitants to feel Ross's visit, 315; effect of repulse at Ghent, 35, 36; depreciation of currency, ix. 62; shares loan of 1815, 102; growth of, 156; steamboat at, 172.
Baltimore riot, July 27, 1812, vi. 406-409.
Bancroft, George, ix. 206.
Bangor, in Maine, plundered by British expedition, viii. 96.
Bank of England, drain of specie from, 1817-1819, ix. 127.
Bank of the United States, Jefferson's hostility to, ii. 130, 131; Gallatin's dependence on, v. 167; bill introduced for rechartering, 207, 208; hostile influence of State Banks, 327, 330, 332, 335, 336; pretexts for opposition to charter of, 328, 329; necessity for, 329; Crawford's bill for rechartering, 332; debate on, 332-336; defeat of, 337; a fatal loss to the Treasury, vii. 386; viii. 214; plan for, with fifty millions' capital, recommended by Dallas in October, 1814, 249, 250; Dallas's plan of, approved by House, October 24, 250; Calhoun's plan of, approved by House, 251; Senate bill, 257; defeated in the House, 257-258; Webster's plan adopted by Congress, 259, 260; vetoed, 260; new bill introduced, passes the Senate Feb. 11, 1815, ix. 56, 57, 82; postponed by the House, 82; recommended by Dallas in his annual report of 1815, 106; Dallas's scheme of 1816, 111; bill for incorporating, 116, 117; bill passes and becomes law, 118; capital subscribed, 131; begins operations, January, 1817, 131.
Banks, State, in Boston in 1800, i. 22; in New York, 25; in the South, 31; hostility to, in 1800, 65; popularity of, in 1812, vi. 208, 209; their capital in 1813, vii. 386; their circulation, 386, 388; of New England financial agents of the enemy, 387; capital of New England, 387; specie in New England, 388; pressure of New England on other, 389; suspend specie payments in September, 1814, except in New England, viii. 213, 214; worthlessness of the suspended notes of, 215, 244-246; suspended notes taken in payment of taxes, 256, 257; of Massachusetts refuse loans to State government, 302, 303; currency of, affected by the peace, ix. 61, 62, 98-103; of Massachusetts drained of specie after the peace, 97; discount on notes of, in the autumn of 1815, 98; special treasury accounts in notes of, 98, 99; resist return to specie payments, 128-130; resume specie payments, Feb. 20, 1817, 131, 132; increase of, in Massachusetts, 157, 158; increase of, in Virginia, 162; increase of, in New York and Pennsylvania, 166.
Bankruptcy, of the national government, in 1814, viii. 213-215; formally announced, Nov. 9, 1814, 244, 245, 252, 254, 260-262.
Baptists in New England, i. 89.

Baptists, ix. 133.
Barataria, smuggling station at, viii. 321; "hellish banditti" of, 325; work guns at New Orleans, 359.
Barbary Powers, war with the, i. 244 et seq.; ii. 425 et seq.
Barbour, James, senator from Virginia, ix 107, 108.
Barbour, Philip P., member of the Fourteenth Congress, from Virginia. ix. 107; on the effect of the Compensation Act, 137; opposes internal improvements, 150.
Barclay, Captain Robert Heriot, of the Royal Navy, sent to command the British squadron on Lake Erie, vii. 119; his fleet, 120; his report of the battle, 124; his losses, 127.
Barclay, John, iii. 231.
Baring, Alexander, ii. 358; on neutral frauds, iii. 52; iv. 69; his reply to "War in Disguise," 317; on British policy, vi. 276; on impressment, vii. 24; correspondence with Gallatin in July, 1813, 343, 349; assists Gallatin to negotiate, 355.
Baring, Sir Francis, at the dinner to the Spanish patriots, iv. 331.
Barker, Jacob, takes five millions of the loan in 1814, viii. 17, 18; fails to make his payments, 213, 241.
Barlow, Joel, i. 69, 99; his "Columbiad," 103 et seq., 106, 182; on Robert Smith's appointment, v. 10; on Smith's opposition to Macon's bill, 187; his defence of the President, 299, 301, 378; appointed minister to France, 359; his instructions on revocation of French Decrees, 427; his departure delayed by Monroe, vi. 50; ready to start, 55; order for his departure countermanded, 56; order finally given, 61; his instructions, 66; his want of success, 217; arrives in Paris, Sept. 19, 1811, 245; his negotiation with Bassano, 248-263; his journey to Wilna, 263, 264; his death, 265.
Barney, Joshua, commands privateer "Rossie," vii. 316; his cruise, 335; commands gunboats in Chesapeake Bay, viii. 127; burns his gunboats, 129, 130; joins Winder's army, 134; ordered to defend the navy-yard bridge, 137; remonstrates and marches to Bladensburg, 139; his battle and capture, 142, 143.
Barron, Captain James, appointed Commodore of the Mediterranean squadron in 1807, iv. 5; replies to Captain Humphrey's note, 13; orders his flag to be struck, 19; blamed by his brother officers, 20; trial of, 21; result of the trial, 22.
Barron, Commodore Samuel, at Tripoli, ii. 428; yields the command to Rodgers, 429.
"Barrosa," 42-gun British frigate, vii. 270.
Bartram, William, i. 124.
Bassano, Duc de. (See Maret.)
Bassett, Burwell, member of Congress from Virginia, v. 206.
Bastrop grant, the, Burr's proposal to Blennerhassett to buy, iii. 256; bought by Burr, 260, 274.
Bath, town-meeting in December, 1808, iv. 409.
Bathurst, Lord, President of the Board of Trade, disapproves of Perceval's general order, iv. 93 et seq., 100, 325; on the Orders in Council, vi. 275, on the right of impressment, vii. 17; sends ten thousand men to Canada, viii. 31; his instructions to Cochrane and Ross regarding an expedition to the Chesapeake, 124, 125; his instructions to Ross regarding an expedition to the Gulf of Mexico, 311-314; approves Ross's Washington cam-

paign, 314; advises severity to Baltimore, 315; sends Pakenham to succeed Ross, 315; his under-secretary commissioner at Ghent, ix. 13; keeps the Ghent negotiation alive, 23; takes charge of the negotiation, 25; his instructions of Sept. 1, 1814, 26, 27; yields the Indian *sine qua non*, 31, 32; claims the basis of *uti possidetis*, 34, 37; hastens the peace, 44; concedes the fisheries, 47, 52.

Baton Rouge, seizure of, v. 305-307; Jackson orders troops to, viii. 332, 333, 336.

Bayard, James A., member of Congress from Delaware, i. 269, 271; his reply to Giles, 291 *et seq.*; beaten by Cæsar A. Rodney, retires to the Senate, ii. 76; re-elected to the House, 201; moves the form of question in the Chase impeachment, 237, 241; senator from Delaware, iii. 339, 461; iv. 146; vi. 229; appointed peace commissioner to Russia, vii. 42; sails for St. Petersburg, 46; nominated and confirmed, 59, 61; arrives at St. Petersburg, 339, 340; obliged to wait at St. Petersburg, 349; goes to London with Gallatin, 355, 363; ix. 1; nominated and confirmed as joint commissioner to Ghent, vii. 371; at Ghent, ix. 14, 15; his remarks to Goulburn, 22; on the Florida policy, 29; Adams's opinion of, 51; secures the success of the negotiation, 52; appointed minister to Russia, 89; his death, 89.

Bayonne Decree. (See Decrees.)

Baynes, Edward, colonel of Glengarry Light Infantry, British adjutant-general, negotiates armistice with Dearborn, vi. 323; commands expedition against Sackett's Harbor, vii. 164, 165; his report, 167

Bayou Bienvenu, selected as line of British advance to New Orleans, viii. 337-339.

Beall, William D., colonel of Maryland militia at Bladensburg, viii. 143, 153.

Beasley, Daniel, commands at Fort Mims, vii. 229; surprised and killed, 230.

Beaujour, Felix de, quoted, i. 46, 165.

Beckwith, Sir Sydney, British major-general, repulsed at Craney Island, vii. 272, 274; captures Hampton, 276.

Beecher, Lyman, ix. 206.

Belden, Lieutenant, iv. 32.

Belknap, Jeremy, i. 93.

Bellechasse, M., of New Orleans, iii. 300, 305 *et seq.*

"Belvidera," British frigate, blockading New York, vi. 364, 365; escapes from Rodgers' squadron, 366; chases "Constitution," 368, 370.

Benedict on the Patuxent, Ross's army lands at, viii. 123, 128; Monroe scouts to, 131.

Bentham, George, commander of British sloop-of-war "Carnation," his part in destroying the "General Armstrong," viii. 202-207.

Benton, Thomas Hart, his opinion of the Louisiana legislation, ii. 119; his brawl with Andrew Jackson, vii. 235.

Berkeley, Admiral George Cranfield, issues orders to search the "Chesapeake" for deserters, iv. 3; approves the attack on the "Chesapeake," 25; recalled and his attack on the "Chesapeake" disavowed, 51.

Berlin Decree of Nov. 21, 1806, iii. 389, 412, 416, 427; enforced in August, 1807, iv. 82, 109; Napoleon's defence of, 221, 295; his persistence in, 295. (See Decrees.)

Bermuda, governor of, licenses im-

GENERAL INDEX. 257

portation from eastern States, vii. 31.

Bernadotte, Jean Baptiste, appointed minister at Washington, ii. 10; Talleyrand's instructions to, 11. (See Sweden.)

Berthier, Louis Alexandre, Napoleon's agent for the retrocession of Louisiana, i. 366.

Beurnonville, Pierre de Ruel, French ambassador at Madrid, ii. 59, 277.

Beverly, town-meeting in January, 1809, iv. 413.

Bibb, William A., member of Congress from Georgia, on the annexation of West Florida to Louisiana, v. 324.

Biddle, James, commander in U. S. navy, commands the "Hornet," vii. 293; ix. 63; captures "Penguin," 71, 72; escapes "Cornwallis," 72, 73.

Biddle, Thomas, captain of artillery in Hindman's battalion, viii. 37; at Lundy's Lane, 53, 56; at Fort Erie, 71.

Bidwell, Barnabas, member of Congress from Massachusetts, iii. 127; supports Jefferson's Spanish message in committee, 132, 137; urged by Jefferson to take the leadership of the Democrats in Congress, 207; in the slave-trade debate, iii. 360, 363; a defaulter, v. 359.

Bigelow, Jacob, professor of medicine at Harvard College, ix. 206.

Bigelow, Timothy, speaker of Massachusetts legislature, iv. 456.

Bingham, A. B., captain of the British corvette "Little Belt," his account of his action with the "President," vi. 30, 31, 33-36.

Birmingham, remonstrates against Orders in Council, vi. 271; treaty of Ghent received at, ix. 54, 55.

Bishop, Abraham, collector of New Haven, i. 226.

VOL. IX. — 17

Bissell, Daniel, captain of the First Infantry, iii. 284, 290: welcomes Burr at Fort Massac, 291; receives a letter from Andrew Jackson warning him to stop expedition, 291; colonel of Fifth U. S. Infantry, promoted to brigadier, vii. 409; his skirmish with Drummond's forces in October, 1814, viii. 116.

Bladensburg, designated as the point of concentration for the defence of Washington, viii. 123, 135, 139, 140; citizens erect works at, 132; the necessary point of British attack, 134, 136, 138; battle-field of, 139, 140; battle of, 141-144; Ross retreats through, 148; relative losses at, ix. 234.

Blakeley, Johnston, commander in U. S. navy, commands the "Wasp" in 1814, viii. 184, 237; cruises in the British Channel, 185; captures British sloop-of-war "Reindeer," 186, 187, 196; sinks the "Avon," 188-192; lost at sea, 193.

"Blakeley," privateer, viii. 194.

Bleecker, Harmanus, member of Congress from New York, vi. 211.

Blennerhassett, Harman, iii. 220, 233; duped by Burr, 247, 256 *et seq.*; his indiscreet talk, 259, 275, 281; returns to his home, 276; driven from his island, 286; rejoins Burr, 291; indicted, 457; keeps a record of Burr's trial, 462 *et seq.*; Allston tries to conciliate, 464; Duane visits, 464.

Blennerhassett, Mrs., iii. 220; sends a warning letter to Burr, 275.

Blockade, law of, ii. 382, 385; preferred by Bathurst to municipal regulations, iv. 95; Napoleon's definition of, v. 149, 227, 250; Pinkney's definition of, 287; vi. 10; Napoleon abandons for municipal regulations, v. 402; alleged by Madison as the third *casus belli*,

vi. 222; offered by American Ghent commissioners for discussion, ix. 12, 18; omitted from treaty, 33, 52.

Blockades, British, of Martinique and Guadeloupe, in 1803, ii. 381.

—— (Fox's) of the French and German coasts, May 16, 1806, iii 398 Pinkney inquires whether still in force, v. 277-279; Wellesley's conduct regarding, 279; express withdrawal of, required by Madison, 318, 383; withdrawal of, demanded by Pinkney. vi. 4, 5, 17 British reply to demand of withdrawal of. 6, 9, 15, 23; becomes the only apparent *casus belli*, 221.

—— of Venice, July 27, 1806, v. 279.

—— of all ports and places under the government of France, April 26. 1809, v. 63, 64, 103, 277; repeal of, demanded by Pinkney, vi. 3, 8; offered by Wellesley on condition that the French decrees should be effectually withdrawn, 9; repeal refused by Wellesley, 14; repeal again asked by Pinkney and refused by Wellesley, 17, 18. (See Order in Council of April 26, 1809.)

—— of the ports and harbors of Chesapeake Bay and Delaware River, Dec 26, 1812, vii. 30, 33; viii. 234; raised, ix. 62.

—— of New York, Charleston, Port Royal, Savannah, and the River Mississippi, May 26, 1813, vii. 262; effects of, 263-265, 334; viii. 214, raised, ix. 62.

—— of New London and Long Island Sound, vii. 262, 278; raised. ix 62

—— of the coast of New England, April 25, 1814, viii. 3, ix. 36; raised, 62.

Blockades, French, of Great Britain, Nov. 21, 1806. (See Decree of Berlin.)

Blockades, *quasi*, of New York, in 1803-4, ii. 396; in 1805, iii. 91-93; in 1807, iv. 143, 144; in 1811, vi. 25, 118, 222.

Blockades of Great Britain by American cruisers in 1813-1814, vii. 332, 333 in 1814, viii. 195-201.

Bloomfield, Joseph, brigadier-general, vi 291; at Plattsburg, 359, 360.

Blount, Willie, governor of Tennessee, orders out two thousand militia for service in Florida, vii. 206; advises Jackson to withdraw from the Creek country, 240; orders out four thousand militia, 251; required to provide for defence of New Orleans, viii 320, 326, 327.

Blue. Uriah, major of Thirty-ninth U. S Infantry, commands expedition to the Appalachicola, viii. 330, 333.

Blyth, Samuel, commander of British sloop-of-war ' Boxer," his death and burial, vii. 282, 283.

Boerstler C. G., colonel of Fourteenth U. S. Infantry, vii. 162; his surrender at Beaver Dam, 163.

Bollman, Eric, to be sent to London by Burr, iii. 248, 251; starts for New Orleans, 255; arrives, 296, 306; reports to Burr, 309; sees Wilkinson, 318; arrested, 319, 338; discharged from custody, 340.

Bonaparte. Jerome, his marriage to Miss Patterson and his reception by the President, ii. 377 *et seq.*

Bonaparte, Joseph, negotiates treaty of Morfontaine, i. 360, 362; scene of. with Napoleon, ii. 35 *et seq.*; crowned King of Spain, iv. 300; driven from Madrid, 315: deserted by Napoleon, v. 27, 28; driven from Spain, vii. 356.

Bonaparte, Lucien, appointed ambas-

GENERAL INDEX. 259

sador at Madrid, i. 371, 373; opposes the cession of Louisiana, ii. 34; scene of, with Napoleon, 35 *et seq.*; offered the crown of Spain, iv. 113; his story of the offer, 124.

Bonaparte. (See Napoleon.)

Bonds, U. S., six per cent., their market value, Feb. 1, 1815, viii. 214, 261, 267; on Feb. 13, 1815, ix. 62; in March, 1815, 160; in 1816, 127, 128.

"Bonne Citoyenne," British sloop-of-war, vi. 384; blockaded at San Salvador, vii. 288.

Bordeaux, Wellington advances on, vii. 373.

Boré, M., of New Orleans, iii. 300

Borodino, battle of, vii. 27.

Boston, population and appearance of, in 1800, i. 20; business, 21; an intellectual centre in 1800, 75; sentiment of, 87; social customs of, in 1800, 91; a summer watering-place, 92; reception of F. J. Jackson in, v. 214, 216; population in 1810, 289; takes one million of loan of 1814, viii. 17, 18, blockaded, ix. 36; welcomes peace, 59; harshly treated by Dallas, 98-100; treasury payments resumed at, 128; growth of, 156; immigrants to, 161; its society in 1817, 182; takes the lead of American literature, 201, 205-207.

Boston town-meeting in January, 1809, iv. 411; town-meeting on Baltimore riot, vi. 409.

Botts, Benjamin, Burr's counsel, iii. 444.

Bowditch, Nathaniel, i. 93.

Bowdoin, James, appointed minister to Madrid, iii. 57; Jefferson's letter announcing appointment, 57; suggestions of plans for his negotiations, 59-61, 71; reveals Talleyrand's plan for a settlement with Spain, 378; letter to, 436.

Bowyer, Fort. (See Fort Bowyer.)

"Boxer," British sloop-of-war, captured by "Enterprise," vii. 281-283.

Boyd, Adam, member of Congress from New Jersey, v. 206.

Boyd, John Parke, colonel of Fourth U. S Infantry, vi. 92, 93; arrives at Vincennes, 94; brigadier-general, vii. 156; Morgan Lewis's opinion of, 162; ordered to cease offensive operations, 179; commands brigade in Wilkinson's expedition, 184; favors moving on Montreal, 185; covers the rear. 187; Brown's and Scott's opinion of, 188; his defeat at Chrysler's Field, 190, 191.

Boyle, John, a manager of Chase's impeachment, ii. 228.

Boyle, Thomas, commands Baltimore privateer "Comet," vii. 316; commands "Chasseur," and notifies a blockade of the British coast, viii. 196, 197.

Brackenridge, H. H., author of "Modern Chivalry," i. 124; ii. 195.

Bradley, Captain, of the "Cambrian," ii. 393, 396; recall and promotion, iii. 48.

Bradley, Stephen R., senator from Vermont, ii. 157, 158, 218, 235, 238, 259; iii. 126, 139; offers a resolution opposing the appointment of a minister to Russia, iv. 466; votes against occupying East Florida, vi. 243.

Brady, Hugh, colonel of Twenty-second Infantry. viii. 35; at Lundy's Lane, 50; wounded, 52.

Brazil, glutted with British goods in 1808, v. 46.

Breckinridge, John, senator from Kentucky, i. 269; moves the repeal of the Judiciary Act, 278, 280; Jefferson's letter to, on the Louisiana purchase, ii. 85; on the

GENERAL INDEX.

admission of Louisiana to the Union 94, 108; his bill for the territorial government of Louisiana, 120; appointed attorney general, iii. 11, 127; his death, 444.

Brenton, E. B., staff officer of Sir George Prevost, his account of the attack on Sackett's Harbor, vii. 167, 168.

Brisbane, major-general in British army, commanding a brigade at Plattsburg, viii. 101.

Bristol, memorial of merchants in September. 1814. viii. 198, 200.

Brock, Isaac. governor of Upper Canada, his career. vi 316; his military precautions, 317 his military force, 317; his civil difficulties, 318, 319; orders expedition to Mackinaw, 320; his proclamation, 320; dismisses his legislature, 320; passes Long Point, 321, 322; arrives at Malden, 329; decides to cross the Detroit River, 330; his march on Detroit, 332; returns to Niagara, 341; his military wishes, 342; distressed by loss of vessels, 347; his force at Niagara, 348; surprised on Queenston Heights, 349; his death, 350; ix. 42.

Broke, P. B. V., captain of British frigate "Shannon," commands squadron, vi. 368, 369 ; chases "Constitution," 370, 371; invites battle with Rodgers, vii. 285 ; challenges "Chesapeake," 286; his qualities, 292; his battle with the "Chesapeake," 293-302; captures "Nautilus," 313; a life-long invalid, ix. 42; his gunnery. 230.

Brooke, Arthur, colonel of the British Forty-fourth Infantry, at the advance on Baltimore, viii. 169 ; succeeds Ross in command, 170; studies the lines of Baltimore, 171; decides to retreat, 172.

Brooke, G. M., major in Twenty-third Infantry, viii. 37.

Brooks, John, elected governor of Massachusetts, in 1816, ix. 133.

Brookville, in Maryland, viii. 156, 157.

Brougham, Henry, his speculations on the cause of English prejudice against America, iv. 73; his hostility to Perceval's orders, 318; at the bar of the House opposing the Orders in Council, 321; organizes agitation against Orders in Council, vi. 271, 280, 283; his speech of March 3, 1812, 276; obliges ministers to grant a committee of inquiry, 283-285; moves repeal, 285.

Brown, Charles Brockden, i. 123.

Brown, Jacob, brigadier-general of N. Y. militia, vii. 164, 408; takes command at Sackett's Harbor, 165 ; his remarks on the battle at Sackett's Harbor, 165, 166, 169 ; appointed brigadier-general in the U. S. army, 170; commands a brigade in Wilkinson's expedition, 177, 184; favors moving on Montreal, 185 ; landed on north bank of the St. Lawrence, 187; clears the bank, 188, 191; his opinion of Boyd. 188; appointed major-general, 408; his fitness described by Wilkinson and Scott, 408, 409; ordered to Sackett's Harbor in February, 1814, viii. 24; carries his army to Niagara, 27; returns to Sackett's Harbor, 28; at Buffalo in June, ordered to capture Fort Erie, 33 ; his forces, 34-38; crosses the Niagara River, 39; fights the battle of Chippawa, 40-42 ; his letter to Commodore Chauncey, 45-46; falls back from Queenston to Chippawa, 47, 48 ; orders Scott to march toward Queenston, 50; his order to Miller at Lundy's Lane, 54; his position at Lundy's

Lane, 57; wounded, 58; orders the army to retire, 59; orders Ripley to return to Lundy's Lane, 64; taken to Buffalo, 66; summons Gaines to Fort Erie. 67; his quarrels with Chauncey and Ripley, 81; his qualities, 82, 218; resumes command, 82, 83; his sortie from Fort Erie. 84-89; asks Izard's aid, 113; meets Izard at Batavia, 114; distrusts Izard, 115; favors attack on Chippawa in October, 1814, 115; sent to Sackett's Harbor, 116; Izard's opinion of, 117; his letter of August 19, 1814, complaining of being left to struggle alone, 218; head of army board for reducing the army, ix. 88; commands northern military district, 88.

Brown, James, secretary of the Louisiana Territory, ii. 220; iii. 219, 280.

Bruff, Major of Artillery, sounded by General Wilkinson, iii. 222, 241; his charge against Wilkinson, 454.

Bruin, Judge, iii. 325.

Bryant, William Cullen, i. 110, 132; his poem "The Embargo," iv. 279; his poem "Thanatopsis," ix. 207, 208, 213, 216, 217, 238.

Buckminster, Joseph, i. 81, remonstrates with Hosea Ballou, ix. 183, 184.

Buckminster, Joseph Stevens, i. 90, 162; ix. 177; his Phi Beta Kappa oration, 199, 204; one of the Anthology Club, 202, 203.

Budd, George, second lieutenant of the "Chesapeake," vii. 293; stationed below, 295; leads boarders, 297.

Buffalo, burned by British, vii. 204.

Bullus, Dr., on the "Chesapeake," iv. 11, 13, 21.

Bülow, Heinrich Wilhelm, i. 41, 48.

Bunker, Elias, captain of the Albany packet "Experiment," i. 6.

Burling, Colonel, iii 313.

Burnt Corn Creek, Indians attacked at, vii. 229, 232.

Burr, Aaron, Vice-President, i. 65, 93, 109, 112: his character, 195, centre of intrigue, 229 *et seq.*, takes the chair of the Senate, 279; votes to recommit the Judiciary Bill, 280; his toast at the Federalist dinner, 282; attacked by the "American Citizen" and "Aurora," 283; in the Pickering impeachment, ii. 154; invoked by Pickering and Griswold, 171; his defence by "Aristides," 172; his interview with Jefferson. 175; nominated for governor of New York, 177; confers with Griswold, 183; defeated, 185; his hostility to Hamilton, 185; his duel with Hamilton, 187 *et seq.*; presides at the Chase impeachment, 227, 238, 368; communicates with Merry, 395; his plan of creating a western confederacy, 402; asks the aid of the British government, 403; Turreau's opinion of. 407; his plan, 408; gives the casting vote against Dr. Logan's amendment to the St. Domingo bill, iii. 88; jealous of Miranda, 189, 218; his conspiracy and connections, 219; on his way to New Orleans, in April, 1805, 220; his plans notorious in New Orleans, 224 *et seq.*; returns and visits Andrew Jackson and Wilkinson, 227; his expectations of aid from England disappointed, 229; his report to Merry, 231; received at the White House, 233; his advances to Yrujo and the Spanish government, 234; his plot to seize the heads of government and the public money, 239; his contempt for Jefferson, 244; his communication with Yrujo, 247;

GENERAL INDEX.

rebuffed by Fox, 250; his imposture. 251, his cipher despatch to Wilkinson, 253; starts for New Orleans with Mrs. Allston and De Pestre, 255; secures Blennerhassett's fortune, 256; arouses opposition in Kentucky, 268; orders the purchase of supplies, 274; denies intention to separate the Eastern from the Western States, 276; attacked in court by District-Attorney Daveiss, 277; a second time accused, 282; acquitted, 282; repeats his disavowal to Andrew Jackson, 287; escapes from Nashville, 289; received at Fort Massac, 291; his relations in New Orleans, 296; his visit to New Orleans in 1805, 302; denounced by Wilkinson, surrenders to Governor Meade, 325 *et seq*; deserts his friends, 327; arrested and sent to Richmond, Va., 327; brought to trial before Chief-Justice Marshall, 441; committed for misdemeanor only, 446; indicted, 459; his demeanor under trial, 464; acquitted, 469; his memoir to Napoleon, v. 239.

Burrows, William, lieutenant in U. S. Navy, captures the "Boxer," vii 281, 282; his death and burial, 282, 283.

Burwell, William A., member of Congress from Virginia, on reducing the army and navy in 1810, v. 202.

CABINET. (See James Madison, Robert Smith, James Monroe, William Jones, Secretaries of State; Albert Gallatin, G. W. Campbell, A. J. Dallas, W. H. Crawford, Secretaries of the Treasury; Henry Dearborn, William Eustis, James Monroe, John Armstrong, A. J. Dallas, Secretaries of War; Robert Smith, Paul Hamilton, William Jones, B. W. Crowninshield, Secretaries of the Navy; Levi Lincoln, John Breckinridge, Cæsar A. Rodney, William Pinkney Richard Rush, Attorneys General.,

Cabot, George, his opinion of democracy, i. 84, 86 *et seq.*: letter of, opposing Pickering's scheme. ii. 164; inclines to Burr, 182; opposed to neutral claims, iii 95. 144; iv. 29: letters from, given to Rose by Pickering, 235, 412; at the head of the Massachusetts delegation to the Hartford Convention, viii. 225, 227, 288; his conservative character, 291, 292; chosen president of the Hartford Convention, 292, 293; authorized to call another meeting, 295; defence of, 305; John Adams's remark about, 308.

Cadore, Duc de (see Champagny).

"Caledonia," 2-gun British brig, captured by Lieutenant Elliott, vi. 347; in Perry's squadron, vii. 116. 120, 122; in Perry's action, 124, 125.

Calhoun, John C., i 154; member of Congress from South Carolina, vi. 122; on Committee of Foreign Relations, 124, 128; his war-speech of Dec. 12, 1811, 143, 144; votes for frigates, 164; warns Quincy of the embargo, 201; on the conquest of Canada, 212; his war-report, 226; his bill declaring war, 228; his speech of June 24, 1812, against the restrictive system, 233; favors war-taxation, 235; opposes compromise of forfeitures under Non-importation Act, 442; favors high import duties, 444; his remark on inconsistency, vii. 374, 375; his plan for a national bank, viii. 250-253; votes against legal tender, 254; accepts Giles's militia bill, 274; not a good judge of treason, 286; in the Fourteenth Congress,

ix. 107; his view of extremes in government, 108, 109; chairman of committee on currency, 111; favors protection, 115; reports bill for a national bank, 116, 117; supports compensation bill, 121; his remark that the House of Representatives was not a favorite with the American people. 134, 137. his defence of the House, 145; his bill for internal improvements, 148, 149, 152, 169.

Callender, James T., his libels on Jefferson, i. 322 *et seq.*

Calvinism, popular reaction against, in New England, i. 82; rupture of church in 1815, ix. 175–187.

"Cambrian," British frigate, iii. 48.

Campbell, George W., member of Congress from Tennessee, ii. 123; a manager in impeachment of Judge Chase, 224, 228, 230; chairman of Ways and Means Committee, iv. 153; challenged by Gardenier, 203, 217; his argument for the embargo, 267; his report to Congress on measures of force, 370; defends his report, 380; his Resolution adopted, 383; opposes fitting out the navy, 426, 441; speech of, on the Non-intercourse Act, 448; his report reaches Canning, v. 49; not a member of the Eleventh Congress, 76; senator from Tennessee, his criticism of Giles, vi. 150, 151; appointed Secretary of the Treasury, vii. 371, 397; negotiates loan in May, 1814, viii. 17, 18; accedes to abandoning impressment as a *sine qua non*, 122; at Winder's headquarters, August 24, 137; goes to Frederick, 152; fails to negotiate loan of six millions in July, 1814, 213; his annual report of Sept. 23, 1814, 240; announces the impracticability of raising loans, 241, 242; makes no suggestion for supplying deficit, 242; resigns, 240; returns to the Senate, ix. 108.

Campbell, John, member of Congress from Maryland, iii. 356.

Campbell, John A., Justice of the Supreme Court, on the Louisiana precedent, ii. 127.

Campbell, Thomas, borrows from Freneau, i. 126; his Declaration of Sept. 9, 1809, ix. 184, 185, 239.

Canada, intended conquest of, vi. 136, 141, 142. 145, 146, 150, 212; invasion planned at Washington, 297; ordered by Eustis, 302; conquest attempted by Hull, 296; invaded by Hull. 302, evacuated, 315; difficulties of defending, 316–319; extent of Upper, 316; military force in 1812, 317, 338; Jefferson and Madison on campaign in, 337; invasion of, at Niagara, 344, 345; Van Rensselaer's attack on, 346-353; Smyth's attempt against, 354–358; Dearborn's march to, 360; British garrisons in, vii. 151, 194–196; reinforcements for, in 1814, viii. 91. 99-102. proper method of attacking, vii. 144–147; difficulties of defence, 145; viii. 91, 93; frontier to be rectified. 94–97; regular troops in, December, 1814, 118; demands of, at Ghent, ix. 7, 8; cession of, asked by Monroe, 11, 12; British reproach about, 29, 30.

Canals in 1800, i 8-10, 26, 29, 38, 94. proposed by Gallatin in 1808, iv. 364. (See Erie Canal.)

Canning, George, rise of, ii. 417; becomes Foreign Secretary, iv. 56; his character, 57, 73; v. 56; his opinion of democrats, iv. 59; his wit, 60; his eloquence, 61; his negotiation with Monroe respecting the "Chesapeake" affair, 40 *et seq.*;

his reasons for disavowing Berkeley's act, 76 et seq.; his opinion on Spencer Perceval's proposed Order in Council, 92, 97; instructs Erskine with regard to the Orders in Council, 99; instructions to Rose, 178 et seq.; opposes interference with the effect of the embargo, 326, his confidence in Napoleon's overthrow in 1808, 331; on the causes of the embargo, 332; replies to Pinkney's conditional proposition to withdraw the embargo, 334 et seq.; letter of, to Pinkney published in the "New England Palladium," 419; his reply to Napoleon and Alexander, v. 23; his notice to Pinkney of possible change in the Orders, 42; his note of Dec. 24, 1808, announcing a change, 43, his anger at Pinkney's reply, 44, 45; his willingness for further relaxations, 45; his discontent with Castlereagh and Perceval, 48, 106; his reception of Erskine's despatches and Campbell's Report, 49, 50, 51; his assertion as to the cause of the embargo, 51; his instructions to Erskine of Jan. 23, 1809, 52-57, 66, 70-73, 90; his influence declining, 57, 58; his speech of March 6, 1809, on the Orders, 61; his remark to Pinkney on the Order of April 26, 64; his disavowal of Erskine's arrangement, 87-95; his statement to the House of Commons, 97, 98; his instructions to F. J. Jackson, July 1, 1809, 98-105; his charge of duplicity against Madison, 99, 100, 114, 125; his resignation, 107; his duel with Castlereagh, 107; his relations with Wellesley, 266, 267; his speech on the renewal of intercourse between the United States and Great Britain, 276; his speech of March 3, 1812, on the Orders in Council and licenses, vi. 277, 278; on the loss of the "Guerriere" and "Macedonian," vii. 6; on the conduct of the war, 10, 11, 23; his failure as a minister, 20, 21; his view of British naturalization acts, 21-23.

"Canons of Etiquette," the, ii. 365.
Cantrelle, M., iii. 300.
Capitol at Washington in 1800, i. 30, 198; designed by Dr. Thornton, 111; the south wing completed, iv. 152, 209, burned, viii. 145; rebuilt, ix. 142.
Caramelli, Hamet, ii. 430, 436.
Carden, J. S., captain of the British frigate "Macedonian," vi. 382, 383.
"Carnation," British sloop-of-war, attacks and destroys the "General Armstrong," viii. 202-207.
"Carolina," American 14-gun sloop-of-war, at New Orleans, viii. 344; her share in the night battle, 346, 347, 349, 350; her fire imprisons the British troops, 352, 355, destroyed, Dec. 27, 1814, 356, 359.
Carroll, William, major-general of Tennessee militia, arrives at New Orleans, viii. 336, 337; his brigade, 344; posted on the Gentilly road, 345.
"Carron," 20-gun British sloop-of-war, sent to Pensacola, viii. 319, 322, attacks Fort Bowyer, 323, 324.
Carronades, their range, viii. 109.
Casa Calvo, Marquis of, iii. 71, 73, 74, 79.
Cass, Lewis, colonel of Ohio militia, vi. 298; refuses to abandon Detroit, 315; his discontent with Hull, 326; detached to open an interior road to the river Raisin, 328; ordered to return, 329; included in Hull's capitulation, 334; brigadier-general U. S. army, vii. 128; treats with Indians, 261.

GENERAL INDEX. 265

Cassin, John, captain in U. S. navy, vii. 270, 271.
"Castilian," British sloop-of-war, cruises in company with the "Avon," viii. 189; her commander's report on the loss of the "Avon," 190-192
Castine, occupied by British expedition, viii. 95, 96; offered to be restored at Ghent, ix. 34.
Castlereagh, Lord, on Howick's Order in Council, iv. 80, 81; becomes War Secretary, 81; urges retaliation on France, 83, 90, 325, 421; his supposed failures as Secretary of War, v. 47, 48, 106, 107; his quarrel with Canning, 56, 57; his duel with Canning, 107; retires from the cabinet, 107; becomes Foreign Secretary, vi. 216; his instructions to Foster of April 10, 1812, 216, 220; announces suspension of Orders in Council, 286; his statement of number of American seamen in British service, 456; his remarks to Jonathan Russell, Aug. 24, 1812, vii. 2, 3; defends course of ministry, 11; his remarks on impressment, 19, 20; his remarks on the Czar's offer of mediation, 29; declines Russian mediation in May, 1813. 340, 345, 346; his letter of July 5, declining mediation, 341, 342; his letter to Cathcart, July 13, offering direct negotiation with United States, 342, 343, 349, 350, 355; lukewarm about the American war, 356, 358, 360; his letter to Monroe, November 4, offering to negotiate directly, 360, 370; his offer accepted by Madison, 363, 371; his irresistible influence, 394; his disposition toward America, ix. 2, 7, 9; his instructions of July 28, 9, 10, 24; his choice of negotiators, 14; delays negotiation until August, 17; his instructions of August 14, 19; keeps the negotiation alive until October, 23; at Ghent, August 19, 24; his letter to Bathurst suggesting immediate peace, 25; at Vienna, embarrassed by the American war, 36; negotiates commercial convention with the United States, 104.
Cathcart, Lord, iv. 64; British ambassador at St. Petersburg, vii. 28; his instructions of July 5, 1813, 341, 342; his comments on the Czar's conduct, 350-354.
Caulaincourt, Duc de Vicence, French ambassador in Russia, v. 412. recalled, 418; congratulates Adams, 419.
Cazeneau, Mr., iii. 379.
Census, of 1800, i. 1, 2; of 1810, Act for, v. 209.
"Centinel," Boston newspaper, of Sept. 10, 1814, quoted, viii. 223, 288, 289, 291, 299, 300; publishes peace. ix. 59, 60.
Cevallos, Don Pedro de, Spanish Minister for Foreign Affairs, i. 371; ii. 23; remonstrates against the sale of Louisiana, 58; refuses to pay for French spoliations, 276, 279; his conditions on ratification of Spanish claims convention, 280; his comments on the Americans, 282, 283; alarmed by Pinckney, 284; complains of Pinckney's conduct, 294; his negotiation with Monroe, iii. 24-36; refuses to countenance Burr's designs, 249.
Chamier, Frederick, lieutenant on the British frigate "Menelaus," his account of house-burning on the Potomac, viii. 164.
Champagny, Jean Baptiste de, succeeds Talleyrand as Minister of Foreign Affairs, iv. 107; his letter of Jan. 15, 1808, declaring war to exist between England and the United States, 221; his instruc-

tions to Turreau in defence of the Decrees, Dec. 10, 1808, v. 31; in defence of the Spanish colonies, 33; his remonstrances to Napoleon against severity to the United States, 138, 139; complains of the Non-intercourse Act, 140; his instructions to Hauterive, June 13, 1809, on concessions to the United States, 140; his note on the right of search and blockade, 149, 150, 250; his efforts on behalf of neutral commerce, 222; his interview with Armstrong, Jan. 25, 1810. 229, 230; his note of Feb. 14, 1810, announcing reprisals for the Non-intercourse Act, 232; his letter of August 5, 1810, announcing that the decrees are revoked, 253-256, 286. 296-302, 383, 414, 415; vi. 7; creates a contract by letter of August 5, v. 342; his report on the decrees. 348, 349, 382, 388; vi. 8; his phrase *bien entendu*, v. 387, 388 declares the decrees revoked on Feb. 2, 1811, 386, 389, 390, removed from office, 401.

Champlain. Lake. (See Plattsburg.)

Champlin, Guy R., captain of the privateer "General Armstrong," vii. 316; his escapes, 325-327.

Chandler, John. brigadier-general in U. S. army, vii. 156. engaged in capturing Fort George, 157; advances to Stony Creek, 159; captured, 160.

Channing, William Ellery. i. 90; his impressions of Virginia manners. 132, 171; takes charge of church at Boston, ix. 178; his letter to Thacher, 178; his Unitarianism, 179-182; his Fast-Day Sermon in 1810, 203-205.

Charles IV. of Spain. his character, i. 341; refuses papal territory, 354; his delight at the offer of Tuscany, 369; refuses to sell Florida, 401; delivers Louisiana to Napoleon, 401; distressed by Napoleon, ii. 56; his demands on Napoleon, 59; withdraws protest against the sale of Louisiana, 277; declares war on England, 309; abdication of, iv. 117, 298.

Charleston, in Maryland, vii. 268.

Charleston, S. C., in 1800, i. 37 *et seq.*, 92, 149. in 1816. ix. 156.

Chase. Samuel, Justice of the Supreme Court, his charge to the Baltimore grand jury, ii. 147; his impeachment, 149 *et seq.*, 158, scene of impeachment, 227; his counsel, 229; the managers of his impeachment, 229; articles of impeachment, 229; the trial, 230 *et seq.;* the votes on the articles, 238; his acquittal, 239.

"Chasseur," privateer, her blockade, viii. 196, 197.

Chateaugay, Hampton's campaign at, vii. 192-197.

Chatillon, Congress of, vii. 394.

Chauncey. Isaac, at Tripoli, ii. 428; captain in U. S. navy, takes command on Lake Ontario, vi. 344; arranges plan of campaign with Dearborn, vii. 152, 153, 154; controls the lake, 153; crosses to Niagara, 155; aids capture of Fort George, 157; returns to Sackett's Harbor, 159: loses control of the lake, 171; recovers control of the lake, 179; dissuades Brown from attacking Kingston, viii. 27, 28; shut up in Sackett's Harbor in the spring of 1814. 28-30, 33; Brown's irritating letters to, 34, 45, 46: sails from Sackett's Harbor, 80; his reply to Brown's letters, 81; carries Izard's army to the Genesee River, 114; loses control of the lake in October, 1814. 115.

Cheetham, James, editor of the "American Citizen and Watch-

GENERAL INDEX. 267

tower," i. 121; attacks Burr, 331; iii. 272, 273.

Cherokee Indians, i. 4; iii. 16; with Jackson in the Creek war, vii 246.

"Cherub," British 18-gun sloop-of-war, viii. 178; assists the "Phoebe" to blockade and capture the "Essex," 179, 180.

"Chesapeake," 38-gun frigate, the desertion of British seamen to, iv. 2; delay in getting her ready for sea, 5; starts for sea, 9; fired on by the "Leopard," 16; strikes her flag, 19; returns to Norfolk, 20; vi. 29, 36; vii. 54, 311; arrives at Boston, April 9, 1813, 285, 287; her force, 292; her action with the "Shannon," 293-303; effect of capture, 303, 309; cause of capture, 337.

"Chesapeake Affair," measures taken by the Cabinet after the, iv. 31, 163; Madison's instructions on, 39, 45; its effect on English society 44; attack disavowed by the British Ministry, 51, 149; Canning's instructions on, 178-182; Rose's negotiation on, ii. 187-197; laid aside, 199; Gallatin's plan for settling, 388; Canning's instructions of Jan. 23, 1809, for settling, v 52. 53; Erskine's settlement of the, 67, 68; settlement disavowed, 88-90; Canning's instructions of July 1, 1809, for settling, 101; Jackson's offer to settle, 126, 130; untouched by Wellesley, 285; Foster's instructions to settle, vi. 23; American indifference to settlement, 37; its effect on the Indians, 79; settled by Foster, 121, 122, 270; remembered too well, ix. 73.

Chesapeake Bay, British naval force in, vii. 14, 24; blockade of, announced Dec. 26, 1812, vii. 30, 33; severity of blockade in, 264, 265; Admiral Cockburn's operations in, 266-269; Admiral Warren's operations in, 277; Cochrane's marauding in, viii. 164; in October, 1814, left to repose, 173; steamboat on, ix. 172.

Cheves, Langdon, member of Congress from South Carolina, asserts contract with Napoleon, v. 342, 343; in the Twelfth Congress, vi. 122; chairman of naval committee, 124; on Committee on Ways and Means, 124; his opinion on the war-power, 160, his motion to build a navy, 162; his argument in favor of seventy-fours, 163; his hostility to non-importation, 205, 230, 232, 446, 447, 448; favors war-taxation, 235; opposes forfeitures under Non-Importation Act, 441, on war-taxes, 444; elected speaker, Jan. 19, 1814, vii. 396, defeats Dallas's scheme for a national bank, viii 259.

Chew, Captain Samuel, deposition of, vi. 193, 196.

Chicago, (See Fort Dearborn)

Chickasaw Bluff, iii. 284, 290, 325

Chickasaw Indians, iii. 16; vii. 216.

"Childers," 18-gun British sloop-of-war sent to Pensacola, viii. 322, in the attack on Fort Bowyer, 323, 324.

Chillicothe in 1800. i. 2.

Chippawa, British force at, viii. 38; Riall takes position at, 39; battle at, 40-45; Brown withdraws to, 47-50; Ripley retreats from, 66, 67; Drummond's delay at, 68; Drummond retires to, 90; Izard's failure at, 116.

"Chippeway," 1-gun British schooner on Lake Erie, vii. 120.

Chittenden, Martin, governor of Vermont, his proclamation recalling the State militia, Nov. 10, 1813, vii. 366; refuses to call out the State militia to defend Plattsburg, viii 222.

GENERAL INDEX.

Choctaw Indians, vii. 216; with Jackson at Mobile, viii. 328; at New Orleans, 346.

Christie, John, lieutenant-colonel of Thirteenth Infantry, vi. 249, 350, 351.

Christophe, i. 394, 395, 416.

Chrystler's Farm, battle at, vii. 188-191.

Cincinnati in 1800, i. 2.

Cintra, convention of, v. 48.

Claiborne, Ferdinand Leigh, brigadier-general of Mississippi militia, vii. 243; penetrates Creek country, 244.

Claiborne, William Charles Cole, appointed governor of Mississippi Territory, i. 295, 403; receives possession of Louisiana, ii. 256; governor of Orleans Territory, 400; character of, iii. 297 et seq.; his anxieties, 304; his ignorance of Burr's conspiracy, 308; warned by Wilkinson and Andrew Jackson, 316 et seq; takes possession of West Florida, v. 310-314; left by Jackson in charge of military defence of New Orleans, viii. 325; his want of authority, 341; commands on the Chef Menteur Road, 369

Claims, American, on France (see French spoliations).

Claims, American, on Spain (see Pinckney), iii. 23-26, 28-30, 32, 35, 107.

Clark, Christopher, a manager of Chase's impeachment. ii. 228.

Clark, Daniel, of New Orleans, iii. 222; in sympathy with Burr and the Mexican Association, 223, 236; his letter to Wilkinson complaining of Burr's indiscretion, 224; Burr's drafts to be drawn in his favor, 231; a correspondent of Burr in New Orleans, 296, 322; his hatred for Claiborne, 300; delegate to Congress, 302, 303; secures affidavits in evidence of his innocence, 306 et seq.; in Washington, 307; preserves silence respecting the conspiracy, 308; Wilkinson's letters to, 321, 322; turns against Wilkinson, 454.

Clark, William, explores Louisiana Territory with Captain Lewis, iii. 12, 215.

Clay, Green, brigadier-general of Kentucky militia, surprises Proctor, vii. 105, 107; commands Fort Meigs, 109, 114.

Clay, Henry, i. 133; Burr's counsel, iii. 278, 282; senator from Kentucky, his war-speech of Feb. 22, 1810, v. 189; his speech on the occupation of West Florida, 320, 321; his speech on the Bank Charter, 333, 334; elected speaker, vi. 122, 124; favors army of thirty-five thousand men, 151; favors war-power, 161; favors navy, 164; supposed to have coerced Madison to war, 196; urges embargo, 201; suppresses discussion in the House, 227; his vote defeats repeal of non-importation, 234; his account of the military efforts of Kentucky, 390-393; his comments on Hull's surrender, 392, 393; opposes compromise of forfeitures under Non-importation Act, 442; elected speaker of Thirteenth Congress, vii. 53; assists Harrison, 73, 74; nominated and confirmed as joint envoy to negotiate peace at Ghent, 371, 393; resigns speakership and sails for Europe, 396; ix. 10; at Ghent, ix. 14, 16; insists that the British will recede, 20, combative, 29; his speeches, 31; drafts Indian article, 32; opposed to recognizing the British right of navigating the Mississippi, 46-48; his opinion of the treaty, 50, 58; his character,

GENERAL INDEX. 269

51, 52; Speaker in the Fourteenth Congress, 107, 108; favors strong foreign policy, 109; favors protection, 113-115; recants his errors in regard to the national bank, 117; attacked on account of the Compensation Act, 136; offered the War Department, 142; supports internal improvements, 149, 150.

Clergy, of New England, their authority, i. 79-82; Jefferson's quarrel with, 313-318; their opinion of Jefferson, 321; their attitude toward the war, viii. 20-23; their division into Orthodox, Unitarian, and Universalist, ix. 175-187.

"Clermont," Fulton's steamboat, makes her first voyage August 17, 1807, iv. 135.

Cleveland in 1800, i. 3.

Clifton, William, i. 98.

Clinton, De Witt, i. 112, 228, 233; resigns his senatorship to become mayor of New York, 266, 281; attacks Burr through Cheetham, 331; his duel with Swartwout, 332, ii. 206; presides over a "Chesapeake" meeting in New York, iv. 28; his attitude toward the embargo, 283; takes electoral votes from Madison, 287; nominated for the Presidency by New York, vi. 215; his canvass, 409, 410; his electoral vote, 413; vii. 48; favors Erie Canal, ix. 168.

Clinton, George, i. 114; governor of New York, 228; ii. 173, nominated for Vice-President, 180; Vice-President, iii. 126; his casting vote confirms Armstrong, 153, 172; renominated for Vice-President in 1808, iv. 226, 287; his hostility to Madison, 227; supported by Cheetham for the Presidency, 227, 284; his opinions reported by Erskine, 385; his opposition to Madison, 428, 430; presides in the Senate, v. 76, 190; his vote against the Bank

Charter, 337; his political capacity, 363, 364; his death, vi. 214.

Clopton, John, member of Congress from Virginia, on the army bill, iv. 212.

Coast survey, appropriation for, by Congress, iii. 355.

Coasting trade under the embargo, iv. 251 et seq.; tonnage employed in 1807-1810, v. 15.

Cobbett, William, i. 46; in Philadelphia, 118; on the "Chesapeake" affair, iv. 44, 73, 329; his "Weekly Register" on the American war, vii. 356.

Cochrane, Sir Alexander, British vice-admiral succeeding Sir John Borlase Warren, communicates with refugee Creeks, vii. 258; joint commander with Ross of expedition in the Chesapeake, viii. 124; his instructions, 124, 125; his orders for general retaliation, 125-127; his letter to Monroe, 128; fails to capture Fort McHenry, 171, 172; sails for Halifax, 173; recommends expedition to Mobile, 311; at New Orleans, 365; suggests canal, 367.

Cockburn, Sir George, British rear-admiral, his operations in Chesapeake Bay, vii. 265-269, 274, 276; at Ocracoke, 277, 329, at Cumberland Island, 277, 278, lands with Ross, and urges attack on Washington, viii. 127; pursues and destroys Barney's flotilla, 129, 130; enters Washington and burns the White House, 145, 146; destroys the type of the "National Intelligencer," 147; an incendiary, 164; at the attack on Baltimore, 170.

Cocke, John, major-general of Tennessee militia, vii. 240: surprises Hillabee village, 241; put under arrest, 252.

Cocke, William, senator from Tennessee, ii. 113; censures Randolph, 240.

Codrington, Sir Edward, British admiral, his account of the artillery battle at New Orleans, viii. 364.

Coffee, John, colonel of Tennessee militia, commands mounted force in Jackson's Creek campaign, vii. 236; destroys Talishatchee, 237; at Talladega, 238; abandoned by his men, 246; wounded at Emuckfaw, 246, 247; engaged at the Horseshoe, 255; his account of the slaughter, 256; marches with Tennessee militia to Mobile, viii. 326, 328; ordered to Baton Rouge, 332, 333; hurries to New Orleans, 336, 337; his brigade, 344, his share in the night battle, 345, 346, 349-351; stationed on the left of Jackson's line, 373.

Coggeshall. George, author of "History of American Privateers," vii. 325; his escape in privateer "David Porter," 325.

Coleman, William, editor of the New York "Evening Post," i. 119.

Coleridge, Samuel Taylor, ix 215.

"Comet," Baltimore privateer, vii. 316.

Colonial system of the European Powers, ii 323.

Colonial trade, ii. 319, 322, 327-329, direct and indirect, 324, 325; West Indian, value of, 331, 332, rule of, established by case of "Essex," iii. 45; distress of, 49; arrangement of, in Monroe's treaty 409, 412, parliamentary report on, iv. 67; the only object of Perceval's Orders in Council, 95.

Columbia College, i. 101.

"Columbiad," the, of Joel Barlow, i. 103 *et seq.*

Commerce, foreign and domestic, in 1800, i. 5, 14; nature and value of American, v. 290, 291.

Commercial Intercourse, Act of May 1, 1810, regarding (see Non-intercourse).

Commercial restrictions, list of measures of, v. 152, 194; Madison's devotion to, 293, 295; Madison's return to, 304.

Compensation Act, ix. 119-122; popular protest against, 134-138; repeal of, 144-146.

"Confiance," British 36-gun ship, on Lake Champlain, viii. 103; her armament and crew, 104, 105, 106; fights the battle of Plattsburg, 108-110; ix. 234.

Congress, the Seventh, first session of, i. 264-307; second session, 427-433; ii. 74-77; the Eighth, first session of, 92, 96-159; second session, 206-242, 396; session of 1804-1805. iii. 9; problems before, December, 1805, 91; meeting of the Ninth, Dec. 2, 1805, 126; close of first session, 196; opening of second session, Dec. 1, 1806, 328; close of, 369; Tenth, character of, iv. 146; meeting of, Oct. 26, 1807, 152; close of the first session, 223; meeting of second session, Nov. 7, 1808, 354, 361; close of, 453, 454; first session of Eleventh, meets, May 22, 1809, v. 76; proceedings of, 77-86; adjourns June 28, 86; second session meets, Nov. 27, 1809, 176; proceedings of, 178-209; adjourns, May 2, 1810, 209, character of, 316, election of Twelfth, 316 ; third session of Eleventh, 319-358; close of Eleventh, 358; first session of Twelfth, meets Nov. 4, 1811, vi. 118; its composition, 122, chooses Henry Clay speaker, 124; war-debate in, 133-153; proceedings of, 133-175, 201, 202, 204; declares war against England, 228, 229; adjourns, July 6, 1812, 235; decline of influence,

437; second session of Twelfth, 435–458; meeting of Thirteenth, May 24, 1813, vii. 53, proceedings of first session, 54–64, 67, 70, 71; meeting of second session, Dec. 6, 1813, 364; proceedings of, 369, 372–379, 381–390; Federalist strength in, viii. 228; meeting of third session, Sept. 19. 1814, 239; proceedings of, 247–262, 266–280; peace legislation of, ix. 82–87; close of, 87, meeting of Fourteenth, 106, 107; superiority of Fourteenth, 108–111, 138; proceedings of first session of, 112–122; close of first session, 125; popular rebuke of, 138; second session of, 143; proceedings of second session, 144–153. (See Acts of.)

"Congress," 38-gun frigate, vi 363; at Boston, 378; her cruise in 1812, 381; returns to Boston, Dec. 31. 1812, vii. 285; goes to sea, April 30 1813, 285; unseaworthy, 287; returns to Boston, Dec. 14, 1813, 310, 311.

Connecticut, i. 105; legislature, action of, in February, 1809, iv. 418, 455; disaffection of, vii. 33, 34; viii. 13; prosperity of, during the war, 15; withdraws militia, Aug. 24, 1814, from national service, 221; appoints delegates to the Hartford Convention, 227; resolutions of legislature against the militia bill, in October, 1814, 278; approves report of the Hartford Convention, 304; regular troops stationed in, 317, elections of 1816, ix. 133, 139; growth of population, 154, 155; increase of wealth in, 157.

"Constellation," 38-gun frigate, at Washington, vi. 364 372, 378; at Norfolk, vii. 269, 270, 274, 287.

"Constitution," 44-gun frigate, at Tripoli, ii. 426; iv. 5: chased by British squadron, vi. 364, 369–372, captures "Guerriere," 373–375; captures "Java," 385, 386; arrives at Boston, Feb. 27, 1813, vii. 285, replaces her masts, 287; goes to sea, Jan. 1, 1814, 311; imperilled by privateering, 337, sails from Boston in December. 1814, ix. 74; her action with the "Cyane" and "Levant," 75–78; escapes British squadron, 78.

Constitution, the (see Virginia and Kentucky Resolutions of 1798, Treaty-making Power, War Power, Militia, Internal Improvement, Amendment, Bank of the United States, Impeachment, Embargo, New England Convention, Marshall, and Story).

Cook, Orchard, member of Congress from Massachusetts, his letter describing Gallatin's plan, iv. 369.

Cooper, Dr. Charles D., his letter or Hamilton and Burr, ii. 178, 186.

Cooper, James Fenimore, i. 110; quotation from "Chainbearer," 43.

Coosa River, home of the Upper Creeks, vii. 217, 224, 234 Jackson's march to the, 237, 238; Cocke's march to the, 240.

Coosadas (see Alabamas).

Copenhagen, the British expedition against, iv. 63; bombardment of, 65.

Copley, John Singleton, ix. 213.

"Cornwallis," British seventy-four, chases "Hornet," ix. 72, 73.

Cordero, Governor, iii. 311.

Cotton, export to France prohibited by England, iv. 101, 219, 322, 323; manufacturers of, v. 16; American, prohibited in France, 151; price of, affected by blockade, vii. 263; value of export in 1815, ix. 94; manufactures depressed by the peace, 96; fabrics, in the tariff of 1816, 111, 114, 116; export in 1816, 126.

"Courier," the, London newspaper, on the American war, vii. 358; on the Americans, 359; on Perry's victory, 359; on Proctor's defeat, 360; on the necessity of retaliation, 362; on privateers, viii. 197; on Madison, ix. 5; on terms of peace, 6, 7, 31, 35; on the news of peace, 54.

Covington, Leonard, brigadier-general in the U. S. army, commands brigade in Wilkinson's expedition, vii. 184; his opinion in council of war, 185; killed at Chrystler's Farm, 189.

Coxe, William S., third lieutenant on the 'Chesapeake," vii. 295; fires the last guns, 298.

Craig, Sir James, governor-general of Canada, calls on the Indians for assistance in case of war with the United States, iv. 137; governor of Lower Canada, 243; warned by Erskine to be on his guard against attacks from the United States, 395; his instructions to John Henry, 460; recalls John Henry, v. 86.

Craney Island, fortified, vii. 271; attacked, 272-275.

Crawford, William H., senator from Georgia, opposes mission to Russia, v. 12; on the message of Jan. 3, 1810, 179; represents the Treasury, 181; votes with Samuel Smith, 191; his character, 331; introduces Bank Charter, 332; his speech on Bank Charter, 332, 333; reports bill for fifty thousand volunteers, 358, party to revolutionizing East Florida, vi. 239; his comments on the conduct of the war, 395; sent as minister to Paris, vii. 49; sails in the "Argus," 304; reason of not being a peace commissioner, 393; appointed Secretary of War, ix. 89; candidate for the Presidency in 1816, 122-124; appointed Secretary of the Treasury, 142.

Creek Indians, Tecumthe visits, vi. 92, 108; their confederacy and grievances, vii. 217-220; Tecumthe's visit to, 220-222; secret excitement among, 222, 223; murders on the Ohio by warriors of, 224; execution of murderers, 225, 226; outbreak of fanaticism among, 227; attacked at Burnt Corn, 228, 229; capture Fort Mims, 229-231; number of hostile warriors among, 233, 244, 245, 249; Andrew Jackson's campaign of 1813 among, 235-240; Cocke's campaign against, 240, 241; Floyd's campaign against, 241-243; Claiborne's campaign against, 243, 244; Jackson's second campaign against, 245-248; Floyd's second campaign against, 249, 250; Jackson's last campaign against, 254-257; number of Red Stick refugees among, 258, 259; Andrew Jackson's capitulation with, 259-261; viii. 317, 318; effect of their war on the Florida difficulties, 318.

Creoles in Louisiana, Claiborne's treatment of, iii. 298; their attitudes toward Burr's conspiracy, 300-309.

Crillon, Count Edward de, his family, vi. 176; acts as John Henry's agent, 177-179; his social success, 178, 180; his evidence, 183; sails for France, 184; an impostor, 185; an agent of French police, 186.

Croghan, George, major of the Seventeenth U. S. Infantry, his defence of Fort Stephenson, vii. 110-114; his expedition against Mackinaw, viii. 32.

Croker, John Wilson, Secretary to the Admiralty, v. 58; on British naturalization laws, vii. 21, 23; on

GENERAL INDEX. 273

the "Chesapeake" and "Shannon," 302; on the captures in British waters, viii. 200, 201.

Crowninshield, Benjamin Williams, appointed Secretary of the Navy, ix. 63.

Crowninshield, Jacob, member of Congress from Massachusetts, declines Navy Department, appointed Secretary, refuses office, remains on records as Secretary of Navy, iii. 10, 11; speech of, in favor of non-importation, 157; Jefferson's letter to, on the Pierce affair, 200; iv. 109; his death, 209; succeeded by Joseph Story, 463.

Cuba, Jefferson's policy toward, iv. 340, 341; v. 37, 38.

Cumberland Island in Georgia, occupied by Admiral Cockburn, vii. 277; again occupied in 1815, ix. 62.

Cumberland Road, iii. 181, 355; v. 209; in 1816, ix. 169.

Currency (see Banks, national and State).

Cushing, Caleb, ix. 206.

Cushing, T. H., Lieutenant-Colonel of Second Infantry, iii. 246, 311; Wilkinson communicates Burr's designs to, 313; orders to, 315; brigadier-general, viii. 221.

Cutts, Charles, senator from New Hampshire, vii. 48.

"Cyane," British corvette, captured by "Constitution," ix. 74–78.

DACRES, J. R., captain of the "Guerriere," vi. 27, 37, 373; his action with the "Constitution," 373–375; censured by the "Times," vii. 5, 14; on the cause of his defeat, 7, 13.

Daggett, David, senator from Connecticut, his speech against Giles's bill for drafting militia, viii. 270, 271.

VOL. IX. — 18

Dalberg, Duc, negotiates with Joel Barlow, vi. 259; his remonstrances to Bassano against Napoleon's treatment of the United States, 262.

Dallas, Alexander James, i. 127, 281; ii. 195–199; letter of, to Gallatin, 198; acts with federalists, iii. 9; his opinion of Jefferson's second administration, iv. 455; his opinion of Armstrong, vii 35; Madison's favorite candidate for the treasury, 396; defeated by senators, 397; author of specifications against William Hull, 415; appointed Secretary of the Treasury, Oct. 5, 1814, viii. 243; his character and temper, 243, 244; his account of the condition of the Treasury in October, 1814, 244; opposes treasury-note issus and recommends a bank, 249, 250–260; ix. 57; describes the condition of the Treasury in November, 1814, viii. 252; describes the condition of the Treasury in December, 1814, 254; describes the condition of the Treasury in January, 1815, 261, 262; sketches financial scheme for first year of peace, ix. 83, 84; acts as Secretary of War to reduce the army. 88; his severity to New England, 98, 99; fails to fund treasury-notes, 100-103; his report of 1815, 105, 106; recommends a national bank and a protective tariff, 111, 112, 114; announces his retirement from the Treasury, 124, 125; restores specie payments, 128-132; his success as Secretary of the Treasury, 140, 141; his death, 141.

Dallas, Alexander James, third lieutenant of the frigate "President," vi. 28, 32.

Dana, Samuel Whittlesey, member of Congress from Connecticut, i. 269; his remark on the dumb legislature, 271; in the Ninth Congress, iii. 143, 242; on repeal of the em-

bargo, iv. 436; senator from Connecticut, vii. 63.
Dane, Nathan, delegate to the Hartford Convention, viii. 292.
Daquin, ———, major commanding battalion of men of color at New Orleans, viii. 345.
Daschkoff, André, Russian chargé at Washington, vii. 41, 211.
Dautremont, M., iii. 379.
Daveiss, Joseph H., United States District Attorney, iii. 268; writes to Jefferson denouncing the Spanish plot, 270; accuses Burr in court of setting on foot a military expedition, 277; renews his motion, 282; removed from office by Jefferson, 234, 309; and censured, 337; offers to serve as a volunteer in Harrison's campaign, vi. 94; urges an attack on Tippecanoe, 99, 101; his death, 103, 104, 107.
"David Porter," privateer schooner, escape of, vii. 325.
Davis, Daniel, brigadier-general of New York volunteers, killed in the sortie from Fort Erie, viii. 87, 88.
Davis, John, an English traveller, i. 122; his account of Jefferson's inauguration, 197.
Davis, Judge John, his opinion on the constitutionality of the embargo, iv. 268 *et seq.*
Davis, Matthew L., i. 231 *et seq.*, 296.
Davy. William R., appointed Major-General, vii. 37.
Dayton, Jonathan, senator from New Jersey, i. 280; ii. 105; in Miranda's confidence, iii. 189; informs Yrujo of Miranda's expedition, 192; his connection with Burr, 219; attempts to obtain funds from Yrujo, 234 *et seq.*; funds received by him from the Spanish treasury, 245; his letter to Wilkinson, 252; at Burr's trial, 463.

Dearborn, Henry, appointed Secretary of War, i. 219; his opinion in the cabinet on Spanish policy, ii. 2; quoted by Eaton, 431; remains in Jefferson's second administration, iii. 10; his remark on Wilkinson, 454; ignorant of Jefferson's instructions to Monroe, iv. 163; appointed collector at Boston, v. 9; his orders, as Secretary of War, to Wilkinson, Dec. 2, 1808, 169; appointed senior major-general, vi. 289; his plan of campaign, 297, 306, 340, 341; reaches Albany, 304; goes to Boston, 305; his difficulties at Boston, 306, 307, 309; returns to Albany, 310; ignorant that he commands operations at Niagara, 310, 322, 339; sends militia to Niagara, 321; negotiates armistice, 322, 323, 340; effect of armistice, 324, 343; armistice rejected by the President, 340; his opinion of Van Rensselaer, 353; his campaign against Montreal, 360; his reflections on the campaign of 1812, 360, 361; Monroe's criticisms of, 396, 397; George Hay's remark on, 421; continued in command, vii. 37, 38, 39; releases Perry's vessels, 117, 159; ordered to attack Kingston, 149; his estimate of British force at Kingston, 151; decides not to attack Kingston, 152, 153, 171; captures York, 154; arrives at Niagara, 155; captures Fort George. 157, 158; devolves command on Morgan Lewis, 161; reports Boerstler's disaster, 163; removed from command, 171, 416; put in command of New York, 407, 416; president of court-martial on William Hull, 417; nominated Secretary of War in 1815, ix. 89.
Dearborn, Fort, at Chicago, murders at, vi. 110; garrison at, 294; evacuated, 334.

GENERAL INDEX. 275

Debt, Public (see Finances).
Decatur, James, killed at Tripoli, ii. 427.
Decatur, Stephen, burns the "Philadelphia," ii. 139; at Tripoli, 427; captain in U. S. navy, on Barron's court-martial, iv. 21, 24; commands squadron, vi. 363; his orders, 363, 364, 368; his advice, 364; his first cruise in 1812, 366, 368, 375 ; his second cruise, 381; captures the "Macedonian," 382, 383 ; returns to port with prize, 383; takes refuge with squadron in New London, vii. 278. 279; reports on blue lights, 279, 280; commands "President," ix. 63; runs blockade, 64; his battle with the "Endymion," 65, 69; his surrender, 70.
Decrees, French, of 1798, vi. 139.
Decree of Berlin, Nov. 21, 1806, declaring Great Britain in a state of blockade, and excluding from French ports all vessels coming from British ports, iii. 389-391; its effect on Monroe and Pinckney's negotiation, 412; its effect in the United States, 427; not enforced until August, 1807, iv. 82; its enforcement notified to Armstrong, Sept. 18, 1807, 109; Napoleon's defence of, 110, 111, 221, 95; his varying objects in using, v. 24.
—— of Milan, Dec. 17, 1807, declaring good prize every neutral vessel that should have been searched by an English ship, or paid any duty to the British government, or should come from or go to a British port, iv. 126; its effect in the United States, 195.
—— of Bayonne, April 17, 1808, directing the seizure of all American vessels entering the ports of France, Italy, and the Hanse Towns, iv. 303, 304; rigorously enforced, 312.

Decrees of Berlin, Milan, and Bayonne, v. 24, 152, 297; their rigid enforcement, 30 ; Champagny's argument in defence of, 31, 32 ; their effect on England, 46; their effect on France, 138 ; Napoleon drafts, June 10. 1809, decree repealing that of Milan, 139-141; lays aside draft of repealing decree, 141; drafts Vienna decree of August, 1809, retaliating the Nonintercourse Act, 143. 144, 150, 230; Louis's resistance to, 148, 240, 241; Napoleon's condition of repeal, 229, 245, 250, 251; null and void for licensed vessels, 248; declared by Champagny revoked on Nov. 1, 1810, 255; declared revoked by Madison, 304, 317, 347, 348 ; Russell's reports on the revocation, 381-396; declared revoked by Champagny for Feb. 2, 1811, 386, 389, 390; not revoked, 394, 395; declared fundamental laws by Napoleon, 397, 407; declared successful by Napoleon, 398; considered suspended by Madison, 400, 401; recognized by United States, 402, 403; their revocation doubted by Russell, 395, 400, 406; their revocation affirmed by Russell, 405; enforced on the Baltic, 426, 427; Barlow instructed that they are considered revoked, 427 ; revocation asserted by Pinkney, vi. 3, 5, 6, 11: evidence of revocation asked by Wellesley, 4; argued by Pinkney, 7, 8; revocation denied by Wellesley, 23; affirmed to be still in force by Foster, 41 ; affirmed by Monroe to be revoked as far as America has a right to expect, 42; their international and municipal characters, 43; argued by Monroe, 44, 45; their revocation unknown to the President, 56; argued by Serurier, 60, disputed by Madison,

64; their revocation a personal affair with Madison, 65; their effect on the northwestern Indians, 83; declared not repealed by British courts, 118 ; their repeal doubted by Madison and Monroe, 120, 187-189; repeal asserted in annual message, 125; repeal assumed by House committee, 133, 134; repeal denied by Monroe, 194, 195, 201; repeal assumed by Monroe, 198; Bassano's report on validity of, 216, 253; repeal assumed by Madison, 218, 224; repeal maintained by Monroe till June, 1812, 232; Bassano's instructions on repeal of, 248-249 ; repeal asserted by Barlow, 252; evidence of repeal required by Barlow, 254; repealing decree produced by Bassano, 255-257; still enforced, 260, 261; revocation unknown to the French authorities, 262, 263; Webster's resolutions on repeal of, vii. 55, 58.

Decree of Rambouillet, March 23, 1810, sequestering American property in retaliation for the Non-importation Act, v. 236, 242, 274.

—— of July 25, 1810, regarding licenses, v. 247; of July 22, 1810, confiscating American property in Dutch and Spanish ports, 258; of Aug. 5, 1810, confiscating American property in France, 258.

—— of St. Cloud, dated April 28, 1811, repealing the Decrees of Berlin and Milan from Nov. 1, 1810, vi. 255-257, 259.

Decrès, Denis, Duc. Napoleon's Minister of Marine, instructions of, to Richepanse and Leclerc, re-establishing slavery, i. 397; defining the boundaries of Louisiana and its administration, ii. 5; his letter to Armstrong respecting the Berlin Decree, iii. 391; asks instructions in the case of American schooner at San Sebastian, v. 142, 143; Marmont's story of, 222.

Defiance, old Fort, vii. 76, 77, 78, 79, 80, 84, 86.

Delaware, growth of population of, ix. 155, 156.

Delaware Indians, murders of, v. 73.

Democrats, denounced by New England clergy, i. 79 *et seq.*; social inferiority, 92; the Northern, 264.

Denmark, Napoleon's demands upon, iv. 63 (see Copenhagen); spoliations of American commerce in, v. 409, 411.

Dennie, Joseph, on democracy, i. 85; editor of the "Portfolio," 119 121; character and influence of his "Portfolio," ix. 198-201.

De Pestre, or Dupiester, one of Burr's officers, iii. 252; starts with Burr as his chief of staff, 255; sent by Burr to report to Yrujo, 261; his message, 264.

Deposit at New Orleans, the right of, granted by treaty, i. 349; taken away, 418 ; restored, ii. 3 ; discussed by Cevallos, iii. 26, 27.

Derbigny, Pierre, creole delegate to Washington, ii. 400, 401; iii. 301; Turreau's opinion of, ii. 406; affidavit of, 408; iii. 219, 305.

De Rottenburg, Baron, forces under his command in Montreal district, viii. 25; one of Brock's successors, 48.

De Salaberry, A., lieutenant-colonel of Canadian voltigeurs, defeats Hampton, vii. 196, 197.

Desertion of British Seamen, ii. 333-335, 345, 346, 392.

Desha, Joseph, member of Congress from Kentucky, insists on reducing the army in 1815, ix. 84-86; on expenses of western members, 120.

Dessalines, i. 416.

GENERAL INDEX. 277

Destréhan, Jean Noel, creole delegate to Washington, ii. 400, 401; iii. 301; Turreau's opinion of, ii. 406.
Detroit, isolation of, i. 14, 15; military situation of, vi. 293, 295, 301; measures for protection of, 296; Hull's difficulties in defending, 315, 322, 324; Hull besieged in, 325–331; Brock's attack on, 332–334; Hull's surrender of, 334, 393 reinforcements for, 391; expedition to recover, to be commanded by Harrison, 392, 393; Harrison receives carte blanche to recover, vii. 74, 75; Harrison's views on military value of, 74, 77, 81, 82, 83; failure of Harrison's campaign against 100, 101; evacuated by Proctor, 131; occupied by Harrison, 132.
"Detroit," 19-gun British ship on Lake Erie, vii. 120; her armament, 121; captured, 127.
De Watteville, major-general in British army, viii. 102. (See Infantry, British regiments of.)
Dexter, Samuel, i. 93; Secretary of the Treasury, 192, 219; his argument against the constitutionality of the embargo, iv. 268, 270; takes the lead in Boston town-meeting, 411, 412; defeats project of State convention in Massachusetts, vi. 402; republican candidate for governor of Massachusetts in April, 1814, viii 9–11; again in 1815, ix. 92; again in 1816, 133.
Dickens, Charles, i. 56.
Dickinson, James, captain of the British sloop-of-war "Penguin," ix. 71; killed in action with "Hornet," 72.
"Diomed," stallion, i. 51.
"Dolphin," Baltimore privateer, captured, vii. 329.
Dos de Maio, the, iv. 300 et seq.; its effect in America, 339 et seq.

Douglas, Sir Howard, on American gunnery, ix. 229, 230, 233, 234.
Douglas, Captain John Erskine, of the "Bellona," iv. 4; reports the affair of the "Chesapeake" to Admiral Berkeley, 25; his letter to the Mayor of Norfolk. 28.
Douglass, David B., lieutenant of engineers, at Fort Erie, viii. 71, 76.
Douglass, George, captain of British sloop-of-war "Levant," his action with the "Constitution," ix. 75–78.
Downie, George, captain in the British navy, commanding flotilla on Lake Champlain, viii. 103; his confidence in the superiority of his fleet, 104, 106; brings his fleet into action, 108; killed, 109.
Drayton, John, of South Carolina, i. 151.
Dresden, battle of, vii. 350.
Dreyer, M., Danish minister at Paris, iv. 106, 107.
Drummond, Gordon, lieutenant-general in British army, and governor of Upper Canada, vii. 202; burns Black Rock and Buffalo, 204; his military career, viii. 48, 49; arrives at Fort George, July 25, 1814, 48, 49; reaches Lundy's Lane, 51; his battle at Lundy's Lane, 51–60; his losses, 62; his delays after Lundy's Lane, 67, 68; moves on Fort Erie, 68, 69; censures his troops at Black Rock, 70; assaults Fort Erie, 71–78; censures De Watteville's regiment, 79; his agony of mind, 80; expects a sortie, 84–86; claims victory, 89; retires to Chippawa, 90; his force, 115, 116; returns to Kingston, 118; compared with Pakenham, 381.
Drummond, ———, lieutenant-colonel of the Hundred-and-Fourth British Infantry, leads assault on Fort Erie, viii. 72, 75; killed in the bastion, 78.

278   GENERAL INDEX.

Dry-dock, Jefferson's plan of, i. 428; ii. 77.
Duane, William, editor of the "Aurora," i. 118; his influence in Pennsylvania, ii. 194, 219; opposes Governor McKean, iii. 9; hostile to Gallatin, 210; visits Blennerhassett in prison, iv. 464; his attacks on Gallatin, v. 361, 364; appointed adjutant-general, vii. 41.
Dudley, William, colonel of Kentucky militia, killed at the Maumee Rapids, vii. 105, 106.
Dunbaugh, ———, sergeant permitted to join Burr, iii. 291.
Dundas (see Melville).
Dupiester (see De Pestre).
Duponceau, Peter S., i. 127; ii. 259.
Dupont, de l'Étang, Pierre, French general, ordered to enter Spain, iv. 121, 122; capitulates, 315.
Dupont de Nemours, commissioned by Jefferson to treat unofficially with Bonaparte, i. 411; letter to, ii. 254.
Duroc, Marshal, iii. 386; iv. 123.
Duval, Gabriel, appointed Justice of the Supreme Court, vi. 429.
Duvall, William P., member of Congress from Kentucky, viii. 276.
Dwight, Theodore, i. 101; his attack on democracy, 225; secretary of the Hartford Convention, viii. 293.
Dwight, President Timothy, quoted, i. 21, 23; his travels, 41; describes popular amusements, 49, 56; on the lack of roads in Rhode Island, 64; his poem, "The Conquest of Canaan" cited, 96 *et seq.*; his "Greenfield Hill," 98; value of his Travels, 100, 310.

"EAGLE," 20-gun brig, in Macdonough's squadron on Lake Champlain, viii. 105; in the battle of Plattsburg, 110.

Early, Peter, member of Congress from Georgia, a manager of Chase's impeachment, ii. 228, 230; chairman of the committee on the slave trade, iii. 356; his bill for the sale of slaves captured on a slave-ship, 357, 362.
Eastern Branch of the Potomac, navy yard in, i. 223, 243, 428; "Chesapeake" lies in, iv. 4; navy-yard bridge over, viii. 131; Winder's position beyond, 132, 134; Winder retreats across, 135; protects Washington on the eastern side, 138; extends to Bladensburg, 139; ships burned in, 145.
Easton, Judge, writes concerning Wilkinson's connection with Miranda, iii. 241.
Eastport in Maine, claimed and occupied by Great Britain, viii. 94, 95.
Eaton, William, his character and career, ii. 429; consul at Tunis, 430; his interviews with Jefferson and the Cabinet, 431; attacks Derne, 433; Burr reveals his plot to, iii. 239; attempts to put Jefferson on his guard, 242, 244, 279, 462.
Eckford, Henry, naval contractor at Sackett's Harbor, viii. 28, 29.
Education in New England, i. 76, 77; in New York, 110; in New Jersey and Pennsylvania, 129; in Virginia, 136; public, favored by Jefferson, iii. 346.
Eel River Miami Indians, vi. 71, 75.
Effectives, rank-and-file present for duty, vii. 151.
Eldon, Lord, his anecdote of King George's reception of Jackson, envoy to Denmark, iv. 65, 96; defends the Orders in Council, 320; on the differences with America, vii. 18.
Election, presidential, of 1800, i. 152, 163; of 1801, 294; ii. 202; in New

England, of 1802, i. 308, 329, 330; State, of 1803, ii. 76; in Massachusetts, May, 1804, 163; in New York, April, 1804, 176, 185; in Pennsylvania, in 1804, 196-200; presidential, of 1804, 201. 202, 204; iii. 8; of April, 1805, in Massachusetts, 9; autumn of 1805, in Pennsylvania, 9; of April, 1806, in Massachusetts, 207; of April, 1807, in Massachusetts, iv. 146; of April, 1808, in Massachusetts, 237-242; of May, 1808, in New York, 283, presidential, of 1808, 285-287; of October, 1808, in Pennsylvania, 286; congressional, of 1808, 287; State, in 1809, v. 12, 13, 158; in 1810, 215, 316; in Massachusetts in April, 1811, vi. 115; in April, 1812, 204; in May, 1812, 209; in New York, May, 1812, 209; presidential, of 1812, 409, 410, 412-414; in the spring of 1813, vii. 49, 51; in the autumn of 1813, 366; in the spring of 1814, viii. 9-13; congressional in November, 1814, 228, 238, 288, 289; of April, 1815, ix. 92, 93; of April, 1816, 132, 133; presidential of 1816, 139.
Electoral College in 1808 and 1812, vi. 413.
Elk River, Cockburn's operations in, vii. 266.
Elliott, Jesse D., lieutenant U. S. navy, vi. 344; cuts out British vessels at Fort Erie, 347; commander in U. S. Navy, commands "Niagara," in Perry's squadron, vii. 120; fails to close with the enemy, 122; Perry's, Barclay's, and Yarnall's remarks on, 123-126; dispute about, 126.
Ellsworth, Oliver, chief-justice, sent to France as envoy extraordinary, vii. 43.
Embargo of March 26, 1794, ii. 323.
Embargo, suggested by Armstrong, in 1805, against Spain, iii. 40; approved by Madison, 75; favored by Senator Jackson in 1805, 149; by John Randolph, 149.
Embargo of Dec. 22, 1807, Jefferson's first draft of message, iv. 168; Madison's draft, 169, 170; bill reported and passed in Senate, 172, 173; moved by Randolph in House, 173; becomes law, Dec. 22, 1807, 175, 176; object of, 175, 176, 186, 332; Senator Adams's resolution on, 187; Jefferson's determination to enforce, 249-271. 273: difficulties of Governor Sullivan regarding, 253-256; difficulties of Governor Tompkins in New York, 259; dissatisfaction of Robert Smith with, 261; demand of "powers equally dangerous and odious" by Gallatin, 262; interference of Justice Johnson in South Carolina, 263, 264; arguments on constitutionality of, 266, 267; decision of Judge John Davis, 268-270; opinion of Joseph Story on, 270; its economical cost, 274. 275; its moral cost, 276; its political cost, 277-284, 288; its failure to coerce, 288, 344; Jefferson's opinion of its relative prejudice to England and France, 309; Jefferson's opinion of its cost, 309, 462; approved by Napoleon, 313; Armstrong's opinion of, 314; its pressure on England, 324, 327-329; Canning's note on, 334-336; W. C. Nicholas's letter on, 345; the alternative to war, 354, 355: repeal of, 438; v. 33; Turreau's complaints of repeal, 34, 35, 37; Canning's note on, 42; revocation of orders attributed to, 75, 77; John Taylor's explanation of repeal, 195, 196; approved by Napoleon, 254; causes France to lose her colonies, 254; its effect on the northwestern Indians, vi. 83.

280 GENERAL INDEX.

Embargo for sixty days, recommended by the President, March 31, 1812, vi. 193, 194, 195, 197, 198; Foster's report on, 199; act passed by Congress, April 4, 1812, 201, 202.

Embargo, of Dec. 17, 1813, rejected by the Senate, vii. 70, 71; recommended by the President, December 9, 367, 368; adopted by Congress, 369; repeal recommended by Madison, March 31, 1814, 373; debate on, 374–377; repealed, 378, 379; viii. 11; effect of, on the currency, vii. 387, 388; effect of, on the elections, viii. 10, 11; on Massachusetts, 14.

"Embargo, The," a satire, by William Cullen Bryant, iv. 279.

Emerson, Ralph Waldo, i. 171, ix. 202, 206.

Emerson, Rev. William, ix. 202.

"Emmanuel," case of, ii. 327.

Emuckfaw, Andrew Jackson's campaign against, vii. 246, 248.

"Endymion," 50-gun British frigate, boats beaten off by the "Prince of Neufchatel," viii. 207-210; her action with the "President," ix. 64-70

Enforcement Act (see Embargo and Acts of Congress).

Engineers. Corps of, established at West Point, i. 301; services of, in the war, ix. 235, 236. (See Walker Keith Armistead, David Bates Douglass, William McRee, Joseph Gilbert Totten, Eleazer Derby Wood.)

England, colonial policy of, ii. 317-332; difficulty with, arising from desertion of seamen, 332–335; her practice of impressment, 335–339; friendly attitude of, in 1801, 339–341; Jefferson's professions of liberality toward, 342–344; outstanding discussions with, 345, 346; cordiality with, 347, 358; change of tone toward, 356, 380, 382, 387; cordial friendship with, iii. 8; change of policy by Pitt in 1804-1805, 43–53 (see Pitt, Perceval, Canning); alliance with, urged by Jefferson, 62–65, 70; Pitt's policy reversed by Fox, 393, 397; unfriendly policy carried to an extreme by Perceval and Canning, iv. 55 *et seq.*; unfriendly feeling in 1808, 331; financial dangers of, in 1809, v. 46, 47; political decline of, 57, 58; distress of, in 1811, vi. 2; apathy of, upon American questions, 24; change of tone between 1807 and 1812, 225, 270, 286; war declared against, 228, 229; distress of, in 1812, 268; attitude toward the war, 405; slow to accept war with United States, vii. 2; sensitive on right of impressment, 3; in consternation at the loss of the "Guerriere," 5–7, 24; angry with United States, 7, 8, 10, 15; her naturalization acts, 21–23; *quasi* blockade of, in 1813, 332, 333; her exultation at Napoleon's overthrow, 356; her indifference in 1813 to the American war, 357–359; her demands at Ghent, viii. 267, 268; her intentions at New Orleans, 313, 314; intoxication of, in the spring of 1814, ix. 1-5, 9; conditions of peace required by, 7–10, 17–20; her reception of the Treaty of Ghent, 54–56.

Enotachopco Creek, Jackson's rout at, vii. 246-248.

"Enterprise," Mississippi steamboat, viii. 341.

"Enterprise," Salem privateer, captured, vii. 329.

"Enterprise," sloop-of-war, captures Tripolitan corsair, i. 245; captures the "Boxer," vii. 281, 282, 312, 313; escapes capture, viii. 193.

"Epervier," British 18-gun sloop-of-war, viii. 182; captured by "Peacock," 182, 184; brought into Savannah, 184.

Eppes, John W., member of Congress from Virginia, ii. 95; opposes suspension of habeas corpus, iii. 339; opposes fortifications, 351; opposes increase of army, iv. 211; supports increase of army, 217; opposes submission to England, 451; chairman of Committee of Ways and Means in Eleventh Congress, v. 76; his appropriation bills for 1810, 200; his bill for reviving non-intercourse against Great Britain, 338; maintains doctrine of contract with France, 341; waits arrival of Serurier, 345; amends his non-intercourse bill, 351, quarrels with John Randolph, 352; defeats John Randolph for Congress, vii. 51; chairman of Ways and Means committee, 53; defeated for the Fourteenth Congress by Randolph, viii. 239; his treasury-note scheme, 247-249; silent about legal tender, 248, 254; reports treasury-note bill, 254; favors doubling taxes, 255; Ticknor's report of his remark to Gaston, 262; moves to reduce term of military service, 279; defeated for the Fourteenth Congress, ix. 93.

Erie Canal, i. 112; ix. 168, 169.

Erie, Fort (see Fort Erie).

Erie, Lake, armaments on, vi. 296, 304, 317, 344; Perry's victory on, vii. 115-129.

Erskine, Lord Chancellor, iii. 393; his speech against the Orders in Council, iv. 320; on the American war, vii. 18.

Erskine, David Montague, succeeds Merry as British minister at Washington, iii. 250, 423; takes Monroe's treaty to Madison, 429; at the White House, iv. 35, 36; his reports on the "Chesapeake" excitement, 37, 78, 142, 143; reports intended commercial restrictions, 144; reports Jefferson's conversation on the "Chesapeake" negotiation, December, 1807, 162; reports an embargo to be imposed in expectation of a retaliatory Order in Council declaring a blockade of France, 175, 176, 332; accompanies Rose to Madison, 193; reported by Rose, 199; interview with Jefferson, Nov. 9, 1808, 351-353; reports the opinion of members of Jefferson's cabinet on the situation in November, 1808, 384; informs Canning of the warlike attitude of the government, 386; reports Gallatin's remarks as to foreign relations, 389; advises Canning that war is imminent, 392, 393; reports Madison for war, 394; his account of the struggle for the repeal of the embargo, 443 *et seq.*; his report, March 17, 1809, of Turreau's anger at the repeal of embargo, v. 34, 35; his threatening despatches of November and December, 1808, 49, 50; his instructions of Jan. 23, 1809, 52-57, 66, 70-72, 90, 94, 111; his reasons for exceeding instructions, 67, 70. 94; his settlement of the "Chesapeake affair," 67, 68; his "Chesapeake" settlement disavowed by Canning, 88, 89; his settlement of commercial disputes, 70-73; his commercial arrangement received in England, 87; disavowed, 90, 95; his explanation of the Order of April 26, 1809, 82, 83; his reply to Canning's criticisms, 94; his recall, 95; effect of his disavowal in the United States, 109; Jackson's opinion of, 119, 120; his farewell audience, 120; effect of his arrangement on Napoleon, 139, 140, 141; comparison between his pledges and those of Champagny, 301.

Erying, George W., as chargé d'affaires replaces Pinckney at Madrid, iii. 37. 377, 388

Erwin, Dr., iii. 263, 265.

"Espiègle," British sloop-of-war, vii 289. 290.

Essex county in Massachusetts, declaration of meeting, July 21, 1812, vi. 402.

Essex Junto, the, i. 89, 314; iv. 29, 401, 403, 405, 412. 442, 462.

"Essex," Sir William Scott's judgment in the case of, iii. 44, 45; received in the United States, 96, 97; Madison's remarks on, reported by Merry, 98; remarks of "a confidential person," 99; effect of, in America, 143; Boston memorial against, 144; Philadelphia and Baltimore memorials. 144.

"Essex," 32-gun frigate, her action with the "Alert," vi. 35, 377; arrives with despatches, 52, 56; sails in July, 1812, 377; returns to port, 378; in the Pacific. vii. 287, 311; viii. 175-177; her force, 178; blockaded at Valparaiso, 179; tries to run the blockade, 179; driven back and captured, 179, 180.

Etiquette at Washington, ii. 362 et seq., 380.

Eustis, Dr. William, member of Congress from Boston, i. 93, 281; his opinion on the political rights of the people of Louisiana, ii. 123, 124; appointed Secretary of War, v. 9; orders Wilkinson not to camp at Terre aux Bœufs, 172, 174; authorizes Harrison to buy Indian land in the Wabash valley, vi. 82; approves Harrison's purchase, 85; orders Harrison to preserve peace with Indians, 88, 93; orders the Fourth Regiment to Indiana, 92. 93; his lost letter of Sept. 18, 1811, to Harrison, 95; appears before the Committee of Foreign Relations, 129; his supposed incompetence, 168, 206. 392, 395, 396, 397, 398; his duties in 1812, 168; on recruiting, 294; his letters to William Hull, announcing war. 290; and ordering conquests in Canada, 302, his orders to Dearborn to repair to Albany, 306, 308, 309; and to take direction of militia at Niagara, 310, 321, 340; resigns, 422; vii. 81, orders out fifteen hundred Tennessee militia for service in Florida, 206

Evans, Oliver, his inventions, i. 68, 71, 182; his experiments with a stern-wheel steamboat, iii. 217.

Evans, Samuel, captain in U. S. navy, commands "Chesapeake," vii. 291.

"Evening Post," the New York, i. 119, 120; ii. 366; Gardenier's supposed letter in, iv. 203.

"Evening Star," London newspaper, on American frigates, vii. 2.

Everett, Edward, ix. 206.

Exchange, turn of, against England, in 1808, v. 47; rates of internal in the United States, 1814-1815, viii. 214; ix. 127, 128; favorable turn of foreign, in 1816. 126, 127.

"Experiment," Albany packet, i. 6.

Exports and Imports in 1800, i. 27. in 1815, ix. 92, 94-96; in 1816, 126; in Massachusetts, 159; in Virginia, 161, 162; in New York and Pennsylvania, 166, 167.

Eylau, the battle of, iv. 62, 105.

FAGAN, ———, agent of Fouché, v. 239.

GENERAL INDEX. 283

Fanning, Alexander C. W., captain of artillery at Fort Erie, viii. 71.
"Fantome," British sloop-of-war, vii 266.
Faragut, David Glasgow, midshipman in U. S. navy, his criticism on Captain Porter, viii. 179.
Faussett, Robert, lieutenant of the British seventy-four "Plantagenet," his affidavit about the "General Armstrong." viii. 203, 204.
"Favorite," British sloop-of-war, arrives at New York with treaty from Ghent, ix. 56, 57.
Fayal, destruction of the "General Armstrong" at, viii. 201-207.
"Federal Republican," Baltimore newspaper, mobbed, vi. 406, 407; of Jan. 28, 1815, on the impossibility that government should stand, viii. 310.
Federalists (see Party).
Fenwick, John R., lieutenant-colonel of Light Artillery, vi. 352.
Ferdinand, Prince of the Asturias (Ferdinand VII.), iv. 290; intrigues against his father, 291; described by Napoleon, 299; proposed kingdom for, in America, v. 239; cedes Florida by treaty of 1819, vi. 236.
Fernandina in East Florida, seized by United States, vi. 240; occupation disavowed and maintained, 242, 243; vii. 206; evacuated, 210, 211.
Ferrand, French general, protests against the contraband trade with St. Domingo, iii. 88.
Fight, the "rough-and-tumble," in the South, i. 52 *et seq.*
Finances, national, in 1801, i. 239 *et seq.*; average annual expenditure, 253; repeal of internal taxes, 270, 272; in 1802, ii. 75, 77; in 1803, 135, 136, 141 (see Mediterranean Fund); in 1804, 206; in 1805, iii. 12, 18; in 1806, 210, 345; in 1807, iv. 148, 156; in 1808, 366; in 1809, v. 163, 178; customs-revenue in 1807, 1808, 1809, 1810, 290, 319; military and naval appropriations of the Eleventh Congress, 257; in 1811, vi. 126; Gallatin's estimates for war, 156-159; war-taxes proposed by Gallatin, 166; approved by the House, 166, 167; laid aside, 167, 168; in 1812, 432, 433; in 1813, 438-448; in 1813, mentioned in annual message, vii. 365; condition of, 385-390, 394; in 1814, viii. 17-19, 213 215; mentioned in annual message, 240; Campbell's annual report on, 240-242; Dallas's account of, in November, 1814, 244. 252; Dallas's account of, in December, 1814, 254; Dallas's account of, in January, 1815, 261, 262; Monroe's account of, in January. 1815, 283; the "Federal Republican's" account of, Jan. 28, 1815, 310; Dallas's sketch of, for the first year of peace, ix. 84; condition of, after the peace, 90, 91, 98-103; Lowndes's report on, January, 1816. 112; Dallas's sketch of, in October, 1816, 140. (See Gallatin, Jones, Campbell, Dallas, Taxes, Loans, Treasury Notes.)
Findlay, James, colonel of Ohio volunteers, vi. 298, 315, 326.
Findley, William, member of Congress from Pennsylvania, favors war, vi. 145; in the Fourteenth Congress, ix. 144.
Finnis, Captain R., of the Royal Navy, commands British squadron on Lake Erie, vii. 116, 118, commands the "Queen Charlotte" in action, 120.
Fischer, British lieutenant-colonel in De Watteville's regiment, leads assault on Snake Hill at Fort Erie, viii. 72-75.

Fisheries, England's wish to exclude the United States from, viii. 4, 268, 287; Governor Strong's views on, 287, 288, to be interdicted to the United States, ix. 6; Newfoundland memorial on, 8; Castlereagh's instructions of July 28 on, 10, 12, 37; discussed by the British commissioners, at Ghent, 18; question of, under the treaty of 1783, 44–50; Adams's struggle for, 45–50; Gallatin's championship of, 46–50; Clay's indifference to, 46–50; British silence regarding, 47; British offer to reserve right, 49; Gallatin's offer regarding, 50; omission of, in the Treaty of Ghent, ix. 52.

Fitch, John, his inventions, i. 66 *et seq.*, 181.

Fletcher against Peck, Marshall's decision in case of, ix. 189, 190.

Florida restored by England to Spain in 1783, i. 353; cession of, asked by Bonaparte in 1800, 367, 413; Bonaparte's demand for, refused by Charles IV., 369; Bonaparte's attempts to secure, 401; Godoy's reasons for refusing Bonaparte's request, 402; cession of, asked by Jefferson, 410, 411, 424, 432, 433, 438; Monroe authorized to buy from France, 442; Livingston's attempt to secure, ii. 44 (see Florida, West); Napoleon's retention of, v. 32, 33; Napoleon insinuates an idea regarding, 408; Foster instructed to protest against the seizure of, vi. 23; his protest, 37; Monroe's reception of the protest, 38, 39; Madison's designs on, vii. 32, 206-209; Russian influence on, 211; supposed sale to England, 212, 213; a southern object, 213, viii. 318; in the negotiation at Ghent, ix. 29, 30.

Florida, East, Madison asks authority to occupy, v. 326, 327; Congress authorizes occupation of, 327; commissioners sent to take possession of, 327; revolutionized, vi. 237–243; bill for occupation of, 243; occupation continued, vii. 206; bill for the seizure of, 208; bill amended, 209; troops withdrawn from, 210, 211.

Florida, West, possession of, necessary for the West, i. 438, 442; not a part of the territory retroceded by Spain to France, ii. 7, 13; claimed by Livingston as part of the Louisiana purchase, 68; Jefferson's anxiety to secure, 245; scheme for seizing, 255; not claimed at the delivery of Louisiana, 256; Randolph's Mobile Act, asserting jurisdiction over, 257, 258, 260-263; claim to, 273, 311, 312; claim adopted by the President, 302; desire of the southern people to acquire, iii. 22; negotiation for, in 1805, 23-37 (see Monroe); Madison's opinion of claim to, 55, 56; not to be turned into a French job, 70, 77; Cabinet decides to offer five millions for, 78; Talleyrand's plan for obtaining, 103; Talleyrand's plan adopted by Jefferson, 106; opposed in Congress, 133 *et seq.*; passage of Two-Million Act for purchasing, 138; Burr's designs upon, 232, 234; source of Talleyrand's plan, 373; Napoleon's attitude, 374, 375; Madison's instructions, 375; Napoleon's defeat of Talleyrand's plan, 376-385, 424, 428; iv. 114; Turreau's views on, iii. 426; American occupation invited by Napoleon iv. 293, 294, 296, 297, 307; invitation acknowledged by Madison, 306; invitation denied by Napoleon, 311; seizure of, intended by Jefferson, 340; revolution in, v. 307-315; Madison orders occupation of, 310-312, 318; Claiborne takes possession of, 313; organized as part of Orleans Territory, 314; protest of British *chargé*, 314, 315; Giles's bill for annexing to Orleans Territory, 320; debate on annexation, 320-323; Macon's bill, admitting, as a part of Louisiana, 323, 324; remains a separate territory, 326; divided by act of Congress, vi. 236; ceded by Spain in 1819, 237. (See Mobile.)

Flour, price of, its effect in repealing the embargo, v. 196; affected by the blockade, vii. 263; affected by peace, ix. 61.

Flournoy, Thomas, brigadier-general, in U. S. army, succeeds Wilkinson at New Orleans, vii. 243.

Floyd, John, brigadier-general of Georgia militia, his campaign to Autossee, vii. 242, 243: his battle at Calibee Creek, 249. 250.

Folch, Governor, of West Florida, iii. 262, 300.

Fontaine, John, lieutenant of artillery in Fort Erie, viii. 76.

Fontainebleau, treaty of, iv. 120.

Forfeitures under the Non-importation Act, vi. 436-443.

Forrest, C. R., major of the British Thirty-Fourth Infantry, Assistant Quarter-Master General before New Orleans, his account of the British batteries, viii. 360, 365; his account of the canal, 374, 375.

Forsyth, Benjamin, major in U. S. Rifle Regiment, vii. 147.

Forsyth, John, member of Congress from Georgia, vii. 53; on bank committee, viii. 252; objects to economy, ix. 85: in the Fourteenth Congress, 107; supports the bank, 117; his remarks on the Compensation Bill, 121.

Fort Barrancas at Pensacola, occupied by British expedition, viii 320; evacuated and blown up, 329

Fort Bowyer, on Mobile Point, constructed by Wilkinson, vii. 215; occupied by Jackson, viii. 319, 322; attacked by British sl ops-of-war, 322-325; captured, 383-385.

Fort Dearborn, Chicago, vi 110, 294, garrison massacred, 334.

Fort Erie, vi. 343, 347, 348, 358; evacuated by British, vii. 117, 159; re-occupied by Drummond, 202; Brown ordered to attack, viii. 33; British garrison at, 38; captured by Brown, 39; Ripley's retreat to, 66; entrenched American camp at, 67, 70, 71; ix. 235; Drummond's repulse at, viii. 71-80; strength of army at, 68, 69, 83; Brown's sortie from, 84-89; Drummond retires from, 89, 90; abandoned and blown up by Izard, 116, 118; in the negotiation at Ghent, ix. 34, 35.

Fort George, vi. 300, 343, 347; vii. 153; Brock's headquarters, vi. 341, 348, 349, 351; captured by Dearborn, vii. 157, 158; held by McClure, 200, 201; evacuated, 202; Riall's headquarters, viii. 38; Brown unable to attack, 45-47.

Fort Harrison, vi. 95, 106, 294; attacked by Indians, vii. 72, 73.

Fort Massac, iii. 222, 284, 290-292.

Fort McHenry, at Baltimore, strength of, viii. 166; bombardment of, 171, 172.

Fort Meigs, constructed in February, 1813, vii. 93, 99, 101; besieged by Proctor. 104-107; siege abandoned, 108; threatened by Proctor, 109.

Fort Mims, surprise and massacre of, vii. 229-231.

Fort Niagara, bombarded, vi. 355; captured by Drummond, vii. 202, 203, 205; British garrison at, viii. 38; cession required, ix. 10, 34.

Fort St. Philip, below New Orleans, viii. 335; bombarded, 383.
Fort Schlosser, on the Niagara River, Brown's base of supplies, viii. 49.
Fort Stephenson, Croghan's defence of, vii. 110–114.
Fort Stoddert, iii. 327; vii. 243.
Fort Strother, on the Coosa, Jackson's base, vii. 238, 239, 240, 245.
Fort Sullivan, at Eastport, Maine, capitulates, viii 94.
Fort Washington (or Warburton), on the Potomac, vii. 56; viii. 120, 137, 138; abandoned, 157.
Fort Wayne, vii. 72.
Fortifications, iii. 179; opposed by southern republicans, 350; appropriation for, in 1809, v. 85; appropriation asked in 1810, 319.
Foster, Augustus John, his description of Jefferson, i. 186; of Madison, 190; appointed British minister to the United States, vi. 16, 21; F. J. Jackson's opinion of, 22; his instructions, 22, 23; arrives at Washington, 37, 52; protests against the seizure of Florida, 37; reports Monroe's language about Spanish America, 38; protests against the non-importation, 39; narrows the issue to Fox's blockade and the Orders in Council, 40, 41; reports Monroe's language on the revocation of the French decrees, 42; threatens retaliation for the non-importation, 44; reports that the Orders in Council are the single object of irritation, 45; settles the "Chesapeake affair," 121, 122; his report of executive temper in November, 1811, 131; his report of Gallatin's language about taxes, 156; his report of the conduct of Federalists in Congress, 172–175; receives instructions, March 21, 1812, 191; communicates them, 192; his report of Monroe's remarks on recent French spoliations, 195, 198; his report of Madison's and Monroe's remarks on the embargo of April, 1812, 199; suggests Madison's reelection, 213; on the American people, vii. 15; his Florida protest, 32.
Fouché, Joseph, Duc d'Otrante, Napoleon's minister of police, v. 222; opposes Napoleon's commercial system, 224; sends an agent to the British government, 238, 239; disgraced and exiled, 241.
"Fox," privateer, in British waters, vii. 332.
Fox, Charles James, ii. 418; accession of, to Foreign Office, iii. 163, 211; recalls Merry, and refuses to listen to Burr's schemes, 250; opens negotiations with Monroe, 394; his blockade, 398; illness of, 406; death of, 407.
France, cause of her influence over the Union, i. 337; her course in 1795, 350; her colonial aspirations, 353; obtains cession of Spanish St. Domingo in 1795, 354; seeks to recover Louisiana in 1797, 354; asks for Louisiana and the Floridas in 1798, 357; makes peace with foreign powers in 1800, 360–362, 373, 374; asks again for Louisiana, 364; and for the Floridas, 368; obtains Louisiana, 369, 370 (see Treaties); her old colonial system, 377–380; loses St. Domingo, 380–387; her attempt to recover St. Domingo, 390–398, 414, 415; her pledge not to alienate Louisiana, 400; presses to obtain the Floridas, 401, 402; Jefferson's first cordiality toward, 404; Jefferson's threats toward, 406–411; Jefferson's forbearance toward, 423–425, 427–446; her intentions regarding Louisiana, ii, 4–12 (see Napoleon, Louisiana, Florida); perfect understanding

GENERAL INDEX. 287

with, iii. 8; Jefferson's alarm at the conduct of, 58-75; her dictatorial tone in 1805, 82-90 (see Decrees); alienation between United States and, v. 28-41, 141-151; difficulties of commerce with, 152, 245: value of spoliations in 1809, 1810, 242, 243; contract with, 339, 340; unfriendly language of the annual message toward, vi. 125; Madison's language regarding, 187, 218, 224; theory of contract with, apparently abandoned, 223; Monroe's language regarding, 232; Napoleon driven back into, vii. 370; invaded, 373, 393, 395. (See Livingston, Armstrong, Barlow, Madison, Monroe, Talleyrand, Champagny, Maret.)

Franklin, Benjamin, i. 60 *et seq.*. 181; citation from Poor Richard, 44.

Franklin, Jesse, senator from North Carolina, vii. 49.

Freeman, Constant, lieutenant-colonel of Artillery, in command at New Orleans, warned by Wilkinson, iii. 314, 315.

Fremantle, Colonel, letter on the situation of Parliament, v. 58.

French Mills, Wilkinson's winter quarters, vii. 199; viii. 24.

French spoliations (see Spoliations. French).

Frenchtown, in Maryland, Cockburn's attack on, vii. 266.

Frenchtown, on the river Raisin, vii. 88. (See Raisin.)

Freneau, Philip, i. 125.

Frere, John Hookham, i. 402.

Friedland, the battle of, iv. 62, 105.

Frigates, American, effect of their captures on England, vii. 5-7, 9, 13-16. 24; cost of, 310; efficiency of, compared with sloops-of-war, 310-312; six new, ordered to be built, 313; their record in 1814, viii. 174-181. (See Navy, "President," "Constitution," "United States," "Chesapeake," "Congress," "Constellation," "Essex," and "Adams.")

"Frolic," American sloop of-war, built in 1813, vii. 313; sails in February, 1814, and is captured April 20 viii. 181.

"Frolic," British sloop-of-war, vi. 379; her action with the "Wasp," 380.

Fugitive-Slave Bill, i. 300.

Fulton, Robert, i. 69, 182; Justice Story's account of, 71; his steamboat, iii. 20. 216; iv. 135; his torpedo, v. 209; his inventions, ix. 236. (See Steamboat.)

GAILLARD, JOHN, senator from South Carolina, ii. 238.

Gaines, Edmund Pendleton, first lieutenant of Second Infantry, commanding at Fort Stoddert, arrests Burr, iii. 327; promoted to brigadier, vii. 409; corrects Brown, viii. 28; takes command at Fort Erie, 67; his force, 73; repulses Drummond's assault, 74-80; wounded, relinquishes command, 82; ordered to Mobile, 331; remains brigadier on peace establishment, ix. 88.

Gallatin, Albert, his opinion of the Connecticut River district, i. 19; on Indian corn. 58; his political doctrines, 72, 115 *et seq.*, 163, 177; personal characteristics of, 190; appointed Secretary of the Treasury, 218; supports M. L. Davis, 232; opposes removals from office, 235; ii. 194; his financial measures of 1801, i. 239; his financial schemes adopted, 272; inserts school and road contract into the law admitting Ohio, 302; Yazoo commissioner, 304-306; underestimates the product of the taxes, ii. 75; his opinion on the acquisition of territory, 79, 131; success of the Treasury Department under, 135; asks Congress for a special tax for the Barbary war, 141, 261; attacked by Duane, 194, 196; by Eaton, 431; remonstrates with Jefferson against allusions to New England in second Inaugural, iii. 6; his policy of internal improvements, 18; iv. 364; his view of Monroe's negotiation with Spain, iii. 65; opposes the idea of war, 67; opposes the offer of five millions for Florida, 78; criticises the draft of Annual Message, November, 1805, 114; success of his financial management, 210; his policy of discharging public debt, 345; his hostility to slavery, 362; prepares for war with England, iv. 32 et seq.; his success with the treasury, 148; modifies Jefferson's Annual Message of 1807, 150; his report Nov. 5, 1807, 156; abandons his dogma against national debt, 157; opposed to Jefferson's gunboat policy, 158, his letter advising that the embargo should be limited as to time, 170; talks freely with Rose, 197; asserts that war is inevitable unless the Orders in Council are repealed, 198; enforces the embargo, 253; requires arbitrary powers to enforce the embargo, 261; thinks the result of the election doubtful, 284; urges Jefferson to decide between embargo and war, 355; his annual report of 1808, 365-367; favors war, 368; his plan, 369, 432; writes "Campbell's Report," 370, 371; his attitude as represented by Erskine, 385; suggests settlement to Erskine, 387, 388; Erskine's report of his conversation, 390; disavows Erskine's report, 391; his legislation to enforce the embargo, 398; presses his measures, 420; defeats bill for employing navy, 425, 426; his analysis of the navy coalition, 428; intended by Madison for Secretary of State, 429; opposed by Giles, 429, 430; his efforts to maintain discipline, 440; explains the Non-intercourse Act to Erskine, 445; his appointment as Secretary of State defeated, v. 4-8; his quarrel with Samuel Smith, 10; his conversation with Turreau about the Floridas, 38, 39; his remarks to Turreau on renewing intercourse with Great Britain, 74; his letters on Erskine's disavowal, 110, 111; his expectations from Jackson's mission, 110, 116, 117; his feud with Giles, Smith, and Leib, 159; his letter of remonstrance to Jefferson, 160, 161, 164; his enemies, 167; his annual report of 1809, 178; his bill for excluding British and French ships, 183 (see Macon); his remarks on Napoleon's secret confiscations, 259; his remarks to Turreau on revival of non-intercourse against England, 303; gives notice of revival of non-intercourse against England, 304; his annual report of 1810, 319; his dependence on the bank, 329, 335; asks an increase of duties, 357; his letter of resignation, 360-366; Serurier's estimate of, vi. 46; his annual report of November, 1811, 126; attacked by Giles, 148, 149; delays his estimates, 156; his war-taxes, 156-159, 165, 166, 204; his war-taxes reported June 26, 235; his loan of 1812, 206, 207; believed to think war unnecessary, 225; complains of Congress, 234, 235; reports tax-bills to Congress, 235; his instructions at the out-

GENERAL INDEX. 289

break of war, 301; his opinion of Eustis, 397, 398; claims department of State, 424; his annual report of Dec. 5, 1812, 433, 438; his views on the forfeiture of merchandise imported in 1812, 439, 440; his attitude toward war-taxation, 446; offended by Duane's appointment, vii. 41; asks to go as peace commissioner to Russia, 42; regards his separation from the Treasury as final, 43; negotiates loan of 1813, 44; settles financial arrangements for the year, 45; sails for Russia, 46; on the incapacity of government, 52; his name sent to the Senate as envoy, 59; his nomination rejected, 60, 355; remonstrates against the seizure of Mobile, 212, 213; objects to special legislation for privateers, 336; arrives at St. Petersburg, 339, 347; writes to Baring, 343; obliged to remain idle at St Petersburg, 348, 349; leaves St. Petersburg and arrives in London, 355, 363; nominated and confirmed as joint envoy to Ghent, 371; his estimate of bank capital, currency, and specie in 1814, 387–389; effect of his letters on the President, viii. 121; Dallas's opinion of, 244; remains in London until June 21, 1814, ix. 1; has interview with the Czar June 17, 8; writes despatch of June 13, 8, 9; his position and authority among the negotiators, 14, 15; abandons hope of peace, 22; takes control of the commission, 28, 29; on the Florida policy, 30; accepts the Indian article, 32; learns Prevost's defeat, 37; becomes champion of the fisheries, 46, 48, 50, Adams's opinion of, 51; his opinion of Adams, 51; appointed minister to France, 89; declines the Treasury, 124, 125, 141.

Gambier, Lord, commands the Copenhagen expedition, iv. 63; bombards Copenhagen, 65; appointed chief British commissioner at Ghent, ix. 13, 14.
Gardenier, Barent, member of Congress from New York, iv. 147; attacks the Supplementary Embargo Bill, 201; his duel with G. W. Campbell, 203; his views on Campbell's Report, 375, 447; his remarks on Jefferson and Madison, v. 79, 80; supports Macon's bill, 185; cause of changing rule of previous question, 353.
Gardiner, John Sylvester John, president of the Anthology Club, ix. 202.
Gaston, William, member of Congress from North Carolina, his reply to Eppes, viii. 262.
Gaudin, Duc de Gaete, orders of, v. 348.
Gelston, Daniel, i. 231.
"General Armstrong," New York privateer brig, vii. 316; escapes the "Coquette," 326; destroyed at Fayal, viii. 201-207.
George III., King of England, character of, i. 342; Eldon's anecdote of, iv. 65; becomes insane, v. 288; vi. 2.
George, Prince of Wales, his Whig associations, vi. 3, 4; becomes Prince Regent, Feb. 6, 1811, 14; retains Spencer Perceval's ministry, 14; his audience of leave for William Pinkney, 16, 18-20; his conditional declaration of April 21, 1812, that the Orders in Council should be withdrawn, 254, 282; his opinion of Major-General Proctor, vii. 93. 94, approves conduct of Major-General Ross, viii. 314
Georgia, State of, in 1800, i. 4, 39; surrenders territory to the United

290 GENERAL INDEX.

States, 303; land speculation in, 303; Rescinding Act, 304; relations with Creek Indians, vii. 218, 219; share in the Creek war, 234, 235; militia campaigns of Floyd, 241-243, 249, 250; militia fail to deal with the Creeks, viii. 219; regular troops in, 316, 317; agitated by British invasion, ix. 63.

German, Obadiah, senator from New York, vii. 48.

Gerry, Elbridge, i. 358; presides over a "Chesapeake" meeting in Boston, iv. 29; elected governor of Massachusetts in 1810 and 1811, v. 215; vi. 115; defeated in 1812, 204; nominated for the Vice-Presidency, 214; elected, 413.

"Gershom," American brig, burned by French squadron, vi. 193, 198.

Ghent, despatches dated Aug. 20, 1814, arrive at Washington from, viii. 267; ix. 23; American commissioners arrive at, ix. 9, 17; first conference at, August 8, 17; second conference at, August 19, 19; despatches of August 20 from, 23; Castlereagh visits, 24; Treaty of, signed December 24, 52; Treaty of, received in England, 54-56; Treaty of, received in America, 57-61; treaty confirmed and ratified, 58, 82; character of treaty, 59; effect of treaty on party politics, 80, 81.

Gholson, Thomas, member of Congress from Virginia, moves new rule of previous question, v. 353.

Gibbs, Sir Samuel, British major-general, appointed second in command of British expedition to New Orleans, viii. 315; commands British right column at the battle of Jan. 8, 1815, 372; attacks and is killed, 375, 381.

Gibson, James, colonel of Fourth Rifles, leads sortie from Fort Erie, viii. 87; killed, 88, 89.

Giles, William Branch, member of Congress from Virginia. i. 209, 261, 267; his political career, 234 *et seq.*; debates the Judiciary Bill, 286 *et seq.*, 299; ii. 142; supports the impeachment of Judge Chase, 221; his view of impeachment, 223, 235, 237, 238, 241; senator from Virginia, iii. 126; introduces a bill to suspend habeas corpus, 338, 340; ready for war, iv. 198; described by Joseph Story, 205; his bill defining treason, 206; his bill conferring power to enforce the embargo, 398; a member of the senatorial cabal hostile to Madison and Gallatin, 428-430; defeats Gallatin's appointment as Secretary of State, v. 4-7; votes for mission to Russia, 11; his report on F. J. Jackson, 178, 179, 182, 183; wishes energy of government, 180, 189; his bill for the annexation of West Florida, 319, 320; his speech on the Bank Charter, 333; his political capacity, 363; reports bill for raising twenty-five thousand troops, vi. 147; his speech attacking Gallatin, 148, 149; his factiousness, 150; his admission of errors, 154; his speech on the volunteer bill, 161; votes for war, 229; votes against occupying East Florida, 243; on seamen's bill, 454; in opposition, vii. 48; votes against Gallatin's appointment to Russia, 59; charged by Monroe with schemes of usurpation, 62; votes against mission to Sweden, 63; no chance of re-election, 399; his bill for drafting eighty thousand militia, viii. 268-280; thinks government cannot stand, 310; resigns seat in Senate, ix. 107.

Gilman, Nicholas, senator from New Hampshire, votes against the Two-Million Bill, iii. 139.

GENERAL INDEX. 291

Girard, Stephen, shares loan of 1813, vii. 44, 45; subscribes for bank-stock, ix. 131.
Gitschin in Bohemia, the Czar's headquarters, vii. 340.
Glasgow, meeting of merchants at, in September, 1814, viii. 198, 199.
Gleig, George R., lieutenant in the British Eighty-fifth Regiment, his account of the capture of Washington, viii. 129, 144; his account of the artillery at New Orleans, 359, 360, 363-366.
Gloucester town-meeting appoints a committee of public safety, iv. 414.
Goddard, Calvin, member of Congress from Connecticut, ii. 160.
Godoy, Don Manuel, Prince of Peace, i. 346 *et seq.*; treaty of 1795 negotiated by, 348, 369, 371; baffles Bonaparte, 374; attempts to conciliate the United States, ii. 21; protests against the sale of Louisiana, 57: conciliates Napoleon, 277; his defiant speech to Erving, iii. 38; offers to accept American advances, 381, 382; opposed to alliance with France, iv. 116, 117, 118, 124; stifles Prince Ferdinand's intrigue, 291; mobbed, 298; described by Napoleon, 299.
Gold, premium in England in 1812, vii. 5. (See Specie.)
Goldsborough, Robert Henry, senator from Maryland, vii. 62, 63; denounces conscription, viii. 273.
Goodrich, Chauncey, senator from Connecticut, iii. 461; iv. 146; delegate to the Hartford Convention, viii. 292, 294.
Goodrich, Elizur, i. 226.
Gordon, Charles, captain in U. S. navy, appointed to command the "Chesapeake," iv. 5: drops down the Potomac, 7; ready for sea, 8; testimony of, 11; prepares for action, 16.

Gordon, James A., captain of British frigate "Seahorse," captures Alexandria, viii. 157, rejoins fleet, 163, 164.
Gore, Christopher, ii. 347; his letter to Pickering on resistance to the embargo, iv. 405; Pickering's reply, 406; elected governor of Massachusetts in 1809, v. 12; invites F. J. Jackson to Boston, 213; defeated in the election of 1810, 215; and in 1811, vi. 115; senator from Massachusetts, his speech on conscription, viii. 272; his letter on State armies, 284, 285; approves report of Hartford Convention, 301; his opinion of the Treaty of Ghent, ix. 59.
Goulburn, Henry, under secretary of state for the colonies, appointed British commissioner at Ghent, ix. 13, 14; presents subjects of discussion, 17; states British demands, 19, 20; reports Bayard's remarks, 22; checked by Castlereagh, 24, 25; anxious for Prevost to move, 27; out of temper, 29, 30, 31; again checked, 31, 32; quite in despair, 36; thinks the fisheries conceded, 47.
"Governor Tompkins," New York privateer schooner, her escape from man-of-war, vii. 327, 328: in the British Channel, viii. 196.
"Grace Ann Greene," American vessel released by Napoleon, v. 391.
Graham, John, sent by Jefferson to inquire into Burr's movements, iii. 280, 281; goes to Chillicothe, 282; to Kentucky, 286; his account of public opinion in Kentucky, vi. 394.
"Grand Turk," privateer, in British waters, vii. 333.
Grandpré, Louis, v. 306, 307.
Granger, Gideon, appointed Postmaster-General, i. 308; an active

politician, ii. 192; agent for the Yazoo claims, 212 ; attacked by Randolph, 213 ; removed from office by Madison, vii. 399-401.
Graydon, Alexander, i. 127.
Great Britain (see England).
Greenleaf's Point (Arsenal), at Washington, viii. 137.
Gregg, Andrew, member of Congress from Pennsylvania, ii. 123; moves a non-importation resolution, iii. 154; the resolution debated, 155-165; the resolution laid aside, 165, 396.
Grégoire, Abbé, i. 105.
Grenville, Lord, ii. 316, 418 ; denounces seizure of Spanish galleons, iii. 46; prime minister, 392, 420; dismissed from office, 421; charges ministers with intending a war with the United States, iv. 70; on Canning, v. 49; on the American government, vii. 10.
Grétry, v. 235.
Grey, Earl (see Howick), denounces seizure of Spanish galleons, iii. 47.
Griswold, Gaylord, member of Congress from New York, on the Louisiana treaty, ii. 96.
Griswold, Roger, member of Congress from Connecticut, i. 269, 299; on the Louisiana treaty, ii. 99. 101 ; on the Vice-Presidency, 133; on the Mediterranean Fund, 142; believes disunion inevitable, 160, 162; his letters to Oliver Wolcott, 162, 169, 180; conference of, with Burr, 183, 390, 391.
Grosvenor, Thomas P., member of Congress from New York, on Webster's bank-bill, viii. 259, 260; in the Fourteenth Congress, ix. 107 ; criticises Webster, 117, 118; on committee for internal improvements, 148.
Grundy, Felix, member of Congress from Tennessee, vi. 122, 137, 196;
on Committee of Foreign Relations, 124, 128; his speech in favor of war, 137-141; favors large army, 152 ; opposes war-power, 161 ; against frigates, 164; on embargo, 201; on the political effects of war, 213; on forfeitures, 443; reports bill for regulation of seamen, 452, 453; on the state of the finances in April, 1813, vii. 390; defeated as Speaker, 396.
"Guerriere," British frigate, vi. 25; "Little Belt" mistaken for, 26-30; Captain Dacres, commander of, 37; joins Broke's squadron, 368; chases "Constitution," 370, captured by "Constitution," 372-375; consternation produced throughout Great Britain by capture of, vii. 5, 6, 24; Captain Dacres on capture of, 7; the "Times" on conduct of, 14; relative loss compared with "Shannon," 299; loss inflicted by, compared with that inflicted by "Cyane" and "Levant," ix. 78, effect of battle of, 229.
Gulf-stream considered by Jefferson as American waters, iii. 129, 405, 424.
Gunboats, arguments for and against, iii. 352; Jefferson's policy adopted by Congress, iv. 158-160; Secretary Hamilton's remarks on, v. 168; attack British frigate "Junon," vii. 270 ; captured on Lake Borgne, viii. 335, 336; ordered to be sold, ix. 87.
Gunnery, naval, of American gunboats in the affair with the British frigate "Junon," vii. 270; of the battery on Craney Island, 274 ; of the "Hornet" and "Peacock," 290; of the "Shannon" and "Chesapeake," 292, 298-301; of the "Argus" and "Pelican," 306-308; superiority of American, 319; viii. 210 ; Michael Scott on, vii.

322; relative superiority at Plattsburg, viii. 106, 109; ix. 234; of the "Peacock" and "Epervier," viii. 183, 184; of the "Wasp" and "Reindeer," 187; of the "Wasp" and "Avon," 190-192; of the "President" and "Endymion," ix. 69, 70; of the "Hornet" and "Penguin," 72, of the "Constitution," "Cyane," and "Levant," 75-78; relative superiority of American, 229-235. (See Artillery.)

HABEAS CORPUS, bill for the suspension of, defeated in Congress, iii. 338, 340.
Halifax, blockaded by privateers in 1814, viii. 194, 195.
"Halifax," British sloop-of-war, desertion of seamen from, iv. 2.
Hall, Basil, i. 164; his account of the practice of the British frigates blockading New York, iii. 92.
Hall, Bolling, member of Congress from Georgia, moves resolutions authorizing issue of legal-tender treasury-notes, viii. 253, 254.
Hall, ———, captain of marines on the "Chesapeake," iv. 11.
Hamilton, Alexander, i. 85, 86, 108, 277; Talleyrand's remark concerning, 352; ii. 168; opposes Burr for governor, 176, 177; not in favor of disunion projects, 184; his opposition to Burr, 185 et seq.; his duel with Burr, 186 et seq.; mourned by the Federalists, 190.
Hamilton, Paul, appointed Secretary of the Navy, v. 9, 206; his orders to Commodore Rodgers of June 9, 1810, vi. 26; of May 6, 1811, 25; his supposed incompetence, 169, 290, 395, 398; his orders to Rodgers, Decatur, and Hull in June, 1812, 363-365, 368; his orders of September, 1812, 378; resigns, 428.
Hammond, George, Under Secretary for Foreign Affairs, v. 45.
Hampshire county-meeting in January, 1809, iv. 410.
Hampton, village of, captured and plundered, vii. 275, 276.
Hampton, Wade, brigadier-general in U. S. army, hostile to Wilkinson, v. 169; takes command at New Orleans, 175; vi. 291; appointed Major-General, vii. 37; sent to Lake Champlain, 174; his hostility to Wilkinson, 175; not under Wilkinson's orders, 175, 176; ordered to prepare winter quarters, 183, 197; his force on Lake Champlain, 192; advances to Chateaugay, 192; reaches Spear's, 193, 194; his force, 196; his check and retreat, 197; offers resignation, 198; falls back to Plattsburg, 199; blamed by Wilkinson and Armstrong, 199, 200; his resignation accepted, 199, 200, 416; fortifies Norfolk, 271; on Hull's court-martial, 415; Armstrong's treatment of, 416.
Hanson, A. C., a victim of the Baltimore riot, vi. 407; on the popularity of the war, vii. 69, 70; his speech, Nov. 28, 1814, on the destitution of government, viii. 252, 253.
Hardin, Benjamin, member of the Fourteenth Congress from Kentucky, moves to repeal the direct tax, ix. 113; on the effect of the Compensation Act, 137.
Hardy, Sir Thomas M., captain in British navy, blockades New York, vii. 278; countenances ship-duels, 286; escorts British expedition to Moose Island, viii. 94.
Harper, Robert Goodloe, ii. 154; one of Chase's counsel, 228, 232; fed-

eralist leader in 1799, vi. 144; senator from Maryland, ix. 108.
"Harpy," privateer, viii. 196.
Harris, Thomas K., member of Congress from Tennessee, on Giles's militia bill, viii. 275.
Harrison, Fort (see Fort Harrison).
Harrison, William Henry, governor of Indiana Territory, his Indian treaty of 1805, iii. 13; appointed governor, in 1800, vi. 68; his account of Indian affairs, 69-73; his treaties of 1804 and 1805, 75, 77; his influence in the dispute about slavery in Indiana, 75-77; his interview with the Prophet in August, 1808, 80; his treaty of Sept. 30, 1809, 83, 84; his interview with Tecumthe of Aug. 12, 1810, 85-88; his letter to Tecumthe, June 24, 1811, 90; his talk with Tecumthe July 27, 1811, 91; instructed to avoid hostilities, 93; raises military forces, 93; sends army up the Wabash valley, 94; constructs Fort Harrison, 95; marches on Tippecanoe, 97; his arrival, 98-100; his camp, 102; attacked, 103; his return to Vincennes, 106; Humphrey Marshall's opinion of, 107; his estimate of the effect of his campaign, 107, 108; appointed by Kentucky to command expedition to recover Detroit, 392, 420; unable to advance, 412; appointed major-general, vii. 37; placed in command by Kentucky, 73, 74; commissioned by the President as brigadier-general, 75; receives *carte blanche*, with no orders but to recover Detroit, 75, 80, 102; his autumn campaign, 75-84; his winter campaign, 84-86, 100, 101; ordered to remain on the defensive, 103; besieged in Fort Meigs, 104-108; attacked at Sandusky, 108-114; his army of invasion, 128; embarks, 129; occupies **Malden**, 131; occupies Sandwich and Detroit, 132; defeats Proctor on the Thames, 137-140; returns to Detroit, 142; sent to Sackett's Harbor, 200; his treaty of peace with Indian tribes, 261; ix. 32; Armstrong's prejudice against, vii. 409; resigns from the army, 410.

Harrowby, Lord, British Foreign Secretary, ii. 418; receives Monroe, 420; instructions as to impressments and the boundary convention, 423 *et seq.*; retires from the Foreign Office, iii. 47.

Hartford Convention (see New England Convention).

"Hartford wits," i. 101.

Harvard College, i. 77, 78, 90; the source of Boston Unitarianism, ix. 176; its influence on Boston, 205, 206.

Hastings, Warren, trial of, ii. 226.

Hauterive, Alexandre Maurice, Comte d', charged with negotiations with Armstrong, v. 140, 141.

Havre de Grace, in Maryland, Cockburn's attack on, vii. 267.

Hawkesbury, Lord (see Liverpool).

Hawkins, Benjamin, Indian agent among the Creeks, vii. 218; satisfied with behavior of Creeks, 220, his report of Tecumthe's address to the Creeks, 221; demands the delivery of Creek murderers, 225; his report on the flight of the Red Sticks, 257, 258.

Hay, George, District Attorney, conducts prosecution of Burr, iii. 445; threatens the court, 466; Monroe's son-in-law, accuses Jefferson of insincerity, iv. 131; his advice to Monroe, vi. 421.

Hayes, John, captain of British 56-gun frigate "Majestic," commanding blockading squadron off New York, intercepts Decatur in the "President," ix. 64.

Head, Sir Francis, ix. 233.

Heath, William, Jefferson's letter to, iii. 8, 9, 58.

Henley, John D., commander in the U. S. navy, his report on the destruction of the "Carolina" at New Orleans, viii. 359.

Henry, John, his letters to H. W. Ryland in March, 1808, iv. 243-248; his letters sent by Sir James Craig to Lord Castlereagh, 246, 248; sent to Boston by Sir James Craig in January, 1809, 460; his reports, 461; his report on disunion, v. 14; recalled, 86; demands money, vi. 176; comes to Boston, 177; employs Crillon to negotiate with Monroe, 178; obtains fifty thousand dollars, 179; sails for Europe, 180; papers of, 182; supposed effect of, in Florida affairs, 241.

Henry, Patrick, i. 143, quoted by Randolph, ix. 110.

"Hermes," 22-gun British sloop-of-war, sent to Pensacola, viii. 319, 322; attacks Fort Bowyer, 323; disabled and burned, 324.

Herrera, General, iii. 300; hostile demonstrations of, 304; movements of, 310.

Hickory Ground, the focus of Creek fanaticism, vii. 234.

Higginson, Stephen, ii. 164.

Hill, Lord, intended to command British expedition to New Orleans, viii. 311.

Hillabee villages, vii. 241, 247.

Hillhouse, James, senator from Connecticut, ii. 160; iv. 146; directs opposition to the embargo, 405; delegate to the Hartford Convention, viii. 292.

Hillyar, James, captain of the British 36-gun frigate "Phoebe," block-ades and captures the "Essex" at Valparaiso, viii. 178-180, 201.

Hindman, Jacob, major of artillery corps, commands battalion in Brown's army, viii. 37; at Lundy's Lane, 56; ordered to withdraw his guns, 59; commands artillery at Fort Erie, 71.

Hinds, Thomas, lieutenant-colonel of Mississippi volunteers, at New Orleans, viii. 345.

"Holkar," New York privateer, captured, vii. 329.

Holland, exempted from the non-intercourse, iv. 446; v. 72, 90-92, 112, restored to independence, vii. 373. (See Louis Bonaparte.)

Holland, James, member of Congress from North Carolina, laments disposition for novelty, iii. 351.

Holland, Lord, negotiates treaty with Monroe, iii. 407, 408-412; on repeal of the orders, vi. 275.

Holmes, John, of Maine, attacks report of Hartford Convention in the Massachusetts legislature, viii. 306.

Holstein, Duchy of, v. 413.

Hope, Henry, captain of the British frigate "Endymion," his report of attack on the "Prince of Neufchatel," viii. 208, 209; his action with the "President," ix. 67.

Hopkins, Lemuel, i. 102.

Hopkins, Samuel, major-general of Kentucky militia, vii. 74. 76, 78; member of the Thirteenth Congress, viii. 279.

Hopkinson, Joseph, one of Chase's counsel, ii. 228, 231; member of the Fourteenth Congress, declares the federal government at its last gasp in January, 1815; viii. 285, 286; represents Pennsylvania, ix. 107.

"Horizon," American ship, condemned by French courts under Berlin Decree, iv. 82; judgment in the case of the, 109.

Horner, Francis, declares the American war unpopular, ix. 43.
"Hornet," sloop-of-war, brings despatches, vi. 215, 217; cruises with Rodgers' squadron, 365, 366; at Boston, 378, 381, her second cruise, 384; blockades the "Bonne Citoyenne," 384; vii. 288; Josiah Quincy's Resolution on victory of, 65, attached to Decatur's squadron, 278; sinks the "Peacock," 289, 290; commanded by Biddle, 291, 293; blockaded at New London, 312; sails from New York, ix. 63, 70; captures "Penguin," 71, 72; escapes "Cornwallis," 73; gunnery of, 230.
Horses and horse-racing in New England, i. 50; in New York and Virginia, 51.
Horse-shoe, of the Tallapoosa River, battle at, vii. 254–257.
Hosack, Dr. David, i. 111.
Hospitals and asylums in 1800, i. 128.
Houston, Samuel, wounded at the Horse-shoe, vii. 256.
Howell, Jeremiah B., senator from Rhode Island, votes against occupying West Florida, vi. 243.
Howick, Lord (Earl Grey), British Foreign Secretary, iii. 407; his order depriving neutrals of coasting rights, 416–421 (see Orders in Council); dismissed from office, 421; iv. 79.
Hull, Isaac, at Tripoli, ii. 428; captain in U. S. navy, commands "Constitution," vi. 364; his orders, 364; chased by a British squadron, 369–371; captures "Guerriere," 372–375; takes command at New York, 383.
Hull, William, governor of Michigan Territory, vi. 292; appointed brigadier-general, 292, 298; his advice regarding the defence of Detroit, 296; his march to Detroit, 298; his loss of papers, 300; arrives at Detroit, 301; invades Canada, 302, 317 ; his proclamation, 303, his required campaign, 311, decides to besiege Malden, 312–314; sudden discovery of his danger, 314, 315; evacuates Canada, 315; his situation at Detroit, 322–329; his capitulation, 332, 334, Jefferson's opinion of, 336, 398; his proclamation, vii. 32; criticised by Harrison, 82; his court-martial, 414, 416; sentenced to death, 417.
Humbert, Jean Joseph Amable, French general, a volunteer at the battle of New Orleans, viii. 380.
Humphreys, S. P., captain of the British frigate "Leopard," iv. 4; his note to Commodore Barron, 12.
Hunt, Samuel, member of Congress from New Hampshire, ii. 160.
Hunt, Major Seth, sounded by General Wilkinson, iii. 222.
"Hunter," 10-gun British brig on Lake Erie, vii. 120.
"Hyder Ali," privateer, viii. 195.

ILLINOIS Territory, population in 1810, i. 289.
Immigration in 1816, ix. 160, 161.
Impeachment (see Pickering and Chase), its political use, i. 256; Jefferson's opinion on the use of, ii. 144, 150; the Senate, in Pickering's trial, sits as a court of, 153, 154; the Senate holds insanity no bar to, 155–157; Giles's doctrine that the Senate is not a court of, 221, 222; doctrine of Chase's counsel that indictable misdemeanors are the only ground for, 223; Campbell's doctrine of an inquest of office for, 224; theory adopted by the House that a mistake in law is

ground for, 225; Hopkinson's argument on, 231; Luther Martin's argument on, 232; Nicholson's view of, 233; Rodney's view of, 234; Jefferson's view of, as a scarecrow, 243; Chase's trial fails to decide the nature of, 244; a farce, iii. 447; Marshall threatened with, 466.

Imports (see Exports).

Impressment of seamen, ii. 335 et seq., 358, 384, 393, 394, 421, 423; act of Congress punishing, 397, 420; severity of, iii. 93, 94; Monroe instructed to require abandonment of, 400; Monroe disregards instructions in, 408, 409; Madison insists on express abandonment of, 422, 429, 432; Samuel Smith on, 434; Madison prepares new instructions on, 438; included in instructions on the "Chesapeake" affair, iv. 39, 45, 47, 162-164; British proclamation on, 52, 166; Jefferson's intentions on, 144, 164, 353; not a voice raised in 1809 against, v. 74; little complaint in 1810, 292; the House refuses to insist upon in February, 1811, 351, 352; not expressly mentioned by Pinkney, vi. 18; or in the annual message, 125; first made a casus belli in the autumn of 1811, 116-118; treated by House Committee of Foreign Relations, 134, 135; mentioned by Grundy, 139; by Madison's war message, 222; only obstacle to peace, 430-432, 450-452; extent of, 451, 452; cost and value of, vii. 19; right of, partially conceded by Monroe's instructions, 47; abandonment of, a *sine qua non*, 47; Alexander Baring's remark on, 343; abandoned by the Cabinet June 27, 1814, as a *sine qua non*, viii. 122; ix. 32, 33; insisted upon by Monroe's instructions of Jan. 28, 1814, ix. 11.

Inaugural Address, first, of President Jefferson, i. 197, 198; its fame, 199; its object, 200; its view of "the strongest government on earth," 201, 202; its ideal of government, 202-207; its deficiencies, 207-209, 212; second, of President Jefferson, iv. 1-8; first, of President Madison, v. 1-4, second, of President Madison, vii. 33, 34.

India, career of Marquess Wellesley in, v. 266.

Indian corn, i. 58; iv. 254.

Indiana Territory, population in 1810, v. 289; created in 1800, vi. 68; its dispute about the introduction of slavery, 75; adopts second grade of territorial government, 76, admitted into the Union, ix. 119; extinction of Indian titles in, 170. (See Harrison).

Indians, in the United States in 1800, i. 4; Jefferson's parallel between Indians and conservatives, iii. 4, 6; cessions of territory in 1805, 14; relations of the northwestern, with Canada, 15, 16; of the southwestern with Florida, 16; in 1810, v 318; in the Northwest, vi. 69, their condition described by Governor Harrison, 69; trespasses on their territory, 70; effects of intoxication upon, 71, 72; murders committed upon, 72, 73; Jefferson's policy toward, 73-75; Harrison's treaties with, in 1804 and 1805, 75; Tecumthe and the Prophet, 78; Jefferson's refusal to recognize them as a confederated body, 79; establishment at Tippecanoe Creek, 79-81; their hostility to cessions of land, 82, 87; their land-cession of Sept. 30, 1809, 83, 84; their outbreak imminent in 1810, 85; outbreak delayed by British influence, 85; their interview with Harrison, Aug. 12, 1810, 86-88; government wishes peace with, 89; of the Six Nations in Upper Canada, wish to remain neutral, 319; their employment in war by the British, 320; murders by, 393, 394; number of, at Frenchtown, vii. 89; at the River Raisin, 94, 95, 96; at the siege of Fort Meigs, 104, 106-108; at the attack on Fort Stephenson, 109-114; at Amherstburg, 130; at the battle of the Thames, 137-139; in the Creek war, 233, 244, 255; at Talishatchee, 237; at Talladega, 238; at the Hillabee towns, 240, 241; of the Six Nations in Porter's brigade at Niagara, viii. 37, 39, 40; in Riall's army, 41, 44; British rations furnished to, in Upper Canada, 92; to be guaranteed in the northwestern territory by treaty, 268; ix. 7, 10, 12; boundary according to the Treaty of Greenville advanced as a *sine qua non* at Ghent, 18-20; boundary abandoned as a *sine qua non*, 25, 27, 28; amnesty accepted as a basis of peace, 31, 32; condition of, in 1816, 170. (See Treaties.)

Infantry, American, First regiment of, at Fort Massac, iii. 290; in 1813, (New Jersey), vii. 73; prisoners from, sent to England for trial, 361; at Lundy's Lane, viii. 53; at Fort Erie, 69.

—— Second, at Natchitoches, iii. 311; at Fort Bowyer, viii. 316, 322; capitulates, 384.

—— Third (Mississippi and Missouri Territories), at Mobile, penetrates Creek country, vii. 243; remains at Mobile, viii. 316, 328, 332.

—— Fourth, ordered to Indiana July, 1811, vi. 92, 93; arrives, 94; part of the expedition to Tippecanoe, 96; losses in the battle, 104; its share in the battle, 107; ordered to Detroit, 110; marches to Detroit, 298; at the battle of Maguaga, 325; at the surrender of Detroit, viii. 36, 37.

—— Sixth (New York), prisoners from, sent to England for trial, vii. 361; at Plattsburg, viii. 100.

—— Seventh (Kentucky), vii. 73; at New Orleans, viii. 316, 333; in the night battle, 344-346, 351.

—— Ninth (Massachusetts), part of Scott's brigade, viii. 35; at Chippawa, 42, 43; at Lundy's Lane, 50, 52, 56; its losses, 63; its strength at Fort Erie, 68; in the assault on Fort Erie, 75; in the sortie from Fort Erie, 76; recruited in Massachusetts, 235.

—— Eleventh (Vermont), part of Scott's brigade, viii. 35, 236; at Chippawa, 42; at Lundy's Lane, 50, 52, 56; its losses, 63; its strength at Fort Erie, 68; in the sortie from Fort Erie, 87.

—— Twelfth, recruited in Virginia, viii. 235.

—— Thirteenth (New York), at Queenston, vi. 345, 349; prisoners from, sent to England for trial, vii. 361.

—— Fourteenth (Maryland), Winder's, vi. 359; at Beaver Dam, vii. 162, 163.

—— Seventeenth (Kentucky), vii. 76, 87; at the River Raisin, 88, 90, 91, 95; at Fort Stephenson, 110; consolidated with the Nineteenth, viii. 36.

—— Nineteenth (Ohio), at Fort Meigs, vii. 107; a part of Ripley's brigade, viii. 36; defend Fort Erie, 75, 77; in the sortie, 87, 88.

—— Twentieth, recruited in Virginia, viii. 235.

—— Twenty-first (Massachusetts), Ripley's, at Chrystler's Field, vii. 188; part of Ripley's brigade, viii. 36; carries the British guns at Lun-

GENERAL INDEX. 299

dy's Lane, 54, 55, 236; its strength at Fort Erie, 69; holds Snake Hill, 71, 74; recruited in Massachusetts, 235.

—— Twenty-second (Pennsylvania), part of Scott's brigade, viii. 35; at Lundy's Lane, 52, 56; its losses, 63; its strength at Fort Erie, 68.

—— Twenty-third (New York), part of Ripley's brigade, viii. 36, 37; breaks the British left at Lundy's Lane, 54-56; its strength at Fort Erie, 69; holds Snake Hill, 71.

—— Twenty-fifth (Connecticut), part of Scott's brigade, viii. 35, 236; at Chippawa, 43; at Lundy's Lane, 51, 56, 58; its losses, 63; at Fort Erie, 68.

—— Thirty-third, recruited in Massachusetts, viii. 235.

—— Thirty-fourth, recruited in Massachusetts, viii. 235.

—— Thirty-fifth, recruited in Virginia, viii. 235.

—— Thirty-ninth (Tennessee), ordered to join Jackson vii. 245, 251; arrives at Fort Strother, 252; storms Indian breastwork at the Horse-shoe, 255; its losses, 256; at Mobile, viii. 316, 328; sent to the Appalachicola, 330, 333; left by Jackson at Mobile, 332.

—— Fortieth, recruited in Massachusetts, viii. 235.

—— Forty-fourth (Louisiana), at Mobile, viii. 316, 328; ordered to New Orleans, 332, 333; in the night battle, 344-346, 351.

—— Forty-fifth, recruited in Massachusetts, viii. 235.

Infantry, British, First Regiment of (Royal Scots), viii. 39; in the battle of Chippawa, 41, 43; at Lundy's Lane, 52, 56; in the assault on Fort Erie, 78; at the sortie from Fort Erie, 88.

—— Third, at Plattsburg, viii. 101.

—— Fourth, at New Orleans, viii. 347, 353; in Gibbs's column, 372, 380.

—— Fifth, at Plattsburg, viii. 101.

—— Sixth, reinforces Drummond at Fort Erie, viii. 80; at the sortie from Fort Erie, 88.

—— Seventh (Fusileers), at New Orleans, viii. 353; at the battle of Jan. 8, 1815, 372, 373, 380.

—— Eighth (King's), at York, vii. 154; at the capture of Fort George, 158; part of Riall's army on the Niagara, viii. 39; in the battle of Chippawa, 41, 43; at Lundy's Lane, 56; in the assault on Fort Erie, 79; at Plattsburg, 101.

—— Ninth, at Plattsburg, viii. 102.

—— Thirteenth, at Plattsburg, viii. 101.

—— Sixteenth, on the St. Lawrence, viii. 102.

—— Twenty-first, at Baltimore, viii. 169; in the night battle at New Orleans, 349; at Villeré's plantation, 353; in the battle of Jan. 8, 1815, 372, 373, 380.

—— Twenty-seventh, at Plattsburg, viii. 101, 102.

—— Thirty-seventh, at Plattsburg, viii. 102.

—— Thirty-ninth, at Plattsburg, viii. 101.

—— Forty-first, at Malden, vi. 312, 314; with Brock in the attack on Detroit, 332; with Brock at Queenston, 348, 349, 351; with Proctor at the River Raisin, vii. 95; at the siege of Fort Meigs, 106; at the assault on Fort Stephenson, 112; on Barclay's fleet on Lake Erie, 119; defeated and captured at the battle of the Thames, 136, 137, 140; at Lundy's Lane, viii. 56; at Fort Erie, 68; repulsed before Black Rock, 69, 70.

—— Forty-third, at New Orleans, viii. 353; in the battle of Jan. 8, 1815, 372, 373, 380.

—— Forty-fourth, at the attack on Baltimore, viii. 169; at New Orleans, 354; in the battle of Jan. 8, 1815, 372, 373, 380.

—— Forty-ninth, Brock's regiment, vi. 316; at Montreal, 317, 338; at Niagara, 348; at Queenston, 350; captures Boerstler, vii. 163; at Chrystler's Farm, 190; at Plattsburg, viii. 101.

—— Fifty-seventh, at Plattsburg, viii. 102.

—— Fifty-eighth, at Plattsburg, viii. 102.

—— Seventieth, on the St. Lawrence, viii. 102.

—— Seventy-sixth, at Plattsburg, viii. 101.

—— Eighty-first, at Plattsburg, viii. 102.

—— Eighty-second, reinforces Drummond at Fort Erie, viii. 80; at the sortie from Fort Erie, 88.

—— Eighty-fifth, in Ross's army, viii. 129; leads the attack at Bladensburg, 141; its losses, 144; leads the advance to Baltimore, 169; leads the advance across Lake Borgne to the Mississippi. 338; in the night battle of Dec. 23, 1814, 347, 348; ordered to the west bank, 371; captures Patterson's battery, 377; losses of, 378, 379.

—— Eighty-eighth, at Plattsburg, viii. 101.

—— Eighty-ninth, at Chrystler's Farm, vii. 190; with Drummond at Niagara, viii. 46; at Lundy's Lane, 51, 52, 56; in the assault on Fort Erie, 79; at the sortie from Fort Erie, 88.

—— Ninety-third, in the night battle at New Orleans, viii. 350; at Villeré's plantation, 354; in the battle of Jan. 8, 1815, 372, 373; its losses, 376, 380.

—— Ninety-fifth, in the night battle at New Orleans, viii. 347, 348; at Villeré's plantation, 354; in the battle of Jan. 8, 1815, 372, 373, 380.

—— Ninety-seventh, reinforces Drummond at Fort Erie, viii. 84, 85, 89.

—— One Hundredth, at the attack on Sackett's Harbor, vii. 165; with Riall, viii. 39; at Chippawa, 41, 43.

—— One Hundred and Second, occupies Eastport, viii. 94.

—— One Hundred and Third, with Riall, viii. 39; at Lundy's Lane, 50, 60; in the assault on Fort Erie, 72, 75, 76, 78.

—— One Hundred and Fourth, at the attack on Sackett's Harbor, vii. 168; in the assault on Fort Erie, viii. 72, 75-78.

—— De Meuron's regiment, at Plattsburg, viii. 101.

—— De Watteville's regiment (German), reinforces Drummond, viii. 68; in the assault on Fort Erie, 72, 74, 75; Drummond's report on their disaster, 79; surprised in the sortie from Fort Erie, 87.

—— Royal Newfoundland, at Malden, vi. 312.

—— First West India (colored), at New Orleans, viii. 354; employed as skirmishers, 372, 373.

—— Fifth West India (colored) at New Orleans, viii. 354; in the action on the west bank, 371.

Ingersoll, Charles Jared, author of a tragedy, i. 123; member of Congress from Pennsylvania, attacks Granger, vii. 400; criticises Calhoun's plan for a bank, viii. 253; calls for previous question on the bank bill, 257, 258; declares the war successful, 278, 279.

GENERAL INDEX. 301

Ingersoll, Jared, ii. 259.
Ingham, Samuel Delucenna, member of Congress from Pennsylvania, opposes Calhoun's plan of a national bank, viii. 251; in the Fourteenth Congress, ix. 107; supports protective tariff, 114; on committee of internal improvement, 148.
Innis, Judge, iii. 274; denies Daveiss' motion against Burr, 278; humiliated by Daveiss and Marshall, 293.
Inns of New England and New York, i. 21.
Inquisitiveness, American, i. 55.
Insane, the, treatment of, in 1800, i. 128.
Insurance, rates of British marine, in 1814, viii. 197-201; ix. 43.
Interior Department, recommended by Madison, ix. 144.
Internal improvements Jefferson's recommendation of a fund for, iii. 2, 346; iv. 364; his anxiety to begin, iii. 19; Gallatin's scheme of, 20; Gallatin's report on, iv. 364; bill for, ix 149-151; vetoed, 151, 169.
Invisibles, the, v. 363.
Ireland, coast of, under the dominion of American privateers, viii. 197.
Irving, Peter, editor of the "Morning Chronicle," i. 121.
Irving, Washington, i. 110; his "History of New York," ix 209-212, 238; his account of Allston, 214.
Isle aux Noix, British force at, viii 26.
Isle aux Poix, British base in Lake Borgne, viii. 337, 338.
Izard, George, major-general in U. S. army, his history, vii. 407; takes command at Plattsburg in May, 1814, viii. 27; his report on intercourse with the enemy, 93; fortifies Plattsburg, 97, 98, 108; suggests moving toward the St. Lawrence, 98; ordered to move, 98; his remonstrance, 99; ordered to Sackett's Harbor, marches Aug. 29, 1814, 100, 113; arrives at Batavia, September 27, 114; his apparent loyalty, 114; moves on Chippawa, October 13, 115; his reports of October 16 and 23, 115, 116; goes into winter quarters, 116; his mortification, 116; recommends Brown to command at Niagara, 117; offers to resign, 117, 118; his career at an end, 118; his effectives, 217.

JACKSON, ANDREW, in 1800, i. 54; his devotion to Burr, iii. 221, 258, his unauthorized order of Oct. 4, 1806, to the Tennessee militia, 258; undertakes the building of boats, etc., for Burr, 274; to be instructed against Burr, 284; requires disavowals from Burr, 287; his letter to Claiborne, 288, 317; his quarrel with Adair, 288; at Richmond, attacks Jefferson, 460; ordered with two thousand men to support the seizure of Florida, vii. 206, 207; ordered to dismiss his force, 209; returns to Tennessee, 210 216; recalls his force into service, 235; penetrates northern Alabama, 236; attacks Talishatchee, 237; relieves Talladega, 238; abandoned by his men, 239; his campaign to Emuckfaw, 245-248; his treatment of Cocke and Woods, 252, 253; captures the Horse-shoe, 254-256; his treaty with the Creeks, 260, 261, appointed major-general in the U. S. army, 410, 411; helpless with militia, viii. 219; his drafts on the Treasury, 283; appointed to command military district No. 7, 317; arrives at Mobile Aug. 15, 1814, 318; attacks Pensacola, 317-330; occupies Mobile Point, 319, 322;

his proclamations to the people of Louisiana, 324, 325; his neglect of New Orleans, 325-334; leaves Mobile November 22, 331; arrives at New Orleans December 2, 333; his military resources, 333, 334; goes down the river December 4, 335; hurries back to the city December 15, 336; surprised December 23, 339; his measures of defence compared with Winder's, 340-343; his military resources at New Orleans, 344-346; his night attack of December 23, 346-351; his entrenchments, 352, 354, 355; his artillery, 358, 361; contrasted with Pakenham, 353; his lines at New Orleans, 368-371; his force, 373, 374; his account of the rout on the west bank, 377, 378; Adair's comments on, 379; contented to let the British escape, 382; his remarks on the surrender of Fort Bowyer, 384; retained on peace establishment, ix. 88; his arbitrary conduct at New Orleans, 89.

Jackson, Mrs. F. J. v. 115, 157.

Jackson, Francis James, his reputation, ii. 360; v. 96; British envoy to Denmark, to demand the delivery of the Danish fleet, iv. 64; Lord Eldon's anecdote concerning, 65; appointed British minister to the United States, v. 97; his instructions, 99-105; sails for America, 105. Gallatin's expectations from, 111, 117; arrives at Washington, 115, 116; his impressions, 117-120; his negotiation, 120-132; rupture with, 132; his anger, 154, 155, his complaints. 156; his reception in Baltimore and New York, 157; discussed before Congress, 176, 178, 179, 182; his letters from New York and Boston. 212-218; returns to England, 219; his treatment by Wellesley. 218, 219, 269, 271, 272; his influence with the British government, vi. 13; his account of Pinkney's "inamicable leave," 20; his opinion of Augustus J. Foster, 22, his death, 22.

Jackson, Jacob, Second Lieutenant of Artillery, commanding at Chickasaw Bluff, iii. 325.

Jackson, James, senator from Georgia, and the Yazoo sale, i. 305; ii. 95, 155, 238; in the Ninth Congress, iii. 126; declares in favor of an embargo, 149, 176; his death, 176.

Jackson, John George, member of Congress from Virginia, ii. 211; replies to Randolph's attack on Madison, 215; attacks Quincy in Congress, iii. 196; opposes war, iv. 378.

Jackson, William, editor of the "Political Register," ii. 265; discloses Yrujo's attempt to use him, 266.

Jacmel, siege of, i. 385.

"Jacob Jones," privateer, viii. 195.

Jamaica blockaded by American privateers, vii. 13; rendezvous for British expedition against New Orleans Nov. 20, 1814, 311, 316, 330.

"Java," British frigate, her action with the "Constitution," vi. 385, 386; effect of capture in England, vii. 15, 16.

Jay, Chief-Justice, i. 108; sent to England by Washington, ii. 323; vii. 43; negotiates treaty with Lord Grenville, 326.

Jay's treaty (see Treaties).

Jefferson, Thomas, describes Virginia roads, i. 13; his agricultural experience, 32; his aversion to cities, 59, 138, 147; his aversion to banks, 65; ii. 131; his political ideals, i. 72, 73, 146, 147, 179; Federalist opinion of, 80 *et seq*., 83, 112, 114; opposed to manufactures, 138; chief author of the Kentucky Resolutions, 140 *et seq* , leader of the Virginia school, 143; characteristics of, 144 *et seq.* ; his political doctrines, 146 *et seq.*, 156 ; Thomas Moore's verses on, 167: visionary, 170; his ideas of progress, 178, 179; personal characteristics, 185 *et seq.*; his dress, 187; ii. 366, 405; social preeminence, i. 188; his inauguration, 191; his antipathy to Marshall, 192, 194; purity ot his life, 196; his Inaugural Address, 199 *et seq.* ; his conception of government, 210 *et seq.*; his foreign policy, 214 *et seq.*; his Cabinet, 218 *et seq.*; his plans for the navy, 222 *et seq.*; his treatment of patronage, 224, 294; his New Haven letter, 226 : his first annual message, 248; his course with regard to the Judiciary, 255 *et seq.*; his abnegation of power, 262; his power, 266; his theory of internal politics, 272; contradictions in his character, 277 ; his hopefulness, 307 *et seq.*; as a man of science, 310; his dislike for New Englanders. 310 *et seq* ; his letter to Paine, 316; attacked by Callender, 322; sensitiveness of. 324; his relations with Callender, 325 *et seq.* ; sends Lear to St. Domingo, 389 : ignorant of Bonaparte's schemes, 403 *et seq.*; his eyes opened, 409; his letter to Dupont de Nemours, 410; writes to Livingston defining his position with respect to France and Spain, 424: his annual message, 1802, 427 ; ignores the war party, 428; replies to their demand for papers touching the right of deposit at New Orleans, 430; quiets the West, 432; attempts the purchase of New Orleans, 432 *et seq.*; his language to Thornton, 436; prefers Natchez to New Orleans as a seat of trade, 443; his apparent inconsistency, 443 *et seq.*; the essence of his statesmanship, 445; proposes alliance with England, ii. 1, 78; instructs Pinckney to offer a consideration to Spain for New Orleans and Florida, 22 ; writes a defence of his use of patronage for the Boston "Chronicle," 82; his amendment to the Constitution regarding Louisiana, 83; his letter to Breckinridge on the subject, 84; to Paine, 86; draws up a new amendment, 86; his reply to W. C. Nicholas, 89; his message Oct. 7, 1803, 92; his bill for the administration of Louisiana, 119; his view of the Louisiana treaty and legislation, 130; requests Congress to enlarge the Mediterranean force, 140; interview with Burr, 175; declines to appoint Burr to an executive office, 176; his knowledge of Federalist schemes, 192; his confidence in his popularity, 202; receives the electoral votes of Massachusetts and New Hampshire, 204; his message November, 1804, 206 ; his disappointment at the acquittal of Justice Chase, 243; his authority in foreign affairs, 245; desires to obtain West Florida, 245; explains to Senator Breckinridge his course toward Spain, 248; his plan to obtain West Florida, 249; instructs Monroe with regard to the Spanish claims, 250; the harvest season of his life, 252; sends troops to Natchez, 254; makes no demand for West Florida when Louisiana is delivered, 256; declares Mobile within the United States, 263; entertains Yrujo at Monticello, 266; his conviction of the power of American commercial interests,

GENERAL INDEX.

330; anxious for friendship with England, 342; his intimacy with Thornton, 347; his opinion of Bonaparte, 347, 353, 381; decides to maintain the neutral rights of the United States more strictly, 356; his social habits, 363; establishes a new social code, 365; receives Merry, 366; invites him to dinner with Pichon, 369; sends list of impressments to the Senate, 384; improves his style of dress, 405; his enemies, 409; his second inauguration, iii. 1; his second Inaugural Address, 1-9; his Cabinet, 10; result of his Spanish diplomacy, 38, 39; his letter to Madison respecting Monroe's mission, 54; his letter to James Bowdoin respecting the Spanish relations, 57; writes to Madison respecting procedure with Spain, 61; suggests a treaty with England, 63; favors Armstrong's advice to occupy Texas, 69; writes to Madison of plan for peaceable settlement by intervention of France, 75; his memorandum of a Cabinet meeting on Spanish relations, 77; the turning-point of his second administration, 80; his conversation with Merry after the British seizures, 101; his memorandum of the new Spanish policy, 106; his aversion to war with England, 108; his annual message, 1805, 111, *et seq.;* announces his intention to retire at the close of his term, 119; his Message applauded by the Federalist press, 129; his secret Spanish message, 130; preserves secrecy in Congress, 147; coerced into sending special mission to England, 150, 152, 433; conciliates opposition in Congress, 165; warns Monroe against Randolph, 165; makes advances to Macon, 167;

Randolph's attack on, 172, *et seq.;* closes American ports to three British cruisers, 200; his character and position described by Turreau, 205; asks Bidwell to take the leadership in the House, 207; his refusal to obey a subpœna, 208, 450; receives Burr at the White House, 233; his seeming indifference to Burr's movements, 266; his memoranda of the situation, 278; sends Graham to inquire into Burr's movements, 281; orders Wilkinson to use active measures, 284; issues a proclamation against Burr, 285; his letter to Secretary Smith regarding naval and military defences, 332; obliged to proceed against Burr, 336; and to defend Wilkinson, 341; his annual message, December, 1806, 345 *et seq.;* advocates internal improvements, 346; would abolish the slave-trade, 347; signs the Act prohibiting the Slave Trade, 365; defied by Spain, 388; his instructions to Monroe and Pinkney regarding the treaty, 401 *et seq.;* determined on commercial restrictions, 423; refuses to submit Monroe's treaty to the Senate, 430 *et seq.;* offers Monroe the government of Orleans Territory, 435; his letter to Bowdoin about Spanish perfidy and injustice, 436; designs to impeach Marshall, 447; his irritation with Marshall and Burr's counsel, 450, 453; supports Wilkinson, 456; his vexation at Burr's acquittal, 470; his proclamation on the Chesapeake affair, iv. 30; preparations for war, 32, his instructions to Monroe, 39; the result of his measures of peaceful coercion, 97; his genius for peace, 130; his personal friendship for Monroe, 130; his confidence in his own theory, 138; domestic opposition to, insignificant, 145 *et seq.*; his strength in Congress, 147; the secret of his success, 148; his annual message, Oct. 27, 1807, 153; his influence, 155; his second message concerning the Burr trial, 156; his policy as to gunboats, 158; yields to Canning, 163, 164; writes an embargo message, 168; signs the Embargo Act, Dec. 22, 1807, 178; his entreaties to Rose through Robert Smith, 188-191; asks Congress for an addition of six thousand men to the regular army, 212; charged with a subserviency to Napoleon, 228; issues a proclamation against insurrection on the Canada frontier, 249; writes a circular letter to State governors respecting the surplus of flour in their States, 252; writes to Governor Sullivan of Massachusetts to stop importing provisions, 253; writes to General Dearborn, 256; his war with the Massachusetts Federalists, 258; his popularity shattered, 269; hatred of, in England, 331; orders Pinkney to offer a withdrawal of the embargo if England would withdraw the Orders in Council, 333 *et seq.*; his attitude toward Spain, 339; decides to propose no new measures in view of his approaching retirement, 356; his language reported by Pickering, 359; his last annual message, 361 *et seq.*; advocates public improvements, 364; desires to maintain the embargo until his retirement, 432; opposition of Joseph Story and others to, 433; his letter to Thomas Mann Randolph, 442; signs the act repealing the embargo, 454; contradictions of his Presidency, 454; insulted by the address of the Massachusetts legislature, 457; his failure to overthrow the New England Federalists, 461; submits in silence to the repeal of the embargo, 462; his letter to Dearborn revealing his mortification, 463; decline of his influence, 464; appoints William Short minister to Russia, 465; the nomination rejected by the Senate, 466; his letter to Short, 468; his style of life and his debts, 469 *et seq.*; quits Washington, 472; his address to his fellow-citizens in Virginia, 473; Turreau's anger with, v. 34, Gallatin's remarks on, 38, 39; the "National Intelligencer" on, 75; Randolph's remarks on, 78: Robert Smith's remarks on, 84; intermediates with Monroe, 161, 162; expenditures of his administration, 200, 205, 206; considered too timid by Robert Smith, vi. 48; his Indian policy, 69, 73-75, 78, 79, 81; his opinion of William Hull, 336, 398; his expectation of the conquest of Canada, 337; his opinion of Van Rensselaer, 398; his letter of sympathy with Madison, Sept. 24, 1814, viii. 231, 232; his letter to Monroe on the capture of Washington, 232; his letter to Short on the defection of Massachusetts, 233; his plan for providing a paper currency, 245, 246, 247; declares that more taxes cannot be paid, 248, 255; thinks it nonsense to talk of regulars, 263; thinks that the war would have upset the government, 308; expects the British to hold New Orleans indefinitely, 309; describes the want of money in Virginia, ix. 60, 61; denounces the Judiciary, 188; reverts to his earlier theories, 192; satirized by Washington Irving, 210, 211; results of his theories, 226.

306 GENERAL INDEX.

Jesup, Thomas Sidney, acting adjutant-general at Detroit, vi. 329; major of the Twenty-fifth Infantry, viii. 35; at Chippawa, 42, 43; at Lundy's Lane, 50-52, 56; wounded, 58, 63, 65; at Hartford, reports on the Convention, 298.

Johnson, James, leads attack at the battle of the Thames, vii. 138.

Johnson, Richard Mentor, member of Congress from Kentucky, his argument in favor of the embargo, iv. 266; opposes war, 376; favors manufactures, v. 197; denounces the timidity of Congress, 203; in the Twelfth Congress, vi. 122; his war speech, 142; on the dangers of a navy, 164; on the treason of opposition, 212; colonel of Kentucky rangers, vii. 129; crosses into Canada, 132; his energy, 137; wins the battle of the Thames, 138, 139; returns home, 142; moves previous question on bank bill, viii. 253; accepts Giles's militia bill, 274; in the Fourteenth Congress, ix. 107; author of the compensation bill, 120, 121, 136; moves for committee on the Compensation Act, 144.

Johnson, Justice William, of South Carolina, issues a mandamus to compel the collector to clear certain ships, iv. 263.

Jones, Evan, iii. 300.

Jones, Jacob, captain U. S. navy, commands the "Wasp," vi. 379; his action with the "Frolic," 380; captured, 381; takes command of the "Macedonian," 383.

Jones, John Paul, vii. 6.

Jones, Walter, his letter to Jefferson on dissensions in Madison's Cabinet, v. 188.

Jones, William, offered the Navy Department in 1801, i. 220; appointed Secretary of the Navy, vi.

428, 429; acting Secretary of the Treasury, vii. 43; recommends legislation to encourage privateering, 336; his treasury report for 1813, 385; hostile to Armstrong, 413; sends Croghan's expedition to Mackinaw, viii. 32, 33; favors abandoning impressments as a *sine qua non*, 122; goes to navy-yard on the morning of Aug. 24, 1814, 137; expects British advance through Bladensburg, 138; permits Barney to go to Bladensburg, 139; orders the vessels at the navy-yard to be burned, 145; accompanies the President into Virginia, 150; causes batteries to be erected on the Potomac, 164; retires from the Navy Department, ix. 63; becomes president of the United States Bank, 131.

Judiciary Act of 1801, i. 274 *et seq.*; repeal of, moved, 278 *et seq.*, 284 *et seq.*; repealed, 298.

Judiciary system, the, Jefferson's recommendations concerning, i. 255; attempt to make an elective, iv. 205.

"Junon," 46-gun British frigate, attacked by gunboats, vii. 270.

Junot, marshal of France, ordered to enter Spain, iv. 117; marches on Portugal, 119; enters Lisbon, 120, 121; capitulates at Cintra, 315.

KEANE, JOHN, British major-general, ordered on the New Orleans expedition, viii. 312; his caution in leading the advance, Dec. 23, 1814, 342; after the night battle, 352; commands assaulting column, Jan. 8, 1815, 372; attacks and is severely wounded, 376.

Keenan, Thomas, member of Congress from North Carolina, iii. 356.

Kempt, ———, major-general in British army commanding brigade at Plattsburg, viii. 102.

Kennedy, Laurence, purser of the "Epervier," viii. 183.

Kentucky in 1800, i. 2, 43; Resolutions of 1798, 140 *et seq.*, 205; enthusiasm for the war, vi. 390; number of men in the field, 391, 393; distaste for the regular army, 391, 394; militia placed under Harrison's command, vii. 73, 74; three regiments at Fort Defiance, 78, 80, 86; march to the Maumee Rapids, 87; advance to the River Raisin, 88, 90; massacred or captured, 95-98; appearance of, 96, 97; failures of, 101; brigade of, sent to Fort Meigs, 105; massacred or captured, 106; two divisions, under Governor Shelby, invade Canada, 128, 129; at the battle of the Thames, 139; State army raised by, viii. 283; twenty-five hundred militia ordered to New Orleans, 327, 333; arrive at New Orleans, 367, 368; ordered to cross the river, 370, 371; in reserve, 373; routed, 377, 379; growth in population, ix. 155.

Kerr, Mr. Lewis, iii. 303.

Key, Philip Barton, ii. 228; member of Congress from Maryland, iv. 147; advises a war policy, 374; favors navigation bill, v. 185.

King, Rufus, American minister in London, i. 109; sends the treaty of the retrocession of Louisiana to Jefferson, 409; ii. 23, 178 *et seq.*; obtains from Pitt a definition of neutral importation, 328, 340; his negotiations with the British government, 345, 347; returns with favorable conventions, 358; opinion of F. J. Jackson and Anthony Merry, 361; leaves England, 410; takes part in meeting on the Pierce outrage, iii. 199; Pickering sends a letter of, to Rose, iv. 234; candidate for Vice-President, 285; letters to Pickering, 348, 457; his supposed opposition to Clinton, vi. 410; elected senator from New York, vii. 48, 49; moves inquiry in regard to Gallatin's mission to Russia, 59; declares a minister in Sweden to be inexpedient, 62, 63; reports bill to incorporate a national bank, viii. 257; defeats Monroe's conscription, 279, 280; to be placed in the Presidency, 306; candidate for the Presidency in 1816, ix. 139; votes for internal improvements, 151.

Kingsbury, lieutenant-colonel of the First Infantry, arrests Adair, iii. 324.

Kingston, on Lake Ontario, vii. 145; Armstrong's plan of attacking, 149; British garrison at, 150, 151; Dearborn decides not to attack, 152, 153; Prevost embarks at, 163, 164, Wilkinson ordered to attack, 176; Wilkinson decides to pass, 178; Armstrong and Wilkinson change opinions regarding, 180-182; Brown ordered to attack, in February, 1814, viii. 27; Prevost visits, in October, 1814, 92, 118; preparations at, for the siege of Sackett's Harbor, 118, 119.

"Knickerbocker" school of literature, ix. 209-212.

LABOUCHÈRE, iii. 379; v. 238, 239.

Lacock, Abner, senator from Pennsylvania, opposes the appointment of Dallas to the Treasury, vii. 397; consents to Dallas's appointment, viii. 243.

Lacolle River, Wilkinson's defeat at, viii. 25, 26; British force at, 26.

Lady "Prevost," 13-gun British

GENERAL INDEX.

schooner on Lake Erie, vii. 120; in action, 124; crippled and captured, 127.

Laffite, Jean, Pierre, and Dominique, of Barataria, viii. 321.

Lambert, Henry, captain of the British frigate "Java," vi. 385, 386.

Lambert, John, Travels of, a description of New York under the embargo, iv. 278.

Lambert, John, British major-general, ordered on the expedition to New Orleans, viii. 314; arrives at New Orleans, 367; commands reserve, 372; his report of the assault, 376, 377; recalls Thornton, 380, 381; escapes, 382; captures Fort Bowyer, 383-385.

"Landrail," British cutter captured in the channel, viii. 195, 196.

Langdon, John, of New Hampshire, offered the Navy Department, i. 220; Jefferson writes to, 330; nominated for the Vice-Presidency, vi. 214.

Lansdowne, Marquess of, moves for a committee on the Orders in Council, vi. 275; on British naval success, vii. 17.

Latour, A. Lacarriere, chief engineer to Jackson at New Orleans, reports to Jackson the numbers of the British advance, viii. 343, 344; lays out lines on the west bank, 370; his services, ix. 236.

Latrobe, Benjamin H., report on steam-engines, i. 68, 70, 112; letter of, to Volney, 130; architect of the Capitol, iv. 152; rebuilds the capitol, ix. 142, 143.

Lauriston, Marquis de, French ambassador to Russia, v. 418.

Laussat, Pierre Clement, French prefect in Louisiana, ii. 5; arrives at New Orleans, 10, 13; defines the boundaries of the Louisiana purchase, 255; declares the Rio Bravo the western limit of Louisiana, 298; iii. 164; his account of the situation, 298.

"Lawrence," Perry's flagship, vii. 120, 127; viii. 111.

Lawrence, James, captain in U. S. navy, commands "Hornet," vii. 287; blockades "Bonne Citoyenne," 288; sinks "Peacock," 289, 290; his previous career, 291; commands "Chesapeake," 291; his defeat and death, 293-302.

Lawrence, William, major of Second U. S. Infantry, commands Fort Bowyer, viii. 322; capitulates, 383-385.

Lea, Thomas, i. 257.

"Leander," British 50-gun frigate, iii. 91, 94; a shot from, kills John Pierce, 199; captures "Rattlesnake," vii. 313.

"Leander," the, Miranda's ship, iii. 190.

Lear, Tobias, consul to St. Domingo, i. 389; quits St. Domingo, 407; negotiates a treaty with the Pacha of Tripoli, ii. 434; quoted as authority on the ownership of Florida, vii. 212.

Leavenworth, Henry, major of the Ninth Infantry, viii. 35; commands right battalion at Chippawa, 42; at Lundy's Lane, 50, 53, 56, 58; wounded, commands brigade, 63, 65; his opinion of Brown's order, 65.

Leclerc, Victor Emmanuel, French general, in command of the expedition against Louverture, i. 378; seizes Toussaint Louverture, 396; insults American shipmasters, 407; reports French losses, 414; blamed by Napoleon, 416; his death, 418; ii. 13.

Lee, Charles, counsel for Chase, ii. 228.

Lee, Henry, crippled by Baltimore rioters, vi. 407, 408.
Legal tender, Jefferson's silence about, in 1814, viii. 247; not a part of Eppes's scheme, 248; denounced by Dallas, 249; rejected by House of Representatives, 253, 254.
Leib, Michael, member of Congress from Pennsylvania, i. 298; ii. 123, 194, 196 *et seq.*; senator from Pennsylvania, v. 181, 189, 191; vi. 229, 243; votes against Bank Charter, 337; his political capacity, 364; in opposition, vii. 48, 59; his vote on seizing West Florida, 209; resigns to become postmaster of Philadelphia, 399, 400; ix. 107.
Leipzig, battle of, vii. 355; news reaches America, 370, 393.
"Leo," privateer, viii. 196.
Leonard, Nathaniel, captain in First Artillery, surprised and captured in Fort Niagara, vii. 203.
"Leopard," the, sent to search the "Chesapeake," iv. 4; accompanies the "Chesapeake" out to sea, 10; hails the "Chesapeake," 11; fires on the "Chesapeake," 16; searches the "Chesapeake," 19.
Leslie, Charles Robert, ix. 213; his account of Allston, 215.
"Levant," 20-gun British sloop-of-war, ix. 74; captured by the "Constitution," 75-77; seized by British squadron in Portuguese waters, 78.
Lewis, Captain, of the "Leander," v. 265.
Lewis and Clark, expedition of, v. 12, 215.
Lewis, Morgan, of the Livingston connection, i. 108; elected in 1804 governor of New York, iv. 283; appointed major-general, vii. 37, 156; on the capture of Fort George, 158; withdraws from Stony Creek, 160; on Dearborn's health, 161; ordered to Sackett's Harbor, 162, 177; commands division under Wilkinson, 184; ill at Chrystler's Farm, 188, 190; commands district, 407.
Lewis, William, i. 127.
Lewis, William, colonel of Fifth Kentucky militia, vii. 88, 89, 91; captured, 96.
Liancourt, Duc de, describes Philadelphia, i. 28, 117; on the Virginians, 33; on life in Pennsylvania, 42, 45, 52; on Virginia culture, 133, 157, 165.
Libraries in 1800, i. 61, 63, 129, 152.
Licenses of trade, British, proposed by Spencer Perceval, iv. 88; favored by Canning, 92; prescribed by Orders in Council, 103, 323; v. 59, 64; scandal of, 273; debate on, 274, 275; Canning's remarks on, 278, 280; Sidmouth's conditions on, 281; Castlereagh proposes to abandon, 221, 282; to be restricted in the war to New England vessels, vii. 31.
Licenses, Napoleon's system of, v. 246-249; promised abandonment of, 392, 393; continued issue of, 400; repudiated by Napoleon, 414, 417, 422; municipal character of, vi. 43; their continued issue, 54; extension of, 250.
Lieven, Prince de, Russian ambassador in London, vii. 340; informs Roumanzoff of Castlereagh's refusal of mediation, 346, 349; ordered to renew the offer, 348, 351, 352; refuses to renew the offer, 353.
Lincoln, Abraham, i. 171.
Lincoln, Levi, Attorney-General, i. 219, 304; ii. 2; on the acquisition of new territory by the United States, 78; resigns, iii. 10; governor of Massachusetts, iv. 416; declines appointment as justice, v. 359.
Lingan, James Maccubin, killed by Baltimore rioters, vi. 407, 408.

Linn, James, member of Congress from New Jersey, i. 295.

Linn, John Blair, i. 123.

"Linnet," British 18-gun brig on Lake Champlain, viii. 103; her armament, 104; in the battle of Plattsburg, 110.

Liston, Robert, British minister, ii. 340, 367.

Literature, American, in 1800, i. 41, 75 et seq., 93; in 1817, ix. 175-218, 238.

"Little Belt," British sloop-of-war, affair of, v. 25-37, 45, 270.

"Little Belt," 3-gun British sloop on Lake Erie, vii. 120.

Little Warrior of Wewocau, joins Tecumthe, vii. 223; murders white families on the Ohio, 224, is put to death, 225.

Livermore, Edward St. Loe, member of Congress from Massachusetts, v. 184.

Liverpool, meeting of merchants at, in September, 1814, viii. 198.

Liverpool, Earl of (Baron Hawkesbury), British Foreign Secretary, ii. 344, 410; his opinion on Spencer Perceval's proposed order, iv. 90; on American partiality to France, v. 50; succeeds Castlereagh at the War Department, 263; his view of American duty, vii. 17, 18; on the opening negotiations at Ghent, ix. 25-27; on the utmost point of concession, 31; on the capture of Washington, 36; writes to Wellington, 40; abandons claim to territory, 41.

Livingston, Edward, district-attorney and mayor of New York, i. 233, 295; ii. 259; at New Orleans, iii. 300; his speech of 1798, viii. 276.

Livingston, Robert R., aids Fulton's steamboat, i. 69, 112; iii. 216; his family connection, i. 108, 109; offered the Navy Department, 219; appointed minister to France, 233, 295, 404; discusses the price of Louisiana, ii. 31; his claims convention, 46; his estimate of the importance of the cession of Louisiana, 67; claims West Florida, 68 et seq.; his plan of gaining West Florida, 246, 275; his situation after the treaty, 289; distrusts Napoleon, 290; succeeded by Armstrong, 291, 303.

Lloyd, George, lieutenant in the British navy, commanding sloop-of-war "Castilian," his report on the loss of the "Avon," viii. 190-192.

Lloyd, James, author of the "Boston Memorial," iii. 144; elected to succeed J. Q. Adams as senator from Massachusetts, iv. 242; senator from Massachusetts, vi. 183; Randolph's letter to, on the Hartford Convention, viii. 230; his reply to Randolph, 306.

Lloyd, Robert, captain of the British seventy-four "Plantagenet," finds the "General Armstrong" at Fayal, viii. 201; his report of the destruction of the "General Armstrong," 202-207, 209.

Loan of 1810, v. 178; of 1812, for eleven millions, vi. 169; partial failure of, 207; of 1813, for twenty millions, 433, 448; for 1813, of sixteen millions, vii. 44; for 1814, authorized for twenty-five millions, 389; threatened failure of, 394; nine millions obtained in May, viii. 17, 18; failure of, in July, 1814, 213, 241, 242; amounts taken in Virginia and Massachusetts, 234; of eighteen millions, in 1815, for funding treasury notes, ix. 84, 100; failure of, in 1815, 100-103.

Lockyer, Nicholas, captain of the British sloop-of-war "Sophie," negotiates with Jean Laffite, viii. 321.

GENERAL INDEX. 311

Logan, George, senator from Pennsylvania, iii. 139; his proposal to prohibit commerce with St. Domingo, 88 ; his bill to prohibit trade with St. Domingo, 140 ; wishes to set Monroe aside, 152 ; an amateur negotiator, iv. 236.

Logan's Act, ii. 259; iv. 236.

Long, Charles, joint paymaster-general of the forces, v. 58.

Longstreet, Judge, author of "Georgia Scenes," i. 52.

Louis Bonaparte, king of Holland, resists Napoleon's decrees, v. 146; his interview with Armstrong, 147, 148; threatened by Napoleon, 236, 237, 240; stipulates seizure of American ships, 240, 274; abdicates, 242.

Louisiana, ceded by France to Spain in 1763, i. 353; retrocession asked by Talleyrand in 1798, 357; retrocession again asked by Bonaparte in 1800, 363-368 ; retroceded by Spain to France in the treaty of San Ildefonso, Oct. 1, 1800, 370; Bonaparte plans an expedition to occupy, 399; boundaries fixed by Decrès, ii. 5; commercial relations and sentiments prescribed toward the United States, 8; ceded by France to the United States, 42 ; price of, 45 ; importance of cession, 49; Napoleon's reasons for selling, 53; Talleyrand's explanation of, 55; treble invalidity of sale, 56; constitutional question debated in Congress, 96 *et seq.*; plans with regard to the status of, 116; admitted without an amendment, 118; bill for temporary government of, 120; Breckinridge's bill defining boundaries and government, 120 *et seq.*; bill defining territorial government of, 125, 130; Spain protests against sale of, 252 *et seq.*; people regarded as unfit for self-government, 399; they urge the execution of the treaty, 400; report of Randolph upon their claims, 400; political effects of purchase of, iii. 17; boundaries of, 33-35; disaffection in, 297 *et seq.*; dislike of Claiborne's administration, 299; admitted to territorial rights, March 2, 1805, 302; first territorial legislature of, 302-304; government offered to Monroe, v. 162; proposed as a kingdom for the French Bourbons, 239; admitted into the Union, 323-326; vi. 235; objects of British expedition to, viii. 313, 314; Nicholl's proclamation to natives of, 320, 321 ; Jackson's proclamation to people of, 324, 325; Jackson's proclamation to free negroes of, 325; Monroe warns Jackson of expedition to, 326, 327; population of, 334; militia in the night battle at New Orleans, 345, 346; militia in want of arms, 368; militia placed on the Chef Menteur road, 369; militia on the west bank, 370, 371; militia routed, 377, 378; to be restored to Spain, ix. 4, 6, 8; Calhoun's question regarding purchase of, 149, 152. (See New Orleans.)

"Louisiana," American 16-gun sloop-of-war at New Orleans, viii. 344; descends the river, 355 ; hauled beyond range of British guns, 356, 359; not brought into action, Jan. 1, 1815, 361; supports Jackson's line, 368; not in action of Jan. 8, 374.

"Louisianacide," Napoleon's, ii. 37.

Louverture, Toussaint, i. 354; story of, 378 *et seq.*; champion of Republican principles, 392 ; seized and sent to France, 396; his dependence on the United States for supplies, 406, 416; his death, ii. 20.

Lowell, John, his pamphlet on disunion, viii. 5; on the condition of

Massachusetts banks, 15; favors a separate peace, 289, 290; on the delegates to Hartford, 291; on H. G. Otis, 294, 295; approves report of Convention, 300.

Lowndes, William, i. 151; member of the Twelfth Congress from South Carolina, vi. 122, 164; his hostility to non-importation, 205, 234, 445, 448; opposes compromise of forfeitures, 442; reports inability to decide between Dallas and Calhoun on a national bank, viii. 252; in the Fourteenth Congress, ix. 107, 108; his report on the revenue, 112; chairman of tariff committee, 114.

Ludlow, Augustus C., first lieutenant on the "Chesapeake," mortally wounded, vii. 295.

Luisa, Queen of Spain, i. 345 *et seq.*

Lumber trade of New England, depressed in 1815, ix. 97.

Lumley, captain of British 32-gun frigate "Narcissus," vii. 313.

Lundy's Lane, Riall advances to, viii. 47; concentration of forces at, 49, 50; battle of, 51-64.

Lyman, Theodore, ii. 169; iv. 411.

Lynnhaven Bay, iv. 4, 9.

Lyon, Matthew, member of Congress from Vermont, i. 295; from Kentucky, his attack on Randolph, ii. 123, 216; votes against the St. Domingo Bill, iii. 143; contractor, 175; favors ships and harbor defences, 180; with Burr, 220; favors defence, v. 358.

MacDonnell, G., major in Glengarry Light Infantry, vii. 147.

Macdonough, Thomas, commander in U. S. Navy, commands flotilla on Lake Champlain, vii. 192; viii. 97; takes position in Plattsburg Bay, 98; his force, 104, 105; his previous career, 106; his forethought in preparing for action, 107; his victory, 109, 110; ix. 234; his losses, viii. 111; his reward, ix. 141, 142.

"Macedonian," British frigate, capture of, vi. 382, 383; effect of capture in England, vii. 6, 7, 9, 13, 16; blockaded at New London, 278, 279, 287, 311; action with, compared with that of "Endymion," ix. 68, 69.

Mackinaw (see Michillimackinaw).

Maclay, William, senator from Pennsylvania, his description of Jefferson, i. 185.

MacNeil, John, major of Eleventh U. S. Infantry, viii. 35; at Chippawa, 42; at Lundy's Lane, 50; wounded, 52, 63.

Macomb, Alexander, colonel of Third Artillery, commands reserve in Wilkinson's expedition, vii. 184; lands on north shore of St. Lawrence, 187; in the advance, 188, 191; promoted to brigadier, 409; takes command at Plattsburg, viii. 100; his account of the British advance, 103; his effectives, 217; retained on peace establishment, ix. 88.

Macon, Nathaniel, of North Carolina, i. 149, 261; chosen Speaker of the House in the Seventh Congress, 267; Speaker of the Eighth Congress, ii. 95, 123; opposed to the impeachment of Judge Chase, 150; Speaker of the Ninth Congress, iii. 128; reappoints Randolph and Nicholson on the Committee of Ways and Means, 128; Jefferson's advances to, 167; defeats Bidwell's amendment by his casting vote, 360; retires from his office, iv. 153; letter on the opinions prevailing at Washington, 368; declares that the embargo is the

GENERAL INDEX. 313

people's choice, 421, 453 ; votes with Federalists, v. 182; his bill for excluding British and French shipping, 183, 184; bill defeated by Senate, 185, 191, 193; Samuel Smith's motives for defeating, 185-188, 192, 193; his bill No. 2, 194, 195 ; adopted by Congress, 197, 198; his remark on manufacturing influence, 197; his speech on reducing the army and navy in 1810, 201; his bill admitting the State of Louisiana, with West Florida, into the Union, 323-326; not candidate for Speaker, vi. 123, 124; his account of the opinions prevailing at Washington, 129; supports war, 145 ; his remark on France and England, 196; his remarks on the repeal of the restrictive system, vii. 377, 378; favors legal-tender paper, 389; viii. 253, 254; senator from North Carolina, ix. 108.

MacRee, William, lieutenant-colonel of artillery, at New Orleans, viii. 345.

Madison, Mrs., iii. 152; her remarks on Congress, vii. 379, 380.

Madison, Bishop, of Virginia, i. 136.

Madison, James, and the Virginia Resolutions, i. 140 et seq., 148, 177; personal characteristics of, 188 et seq.; appointed Secretary of State, 218 ; makes no removals in the Department of State, 236; distrust of, 248, 261; a commissioner in the Yazoo sale, 304, 322, 332; instructions of, respecting the retrocession of Louisiana, 405 ; asks Pichon to remonstrate with Leclerc, 408; writes to Livingston, 423, 426; his orders to Pinckney, 427, 433 ; invokes Pichon's aid, 438, 439, 441; writes instructions for Livingston and Monroe, ii. 2; conversation with J. Q. Adams respecting the Louisiana treaty, 117 ; favors Yazoo compromise, 211; instructs Monroe to bargain with Spain for West Florida, 248, 251; explains the failure to demand West Florida, 256; sends the ratified claims convention to Madrid, 260, 278, 279; hopes to be relieved of Yrujo, 267; communicates with Livingston respecting West Florida and Yrujo, 262; attempts to cajole Turreau, 273 ; Turreau's description of, 274; compromised by Pinckney, 276 ; recalls Pinckney and hurries Monroe to Spain, 286; denies that the Government aids desertion of seamen, 345 ; communications to Thornton, 362; proposes a convention with regard to impressments and the blockade, 385; remonstrates with Merry respecting impressments, 393 ; remains Secretary of State in Jefferson's second administration, iii. 10; writes to Jefferson respecting the claim to West Florida, 55, 60; his letter to Jefferson concerning Monroe's failure at Madrid, 59 ; proposes negotiations and diplomacy, 70; his character as a diplomatist, 74; his pamphlet, "Examination of the Brit sh doctrine," 102, 110; to be Jefferson's successor, 120; his altercation with Casa Yrujo, 185 et seq.; his complication with Miranda, 190 et seq.; Turreau demands an explanation from, 195; imposes impossible conditions on Monroe, 402; writes to Jefferson respecting the new instructions to Monroe, 438; arranges with Rose a "bridge" for Jefferson, iv. 191; sends his last reply to Rose, 196; notifies Erskine that the "Chesapeake" affair has lost consequence, 199; the caucus for, in Virginia and Washington, 226;

elected President, 287; sends Armstrong instructions in response to Champagny's letter of Jan. 15, 1808, 305; his anger with Perceval's order of April 11, 1808, 327; threatens a declaration of war, 386; his opponents in Congress, 428; inaugurated, 472; v. 1; his Inaugural Address, 2, 3, 4; offers the Treasury to Robert Smith, 7, 379; appoints Robert Smith Secretary of State, 8; his Cabinet, 9, 10; nominates J. Q. Adams to Russia, 11; his letter to Erskine accepting settlement of the "Chesapeake" affair, 68–70, 89; issues proclamation renewing intercourse with England, 73, 74; his views of the change in British policy, 75, 76, 81, 83; his message of May 23, 1809, 76, 77; his popularity, 80, 85, 86; on the disavowal of Erskine's arrangement, 112; revives non-intercourse against England, 114; his negotiation with F. J. Jackson, 117, 122–132; described by Jackson, 120; his message of Nov. 29, 1809, 176, 177; special message of Jan. 3, 1810, asking for volunteers, 179; his opinions of Samuel and Robert Smith, 186; dissensions in his cabinet, 188; remarks on the experiment of unrestricted commerce, 210, 211; his reply to Napoleon's note on the right of search and blockade, 250, his anger at Napoleon's confiscations, 292; his instructions of June 5, 1810, to Armstrong on Champagny's reprisals, 293, 294; his devotion to commercial restrictions, 293, 295; his instructions of July 5, 1810, to Armstrong requiring indemnity, 295, 296, 297, 299; his decision to accept the conditions of Champagny's letter of August 5, 296–301; revives non-intercourse against Great Britain, 303, 304; takes military possession of West Florida, 308–312, 318; his supposed character, 310; his annual message of Dec. 5, 1810, 314, 317–319; asks authority to take possession of East Florida, 327; appoints commissioners for East Florida, 327; decides to enforce the non-intercourse against Great Britain, 347; his doubts regarding Napoleon's folly, 350; his irritation at Smith's proposed inquiry from Serurier, 350, 351; offers the State Department to Monroe, 366, 372, 374; his parting interview with Robert Smith, 375–377; his anger with Smith, 378; his translation of *bien entendu*, 387, 388; his success in maintaining his own system in the Cabinet, vi. 61, 62; his discontent with Napoleon's conduct, 63, 64, 125, 187, 218, 224; his orders to maintain peace with the northwestern Indians, 88, 93; his attitude toward war with England, 118, 125, 129, 131, 175, 196, 197, 213; his annual message of Nov. 5, 1811, 124; entertains Crillon, 179, 185; his message communicating Henry's papers, 181; his embargo message, 193, 198, 199; his comments on the conduct of the Senate, 203; sustains non-importation, 205; renominated for the Presidency, 214; perplexed by the French decrees, 218; his letter to Barlow threatening war on France, 218, 259; his view of the "immediate impulse" to war with England, 220, 226: his war message, 221–226; signs declaration of war, and visits departments, 229: his measures regarding East Florida, 237, 239, 241, 243; his remarks on Napoleon's Russian campaign, 265; his remarks in August, 1812, on the Canadian campaign, 337; re-elected President, 413; wishes Monroe to command western army, 419, 420, 425; his annual message of 1812, 430-433; his "fair calculation" on Napoleon's success, vii. 2; his message on British "demoralizing and disorganizing contrivances," 31, 32; his second Inaugural Address, 33; his relations toward Gallatin and Monroe, 39; consents to Gallatin's departure, 42, 43; his annual message, May 25, 1813, 53, 54; dangerous illness of, 55, 58; his reply to the Senate in regard to Gallatin's absence, 59, 60; his skill in overthrowing an enemy, 64; goes to Montpelier, 70; his annual message of Dec. 7, 1813, 365, 366; his embargo message of Dec. 9, 1813, 367, 368, 372, 392; accepts Castlereagh's offer of direct negotiation, 371; nominates commissioners and a Secretary of the Treasury, 371; his obstinacy, 372, 393; abandons system of commercial restrictions, 373, 374, 379; causes of his abandonment of commercial restrictions, 373, 374, 377, 394, 395; his language about Napoleon, 392; appoints G. W. Campbell Secretary of the Treasury, 396, 397; appoints Richard Rush attorney-general, 398; appoints R. J. Meigs postmaster-general, 401; overcomes his party enemies, 402; his dislike of Armstrong, 405, 406, 414; offended by Armstrong's letter appointing Andrew Jackson a major-general, 410, 411; his court-martial on William Hull, 415-417; his mode of resisting usurpations on State rights, viii. 8; irritated by Armstrong's neglect to defend Washington, 121; calls a cabinet meeting, June 23, 1814, 121; selects General Winder to command at Washington, 122; calls for militia, 131, 132; reviews the army at the Old Fields, 134; goes to Winder's headquarters at eight o'clock on the morning of August 24, 137; arrives on the battle-field at Bladensburg, 140; his movements, August 24-27, 149-151, 156, 157, 300; ix. 21; charges Monroe with the war department in Armstrong's absence, viii. 158; his interview with Armstrong, August 29, 160, 161; greatly shaken by the capture of Washington, 160, 230, 231; appoints Monroe Secretary of War, 163; his unpopularity, 229, 230; his disappointments, 237, 238; his annual message of Sept. 20, 1814, 239, 240; vetoes bill for incorporating a national bank, 260; to be coerced into retiring, 306, 309; ix. 3, 4; characterized by the London press, ix. 2-6; decides to omit impressment from treaty, 33; Lord Liverpool's remark on, 36, sends treaty of peace to the Senate, 58 recommends preparation for war, 82, 83; his annual message of 1815 105, 106; his annual message of 1816, 143, 144; his veto of internal improvements, 151, 169, 192, 220; his retirement, 153.

Maguaga, battle of, vi. 325.

"Maidstone," 36-gun British frigate, vii. 266.

Mail routes in 1800, i. 15; in 1816, ix. 170, 171.

Maine, District of, a part of Massachusetts, i. 20; boundary of, disputed, ii. 358, 383, 392; viii. 4, 94, 95; two counties of, occupied by British expedition in 1814, viii. 95, 96, 267, 272; ix. 17; portion of, demanded by Great Britain, viii. 268, 287; concessions proposed by Governor Strong, 288; territory of, required by England, ix. 8; cession assumed by the *uti possidetis*, 10; claimed at Ghent, 19, 25; claim partially abandoned, 34, 35; claim rejected, 37; claim wholly abandoned, 42, 52; relative prosperity of, 155, 157, 160.

Maitland, General, at St. Domingo, i. 385.

"Majestic," 56-gun British frigate, intercepts the "President," ix. 64, 66, 67.

Malbone, Edward G., i. 149; his painting, ix. 214, 215.

Malden, British trading post on the Detroit River, vi. 73, 80, 85, 300; to be besieged by Hull, 303, 314; British force at, 312, 313; evacuated by Proctor, vii. 130, 131; occupied by Harrison, 132; in the negotiation at Ghent, ix. 34.

Malmesbury, Lord, patron of F. J. Jackson, iv. 64.

"Mammoth," privateer, in British waters, viii. 196.

Manhattan Company of New York city, i. 65, 70.

Manners and morals, American, in 1800, i. 48 *et seq.*

Manners, William, captain of the British sloop-of-war "Reindeer," his action with the "Wasp," viii. 186-188.

Mannheim, proposed Congress at, vii. 373.

Manufactures in New England in 1800, i. 22; growth of, in 1809-1810, v. 15-19; political influence of, 197; protection of, 319; stimulated by the war, viii. 14; depressed by the peace, ix. 95, 96; protection of, recommended by Madison, 105; protective tariff recommended by Dallas, 106; Dallas's scheme for protecting, 111, 112; protection opposed by Randolph, 112, 113; protective tariff of 1816, 114-116; value of, 160.

Marblehead, privateersmen from, vii. 337.

Marbois, Barbé, favors the cession of Louisiana, ii. 26; removed from office, iii. 371-374.

Marbury against Madison, case of, ii. 145 *et seq.*

Maret, Hugues Bernard, Duc de Bassano, Napoleon's secretary, v. 143; succeeds Champagny as Minister of Foreign Affairs, 401; his report to Napoleon of March 10, 1812, vi. 216, 253; his negotiation with Joel Barlow, 248-263; his instructions to Serurier of October, 1811, on the revocation of the decrees, 248, 249; communicates Decree of St. Cloud to Barlow and Serurier, 255-257; his instructions to Dalberg, 260; invites Barlow to Wilna, 263; dismisses his guests, 264.

Marietta, Ohio, in 1800, i. 2.

Marlboro, in Maryland, Ross camps at, Aug. 22, 1814, viii. 130; returns to, Aug. 26, 148.

Marmont, Marshal, his story of Decrès, v. 222.

Marriatt, Joseph, his pamphlet in 1808, iv. 333.

Marshall, Humphrey, of Kentucky, i. 268; on W. H. Harrison, vi. 107.

Marshall, John, Chief-Justice, i. 133; Jefferson's antipathy to, 192; personal characteristics of, 193; detests Jefferson, 194; his constitutional views, 256; his influence on Story, 260; his opinion of Jefferson, 262; his appointment obnoxious to Jefferson, 275, 290; ii. 145; fear of his decisions, i. 298; ii. 143; opinion of, respecting the powers of Government in the Louisiana case, ii. 125; his decision in the Marbury case, 146; his decision in the Yazoo case, 214; his definition

GENERAL INDEX. 317

of treason in the case of Bollman and Swartwout, iii. 340, 443; presides over the trial of Burr, 442; refuses to commit Burr for treason, and rebukes the Government for laxity in procuring proof, 445; threatened with removal from office, 447; and impeachment, 466, 470, 471 ; his alleged sympathy with Burr, 461; his decision in the Burr trial, 467 *et seq.;* iv. 147; menaced in Jefferson's annual message of 1807, 155; Jefferson's desire to punish, 205; his decision in the case of the United States *v.* Fisher *et al.*, 270; inclines to Pickering's view of Jefferson, 348; his judicial opinions, ix. 188-191.

Martin against Hunter's Lessee, Story's opinion in case of, ix. 190-192.

Martin, Luther, Chase's counsel, his view of impeachment, ii. 223, 227, 231; Burr's counsel, iii. 444; attacks Jefferson, 449; angers Jefferson, 453; his speech in the Burr trial, 465.

Maryland, her electoral vote, vi. 406, 413; affected by the blockade, vii. 264; Admiral Cockburn's operations against the shores of, 265-269; election of 1814, viii 228; creates a State army, 282; growth of population, ix. 155, 161; increase of wealth in, 163.

Mason, Armistead, succeeds Giles as senator from Virginia, ix. 107.

Mason, George, i. 133.

Mason, Jeremiah, elected senator from New Hampshire, vii. 48; votes against a mission to Sweden, 63; his speech against Giles's bill for drafting militia, viii. 271; votes for internal improvements, ix. 151.

Mason, John Thompson, declines appointment as attorney-general, iii. 11.

Mason, Jonathan, iv. 411; his letter to Nicholas on the alternative to disunion, viii. 306, 307.

Massa, Duc de, letter from, v. 347.

Massac (see Fort Massac).

Massachusetts, population of, in 1790 and 1800, i. 20; valuation of, 23; society of, in 1800, 76; political divisions of, 76, 82; suffrage in, 86; intellectual activity of, 93; separatist tendency in, 138; judicial tenure in, 256; Jefferson's conception of, 310, 315, 329; the necessary head of a New England Confederation, ii. 163; election of May, 1804, 163; political apathy in, 165-168, 170; chooses republican electors in 1804, 201, 204; anxiety for settlement of eastern boundary, 392; militia of, iv. 210; feelings of, toward Virginia in 1808, iv. 409-420, 433; proceedings of legislature in February, 1809, 416; address of legislature in March, 1809, 456; "Patriotick Proceedings" of, in 1809, 458, 459; tonnage of, v. 15; manufactures of, 17-19; resolutions of legislature regarding F. J. Jackson, 214; election of 1810, 215; republican control of, in 1810 and 1811, vi. 115; Federalists recover control in 1812, 204; gives trouble to Dearborn, 305; refuses obedience to call for militia, 309; temper of, in 1812, 399-402; federalist majority in the elections of 1812, 413; disaffection of, vii 33; election in April, 1813, 50; delays action, 52; reports and resolutions of legislature in 1813, 64-66; banks of, their condition and influence, 386-389; expression of legislature in January, 1814, viii. 2, 3; blockaded April 25, 1814, 3; in danger from both sides, 4; town meetings in January, 1814, 5-7;

report of legislature on a New England Convention, Feb. 18,1814, 8; election in April, 1814, 9–11, 13; prosperity in 1814, 14; expressions of clergy, 20–23; regular troops in, vii. 284; viii. 95, 316; territory of, occupied, 95, 96; object of, in dependence on militia, 220; places militia under State major-general, 221, ix. 160; "dangerous and perplexing" situation of, viii. 222–224; calls a New England Convention at Hartford, 225–227, 287; election of November, 1814, a federalist triumph, 228, 288, 289; Jefferson's remark that Virginia got no aid from, 233; money furnished by, 233–235; men furnished by, 235, 236; moral support furnished by, 236, 237; arrears of internal taxes in, 255, 256; legislature of, refuses to co-operate in expelling enemy from Maine, 272, 304; creates a State army of ten thousand men, 272, 282; her delegation to the Hartford Convention, 290–292; accepts the report of the Hartford Convention, 295, 301; banks refuse to lend money to the State, 302; suspends organization of State army, 303; disunion sentiment of, 305–308; her indifference to the negotiation at Ghent, ix. 16, 45; alone interested in the obstacles to a treaty, 49; election of April, 1815, 92; interests affected by peace, 95, 97; suffers from Dallas's arrangements, 98–103; election of April, 1816, 133; legislature denounces Compensation Act, 137; in Presidential election of 1816, 139.

Massassinway, council at, vi. 111.

"Matilda," privateer, captured, vii. 330.

Mathews, George, appointed commissioner to take possession of East Florida, vi. 237; his proceedings, 238–240; disavowed, 240-242.

McArthur, Duncan, colonel of Ohio militia, vi. 298, 326, 328, 332, 334; brigadier-general, vii. 128.

McClure, George, brigadier-general of New York militia, commands at Niagara, vii. 200; evacuates Fort George and burns Newark, 201, 202.

McDonald, William, captain in Nineteenth U. S. Infantry, on Ripley's staff, his account of the battle of Lundy's Lane, viii. 55, 57.

McDonogh, P., lieutenant of artillery in Fort Erie, viii. 76.

McFarland, D., major of Twenty-third U. S. Infantry, viii. 35; at Chippawa, 42; at Lundy's Lane, 50; wounded, 52, 63.

McKean, Thomas, Governor of Pennsylvania, i. 228; iii. 210; declines to remove Judge Brackenridge, ii. 196, 259.

McKee, John, vi. 237.

McLean, John, member of Congress from Ohio, ix. 107.

McQueen, Peter, half-breed Creek Indian, visits Pensacola, vii. 228; attacked at Burnt Corn, 229; captures Fort Mims, 229–231; claims forty-eight hundred gun-men, 233; escapes to Florida, 257.

McRae, Alexander, counsel for Burr, iii. 445.

McRee, William, major of engineers, advises Brown to move against Riall, viii. 47; directs entrenchments at Fort Erie, 67, 76; ix. 235.

Meade, lieutenant of the British frigate "Leopard," iv. 12.

Meade, Cowles, governor of Mississippi Territory, iii. 304; arrests Burr, 326.

Meade, William, bishop of Virginia, i. 193.

Mecklenburg, Grand Duchy of, closes

GENERAL INDEX. 319

its ports to American commerce, v. 413.

Mediterranean Fund, the, ii. 141; iii. 137, 182, 183.

Meigs, Return Jonathan, appointed postmaster-general, vii. 401.

"Melampus," British frigate, iv. 2, 23; vi. 25.

Melville, Viscount, First Lord of the Admiralty, iii. 235, 238.

"Menelaus," British frigate, engaged in house-burning on the Potomac, viii. 164; off Sassafras River, 165.

Merry, Anthony, appointed British minister to the United States, ii. 360; his arrival and reception by Jefferson, 361 *et seq.*, 380, 381, 390; dines at the White House, 369; affronted and declines the President's invitations, 375; union of, with Burr, 390; writes to his Government on the boundary question, 392; remonstrates with Madison respecting the enlistment of deserters, 393; receives a message from Burr, 395; inquires meaning of impressment act, 397, 398; communicates Burr's plan to his Government, 403; his instructions in November, 1804, 422–424; writes to his Government concerning the failure of the Spanish mission, iii. 96; his account of Madison's conversation, 98; of Jefferson's, 101; his report of the sensation produced by the seizures, 109; informs his Government respecting the Non-importation Resolutions, 150; takes Yrujo's part, 188 ; his report to his Government of the apprehensions of the Americans, 198; advises Fox against concessions, 202; upholds Burr, 219; alarmed by the publicity of Burr's schemes, 226; confers with Burr respecting his journey to the west, 230 *et seq.*; recalled by Fox, 250; his last interview with Burr, 250 ; Jackson's allusions to, v. 118–121.

Message, annual, of 1801, i. 248–263; annual, of 1802, 427–429; special, of Dec. 22, 1802, on violation of the right of deposit, 430; annual, of 1803, ii. 92; special, of March 20, 1804, on the loss of the frigate "Philadelphia," 140; special, of Feb. 3, 1803, inviting the impeachment of Judge Pickering, 143; special, of Dec. 21, 1803, on the Spanish claims, 259; annual, of Nov. 8, 1804, 206-208, 263; annual, of 1805, iii. 111 *et seq.*, 128, 129; special, on Spanish relations, Dec. 6, 1805, 115–118, 130 *et seq.*; special, on British spoliations, 145; referred, 146; annual, of 1806, 329, 345; special, of Jan. 22, 1807, on Burr's conspiracy, 337; annual, of 1807, iv. 149, 150, 153–156; special, of Nov. 23, 1807, on the failure of Burr's trial, 156; special, of Dec. 18, 1807, recommending an embargo, 168–170, 228, 229; special, of Feb. 25, 1808, recommending an increase of the regular army, 212; special, of March 22 and 30, 1808, communicating papers relating to England and France, 218; annual, of Nov. 8, 1808, 361, 364; first annual, of President Madison, May 23, 1809, v. 76; annual, of Nov. 29, 1809, 176-178; special, of Jan. 3, 1810, asking for volunteers, 179; annual, of Dec. 5, 1810, 317–319; special, of Feb. 19, 1811, on the revocation of the French decrees, 347, 348; annual, of Nov. 5, 1811, vi. 124–126 ; special, of March 9, 1812, communicating John Henry's papers, 181; special, of April 1, 1812, recommending an embargo for sixty days, 198; of April 24, 1812, asking for two assistant Secretaries of War, 206; of June 1, 1812, recommending a declaration of war with England, 221-226; annual, of Nov. 4, 1812, 430-433; special, of Feb. 24, 1813, on British licenses of trade with New England, vii. 31, 32; annual of May 25, 1813, 53, 54; annual of Dec. 7, 1813, 365; ix. 5; special of Dec. 9, 1813, asking for an embargo, vii. 367, 368, 372; special of March 31, 1814, recommending abandonment of commercial restrictions, 373, 374; annual of Sept. 20, 1814, viii. 239; veto, of Jan. 30, 1815, on the bill to incorporate the United States Bank, 260; special, of Feb. 20, 1815, transmitting treaty of peace, ix. 82; annual, of Dec. 5, 1815, 105; annual, of Dec. 3, 1816, 143, 144; special, of March 3, 1817, vetoing bill for internal improvements, 151.

"Messenger," stallion, i. 51.

Mexico, Jefferson's language to, iv. 340, 341.

Michigan Territory, iii. 176; population in 1810, v. 289. (See Detroit.)

Michillimackinaw, Island of, vi. 294; captured by British expedition, 314, 320; Croghan's expedition against, viii. 32; demanded by British at Ghent, ix. 34.

Milan Decree (see Decrees).

Militia, condition of, in 1808, iv. 210, 213; appropriation for, 224; constitutional power of Congress over, vi. 159, 160, 400; Cheves's opinion on the war power, 160; act authorizing call for one hundred thousand, 204, 390; refuses to cross the frontier, 351, 352, 360; of Kentucky, 391, 393 (see Kentucky, Tennessee, Georgia, Washington City); praised by political parties, viii. 217; system a failure in 1814, 217-219; tainted with fraud, 219; intended for overthrowing the national government, 220; of Massachusetts and Connecticut withdrawn from national service in September, 1814, 220, 221; of Vermont refused for defence of Plattsburg, 222; views of the Massachusetts Senate regarding, 226; Monroe's complaints of, 264; Monroe's scheme for drafting from, 265, 266; Giles's bill for raising eighty thousand by draft, 269-280; Troup's opinion of, 274; Madison's recommendation for, ix. 105.

Mill, James, his reply to Spence and Cobbett, iv. 329.

Milledge, John, Governor of Georgia, and the Yazoo sale, i. 305.

Miller, James, lieutenant-colonel of Fourth U. S. Infantry, at Detroit, vi. 326, 328; appointed colonel of the Twenty-first Infantry, viii. 36; at Lundy's Lane, captures the British guns, 54, 55, 60; promoted to brigadier, takes command of Scott's brigade, 87; carries British battery in sortie from Fort Erie, 87, 88.

Miller, John, colonel of Nineteenth U. S. Infantry, leads sortie at Fort Meigs, vii. 107.

Miller, Morris S., member of Congress from New York, on the States taking care of themselves in 1814, viii. 276.

Miller, Samuel, captain of marines, at Bladensburg, viii. 143.

Minor of Natchez, iii. 224, 225, 315.

Mint, opposition to, i. 299; ii. 77.

Miranda, Francesco de, his plans to revolutionize Colombia, iii. 189 *et seq.;* distrusted by Burr, 189, 238; visits Washington, 190; his letter to Madison, 191; sails, 191; defeated by the Spaniards, 209; returns to New York, 238.

GENERAL INDEX.

Miró, Governor, iii. 269.

Mississippi, district of, created, ii. 257.

Mississippi militia, with Jackson at Mobile, viii. 328; at New Orleans, 333, 337, 344-346.

Mississippi River, British right of navigating, under the treaty of 1783, ix. 44-46, 52.

Mississippi Territory, admitted into the Union, ix. 119.

Mitchell, D. B., Governor of Georgia, vi. 242.

Mitchill, Dr. Samuel L., i. 69, 93, 110; in the Seventh Congress, 264; in the Eighth Congress, ii. 153, 218, 238; senator from New York, iii. 126, 139, 430, 431.

Mobile, intended to be seized at the outbreak of the war, vii. 206, 207; Congress authorizes seizure of, 208, 209; Gallatin's remonstrance against seizure of, 211-213; Armstrong orders seizure of, 213, 214; Wilkinson takes possession of, 217; Vice-Admiral Cochrane recommends expedition to, viii. 311; Andrew Jackson arrives at, Aug. 15, 1814, 319, 320; Jackson waits at, 320-331; Jackson leaves for New Orleans, Nov. 22, 1814, 331-333.

Mobile Act, annexing Mobile to the Union, ii. 255, 257, 260-263, 291, 293, 304, 380; vi. 236; criticised by Cevallos, iii. 25; explained by Jefferson, 56; Randolph's explanation of, 163.

"Modern Chivalry," i. 125.

"Mohawk," British sloop-of-war, vii. 266.

Mollien, Nicholas François, appointed Minister of the Treasury by Napoleon, iii. 371.

Money, Captain, of the British ship "Trave," commands sailors at the battle of Jan. 8, 1815, wounded, viii. 379.

Monroe, James, and the Callender scandal, i. 325; nominated minister extraordinary to France and Spain, 433; accepts, 436; his language to Pichon, 440; his instructions, 442; sails for France, ii. 1; his arrival in France, 26; illness of, in Paris, 39; his draft of claims convention, 41; his share in the negotiation, 50; under the influence of other men, 67; commissioned to negotiate with Spain for West Florida, 248; takes Rufus King's place in London, 275, 288, 410; distrusts Livingston, 289; returns to Paris, 292, 301; is instructed to insist upon the right to West Florida, 301; writes to Talleyrand, 304; starts for Madrid, 307, 422; receives answer from Talleyrand, 313; in ignorance of Pitt's schemes, 419; interview with Lord Harrowby, 420; warns the President to expect a change in British policy, 422; envoy extraordinary to Spain, arrives in Madrid Jan. 2, 1805, iii. 23; his correspondence with Cevallos, 23-36; his letter to Armstrong, March 1, 1805, threatening a quarrel with France, 30; leaves Spain, 37; adopts Armstrong's views, 40; returns to London, 42, 47; intends to return home in November, 1805, 43; expects a change in British policy, 43; negotiations with Mulgrave, 47; advises the President to press on England and France at once, 49; his Spanish failure discussed in Cabinet, 58, 65-67; favored by Randolph for the Presidency, 122, 166; affected by Senate scheme for a special mission, 150-152; warned by Jefferson against Randolph, 165; has his first interview with Fox, 393; hurt by the appointment of Pinkney as his associate, 400, 414; his instructions regarding the treaty, 400 *et seq.*; disregards instructions, and signs treaty, 408 *et seq.*; embarrasses Jefferson by his treaty, 411, 434; his letter to Colonel Taylor of Caroline defending his treaty, 413; unfortunate in diplomacy, 415; negotiates with Canning with regard to the "Chesapeake" affair, iv. 42 *et seq.*; leaves London, 51; warns Jefferson of danger from England, 71; sails for home, 128; Jefferson's friendship for, 129; Pickering's opinion of, 130; reaches Washington, Dec. 22, 1807, 183; goes into opposition, 194; caucus for, 226, 284; his letter to Nicholson on support asked for the embargo, 346; Madison's advances to, v. 159, 161, 162; his state of mind, 162; offered the State Department, 366; his acceptance and policy, 368-374; takes charge, 380; Secretary of State, April 1, 1811, vi. 50; his sensitiveness about the title to West Florida, 38; his reply to Foster's protest against the seizure of Florida, 38, 39; blames Jonathan Russell for questioning the revocation of the French decrees, 42; asserts the revocation of the French decrees, 42, 43; abandons task of reconciliation with England, 44; requires revocation of the Orders in Council, 45; delays Barlow's departure, 50; his remonstrances to Serurier about Napoleon's conduct, 51, 54, 188, 189, 194, 195, 200, 217; his remarks on protection accorded to commerce, 58; his acceptance of Madison's policy, 59-61; affirms to Foster the repeal of Napoleon's decrees, 65; his letter of June 13, 1812, to John Taylor of Caroline, 66; his language to Serurier, in October, 1811, 120; informs Serurier in November of executive plan, 129; agrees to assist the independence of Spanish America, 130; negotiates purchase of Henry's papers, 178-180; his remarks to Foster on Wellesley's instructions, 192; his conference with House Committee of Foreign Relations, March 31, 1812, 197; his remarks on the embargo, 199, 200, 202; his relations toward Matthews and the occupation of East Florida, 238, 240, 241, 242; his criticisms on the conduct of the war, 396, 397; assures Serurier he will not negotiate for peace, 415; proposes to negotiate, 416; proposes to take a military commission, 419, 420; hesitates between civil or military control of the war, 421-423; becomes acting Secretary of War, 423; excites jealousy, 424, 425; abandons military career, 425, 426; offers to prohibit the employment of foreign seamen, 451; expected to command the army, vii. 35, 37; declines commission as major-general, 37; his protest against Armstrong's military control, 37, 38; his reply to the Czar's offer of mediation, 41; acquiesces in Gallatin's departure, 42; his instructions to the peace commissioners in April, 1813, 47, 211; goes as scout to the lower Potomac, 56; acting Secretary of War, 81; his views on the force required for conquering Canada, 148; instructs commissioners to assert right to Florida, 211; his views on the seizure of Florida, 212, 213; his remarks to Serurier on intercourse with Canada, 392; his antipathy to Armstrong, 411; advises the President to remove Armstrong, 412, 413; charges Armstrong with improper ambition, 414; friendly to

GENERAL INDEX. 323

Izard, viii. 114; irritated by Armstrong's indifference to the defence of Washington, 121; accedes to the abandonment of impressment as a *sine qua non*, 122; acts as a scout, August 19 and 20, 131; joins Winder, August 21, 133; notifies Madison and Serurier of expected battle at Bladensburg, 133, 138; goes to Winder's headquarters on the morning of August 24, 137; arrives first on the battle-field at Bladensburg, 139; changes the order of troops, 140; returns to Washington, 152; at Rockville, 156; returns with the President to Washington, 157; takes charge of the War Department, 158, 160; effect of his course on Armstrong, 159; claims the War Department, 161, 162; appointed Secretary of War in September, 1814, 163; admits failure of recruiting service, 216, 266; declines to receive Massachusetts militia into national service under a State major-general, 221; asks Congress for one hundred thousand regular troops in October, 1814, 264; recommends a draft, 265; borrows national loans on his private credit, 283, 284; warns Jackson Sept. 25, 1814, of British expedition against Louisiana, 326, 329; his measures for the defence of Louisiana, 326–328; forbids attack on Pensacola, 327; orders Gaines to Mobile, and Jackson to New Orleans, 331; his instructions to the Ghent commissioners, ix. 10–12; his instructions of June 27, to omit impressment, 33; recommends a peace establishment of twenty thousand men, 83; returns to State department, 87, 88; nominated for the Presidency, 122–124; elected President, 139.

Montalivet, Comte de, Napoleon's Minister of the Interior, v. 221; his efforts for American commerce, 223, 224.

Montgomery Court House (see Rockville).

Montreal, Wilkinson decides to attack, vii. 178; Amherst's expedition against, in 1760, 178; Armstrong and Wilkinson change opinions about, 180–182; Hampton's advance toward, 192–194; British forces in district of, 194–196; British forces about, in January, 1814, viii. 25.

Moore, Sir John, his Spanish campaign, v. 26, 47, 48.

Moore, Thomas, i. 48; lines of, on the Philadelphia *literati*, 122; his verses on Jefferson, 167.

Moose Island, occupied by British troops in July, 1814, viii. 94; disputed territory, 95; claimed at Ghent by England, ix. 10, 20, 25, 34, 49, 52.

Morales, Don Juan Ventura, Spanish Intendant at New Orleans, officially declares the right of deposit at end, i. 419-421; blamed by Yrujo, 427; blamed by Cevallos, ii. 60; defended by Cevallos, iii. 26; remains at New Orleans, 72-79, 300.

Moravian town, Proctor's defeat at, vii. 131-142.

Moreau, Jean Victor, Turreau's note about, iii. 82, 83; death of, vii. 351.

Morfontaine, treaty of, i. 362, 370, 388; ii. 21, 42, 46, 47, 293, 296, 297, 383. (See Treaties.)

Morgan, David, brigadier-general of Louisiana militia, commands on right bank at New Orleans, viii. 370; driven back, 377.

Morgan, George N., warns Jefferson of Burr's declarations, iii. 255, 279.

Morgan, L., major of First Rifles,

repulses British attack on Black Rock, viii. 69.

Morier, J. P., British chargé at Washington, v. 219; his protest against the seizure of West Florida, 315.

"Morning Chronicle," the, on the "Chesapeake" affair, iv. 41, 54, 70; silent toward the American war in 1813, vii. 356; on American privateers, viii. 197; on the failure of the war, ix. 35, 43; on the Ghent correspondence. 43; on the news from Ghent, 54; on the treaty, 55.

"Morning Post," the, on the "Chesapeake" affair, iv. 41, 44, 53, 54, 70 *et seq.*, 76; on the principle of retaliation, 132. 317; on the American frigates, vii. 13; calls for execution of British subjects taken in arms, 362; on the American government, ix 4, 5

Morocco, ii. 137.

Morris, Charles, captain in U. S. navy, commands corvette "Adams," viii 95; destroys his ship in the Penobscot, 96.

Morris, Commodore Richard Valentine, dismissed, ii. 137.

Morris, Gouverneur, i. 93; senator of the United States, in the judiciary debate, 279; assails the Government, 435; on the right of deposit, 435; ii. 283; on the Louisiana purchase. ii. 99, 101; his oration on the overthrow of Napoleon, viii. 19, 20; his letter on the Hartford Convention, 299; assists Erie Canal, ix. 168.

Morrison, J. W., lieutenant-colonel of British Eighty-ninth Regiment, commanding at Chrystler's Farm, vii. 189, 190; reinforces Drummond, viii. 46.

Morse Jedediah, i. 78, 93.

Moscow, occupied by Napoleon, vii. 4, 27; abandoned, 9, 30.

Moseley. Jonathan Ogden, member of Congress from Connecticut, viii. 277.

Mountmorris, Lord, v. 265.

Mulcaster, W. H., captain in British navy, commands flotilla in Wilkinson's rear. vii. 187, wounded in attacking Oswego, viii. 29, 30.

Mulgrave, Lord, British Foreign Secretary, his reception of Monroe's complaints in 1805, iii. 47; his indifference to American affairs, 48; affirms the Rule of 1756, 48; fails to answer Burr's inquiries, 229, 232.

Murray, Sir George, British major-general, succeeds Prevost as governor-general of Canada, viii. 118, 267.

Murray, J., colonel in British service, retakes Fort George, vii. 202; captures Fort Niagara, 203.

Murray William A., Lieutenant of Artillery, his report of conversation in New Orleans respecting Burr's conspiracy, iii. 303

Muscogee Indians (see Creeks).

NANTUCKET, British naval station, vii. 278, viii. 287; relieved from operation of the embargo in 1814, 369.

Napier, Charles James, lieutenant-colonel of British infantry, vii. 272; his remark on the Craney Island affair, 274; on the affair at Hampton, 276; on plundering the Yankees, 278.

Napoleon, i. 334; and Talleyrand, 357, 359; restores peace in Europe, 360, 363, 370, 373, 374, 395; obtains retrocession of Louisiana, 363-370; his anger with Godoy, 373-375; makes peace with England, 374; parallelism with Louverture, 383, 387, 388; attacks Louverture,

GENERAL INDEX. 325

390; his explanations to the British Government, 391; his letter to Louverture, 392, 393; his instructions to Leclerc, 397, 398; orders the occupation of Louisiana, 399 400; attempts to obtain Florida, 402; Jefferson's messages to, 404, 410, 411, 413, 443; his account of his miscarriage at St. Domingo, 416; fears a war with the United States, ii. 2; abandons his colonial system, 14 et seq.; scene with Lord Whitworth, 19; reveals his determination to cede Louisiana, 25-28; angry scene with his brothers, 34 et seq.; his projet of a secret convention respecting Louisiana, 40; objects to the payment of claims, 51; his inducement to sell Louisiana, 52; his conduct toward Spain, 56; his avowal as to the sale of Louisiana, 61; his reasons for betraying Charles IV., 63; for selling Louisiana, 63 et seq., repudiates drafts on the public Treasury, 270; prepares for a descent on England, 291; weary of Talleyrand. 310, 312; Jefferson's language about, 348, 353, 381; his irritation at Jerome's marriage, 379; his intervention in Monroe's Spanish negotiation, iii. 26, 29, 30, 32, 41, 82; not influenced by corruption of his subordinates. 42; begins war with Austria and Russia, 73, 76, 77, 103; forbids trade with St. Domingo, 89; captures Ulm and enters Vienna, 106, 370; returns to Paris, 371; his financial measures in 1806, 372-375; defeats Talleyrand's plan for a settlement between Spain and the United States, 383; wins the battle of Jena, 388; issues the Decree of Berlin, 389; makes the treaty of Tilsit, iv. 62, 105; attacks Portugal and Denmark, 106, enforces his Berlin Decree against the United States, 109. 110; Armstrong's story about his attitude toward Florida, 114; orders his armies into Spain, 117; his proposed division of Portugal, 119; offers Lucien the crown of Spain, 124; issues the Decree of Milan, 126; treats the United States as at war with England, 221, 292, 295, 312; seizes the Spanish Court, 298; crowns Joseph King of Spain, 300; his Spanish plan for conquering England, 303. issues the Bayonne Decree, 304; his Spanish campaign. v. 22-28; his severity toward American commerce, 30-32; withholds Florida, 32, 33; his causes for rupture with the United States, 39, 40: his war with Austria in 1809, 106, 134; learns the repeal of the embargo and of the British Orders. 136; his first reply to Armstrong's communication, 137, drafts decree withdrawing the Milan Decree, 139; cause of his hesitation, 140, 141; lays aside his repealing decree, 141; his view of the right of search, 137, 145, 149; his draft of Vienna Decree of Aug. 4, 1809, 143, 144, 230, 233, 236: quarrels with his brother Louis, 146, 147; his increased severity toward the United States, 150-152, 220; calls a Cabinet council on commerce, Dec. 19. 1809, 220, 221; discussions with Montalivet. 221, 223; his note to Gaudin on American ships, 224; his want of money. 225, 226, 237; calls for a report from Champagny, Jan 10, 1810, 226, 227; his dislike for Armstrong. 228, 229; his condition for the revocation of his decrees, 229; his draft of note asserting retaliation on the Non-intercourse Act, 230, 231; his reply to Armstrong's remonstrances, 234, 235; his memory,

326 GENERAL INDEX.

235; his Decree of Rambouillet, 236; his threats of annexing Holland, 238, 246; his annexation of Holland, 241, 242; his reflections on Macon's act, 244, 245; his license system, 246; his instructions to Champagny ordering announcement that the decrees will be withdrawn, 253; dictates letter of Aug. 5, 1810, 253; his idea of a trap, 257, 383; his instructions of Dec. 13, 1810, on the non-intercourse and the Floridas, 384; on commercial liberties, 386; his address of March 17, 1811, to the deputies of the Hanse Towns, 396, 397, his address of March 24, 1811, to the Paris merchants, 398 399, 420; appoints Maret in place of Champagny, 401; orders a report on American commerce, 402, 403; admits American cargoes, May 4, 1811, 404; his instruction of Aug. 28, 1811, about Spanish America and Florida, 407, 408; his rupture with Russia and Sweden, 408-427, his order of May 4, 1811, opening his ports to American commerce, vi. 44, 59; probable amount of his spoliations, 247; his restrictions on American commerce, 247; goes to Holland, Sept. 19, 1811, 248; his interview with Joel Barlow, 249; his extension of the license system in January, 1812, 250; his seizure of Swedish Pomerania, 251, 252; his Decree of St. Cloud, April 28, 1811, 255, 256; his departure for Poland, May 9, 1812, 258; enters Russia, 259, 288; his battle at Borodino, Sept. 7, 1812, 263: enters Moscow, Sept. 15, 1812, 263; begins his retreat, 264; his passage of the Beresina, 264; his return to Paris, December, 1812, 265; enters Moscow, vii. 4, 26, 27; begins retreat, 9; leaves his army, 11; returns to Paris, 30; organizes a new army, 339; wins battles of Lützen and Bautzen, 340, 344, 391; makes armistice, 340, wins battle at Dresden, 350; overthrown at Leipzig, 355, 360, 370, 393; approaching fall of, 362, 393; effects of overthrow on Congress and the President, 393-395; his return from Elba, ix. 56, 83; overthrown at Waterloo, 104

"Narcissus," British 32-gun frigate, captures "Viper," vii. 313.

Nash, Thomas, ii. 333.

Natchez delivered to the United States, i. 355.

"National Intelligencer," origin of, i. 121; publishes Paine's letters, 328; prints the British Impressment Proclamation, iv. 166, 172, 186; publishes the Milan Decree, 195; on renewal of intercourse with Great Britain, v. 75; on Erskine's disavowal, 109, 110; Joel Barlow's letter in, 299; office destroyed by Cockburn, viii. 147.

Naturalization, the law of, in England and America, ii. 337 *et seq*; British laws of, vii. 21-23; issue raised, 360

Naturalization law adopted, i. 301.

"Nautilus," East India Company's cruiser, ix. 73.

"Nautilus," sloop-of-war captured, vi. 369 386; vii. 312, 313.

Navigation, British law of, ii. 318, 321, 413

Navigation Act, moved by Macon, v. 183.

Navigation Act of 1816, ix. 146, 147.

Navy, British, cost and pay-roll of, vii. 20.

Navy Department (see Samuel Smith, Robert Smith, Paul Hamilton, William Jones, B. W. Crowninshield).

Navy of the United States, Jefferson's opinion of, i. 222, 223, 238; Gallatin's views on, 222, 240, 252; Giles's views on, 287; Leib's proposal to abolish, 299 ; condition in 1801, 242-245; economies in, 272; four sloops-of-war and fifteen gunboats built in 1803, ii. 77; cost and estimates, 77, 136; at Tripoli, 137- 141, 425-436 ; Jefferson suggests ships-of-the-line for, iii. 113, 178. 201; fifty gunboats voted in 1806, 181 ; favored by Jefferson. 201; arguments for and against gunboats, 352; gunboats adopted in 1807, iv. 158. 159; frigates to be laid up in case of war, 159; frigates to be used to serve gunboats, 427; in 1809, v. 168, 169 ; reductions in 1810, 200-207; opposed by Republican party, vi. 162 : increase refused by Congress in January, 1812. 164 ; condition of, in June. 1812, 363, 364; distribution of, in September, 1812, 377, 378; movements and battles of, in 1812. 362- 387; increase of, 436, 449; condition of, in 1813, vii. 287; appropriations for, in 1814, 384, 385, legislation for, in November. 1814, and February, 1815, viii. 281; war establishment retained in peace, ix. 87, 119. (See Gunnery, "Constitution," "President," "United States," "Constellation," "Chesapeake," "Congress," "Essex," "Adams," "Wasp," "Hornet," "Argus," "Peacock," "Syren," "Nautilus," "Louisiana," "Carolina.")

Navy-yards, incompetency of, iv. 6.

Nelson, Roger, member of Congress from Maryland, ii. 229 ; favors abandoning cities in case of attack, iii. 350, 353; on reduction of armaments in 1810, v. 202, 203.

Negril Bay (see Jamaica).

Nesselrode, Count, accompanies Czar Alexander as foreign secretary. vii. 344; his despatch of July 9 to Lieven, 346, 349; ignorant of the Czar's orders to Roumanzoff, 349, 352, 354.

Neutrals, admitted to colonial ports of France and Spain, ii. 321; British doubts whether to recognize trade of, with colonies of belligerents, 321, 322 (see Rule of 1756); affected by practice of blockade, 322, 399; forbidden by England in 1793 to trade with belligerent colonies, 322, 323; permitted in 1794 to trade with belligerent colonies, 324, 327, 328; prosperity of United States as, 329, 332; neglect of obligations of. 337; Madison's demands for, in December, 1803, 385, 386, 419 420, 423; British West Indies'hostile to, 416; British measures of 1805 hostile to, iii. 44- 46; James Stephen's pamphlet on frauds of, 50-53; practice of blockading ports of, 91-94, 199, 200; anger of the American merchants at British restrictions on, in 1805, 95-98, 143, 144, 151; Madison's pamphlet on rights of, 102; Madison's remonstrances on infringement of rights of, 109, 110; Jefferson's annual message of 1805 regarding, 112, infringement by Miranda of law of, 190-195, 208; British disregard of rights of, 202, 203; Jefferson's scheme of alliance to protect, 204; Napoleon's Berlin Decree retaliating on England's violations of law of, 389, 391; Fox's blockade a concession to, 398, 399; Madison's demands for, in 1806, 401; Monroe's compromise of rights of, 408-412; Howick's Order in Council restricting trade of, 416-421, 435; rights of, to depend on France and Russia, 437; aggression against, by British frigate "Leopard," iv. 1-30; nature of reparation demanded for, 31, 39, 45, 46, 62 (see "Chesapeake" affair); the United States in 1807 almost the only, 66; West India report on trade of, 67-69; British lawyers on violations of law of, 77; Spencer Perceval's Orders in Council restricting rights of, 79-104 (see Orders in Council); Napoleon's Milan Decree, making war on, 126 (see Decrees); British disregard of law of, in America, 136, 137; Napoleon's idea of, as exempt from interference, v. 137, 149; list of restrictions on commerce of, 152; of 1809, 165; Napoleon's declaration that, after the Milan Decree, there were no more, 227 (see Napoleon); defence of, by Russia and Sweden, 409-428 (see Impressment, Licenses, Spoliations); Madison's indifference to duties of, in West Florida, 309, 310 (see Florida, East and West); Act of 1816, to preserve relations of, ix. 147.

Newark, on the Niagara River, burned by McClure, vii. 202.

Newbury, memorial of town-meeting in January, 1814, viii. 6.

Newburyport town-meeting in January, 1809, iv. 410.

New England in 1800, i. 18; schoolhouses, 19; population, 20; poverty, 21; commerce and manufactures, 21 *et seq.*; social system, 76; schools, 76; society, organization of, 108, temper of, toward Jefferson in 1802, 308-330; conspiracy of 1804 in, ii. 160-190, 391, 392; its conservatism, Jefferson's second Inaugural on, iii. 5-9; townships, Jefferson's opinion of, iv. 441; prosperity of shipping in, 1807-1810, v. 15; prosperity of manufactures in, 16-21; encouragement of manufactures in, 196, 197; F. J. Jackson's reception in, 213-217; refuses to take the war loan of 1812, vi. 207; favored by British government in the war, vii. 31, 32; furnishes money and supplies to Canada, 146, 367, 368; benefited by the British blockade, 264, 283, 367, military force assigned to, 284; banks, their condition and influence, 387, 389; viii. 15; blockaded, April 25, 1814, 3; attitude toward the war in January, 1814, 13; prosperity in 1814, 14; attitude of clergy, 21-23; banks maintain specie payments, 214; frauds in militia system of, 219; practically independent in September, 1814, 222 (see New England Convention); congressional elections of November, 1814, in, 228; effect of sedition on Madison, 231; furnishes thirteen regiments, 235; supplies Scott's brigade, 236; supplies Blakeley's crew, 237; burden of taxation thrown on, 257; probable consequence of her proposed action, 318; delighted by news of peace, ix. 59, 60; disastrous effects of peace on, 95-103, 126; church of, in 1816, 133; representatives of, oppose internal improvements, 150, 151; increase of population in 1817, 154, 155; increase of wealth in, 157-160; division of church in, 175-187. (See Massachusetts, Connecticut, etc.)

New England Confederation, tendency to, iv. 403.

New England Convention, project of, in 1804, ii. 162-188; in 1808, iv. 239, 246, 402-407; in 1812, vi. 402; in 1814, viii. 4-13; project realized in October, 1814, 225, 287; Massachusetts delegates to, 226, 227, 290-292; Rhode Island and Connecticut send delegates to, 227; Vermont declines invitation to, 227, project approved by the people in the November election, 228-230; its intention to sequester the government taxes, 257; its demand for State armies conceded by the national government, 284; assembles at Hartford, Dec. 15, 1815, 292; character of members of, 292, 293; proceedings of, 293-298; report of, approved by Massachusetts and Connecticut, 300, 301, 304, 305; commissioners appointed to effect the arrangement proposed by, 301, 302; commissioners start for Washington, ix. 56; met by news of the battle of New Orleans, 57; return home, 81; sarcasms about, 81, 103, 160.

New Hampshire, opposed to disunion in 1804, ii. 162, 169, 204; becomes Federalist in 1809, v. 13; sends no delegates to the Hartford Convention, viii. 227; prosperous, ix 160.

New Haven, i. 75.

New Jersey, election in 1814, viii. 228; increase of population in, ix 154.

New London, blue lights seen from, vii. 279

New Orleans delivered by Spain to the United States, Dec. 20, 1803. ii. 256; sends deputies to Washington, 400; menaced by Spain in 1805, iii. 17; Burr's confederates in, 236; concentration of troops at, in 1809, v. 169, 170; to be occupied by British expedition in 1814, viii. 312-314; military defences of, 316, 317; Jackson's delay in going to, 318-320; Nicholl's talk of attacking, 321; Jackson's neglect of, 325-330; Monroe's anxiety for, 331; Jackson arrives at, Dec. 2, 1814, 333; population of, 334; Jackson's measures at, 335; news of British capture of gunboats reaches, 336; martial law proclaimed at, 336, 337; in danger, 342; its defences, 344, 345; volunteer companies of. 344, 345; volunteers of, in the night battle of Dec. 23, 1814, 346, 347, 351; night battle of Dec 23, 1814, 347-351; artillery battle of Jan 1, 1815, 358-366; supplies militia, 368; in danger from the west bank, 371; battle of Jan. 8, 1815, 375-381; news of battle reaches the government, ix. 57; civil authority restored at, 89, 90; growth of, 157; fortifications at, 236.

"New Orleans packet," seized under the Berlin and Milan Decrees, vi. 8; by a " municipal operation," 42, 43.

Newport, fort at, iv. 210.

Newspapers, American, in 1800, i. 41, 120.

Newton, Gilbert Stuart, ix. 213-215.

New York city in 1800, i 24; expenses and sanitary condition, 25; business, 25 *et seq.*; blockaded by British frigates, iii. 91, 203; debate in Congress on the propriety of fortifying, 351, 355; described by F. J. Jackson, v. 213; population in 1810, 289; affected by the blockade, vii. 264; depreciation of currency, ix. 62; increase of exports, 126; increase of population, 155, 156; immigrants to, 161; exports and imports of, 166, 167; steamboats in 1816, 171, 173.

New York State in 1800, i. 3, 6, 23, 108-114; politics in 1802, 331, 332; politics in 1804, ii. 170-190; election of 1809, v. 13; insurrection in, on account of the embargo, iv. 259; position of, in census of 1810, v. 289; banking mania in, vi. 208; election in May, 1812, 209; nominates De Witt Clinton to the Presidency, 215; recruiting in, 305; politics of, in 1813, vii. 48, 49; suffrage in, 50; jealousy of Virginia, 402, 403; elections in April, 1813 and 1814, viii. 11, 12; banks suspend payment, 214, soldiers furnished by, 235; arrears of internal taxes in, 256; creates a State army, 282; elections in April, 1815, ix. 93; election in April, 1816, 132, 133; growth of population, 1800-1816, 154, 167; growth of wealth in, 166, 167; begins the Erie Canal, 167-170.

"Niagara," 20-gun brig on Lake Erie, commanded by Jesse D. Elliott, vii. 120; her armament, 121, 122, taken command of by Perry, 123, 124; ill-fought by Elliott, 125.

Niagara, Fort (see Fort Niagara).

Niagara frontier, military importance of, vi 304, 310; force at, 311, 320, 341, 344; force raised to six thousand men, 345; Van Rensselaer's campaign at, 346-353; Alexander Smyth's campaign at, 353-358; sickness of troops at, 359; Brown's campaign at the, viii. 24-90; British force at the, in June, 1814, 38, 39; victories fail to stimulate enlistments, 217, 218; cession required as a condition of peace, ix. 7.

Nicholas, Wilson Cary, i. 221; senator from Virginia, dissuades the President from raising Constitutional question, ii. 87, 88, 94, on the Louisiana treaty, 111; retires from the Senate, 221; helps to set Monroe aside. iii 152; on Randolph's philippic 173; writes to Jefferson doubting the possibility of longer embargo, iv. 345, 346; file-leader of the House, 428; urges Giles to withdraw opposition to Gallatin, 429, 430; his resolution to repeal the embargo, 435, 438; on the appointment of Gallatin as Secretary of State, v. 4, 5, 6; resigns from Congress, 76; his letter to Jonathan Mason in 1814, viii. 306, 308.

Nicholl, Sir John, King's advocate, iii. 417; iv. 96.

Nicholls, Edward, major of the British marines occupies Pensacola, viii. 319, 320; issues proclamation to the natives of Louisiana, 320, 321, 325; distracts Jackson's attention, 321, 322; evacuates Pensacola and goes to the Appalachicola, 330.

Nicholson, Joseph Hopper, member of Congress from Maryland, i. 261, 268, 433; ii. 95, 100, 124, 144; invited to attack Judge Chase, 149; a manager of the impeachment, 225, 228; offers an amendment to the Constitution, 240; in the Ninth Congress, iii. 127, 133, 135, his non-importation resolution, 154; his resolution adopted, 165; appointed State Judge, 167, 180; remonstrates with Gallatin, iv. 32.

Nicklin and Griffith, iii. 153.

Non-importation (see Non-intercourse).

Non-intercourse, list of acts, v. 194. partial, moved by Senator Samuel Smith in February, 1806, iii. 146, debate on, 147; favored by Madison, 148, 426; opposition to, 150; Smith's resolutions adopted, 151; Gregg's resolution of Jan. 29, 1806, 154, 155, 165. Nicholson's resolution, Feb. 10, 1806, 154, 155; Nicholson's resolution adopted, 165, 166; Non-importation Bill reported, March 25, 1805, 175; becomes law, April 18, 1806, 175; suspended, Dec. 19, 1806, 349; effect of, in England, 394, 399; conditions of its repeal, 401, 436; to remain suspended, 430, 436, 437; favored by Jeffer-

GENERAL INDEX. 331

son after the "Chesapeake" affair, iv. 34, 36; expected by Erskine, 144; Non-importation Act goes into effect, Dec. 14, 1807, 165 (see Embargo); not avowed as a coercive policy in Congress, 203; or by Jefferson, 176, 204; bill for total non-intercourse introduced, 444; becomes law, March 1, 1809, 453.

Non-intercourse Act of March 1, 1809, its effect on commerce, v. 35, 36; English view of, 62; affected by Erskine's arrangement, 80, 88, 90; revived by Erskine's disavowal, 111, 114, 115; communicated to Napoleon, 135; communication denied by Napoleon, 232, 234, 235, 254; Champagny's complaints of, 140; Napoleon's retaliation on, 143, 150, 151, 230, 232, 254, 255; its mischievous effects in America, 164, 165, 166, 178, 184; about to expire, 183; suspended, 195-198, 210; revived by proclamation of Nov. 2, 1810, 302, 303, 304.

—— of May 1, 1810, its passage, v. 194-198, 274; its effect on Napoleon, 220, 244, 255; its effect in England, 273-276; its condition precedent to reviving non-intercourse, 297; creates a contract, 342, 395, 396.

—— of March 2, 1811, reviving Act of March 1, 1809, moved by Eppes, Jan. 15, 1811, v. 338; decided upon, 347; amended, 351; reported, 352; passed, 354, 391; its effect on Napoleon, 393, 394, 400, 404; Foster's instructions on the, vi. 23; his protest against, 39; his threat of retaliation, 44, 124; not noticed by Napoleon, 56; an intolerable burden to the United States, 140; efforts to suspend, 205, 230-234, 447; not retaliated by England, 270; forfeitures under, 438-443; Calhoun on, 444; bill for stricter enforcement of, 448.

Norfolk, the mayor of, forbids communication with the British squadron, iv. 27; exposed to attack, vii. 269; fortifications of, 271; attacked by British expedition, 272-275; sickness among militia at, viii. 219.

"North American Review," ix. 207.

North Carolina in 1800, i. 36; cotton-planting, 37, 148; in 1816, growth of population, ix. 154, 155, 161; growth of wealth, 163; legislative report on internal improvements, 164.

Norton, Rev. Andrews, ix. 182.

Nottingham, in Maryland, Ross's camp, Aug. 21, 1814, viii. 129.

OCAÑA, battle at, v. 268.

Ocracoke Inlet, captured by Admiral Cockburn, vii. 277.

Offices, Jefferson's removals from, i. 230 *et seq.*

Ogden, owner of the "Leander," iii. 190; indicted by Jefferson, 195.

Ogden, Aaron, appointed major-general, vii. 37.

Ogden, Peter V., iii. 252, 255; carries despatches to Burr's friends in New Orleans, 295; arrested at Fort Adams, 319; discharged from custody, 340.

Ogdensburg, captured in 1813, vii. 147; passed by Wilkinson, 185.

Ohio, admitted into the Union, i. 302; ii. 76; population in 1810, v. 289; militia, vii. 102; growth of, ix. 155.

Ohio River settlements in 1800, i. 2.

Ohio, Territory of, ii. 121.

Olcott, Simeon, senator from New Hampshire, ii. 160.

Old Fields, Winder's army camps at, vii. 134; retreat from, 135.

Olmstead, Gideon, case of, v. 13; Marshall's opinion in case of, ix. 188, 189.
Ontario, Lake, armaments on, vi. 342, 344. (See Sackett's Harbor.)
Order in Council, of Jan. 7, 1807, called Lord Howick's Order, prohibiting neutral trade from one belligerent port to another, iii. 416-421; iv. 79, 80, 83, 93, 102, 144, 154, 318; arrives in America, iii. 435.
—— of Nov. 11, 1807, called Spencer Perceval's Order, prohibiting neutral trade with any port from which British trade was excluded, iv. 79-103; its publication in England, 132; arrives in America, 186; a cause of the embargo, 168, 175, 176, 186, 332; its object explained by Erskine, 219; debate in Parliament in 1808, 317-321; parliamentary inquiry into, 322; asserted by Canning not to have caused the embargo, v. 51; Canning's conditions of repealing, 53, 54, 56, 70-73, 90, 94, 101, 102; Grenville and Sidmouth's language regarding, 59, 60; debate on, March 6, 1809, 60-62; Erskine's arrangement withdrawing, 70-73; disavowal of Erskine's arrangement, 87-95, 109-113.
—— of April 11, 1808, protecting neutral vessels trading with British ports, proposed by Perceval, iv. 324; approved by Bathurst, 325; opposed by Castlereagh and Canning, 325, 326; issued, 327; Madison's indignation at, 327.
—— of Dec. 21, 1808, suspending export duties on foreign produce, v. 43, 44; further relaxations proposed, 45; their effect on English trade, 46.
—— of April 26, 1809, establishing a general blockade in place of the Orders of November, 1807, v. 63, 64, 65, 81, 103, 113, 126, 152; issue chosen by Madison and Monroe, vi. 39, 40, 45, 121, 188; conditions of repeal, 124, 220; enforced by British prize-courts, 118, 124, 267; alleged as Madison's fourth complaint, 222; revocation promised by Prince Regent on formal revocation of French decrees, 254, 282; popular agitation against, 271, 281, 283; debate of Feb 28, 1811, in House of Lords, 275; debate of March 3 in House of Commons, 276; Rose's definition of, 276, 283; Canning's remarks on, 277, 278; Perceval's account of, 279; ministers grant a committee on, 283, 284; suspension of, June 16, 1812, 286, 287, 403; suspension not satisfactory to the President, 404; repeal susceptible of satisfactory explanations, 431.
—— of May 24, 1809, repudiating Erskine's arrangement, and protecting vessels sailing under it, v. 93, 95; Canning's instructions of July 1, 1809, to F. J. Jackson, on, 101-105.
—— of Oct. 13, 1812, directing general reprisals against the United States, vii. 4.
"Orders in Council," privateer, captured, vii. 330.
Ordronnaux, John, captain of the privateer "Prince of Neufchatel," viii. 209.
Orleans, Territory of, created, ii. 121, 399-409; iii. 223, 224, 296-325. (See Louisiana.)
"Orpheus," British 36-gun frigate, sent to communicate with Creek refugees, vii. 258; captures "Frolic," viii. 181.
Osgood, David, minister of Medford, viii. 21; ix. 202.
Osgood, Samuel, i. 108.

Oswego attacked in May, 1814, viii. 29, 30.
Otis, Harrison Gray, Speaker of Massachusetts legislature, ii. 163; president of Massachusetts Senate, J. Q. Adams's letter to, iv. 241; his letter to Josiah Quincy suggesting a New England Convention, 403; signs Address to the People, 456; supports State convention in 1812, vi. 402; supports Clinton for President, 440; his report of Oct. 8, 1814, on controlling their own resources, viii. 224; reports in favor of a New England Convention, 225; chosen a delegate, 227, 292; publishes journal of, 293; his activity in, 294, 295; Lowell's opinion of, 294; appointed commissioner for, 302.
Otter Creek in Vermont, station of Macdonough's flotilla in May, 1814, viii. 97.
Ouvrard, Gabriel Julien, agent of the French treasury, i. 239; obtains from Spain financial concessions, iii. 372; ruined by Napoleon, 374; his scheme, 378.

PAINE, ROBERT TREAT, i. 330.
Paine, Thomas, Jefferson's letter to, i. 316-318; arrives from Europe, 327; his letters in the "National Intelligencer," 328.
Pakenham, Sir Edward, British major-general, ordered to command the expedition to New Orleans, viii. 315; his instructions, 316; his armament leaves Jamaica, 331, 332; on the way to Louisiana, 333; makes land, Dec. 10, 1814, 335; takes command Dec. 25, 1814, before New Orleans, 352; contrasted with Jackson, 353; sends for field-pieces, 355, 356; halts before Jackson's breastworks, Dec. 28, 1814, 357; sends for heavy guns, 358; digs canal, 367; his plan of attack, 371-374, killed in the assault, 375, 376; his assault compared with Drummond's, 381.
Palfrey, John Gorham, ix. 206.
"Palladium," the, i. 314.
"Panoplist," the, ix. 178.
Papenberg, v. 165.
Paris, capitulates, March 31, 1814, ix. 6; pleased with the victory at Plattsburg, 35, 36; Napoleon's return to, 56.
Parish, David, shares loan of 1813 vii. 44, 45.
Parish, Elijah, his Fast-Day sermon of April 7, 1814, viii. 21, 22; ix. 202.
Parker, Admiral, ii. 340.
Parker, Daniel, offers the two Floridas, iii. 379.
Parker, Sir Peter, captain of British frigate "Menelaus," his death, viii. 164, 165.
Parliament (see Acts of) imposes unequal duties on exports to the United States, ii. 399; to lodge in the King in Council the power of regulating commerce with America, 423; in 1804-1805 passes acts regulating West India commerce, iii. 44; debates Howick's Order in Council, 417; dissolved, April 27, 1807, iv. 55; meets June 22, 1807, 55; report to, on the West Indies, 67, 68, 81; prorogued, Aug. 14, 1807, 81; meets Jan. 21, 1808, 317; debates the Orders in Council, 318-322; meets Jan. 19, 1809, v. 49; debates the Orders in Council, 49-52, 58-62; on the Duke of York, 57, 58; prorogued June 21, 1809, 98; prorogued June 15, 1810, 275; passes the Regency bill, January, 1811, vi. 13, 14; meets Jan. 7, 1812, 270; debates in, 270-280; orders a committee of inquiry into

334 GENERAL INDEX.

the Orders in Council, 282, 284; meets Nov. 24, 1812, vii. 10; debates on the speech from the throne, 10; debates the American war, Feb. 18, 1813, 17-24; debate of Nov. 19, 1814, on the Ghent correspondence, ix. 43.

Parma, Duchy of, i. 363, 371.

Parsons, Theophilus, chief-justice of Massachusetts, i. 48, 87, 89, 93; ii. 164; iv. 29; his opinion of the unconstitutionality of the embargo, 411; his opinion on the power of a State over its militia, vi. 400; his assurance to Pickering, vii. 52.

Party, the Federalist, in New England, i. 76, 82-89, 329; ii. 160, 170, 202; in New York, i. 109; ii. 171, 191; views on government, i. 252; on the Judiciary, 273-275, 279, 290, 297; on the treaty-making power, 99, 100, 105, 110, 111; their attitude toward Jefferson and the embargo, iv. 228, 232, 240, 242, 283, 286, 408; deprived of grievances, v. 77; praise Madison, 78, 158; makè common cause with Jackson, 158; described by Giles, 180; in Congress, Foster's reports of their conduct and advice, vi. 171-175; their reception of Henry's documents, 183, 184; cease attempts to discuss war, 227, 228; their attitude toward the war, 398, 399; support Clinton for the Presidency, 410; strength of, in 1813, vii. 51; encouraged by overthrow of Napoleon, 370; divided on protection to manufactures, 376; their inert perversity, viii. 1, 2; divided on the question of a New England Convention, 9-13; praise militia, 217; of New England believe the crisis arrived in September, 1814, 220; call New England Convention at Hartford, 225; victorious in the congressional elections of November, 1814, 228; a majority of the members of Congress north of the Potomac, 229; oppose tax-bills, 255; approve report of Hartford Convention, 301; influence British press, ix. 2; affected by peace, 92, 93.

Party, the Republican, in New England, i. 76, 329, 330; ii. 81, 201, 202; in New York, 108, 109, 113, 229-236, 331; ii. 171-191; in Pennsylvania, i. 116, 194-200; in Virginia, 138-143, 145-148, 179; in North Carolina, 148; in South Carolina, 152-154; political principles of, 199-217, 238-243, 247, 251, 272, 287; ii. 77, 78, 130, 134, 142, 203, 205, 254-262, leaders of, in Congress, i. 264-269; views of, on the Judiciary, 275, 276, 288-290, 297; ii. 143-159, 221-244; on the treaty-making power, 78-80, 83-91, 94-99, 100-104, 106-112; on the power of Congress over territories, 116-129; on exclusive privileges, 208-210; on British relations, 349, 355, 356; success in 1803, 74-77; in 1804, 201; in 1805, iii. 9, 122, 127; Randolph's schism in the, 132-138. 147, 157-164, 166-171, 181-184, 197; Jefferson's attempts to restore harmony in 1806, 344-350; its hostility to fortifications and cities, 350-355; its attitude toward the slave trade, 356-369; Monroe's schism, iv. 128-131, 147, 226, 286; cause of success, 148, 149; its hostility to a standing army, 209-212; its change of attitude toward a standing army, 212-217, 259: its Presidential candidates in 1808, 226-228; its attitude toward the Constitution in the embargo, 261-271; its success in 1808, 284-288; its attitude toward Spain, 339-343; revolts against Jefferson in 1808, 357, 358, 382, 432-434, 440-

442, 455; its attitude toward the manufacturing interest in 1809, 449; v. 196, 197; attempt to restore its purity in 1810, 199-206; its attitude toward the Bank, 207-209, 327-337, 356; its attitude toward the Constitution in Florida, 236-244, 320-326; its attitude on the previous question in Congress, 351-356; its attitude toward war in 1811, vi. 137-158, 170, 171; its attitude toward the militia, 159-161; its attitude toward a navy, 162-164; its attitude toward taxation, 166-168; its attitude toward war in 1812, 201-213, 226-229; its caucus of 1812, 214, De Witt Clinton's schism, 215, 410; its success in the election of 1812, 412-414; its change of attitude toward a navy, 436; its treatment of war-taxation, 447.

Passamaquoddy Bay (see Moose Island).

Patapsco River, at Baltimore, viii. 168.

"Patriotick Proceedings" of Massachusetts legislature in 1809, iv. 458.

Patronage, public, Jefferson's course regarding, i. 224, 294.

Patterson, Daniel T., commander in U. S. Navy, brings the "Carolina" into action at New Orleans, viii. 346; establishes battery on west bank, 358. 359-361, 369, 370, 374; abandons battery and spikes guns, 377, 378.

Patterson, Elizabeth, ii. 377.

"Paul Jones," privateer, captured, vii. 329, 332.

Paulus Hook, i. 11.

Peace, Prince of (see Godoy).

"Peacock," American 22 gun sloop-of-war built in 1813, viii. 181; goes to sea in March, 1814, 182, 183; captures "Epervier," 182, 183;

returns to port October 30, 184, 193; sails from New York, ix. 63, 70; fires into "Nautilus," 73.

"Peacock," British sloop-of-war, vii. 289; sunk by "Hornet," 290.

Pechell, S. G., captain of the British 74-gun ship "San Domingo," repulsed at Craney Island, vii. 272, 273.

Peddie, John, British lieutenant in Twenty-Seventh Infantry, deputy-assistant-quartermaster-general, reconnoitres Bayou Bienvenu, viii. 338; his sketch of battle-fields at New Orleans, 359, 360.

Pêle-Mêle, ii. 365, 372, 390.

"Pelican," British sloop-of-war, her force, vii. 305; captures "Argus," 306-308.

Pellew, Captain, of the "Cleopatra," ii. 340.

"Penguin," British sloop-of-war, her action with the "Hornet," ix. 71, 72, 230.

Pennsylvania in 1800, i. 29, 114, 115; schism, the, ii. 194 *et seq.*; politics in 1805, iii 9; in 1808, iv. 286; resists mandate of Supreme Court, v. 13; decides Presidential election of 1812, vi. 412; affected by blockade, vii. 264; creates forty-one banks in 1814, viii. 16; election of 1814, 228; arrears of internal taxes in October, 1814, 256; creates a State army. 282; bank circulation in 1816-1817, ix. 130; growth of population, 1800-1816, 154, 155; increase of wealth in, 166, 167; internal improvements in, 168, 169, 171.

Pensacola, visited by Creek Indians, vii. 228; object of Jackson's Creek campaigns, viii. 318, 319; occupied by Nicholls, 319, 320, 322; seized by Jackson, 326, 329, 330.

Perceval, Spencer, his comments on Howick's Order in Council, iii.

417, 421; iv. 80; Chancellor of the Exchequer, 55; character of, 56; Sydney Smith's caricature of, 56 *et seq.*, 73; takes office as Chancellor of the Exchequer, 81; his paper on the policy and justice of retaliation, 83 *et seq.*; submits his paper on retaliation to the Ministry, 88; his letter to Charles Abbot, 97; his orders approved in Council, 102; prohibits the export of cotton and quinine, 323; affected by the embargo, 324; his plan to conciliate the Federalists, 324; carried into effect, 327; his relaxations of the Orders in Council, v. 42, 45, 63; decline of his authority in 1809, 57, 58, 62, 63; his difficulties with Canning and Castlereagh, 107; becomes First Lord of the Treasury, 263; invites Wellesley into the Cabinet, 267; Wellesley's opinion of, 281, 282, 283; prime minister of England, becomes ruler after the insanity of George III., vi. 2, 3; retained as prime minister by the Prince Regent, 14; his indifference to Wellesley's advice, 268; his remarks on an American war, 271; his persistence in the system of commercial restriction, 272; his remarks on licenses, 274; his silence toward Canning, 280; his bargain for Sidmouth's support, 281; concedes a committee on the Orders in Council, 283; his assassination, 284.

Percy, W. H., captain of British 22-gun sloop-of-war "Hermes," viii. 322, 325; attacks Fort Bowyer, 323; abandons his ship, 324.

Perkins, Jacob, i. 182.

Perkins, Thomas Handasyd, iv. 411.

Perry, Oliver Hazard, commander in U. S. Navy, ordered to Lake Erie, vii. 115; creates squadron, 116-118; destroys British fleet, 120-127; his despatch of Sept. 10, 1813, 128; effect of his victory on the Creek war, 232; its effect in England, 355, 359, 360; erects batteries on the Potomac, viii. 164; his rewards, ix. 141, 142.

Petry, M., v. 228, 229.

Philadelphia in 1800, i. 28, 29; library company, 61; intellectual centre in 1800, 117; population of, in 1810, v. 289; banks suspend payment, Aug. 31, 1814, viii. 214; depreciation of currency, ix. 62, 98; allotted share in loan of 1815, 102; growth of population of, 156; immigrants to, 161; steamboats in 1816, 172.

"Philadelphia," 38-gun American frigate, captured, ii. 138.

Phillimore, Dr. Joseph, his pamphlets on the license system, vi. 274.

Physick, Dr. Philip Syng, i. 127.

Piankeshaw Indians, vi. 71, 75.

Pichon, Louis André, French *chargé d'affaires*, remonstrates with Leclerc and is superseded, i. 408; ii. 268; complains to Talleyrand of the attitude of the United States, i. 437, 439; observes Jefferson's close relations with Thornton, ii. 354; invited by Jefferson to meet Merry at dinner, 369.

Pickering, Judge John, impeachment of, ii. 143 *et seq.*; trial of, 153 *et seq.*; irregularity of trial, 158.

Pickering, Timothy, senator from Massachusetts, i. 88; ii. 110; quarrels with Yrujo, i. 425; on the admission of Louisiana to the Union, ii. 105 *et seq.*, 160; his letter to George Cabot on the impending dangers, 161, 164; receives Cabot's reply, 166 *et seq.*; letter of, to Rufus King on Burr's candidacy for the governorship, 179, 390, 391; votes for Adams's resolution, iii. 151; willing to let the ship run aground, 210; silent about the "Chesapeake" affair, iv. 29; his party in the Senate, 146; praises Monroe, 129, 167; won by Rose, 184 et seq.; cultivated by Rose, 232; exerts himself to form a coalition with the British ministry, 234; his letter to Governor Sullivan, 237 et seq.; effect in England of his letter to his constituents, 333; declares Jefferson a tool of Napoleon, 347, 442; reports Jefferson's language about the embargo, 359, 442; his triumph, 401, 409; described by John Adams, 402; maintains relations with Rose, 460; his toast at Jackson's dinner, v. 217; his speech on the occupation of West Florida, 321, 322; loses his seat in the Senate, vi. 116; his attempt to call a State convention in 1812, 402; favors disunion, viii. 4, 5; urges a New England Convention in January, 1814, 5-7; exhorts Governor Strong to seize the national revenues, 223, 224; acquiesces in British demands, 288; suggests doubts of George Cabot's earnestness, 290, 291; approves the report of the Hartford Convention, 300, 301; considers the Union dissolved, 300, 309; member of the Fourteenth Congress, ix. 107; on the power of internal improvement, 149.

Pierce, John, killed by a shot from the "Leander," iii. 199, 211.

Pigot, H., captain of British frigate "Orpheus," reports number of Creek warriors, vii. 258.

Pike, Zebulon Montgomery, lieutenant of First Infantry, explores the sources of the Mississippi, iii. 213; and of the Arkansas and Red rivers, 214, 223; brigadier-general, vii. 152; captures York, 154; killed, 155.

Pilkington, A., lieutenant-colonel commanding British expedition to Moose Island, viii. 94.

"Pilot," British newspaper, on the American frigates, vii. 16.

Pinckney, Charles, i. 152; appointed minister to Madrid, 294, 427; obtains a convention for Spanish depredations, ii. 249 et seq.; indiscretions of, at Madrid, 275; compromises Madison, 276; adopts a high tone with Cevallos, 279; sends him a threatening letter, 280; excuse for his conduct, 281; in an awkward situation, 284; his recall asked for, 286; asks the Spanish government to be permitted to resume relations, 315; recalled, but associated by Monroe in negotiation, iii. 23; returns home, 37.

Pinckney, C. C., his treaty with Spain, i. 348-350; iii. 38; candidate for President, iv. 285.

Pinckney, Thomas, appointed major-general, vi. 290; ordered to prepare for seizing St. Augustine, vii. 207; ordered to withdraw troops from Amelia Island, 210; his difficulties in the Creek war, 234; his estimate of the hostile Indians, 244, 245; orders the Thirty-ninth Regiment to join Jackson, 245; prepares army against Creeks, 251; joins Jackson, 257.

Pinkney, William, author of the Baltimore "Memorial," iii. 144; appointed to aid Monroe in London, 152, 165, 169; iv. 354; arrives in London, iii. 400; sole minister in London, iv. 162; remonstrates against the tax on American cotton, 322; his reply to Canning, 338; publication of Canning's personal letter to, 419; his reply, Dec.

28, 1808, to Canning's first advance, v. 43, 44, 45; his reception of Canning's further advances, 49, 51, 52; opinion attributed to, by Canning, 54; his pleasure at the Order of April 26, 1809, 63, 64; his opinion of Francis James Jackson, 96; his intimacy with Wellesley, 270, 275; his reports of Wellesley's intentions, 271; inquires whether Fox's blockade is in force, 277-280; notifies Wellesley of Champagny's letter of Aug. 5, 1810, 286; his "republican insolence," 287; demands repeal of the Orders, Nov. 3, 1811, vi. 3; his argument that the French decrees were revoked and that Fox's blockade was illegal, 5, 6, 7, 9. 10, 11; his definition of blockade, 10; his demand for an audience of leave, 12, 15; his hesitation, 16; his note of Feb. 17, 1811, to Wellesley, 17; insists on "an inamicable leave," 18, 20; his final audience, 19, 20; his character as minister, 20, 21; sails for America, 21; appointed attorney-general, 429; resigns attorney-generalship, vii. 398; member of the Fourteenth Congress, ix. 107.

Pitkin, Timothy, member of Congress from Connecticut, votes for war measures, vi. 147; on the bank capital of the Union, vii. 386; opposes national bank, ix. 118.

Pitt, William, ii. 316, 320, 324, 326, 328, 330, 336, 342; restored to power, 396, 418; determined to reestablish the former navigation laws, 419; his measures in 1804 and 1805 for restricting American commerce, iii. 44, 45; his coalition with Austria and Russia, 73; Burr expects support from, 235, 238; death of, 163, 211, 245; his patronage of young men, v. 264, 265.

Pittsburg in 1800, i. 2; growth of, in 1816, ix. 157; steamboats built at, 172.

"Plantagenet," British seventy-four, at Fayal, viii. 201-207.

Plattsburg, on Lake Champlain, military force at, in October, 1812, vi. 344; Dearborn's campaign from, 360; plundered by British expedition in July, 1813, vii. 192; Wilkinson's headquarters in March, 1814, viii. 25; fortified by Izard, 98, 99; garrison at, 100; British armament against, 101-105; battle of, 106-113; effect of battle in England, 112; saved by engineers and sailors, 218; ix. 236; effect of battle at London, Paris, and Ghent, ix. 35-37, 55; at Washington, 57.

Plauché, ———, major of New Orleans militia, viii. 345.

Plumer, William, senator from New Hampshire, ii. 160, 364, 405; Republican candidate for governor of New Hampshire, viii. 11.

Plymouth town-meeting in January, 1809, vi. 414.

Poland, v. 257.

"Polly," case of the, ii. 328, 340; rule established by case of, set aside, iii. 45.

"Pomone," British 38-gun frigate, ix. 64; extracts from her log, 66, 67; Decatur's surrender to, 70.

Population of the United States in 1800, i. 1; centre of, near Baltimore, 1; west of the Alleghanies in 1800, 3; of cities, 59; in 1810, v. 289; of the Union in 1817, ix. 154; movements of, 1800-1817, 154-157, 161, 163, 164.

Porter, David, captain in U. S. navy, commands "Essex," vi. 377; captures "Alert," 377; returns to port, 378; sails again, 384; erects batteries on the Potomac in August, 1814, viii. 164; his cruise in the Pacific with the "Essex," 175-

GENERAL INDEX. 339

177; blockaded at Valparaiso, 179; attacked and obliged to surrender, 180.

Porter, Moses, major of artillery, iii. 246; colonel of Light Artillery, brevet brigadier-general, commands artillery in Wilkinson's expedition on the St. Lawrence, vii. 184; his opinion on moving against Montreal, 185; intended by Armstrong to command at Washington, viii. 122.

Porter, Peter Buell, member of Congress from New York, vi. 122; on Committee of Foreign Relations, 124, 128; his report favoring war, 133-136; his war speech, 136; favors small army, 151 ; asks for provisional army, 165; introduces embargo bill, 201 ; calls for volunteers, 355; charges General Smyth with cowardice, 358 ; his duel with Smyth, 358; raises volunteer brigade under Brown, viii. 34; strength of his brigade, 37 ; at Chippawa, 40, 41, 44; at Lundy's Lane, 53, 56, 58, 64 ; at Fort Erie, 71, 83; brings volunteers to Brown, 85; leads sortie from Fort Erie, 87, 88; wounded, 88; fails to create a brigade respectable in numbers, 218; in the Fourteenth Congress, ix. 107; helps to defeat Crawford, 123; assists Erie canal, 168.

"Portfolio," the, i. 85, 119, 121; its character and influence, ix. 198-201.

Portland, Duke of, Prime Minister of England, iv. 55; his opinion on Spencer Perceval's proposed Order in Council, 88; his death, v. 107.

Portugal, her ports ordered to be closed, iv. 106; forced into war, 118 ; divided by Napoleon into three parts, 121.

Postal System of the United States in 1800, i. 61 ; in 1816, ix. 170, 171.

Postmaster - General (see Gideon Granger, R. J. Meigs).

Potomac (see Eastern Branch).

Pottawatomies, charged by Tecumthe with bad conduct, vi. 111, 112.

Potter, Elisha, member of Congress from Rhode Island, v. 167; vi. 447 ; opposes the repeal of the restrictive system, vii. 376.

Power, ———, major-general in British army, commanding brigade at Plattsburg, viii. 101.

Pozzo di Borgo, ii. 66.

Prairie du Chien, captured by British expedition, viii. 32.

"Preble," 7-gun sloop in Macdonough's fleet on Lake Champlain, viii. 105; in the battle of Plattsburg, 109.

Preble, Commodore Edward, appointed in command of the Mediterranean squadron, ii. 137; at Tripoli, 426.

Prescott, opposite Ogdensburg, vii. 147; British garrison at, 151; passed by Wilkinson, 185.

Prescott, William, delegate to the Hartford Convention, viii. 292.

Prescott, William Hickling, ix. 206.

"President," American 44-gun frigate, ordered to sea, May 6, 1811, vi. 25, 26; chases a British war-vessel, 27; fires into the "Little Belt," 30; at New York, 363, 365; goes to sea, 366; cruise of, 366, 368; returns to Boston, 375, 378; sails again, 381; returns to Boston, Dec. 31, 1812, 381; vii. 285; goes to sea, April 30, 1813, 285; returns to Newport, Sept. 27, 1813, 310 ; goes to sea, Dec. 4, 1813, 311; in British waters, 333; captured by British squadron, Jan. 15, 1815, ix. 63-70.

Press, Jefferson's remarks on the, iii. 7. (See Newspapers.)

340   GENERAL INDEX.

Previous question, the rule of, adopted, v. 353-356; denounced by Stanford, vi. 146.
Prevost, Sir George, governor general of Canada, vi. 317; his report on the lukewarm and temporizing spirit in Upper Canada, 318, 319; negotiates armistice with Dearborn, 323; ix. 33; his military superiority in August, 1812, vi. 338, 339; unable to assist Proctor, vii. 108; on Proctor's defeat at Fort Stephenson, 113; unable to man the British fleet on Lake Erie, 118, 119; his difficulties of transport, 145; his remarks on supplies from Vermont, 145; viii. 93; charged with timidity, vii. 147; visits Kingston in March, 1813, 150; his supposed force at Kingston, 151, 153; comes to Kingston in May, 1813, 163, embarks for Sackett's Harbor, 164; attacks Sackett's Harbor, 165; repulsed, 166-168; charged with want of courage, 168-170; his remarks on Hampton's movement, 193; his force for the defence of Montreal, 194-196; shows timidity toward Hampton, 197; his proclamation on the burning of Black Rock and Buffalo, 204; his letter to Wilkinson on the execution of hostages, 361; reinforced by ten thousand troops in July, 1814, viii. 31, 91; his letter of Oct. 18, 1814, on the impossibility of supplying an army in Upper Canada, 92; his expedition against Plattsburg, 101-105, 107-113, 172; recalled to England, 118; asks Cochrane to retaliate for American outrages in Canada, 125; at Kingston, 267; effect of his campaign on the negotiation at Ghent, ix. 27, 34-36.
Prevost, J. B., appointed judge at New Orleans, ii. 220; iii. 219; one of Burr's correspondents in New Orleans, 296, 319, 324.
Prices of American produce, affected by blockade, vii. 263; speculative, in imported articles, 263.
Priestley, Dr. Joseph, i. 157, 311.
"Prince of Neufchatel," in the Irish Channel, viii. 196; beats off the "Endymion's" boats, 207-209.
Prince of Peace (see Godoy).
Prince Regent (see George, Prince of Wales).
Princeton College in 1800, i. 129.
Pringle, John Julius, declines appointment as attorney-general, iii. 11.
Prisons in 1800, i. 128.
Privateers, American, their depredations in the West Indies in 1812, vii. 12; types of, 314-317; qualities of, 318, 320, 324; modes of capturing, 328, 329, 330; number of, 330, 331; in British waters, 332, 333; disadvantages of, 333-338; in 1814, viii. 194-209; their value as a test of national character, ix. 228, 229.
Privateers, French, not received in American ports, vii. 395.
Prizes, number captured in 1813, vii. 331; American success in taking, in 1814, viii. 198, 199.
Proclamation by President Jefferson, of May 30, 1804, in pursuance of the Mobile Act, ii. 263; of May 3, 1806, against the "Leander," "Cambrian," and "Driver," iii. 200, 201; of Nov. 27, 1806, against Burr, 283, 285, 289, 290, 292, 325, 328, 330; of July 2, 1807, on the "Chesapeake" affair, iv. 30, 32, 34, 46, 187, 188, 192; v. 51; by the King of England, of Oct. 16, 1807, asserting the right of impressment. iv. 52, 166, 168, 169; by President Jefferson, of April 19, 1808, declaring the country on the Cana-

dian frontier in a state of insurrection, 249; by President Madison of April 19, 1809, renewing intercourse with Great Britain, v. 73, 115; of Aug. 9, 1809, reviving the Non-intercourse Act against Great Britain, 114, 115; of Nov. 2, 1810, reviving the non-intercourse against Great Britain, 302, 303, 304, 338, 400; of Oct. 27, 1810, ordering the military occupation of West Florida, 310, 311; of Nov. 2, 1810, announcing the repeal of the French decrees, vi. 4, 56; by William Hull, of July 12, 1812, on invading Canada, 303, 320; by Isaac Brock in reply to Hull, 320; of Aug. 8, 1814, summoning Congress to meet Sept. 19, 1814, viii. 239; of Aug. 29, 1814, by Major Nicholls of the Royal Marines, to the natives of Louisiana, 320, 321; of Sept. 21, 1814, by Andrew Jackson, to the people of Louisiana, 324, 325.

Proctor, Henry, colonel of the Forty-first British Infantry, arrives at Malden, vi. 314; disapproves Brock's measures, 330: major-general, his incapacity officially censured by the Prince Regent, vii. 93, 94, 142; his victory over Winchester at the River Raisin, 94-98; returns to Malden, 99; besieges Fort Meigs, 103-107; repulsed at Fort Stephenson, 109-113; evacuates Malden and Detroit, 130, 131; his retreat, 133-135; his defeat on the River Thames, 136-140; his report, 142.

Prophet, the Shawnee, begins Indian movement at Greenville, vi. 78; removes to Tippecanoe Creek, 79; his talk with Gov. Harrison in August, 1808, 80; charged with beginning hostilities, 95; sends Indians to Harrison, 97, 100; blamed for the affair at Tippecanoe, 108.

Protection to American manufactures, measure of, recommended by Madison for two years, vii. 374; promised by Calhoun, 375; opposed by Webster, 376; urged by Potter, 376; recommended by Madison and Dallas in 1815, ix. 105, 106, 111; opposed by Randolph, 112, 113; debated in Congress, 114, 115; avowed in tariff of 1816, 116.

Prussia, spoliations by, v. 226; closes ports to American vessels, 413, 416; king of, visits London, ix. 8.

Putnam, Samuel, correspondent of Pickering, viii. 6.

"QUEEN CHARLOTTE," 17-gun British ship on Lake Erie, vii. 120; in action, 124; captured, 127.

Queenston, battle at, vi. 349-352.

"Querist," papers by Blennerhassett, iii. 257, 273, 275.

Quincy, Josiah, member of Congress from Massachusetts in the Ninth Congress, iii. 128, 142; in favor of voting money for ships and harbor defences, 179; presents memorials to Congress in favor of Smith and Ogden, 195; irritates opponents, 354, 360, 363; iv. 147; his contempt for Jefferson, 356; attacks Campbell's Report, 372; attacks the advocates of the embargo, 422; declares that the Republicans "could not be kicked into" a declaration of war, 423; on the distraction among the Democrats, 440; requires total submission to Great Britain, 446, 453; his account of John Henry, 461; declares the admission of Louisiana a virtual dissolution of the Union, v. 325, 326; votes for war-measures, vi.

342   GENERAL INDEX.

147, 152; gives warning of embargo, 201; moves that the war-debate be public, 227; opposes enlistment of minors, 435; opposes forfeitures, 443; his Resolution on the "Hornet's" victory, vii. 65, 66; viii. 1; his opinion on the temper of Massachusetts, 223; on the Boston "Anthology," ix. 201.

RAISIN, River, defeat and massacre at the, vii. 88-97, 100.
Rambouillet, Decree of (see Decrees).
"Ramillies," Sir Thomas Hardy's flagship, viii. 94.
Ramsay, David, i. 151.
Randolph, Edmund, Burr's counsel, iii. 444.
Randolph, John, i. 143, 209; in favor of anti-Federal declarations, 260, 267, 296, 338; demands papers relating to the right of deposit at New Orleans, 429; ii. 95; defends the Louisiana treaty in Congress, 97; defends the Louisiana legislation, 120, 124; favors abolition of the Vice-Presidency, 133; favors impeachments, 142, 144; impeaches Judge Chase, 151; opposes remission of duties on school-books, 208; decline of his influence, 210; on the Yazoo claims, 210; his violent temper, 213; supported by the Administration 220; opens the trial of Judge Chase, 229; his closing speech, 236; his amendment to the Constitution, 240, 241; asserts title to West Florida, 255; iii. 163; complains of Jefferson's credulity, ii. 409; his attitude in 1805, iii. 3. 20, 23; his antipathy to Madison, 119. 120, 126; his reception of Jefferson's secret Spanish message, 132; his war on Madison, 134; opposes Jefferson's plan of buying Florida, 136; favors an embargo, 149; opposition of, 154; his speech against the Non-importation Resolution of Gregg, 158; attacks the Administration, 159; his account of the Mobile Act, 163; goes formally into opposition, 164; philippics against the government, 172 *et seq.*; his resolutions against the union of civil and military powers, 175; makes public Jefferson's secret message, 179; his dislike to Robert and Samuel Smith, 180; his schemes to reduce the revenue, 182; his object to make Madison contemptible, 182; writes to Monroe respecting Burr, 333; moves a resolution of inquiry, 335; his dictatorial tone in Congress, 349; favors abandoning New York in case of attack, 351; attacks the coastwise prohibition of slave-trade, 364; his qualities and faults, 367; his influence destroyed, 368; foreman of the jury in Burr's trial, 448; desires to indict Wilkinson, 457; his letters to Nicholson, 457; calls Jefferson's proclamation in the "Chesapeake" affair an apology, iv. 32; upholds Monroe, 129; fails to be reappointed on the Ways and Means Comm'ttee by Speaker Varnum, 153; advocates and then denounces the embargo, 174; opposes Jefferson's request for an increase of the regular army, 215, 374; his speech on war, 380; discord his object, 438; claims to have prevented war, 451; his opinion of Jefferson's second administration. 454; his remarks on Jefferson. v. 78; on Erskine's arrangement, 79; on Madison's message, 177; his attempt to reduce expenditures in 1810, 199-207; on the incapacity of government, 209; on the contract with Napoleon, 344, 345; his quarrel with Eppes,

352; denounces the previous question, 353; his remarks on President and Cabinet, February, 1811, 360, 361; supports the Bank Charter, 362; his opinion of "the cabal," 363, 364; his quarrel with Monroe, 367; his report on slavery in Indiana, vi. 76; replies to Grundy on war, 142, 145; ridicules army bill, 153; declares war impossible, 202; his comments on Eustis and Hamilton, 206; his remarks on war, 211; criticises Gallatin, 446; defeated for Congress, in 1813, vii. 51; quoted by Pickering, viii. 5; his letter to Lloyd on the Hartford Convention, 230, 306; elected to the Fourteenth Congress, 230; ix. 93; suggests inquiry of Monroe's opinions in 1800, viii. 265; in the Fourteenth Congress, ix. 107; leads minority, 109-111; opposes manufacturers, 112, 113, 115; hostile to State banks, 116, 117; supports Compensation Bill, 121; not a friend of Monroe, 124; on the popular action against the Compensation Act, 136; his oratory, 217.

Randolph, T. J., Jefferson's letter to, iv. 138, 139.

Randolph, Thomas Mann, member of Congress from Virginia, ii. 95, 124; iii. 183, 356.

Rank-and-file, mode of stating strength of armies, vii. 150.

Ratford, Jenkin, a deserter from the "Halifax," iv. 2; taken from the "Chesapeake," 19; hanged, 25.

"Rattlesnake," American 16-gun sloop-of-war, vii. 312; captured, 313; viii. 193.

"Rattlesnake," privateer, in British waters, vii. 333.

Rawle, William, i. 127; ii. 259.

Reading in Massachusetts, town of, votes to pay no more taxes, viii. 299.

Red Clubs, hostile Creeks, vii. 227; their flight to Florida, 257; their number, 258; assisted by British, 320, 330; viii. 311, 319, 320; pursued by Jackson, 319, 330.

Reeve, Judge Tapping, ii. 168.

Regiments (see Infantry).

Regnier, Grand Judge, announces the enforcement of the Berlin Decree, iv. 169.

Reid, Samuel C., captain of privateer "General Armstrong," his battle at Fayal, viii. 202-207.

"Reindeer," British 18-gun sloop-of-war, captured by the "Wasp," viii. 186-188; ix. 230.

"Reindeer," privateer, built in thirty-five days, viii. 194.

Remusat, Mme. de, v. 235.

Representation, ratio of Congressional, fixed, i. 301.

Republicans (see Party).

Retaliation acts, ii. 397 *et seq.*

"Revenge," the, sails with instructions to Monroe respecting the "Leopard" outrage, iv. 39; returns, 133, 166.

Revenue (see Finances).

Rhea, James, captain in the First United States Infantry, vii. 73.

Rhea, John, member of Congress from Tennessee, on the annexation of West Florida to Louisiana, v. 324; asserts contract with Napoleon, 343.

Rhine, passed by the allied armies, vii. 373.

Rhode Island, roads in, i 64; appoints delegates to the Hartford Convention, viii. 227; elects federalist congressmen in November, 1814, 228; cotton manufactures of, depressed by the peace, ix. 96; federalist in 1816, 133.

Riall, P., British major-general, his force, viii. 38; takes position behind the Chippawa River, 40; advances in order of battle, 41; his report of his defeat, 43, 44; his loss, 45; retires toward Burlington, 45; advances to Lundy's Lane, 47, 49; orders retreat, 51; wounded and captured, 52.

Rice, value of export of, in 1815, ix. 94; in 1816, 126.

Richardson, ———, lieutenant of Canadian militia, his account of the capture of Detroit, ii. 332; his description of Kentucky militia, vii. 96, 97.

Rifles, efficiency of, vii. 95; ix. 231; First Regiment of, viii. 69; at Fort Erie, 71, 83; Fourth Regiment of, at Fort Erie, 83; in the sortie, 87-89.

Rigaud, i. 384, 386.

Ripley, Eleazar Wheelock, colonel of Twenty-first U. S. Infantry, at the battle of Chrystler's Farm, vii. 188; promoted to brigadier and sent to Niagara, 409; his previous history, viii. 35; his brigade, 36; crosses the Niagara, 39; arrives at Chippawa, 40; not in battle of Chippawa, 43; advises advance on Burlington Heights, 47; strength of his brigade, 47; arrives on the battle-field at Lundy's Lane, 53; captures the British position, 54-56; holds the hill-top, 58; ordered to retreat, 59; his losses, 64; ordered to regain the field of battle, 64, 65; marches out and returns, 65; retreats to Fort Erie, 66, 70; his quarrel with Brown, 66, 67, 81, 85; fortifies Fort Erie, 67; strength of his brigade, 69; repulses assault, 71, 72, 74; discourages sortie, 85; desperately wounded in sortie, 88, 89; retained on peace establishment, ix. 88.

Ritchie, John, captain of artillery in Hindman's battalion, viii. 37; at Lundy's Lane, 53; killed, 58.

Roads, in 1800, i. 2, 5, 11 et seq., 14, 63, 64; over the **Alleghanies** in 1800, 2; Jefferson's proposed fund for, iii. 2, 345; through the Creek and Cherokee country, 14; Jefferson's anxiety to begin, 19; Cumberland, 181; proposed by Gallatin, iv. 364, 365; and canals, national, recommended by Madison, ix. 105; encouraged by Virginia in 1816, 163-165; popular demand for, 168, 169.

Robbins, Jonathan, case of, ii. 333.

Roberts, Jonathan, elected senator, vii. 401.

Robertson, Thomas Bolling, member of Congress from Louisiana, favors protection to sugar, ix. 114.

Robinson, W. H., British commissary-general, his report on the failure of supplies for Upper Canada, viii. 92.

Robinson, ———, major-general in British army, commands light brigade at Plattsburg, viii. 101; moves on the works, 110, 111.

Rochambeau, General, succeeds Leclerc at St. Domingo, ii. 15; iii. 87.

Rockingham, in New Hampshire, county meeting of, vi. 403, 409.

Rockville, or Montgomery Court House, sixteen miles from Washington, viii. 142; Winder arrives at, 154, 156.

Rodgers, John, captain in the United States navy, at Tripoli, ii. 429; president of Barron's court-martial, iv. 21; ordered to sea in the "President," May 6, 1811, vi. 25; chases the "Little Belt," 26, 27; mistakes the "Little Belt" for the "Guerriere," 29, 30; his action with the "Little Belt," 28-36; his orders in June, 1812, 363, 365, 367, 368, chases the "Belvidera," 366; arrives with his squadron at Boston, 375; sails again with squadron, 378, 381; returns, Dec. 31, 1812,

381; goes to sea April 30, 1813, vii. 285, 287; erects batteries on the Potomac, viii. 164.

Rodney, Cæsar A., elected to Congress in place of James A. Bayard, ii. 76, 95; a Republican leader, 100; defends the Louisiana treaty, 102; reports Jefferson's bill for administering Louisiana, 119; shares in the trial of Judge Chase, 219, 228, 234; attorney-general, undertakes the prosecution of Burr, iii. 444; points out the consequences to the Administration of convicting Wilkinson, 455; his opinion concerning Judge Johnson's *mandamus*, iv. 264; his report on slavery in Indiana, vi. 76; resigns attorney-generalship, 429.

Rose, George, vice-president of the board of trade, ii. 419; his view of the Orders in Council, iv. 100, 102; on the Orders in Council, vi. 276, 277, 281, 283, yields to an inquiry, 283.

Rose, George Henry, sent as envoy for the adjustment of the "Chesapeake" affair, iv. 104; v. 112; his ignorance of the Orders in Council, iv. 133; arrives at Norfolk on the "Statira," 178; his instructions, 178–182; his character and qualities, 182; his description of Congress, 184; explains to Madison that Jefferson's proclamation is a stumbling-block, 187; his letter to Canning, 188; suggests withdrawal of the proclamation, 190; explains the new proposals of Jefferson to Canning, 192; difficulties in the way of following his instructions, 192; reveals the further disavowals expected, 193; breaks off negotiation, 196; makes his parting visits, and has free conversation with Gallatin and Smith, 197; writes to Canning under Pickering's influence, 232; intended as minister to the United States to succeed Erskine, v. 95.

Rosily, Admiral, iv. 298.

Ross, Robert, major-general of the British army, commands expedition to America, viii. 124; arrives in the Potomac, 127; lands in the Patuxent, August 19, 1814, 128; camps at Nottingham, August 21, 129; camps at Marlboro, August 22, 130; camps at Old Fields, August 23, 131; his report of losses at Bladensburg, 144; enters Washington, 145; ix. 21; reported by Serurier as setting fire to furniture in the White House, viii. 146; retires from Washington, 147, 148; takes part in incendiarism, 164; lands his army before Baltimore, 168; killed, 170; ix. 42; intended for command of New Orleans expedition, viii. 311–313; his capture of Washington highly approved by the Prince Regent, 314, 315; his movements synchronous with Jackson's, 318.

"Rossie," Baltimore privateer, vii. 316, 335.

"Rota," British 38-gun frigate, viii. 205, 206.

Rottenburg (see De Rottenburg).

Roumanzoff, Count Nicholas, chancellor of the Russian empire, his language about Austria, v. 134; declines to interfere in Danish spoliations, 409, 410, 411; declines to release vessels at Archangel, 415; protests against ukase, 418; offers the Czar's mediation, vii. 27, 29; left at St. Petersburg, 344. 345, receives Castlereagh's refusal of mediation in May, 345, 346; favors renewing offer, June 20, 347; authorized by the Czar, July 20, to renew offer, 348; his conduct perplexes the American commissioners, 349; his motives, 350; renews offer of mediation in note of August 28, 351, 353; mortified by the Czar's treatment, 353, 354; assures Gallatin that mediation was the Czar's idea, 353; resigns and retires, 354, 355.

Roume, Citizen, French agent in St. Domingo, i. 384, 387.

Round Head, Indian chief, at the River Raisin, vii. 94; captures Winchester, 96.

Rouse's Point, difficulty in fortifying, viii. 97, 98.

Rovigo, Duc de (see Savary).

Rule of the war of 1756, that trade illegal in peace should not be permitted in times of war, ii. 322, 323, 329; affirmed by Lord Mulgrave, iii. 48: assumed by James Stephen, 51, 53; applied by the Whigs, 419; insufficient to protect British trade, iv. 100, 319; Erskine reports Gallatin ready to concede, 389; Canning's demand for express recognition of, v. 53, 55, 72, 104.

"Running ships," vii. 315.

Rush, Richard, comptroller of the Treasury, vi. 229; on the loss of the "Chesapeake," vii. 303; offered the Treasury, 397; appointed attorney-general, 398, 399; attends the President to Bladensburg, viii. 137, 140; and in the subsequent flight, 149, 150; returns to Washington, 157.

Russell, Jonathan, charged with legation at Paris, v. 260, 380; his reports on the revocation of the decrees, 381-395; blamed by Monroe for questioning the revocation of the French decrees, vi. 42; blamed by Serurier for his tone, 53; sent as chargé to the legation at London, 252, 282; asks proofs that the French decrees are repealed, 252; his reports from London, 283; his interview with Castlereagh, Aug. 24, 1812, vii. 2, 3; nominated minister to Sweden, 59; nomination not confirmed by the Senate, 62, 63, 71; confirmed 64, 371; at Ghent, ix. 14, 16, 46.

Russia, wishes to exchange ministers with the United States, iv. 465; declined by Senate, 466; mission to, declared inexpedient, v. 11; minister to, appointed, 86; her rupture with France in 1811, 385, 398, 399, 412-423; annoyed by American war, vii. 1, 26; loses and recovers Moscow, 9, 26, 27, 30; drives Napoleon from Poland and Prussia, 11, 30; offers mediation to the United States, 28, 29, 41. (See Alexander, Roumanzoff, Nesselrode.)

Rutledge, John, member of Congress from South Carolina, i. 269, 271.

Ryland, Herman W., secretary to Sir James Craig, iv. 243, 460; v. 86.

SACKETT'S HARBOR, military importance of, vi. 342, 343; force concentrated at, in March, 1813, vii. 149, 150; denuded of troops, 156, 163; attacked, 164, 165; attack repulsed, 166-170; garrison at, in 1814, viii. 91; to be besieged in the spring of 1815, 92, 118, 119.

Sailors (see Seamen).

St. Augustine (see Florida, East).

St. Cyr, Gouvion, French ambassador at Madrid, pledges France never to alienate Louisiana, i. 400; ii. 61.

St. Domingo ceded to France, i. 354, 378 *et seq.*; destruction of the French army in, 414; relations of United States to, ii. 326; independence declared, iii. 87; armed trade with, 87; Napoleon's prohibition

of, 89; trade with, prohibited by act of Congress, 141; character of the act, 142; Southern reasons for approving, 142.
"St. Lawrence," British line-of-battle ship, on Lake Ontario, viii. 93.
St. Lawrence River, strategic importance of, vii. 144-147; Wilkinson's expedition down, 178-191; difficulties of transport on, viii. 92; both banks to be Canadian, ix. 7, 10, 31.
St. Mary's, seized by British, ix. 62.
St. Mary's River, v. 165.
Salaberry (see De Salaberry)
Salaries of cabinet officers, vii. 398; of public officials, ix. 119-122.
Salt, repeal of duty on, iii. 182, 183; vi. 149, 150; tax to be re-enacted, 157, 166, 167.
"San Domingo," British ship-of-the-line, vii. 272.
Sandusky River, base of Harrison's campaigns, vii. 76, 78, 79, 84, 108, 109. (See Fort Stephenson.)
Sandwich, opposite Detroit, vi. 302; occupied by Harrison, vii. 132.
Saratoga, i. 92; Armstrong's idea of renewing the scene of, vii. 173; viii. 101.
"Saratoga," Macdonough's flag-ship on Lake Champlain, viii. 104; her armament, 105; in the battle of Plattsburg, 107-110; her losses, 111; ix. 234.
Sargent, Daniel, iv 413.
Sassafras River, in Maryland, Cockburn's expedition to, vii. 268; Sir Peter Parker stationed off, viii. 165.
Sauvé, Pierre, ii. 401, 406; iii. 301.
Savannah, threatened by British, ix. 63.
Savary, Duc de Rovigo, v. 241.
Sawyer, British vice-admiral, vi. 368.
Sawyer, Lemuel, member of Congress from North Carolina, v. 184.

Scheldt, British expedition to, v. 107.
Schooner, the swiftest sailer in the world,' vi. 48; privateer, vii. 315, 316; a wonderful invention, 319, 320; ix. 228, 236; the triumph of the war. vii. 322, 323.
Schuylers of New York, the. i. 108.
Scott, ———, British colonel of the Hundred-and-third Regiment, at Lundy's Lane, viii. 50; leads assault on Fort Erie, 72, 75; killed. 76. 78.
Scott. Charles, governor. of Kentucky, vii. 73.
Scott, Dred, case of. ii 126, 129.
Scott, Michael, author of "Tom Cringle's Log," vii. 321; his remarks on Yankee 'sailors and schooners, 321-323.
Scott, Walter, i. 126; ix. 212.
Scott, Sir William, his judgments in admiralty cases, ii. 327; his judgment in the case of the "Essex," iii. 44, 45, 47; news of judgment received in America, 95, 96; opposes reforms in his court, iv. 96; his remarks on the right of retaliation, 321; decides the French decrees to be still in force, vi. 267.
Scott. Winfield, captain of artillery in 1808, vi. 292; his description of the army, 292; lieutenant-colonel at Queenston Heights, 351; surrenders, 352; colonel of Second U. S. artillery, chief-of-staff to Dearborn, vii. 156, 161; captures Fort George, 157, 158; his opinion of Wilkinson, 173; his opinion of Hampton, 174; his opinion of Brown, 409; promoted to brigadier, 409; drills his brigade at Buffalo, viii. 28, 36; organization and strength of his brigade, 35; lands below Fort Erie, 39; marches on Chippawa, 39, 40; fights the battle of Chippawa, 41-45; ordered to march toward Queenston, 50; at-

tacks British army at Lundy's Lane, 51–53; wounded, 58, 66; his brigade, 236; retained on peace establishment, ix. 88.

"Scourge," privateer, in British waters, vii. 333.

Seamen, British, their desertion to American service, ii. 332–339; in the American marine, iii. 94; desertion of, iv. 1; foreign, in the American service, vi. 455–457; foreign, to be excluded from American vessels, vii. 47.

Search, right of, ii. 322; as understood by Napoleon, v. 137, 145.

Seaver, Ebenezer, member of Congress from Massachusetts, vi. 400.

Sebastian, Judge, iii. 274; resigns, 293.

Sedition Law (see Acts of Congress).

Seminole Indians, vii. 217, 218.

Semonville, Comte de, his official address, v. 382, 388; vi. 8.

Senate (see Congress).

"Serapis," British 44-gun frigate, vii. 6.

Sergeant, John, member of Congress from Pennsylvania, ix. 107; opposes bank, 118; sent to Europe, 131.

Serurier, Jean Matthieu Philibert, succeeds Turreau as French minister at Washington, v. 345, 346; his first interview with Robert Smith, 346; reports the government decided to enforce non-intercourse against Great Britain, 347; his estimates of Gallatin and Robert Smith, vi. 46–50; the crisis of his fortune, 52; reports Monroe's anger at Napoleon's conduct, 51, 53, 54, 57; remonstrates at Barlow's delay, 55; his letter of July 19, 1811, on the repeal of Napoleon's decrees, 60; his report of Monroe's and Madison's remarks on Napoleon's arrangements, July, 1811, 63, 64; his report of Madison's warlike plans in November, 1811, 129, 130; his reports on Crillon and John Henry's papers, 178–181; his report of Madison's language on the French spoliations, 187; his report of Monroe's language regarding the repeal of the French decrees, 188, 189, 194, 195; his report of Monroe's remarks on the embargo and war, 200; remonstrates against suspension of the Non-importation Act, 205; his remarks on the failure of the loan, 208; his report of angry feeling against France, 217; his report of Monroe's complaints in June, 1812, 231; his report of Monroe's language about the occupation of East Florida, 241; his report of Monroe's language about negotiation for peace, 415, 416; his report of Monroe's military prospects, vii. 35, 36; his report of fears for the safety of Washington, in July, 1813, 56; his reports in 1813–1814, 391–395; his explanation of the abandonment of the restrictive system by Madison, 393–395; his report of the burning of Washington, viii. 145, 146.

Shaler, Nathaniel, captain of privateer "Governor Tompkins," vii. 327; his escape from a man-of-war, 328.

"Shannon," British frigate, vi. 368; chases "Constitution," 370; stationed off Boston, vii. 281; captures the "Chesapeake," 285–303.

Sheaffe, Sir R. H., major-general of the British army in Canada, vi. 349, 351; his force in the district of Montreal, vii. 194, 195; Brock's successor in Upper Canada, viii. 48.

GENERAL INDEX. 349

Sheffield, Earl of, his devotion to the British navigation laws, ii. 413; iv. 73.

Shelburne, Lord, his negotiation of 1783, ix. 14.

Shelby, Isaac, governor of Kentucky, vii. 74; commands the Kentucky volunteers in Canada, 128, 139; remonstrates against Harrison's resignation, 410, 411; his letter of April 8, 1814, on the necessity of peace, viii. 13; sends Kentucky militia to New Orleans, 327.

Sherbrooke, Sir J. C., British governor of Nova Scotia, occupies Castine and Machias, viii. 95, 96, 174.

Sheridan, Richard Brinsley, v. 265.

Sherman, Roger Minot, delegate to the Hartford Convention, viii. 292.

Shipherd, Zebulon R., member of Congress from New York, on the approaching fall of the national government in 1814, viii. 277.

Shippers, British, ii. 318, 320.

Shipping, character of, in 1800, i. 6; American, increase of, ii. 325; its prosperity in 1809-1810, v. 15, 290; protection of, 319; growth of, in Massachusetts, 1800-1816, ix. 159.

Short, William, sent by Jefferson as minister to Russia, iv. 465; appointment negatived, 466; v. 11.

Sidmouth, Lord (see Addington), Lord Privy Seal, iii. 393; iv. 73; speech on the Orders in Council, v. 59; his weariness of the orders, 282, 283; enters Cabinet, vi. 281.

Silliman, Benjamin, Professor of Chemistry at Yale College, i. 310.

"Siren," privateer, captures "Landrail," viii. 195, 196.

Skipwith, Fulwar, U. S. consul at Paris, attacks Livingston, ii. 289; iii. 379.

Slave representation, iv. 458.

Slave-trade, restrictions of, in Louisiana, ii. 122; Jefferson recommends its abolishment, iii. 347; debate in Congress on the abolition of, 356.

Slavery, i. 134-136, 150, 154; in Indiana, vi. 75-77; stimulus to, in 1815, ix. 94.

Sloan, James, member of Congress from New Jersey, iii. 160, 174, 183, 357; moves that the seat of government be moved to Philadelphia, iv. 208.

Sloops-of-war, in the U. S. navy (see "Wasp," "Hornet," "Argus," "Syren," "Nautilus"); act of Congress for building six, vi. 449; their cost, vii. 310; their size and force, 311; their efficiency compared with frigates, 312; six new, ordered to be built, 313; twenty authorized by Act of November 15, 1814, viii. 281; their record in 1814, 181-193.

Smilie, John, member of Congress from Pennsylvania, iii. 359, 362; iv. 213; v. 204.

"Smith Faction," the, in Congress, iv. 428.

Smith, Senator Israel, of Vermont, ii. 218.

Smith, John, senator from Ohio, ii. 218; iii. 175; under the influence of Burr, 220; sends letter to Burr by Peter Taylor, 275; Burr's reply, 276; refuses to testify, 282; his complicity in Burr's schemes investigated, iv. 208.

Smith, John, senator from New York, ii. 153, 218.

Smith, John Cotton, member of Congress from Connecticut, i. 269; iii. 132, 143, 242; governor of Connecticut, on the report of the Hartford Convention, viii. 304, 305.

Smith, John Spear, chargé in London, vi. 21, 267.

350   GENERAL INDEX.

Smith, Nathaniel, delegate to the Hartford Convention, viii. 294.

Smith, Robert, appointed Secretary of the Navy, i. 220 *et seq.*; promises economies, 272; dissuades Jefferson from proposing constitutional amendment, ii. 83; consents to reduction of navy estimates, 136; *homme fort poli*, 373, 374; uncle of Mrs. Jerome Bonaparte, 377–379; a gentleman and a soldier, 431; asks to be made attorney-general, January, 1805, appointed and commissioned as attorney-general, but continues Secretary of the Navy, iii. 10–12; his opinion on Monroe's Spanish negotiation, 68; his letter to Jefferson on Burr's conspiracy, 331; wishes a call of the Senate to consider Monroe's treaty, 432; acts as Jefferson's intermediator with Rose, iv. 188–191; talks freely with Rose, 197; dislikes the embargo, 261; his opinions reported by Erskine, 384; regarded as extravagant by Gallatin, 425, 428; offered the Treasury Department, v. 7, 379; becomes Secretary of State, 8, 10; his language about war with France, 35; his letter to Erskine accepting settlement of the "Chesapeake" affair, 68, 69, 89; his replies to Canning's three conditions, 71–73; his remarks to Turreau on Jefferson's weakness and indiscretions, 84; introduces F. J. Jackson to the President, 120; his interviews with Jackson, 122–124, 126; his incompetence, 159; Madison's resentment of his conduct on Macon's bill, 186, 187; his supposed quarrels in the Cabinet, 188; opposed to Madison's course toward France, 296, 297, 366, 374, 375, 378; notifies Turreau of the President's intention to revive the non-intercourse against England, 302, 303; explains to Turreau the occupation of West Florida, 313; his first interviews with Serurier, 340, 347; irritates Madison by questioning Serurier, 350; his abilities, 363, 376; his removal from the State Department, 375–377; his Address to the People, 378; his retort against Madison, 379; Serurier's estimate of, vi. 46–50; his remark about American schooners, 48; his comments on Jefferson, Madison, and Clinton, 48; his pamphlet reveals secrets annoying to Madison, 54.

Smith, Samuel, member of Congress from Maryland, appointed temporarily Secretary of the Navy, i. 219, 245; his character, 267; moves to purchase Louisiana, 433; his vote on Chase's impeachment, ii. 238; his wish to be minister to Paris, 378; senator from Maryland, iii. 83, 126; his Non-importation Resolutions, 146, 150, 151; his wish for diplomatic office, 152, 153; his opposition to Armstrong's appointment defeated, 153, 172; punished by Jefferson, 168, 170; his view of the President's course, 169, 170; writes to Nicholas respecting Burr's conspiracy, 335; annoyed at Jefferson's ignoring the army in annual message, 348, 349; his letters to W. C. Nicholas respecting Jefferson's rejection of Monroe's treaty, 431 *et seq.*; on the embargo committee, iv. 172; his hostility to Gallatin, 425, 428; defeats Gallatin's appointment as Secretary of State, v. 4–7; his quarrel with Gallatin, 10, 11; votes for mission to Russia, 11; re-elected to the Senate, 159; his support of Giles, 180; defeats Macon's bill, 185, 192, 193; his motives, 185, 186, 187, 192; re-

GENERAL INDEX. 351

ports bill of his own, 197, 198; moves censure of Pickering, 322; his speech on the Bank Charter, 335, 336; his abilities, 363; opposes every financial proposal, vi. 234; votes against occupying East Florida, 243; in opposition, vii. 48; votes against Gallatin's Russian mission, 59; opposes seizure of East Florida, 209; no chance of re-election, 399; major-general of Maryland militia, refuses to yield command of Baltimore to Winder, viii. 167, 168; sends Stricker's brigade to meet the enemy, 169; member of the House in 1815-1817, ix. 107; supports Bank, 116.

Smith, Thomas A., colonel of Rifles, promoted to brigadier-general, vii. 409.

Smith, William Steuben, surveyor of the Port of New York, in Miranda's confidence, iii. 189; removed from office and indicted, 195, 208; his trial, 208; his acquittal, 209; connected with Burr, 263, 265.

Smith and Ogden, case of, iii. 208, 450.

Smyth, Alexander, inspector-general of United States army, with rank of brigadier, vi. 353; arrives at Buffalo with brigade, 346;. his disagreement with Van Rensselaer, 346, 348; ordered to take command, 353; his Niagara campaign, 354-358; dropped from the army-roll, 358.

Snake Hill, western end of the American lines at Fort Erie, viii. 71, 86; assaulted, 72-75, 79.

Snyder, Simon, chosen governor of Pennsylvania, iv. 286; v. 13; vetoes bill creating forty-one banks, viii. 16.

Somers, Lieutenant, at Tripoli, ii. 427.

"Sophie," 18-gun British sloop-of-war, appears off Barataria, viii. 321; attacks Fort Bowyer, 322-324.

South Carolina in 1800, i. 37; brilliant prospects of, 39, 149 *et seq.*; decides the election of 1800, 150; contrast in the character of its people, 153 *et seq.*; creates a State army, viii. 283.

Spain, relations of, with the United States, i. 337 *et seq.*; clumsiness of her colonial system, 419; declares war with England, ii. 303; Jefferson's expectation of bickering with, iii. 8; Monroe's negotiation with, 23-36; effect of Monroe's negotiation with, on Jefferson and Madison, 54-79; expected war with, 61, 62, 99, 118, 128, 189; Gallatin's opinion of Monroe's negotiation with, 66; Robert Smith's opinion, 68; negotiation with, not to be converted into a French job, 70, 77; Cabinet decision to transfer negotiation to Paris, and offer five millions for West Florida, 78; Merry's report on, 96; Madison's remarks to Merry, 98; Talleyrand's proposed settlement with, 103, 106; accepted by Jefferson, 106; notice of unfriendly relations with, in Jefferson's annual message of 1805, 121; Jefferson's comments on, to Turreau, 125; Jefferson's secret message on, Dec. 6, 1805, 130, 177; Randolph's remarks on the policy toward, 178; relations with French finance, 372; her "perfidy and injustice," 437; her condition in 1807, iv. 115, 116; occupied by French armies, 119, 122, 293, 297; collapse of government in, 298; Joseph Bonaparte crowned king of, 300; revolution of the Dos de Maio, 300-302, 315; its effect in America, 339-343; Napoleon and Moore's campaigns in, v. 22-28; Wellesley's campaigns in, 268.

GENERAL INDEX.

Spanish America, Napoleon's policy toward, ii. 54; iv. 300-303, 316; v. 32, 33, 384, 385, 407; Jefferson's wishes regarding, iv. 340-342; v. 37, 38; Madison's policy toward, 38, 39, 305-315; Spencer Perceval's policy toward, 269, 283, 284; movements for independence in, 305; Henry Clay's policy toward, ix. 109.

Spanish claims convention, ii. 249; defeated in the Senate, 250; ratified, 278; conditions on ratification imposed by Spain, 280; conditions withdrawn by Spain, iii. 26.

Specie in the United States in 1810, v. 330; large sums of, sent to Canada, vii. 146, 389; viii. 94; drain of, to New England, 1810-1814, vii. 387-389; viii. 15, 16; premium on, in New York, Philadelphia, and Baltimore, Feb. 1, 1815, 214; premium on, in the autumn of 1815, ix. 98; influx of, in 1816, 127.

Specie payments, suspended in August and September, 1814, by State banks, except in New England, viii. 213, 214; suspended by Treasury of the United States, 215; power to suspend, in Dallas's scheme for a national bank, 251; ix. 117; ordered to be resumed by the Treasury, on Feb. 20, 1817, ix. 118, 119, 128; resisted by State banks. 129; resumed Feb. 20, 1817, 131, 132.

Spence, Lieutenant, carries letters from Bollman to Burr, iii. 309.

Spence, William, iv. 69; his pamphlet "Britain independent of Commerce," 329.

Spencer, Ambrose, i. 109, 112, 228, 233.

Spencer, P., captain of the British sloop-of-war "Carron," reconnoitres Bayou Bienvenu, viii. 338.

Spoliations, British, in 1805, i. 45, 73, 108; sensation excited by, 109, 118, 125; indemnities asked for, at Ghent, ix. 18; abandoned, 52.

—— French, on American commerce within Spanish jurisdiction in 1797-1798, i. 350; excluded from the treaty of 1800, 361-363; included in Louisiana treaty, ii. 30, 31, 40-42, 46-50, 51, 60, 61; of every kind, indemnified by treaty of 1800, 297; insisted upon by Monroe, iii. 23, 25, 29, 30; forbidden by France, 32; Monroe's proposition regarding, 35; Madison's suggestion regarding, 60; Cabinet decision regarding, 107; in 1807-1808, iv. 292, 293, 312; v. 30; in 1809, v. 151, 152, 220, 255; value of, 242, 243; Madison's anger at, 292; Madison's demand for indemnity, 295, 296; their municipal character, 299; their justification as reprisals, 230, 232, 234, 237, 254, 258, 259, 388, 391, 396; in Denmark, 409, 411; not matter of discussion, vi. 54, 125; Madison's language regarding, 187; Monroe's language regarding, 188, 189; new, reported in March, 1812, 193, 224, 251; in June, 231; probable value of, 247.

—— Spanish, in 1805, iii. 37, 67, 78, 107.

Spotts, Samuel, first lieutenant of artillery, in the night battle at New Orleans, viii. 345.

Stage-coaches, travel by, i. 11 et seq.

Stanford, Richard, member of Congress from North Carolina, on armaments in 1808, iv. 214; votes against Giles's resolution, v. 182; his retort on Calhoun, vi. 144; his speech on war, 146; votes for legal tender paper, viii. 254; in the Fourteenth Congress, ix. 107, 118.

Stanley, Lord, vi. 283.

Stansbury, Tobias E., brigadier-general of Maryland militia commanding brigade at Bladensburg, viii. 140, 156; criticises Monroe, 151.

State armies, created by Massachusetts, viii. 221, 225, 272, 282; one of the causes that led to the Constitution of 1789, 282; created by New York, 282; by Pennsylvania and Maryland, 282; by Virginia, South Carolina, and Kentucky, 283; demanded by Hartford Convention, 284, 297; Joseph Hopkinson's remarks on, 286; of Massachusetts, suspended for want of money, 303.

State Department (see James Madison, Robert Smith, James Monroe).

State rights, asserted by Virginia, i. 138-140; by Kentucky, 140-143; by Georgia, 304; ii. 215; affected by Jefferson's acts, i. 203, 205, 254, 255, 260, 263, 298; ii. 78, 85, 90, 114, 118, 125, 130, 203, 205, 210; Gallatin's attitude toward, i. 116; ii. 79, 80; Bayard on, i. 292; Randolph on, ii. 97, 98, 104, 120, 209, 211; Nicholson on, 102, 209; Rodney on, 103, 119; Pickering on, 105; John Taylor of Caroline on, 105-107; Breckenridge on, 109, 121; W. C. Nicholas on, 111-113; Chief-Justice Taney on, 127; Justice Campbell on, 127-129; affected by Jefferson's acts, iii. 3, 18, 19, 346; iv. 363, 364, 454; affected by Acts of Congress, iii. 142, 355, 361, 364, 366; affected by the system of embargo, iv. 251-271, 273, 408-419, 456-459; mentioned in Madison's Inaugural Address, v. 4; affected by the use of militia in war, vi. 159, 160; affected by the war, vii. 67; asserted in Massachusetts in February, 1814, viii. 5-8; asserted by New England in September, 1814, 220-228; championed by Randolph in the Fourteenth Congress, ix. 110, 111; affected by decisions of Supreme Court, 188-192; affected by consistent action of government, 193.

"Statira," British frigate, viii. 316.

Status ante bellum, the best terms of peace obtainable, ix. 9; not offered by Madison, 12; not offered by England at Ghent, in August, 1814, 21; opposed to *uti possidetis*, 33, 34; offered by American commissioners, 37, 49.

Steam-battery, appropriation for, vii. 385.

Steamboat, Fulton's, i. 69, 71, 182; iii. 20, 216; iv. 135; experiments of Evans and Stevens, iii. 217; use of, in 1816, ix. 167, 168, 170-172; relative character of invention, 236.

Steam-engines in America in 1800, i. 66, 68, 70.

Stephen, James, author of "War in Disguise," iii. 50-53; reprints Randolph's speech, 396; assists in framing Spencer Perceval's Orders in Council, iv. 57, 100, 102; his opinion of Brougham's speech on the orders, 323; his speech of March 6, 1809, v. 60, 65; his remarks on Erskine's arrangement, 98; on the orders, vi. 276; yields to a parliamentary inquiry, 284.

Stevens, Edward, consul-general at St. Domingo, i. 385 *et seq.*, 389.

Stevens, John, his character and social position, i. 69, 182; his experiments with a screw-propeller in 1804, iii. 217; relative merit of his invention, ix. 236.

Stewart, Charles, at Tripoli, ii. 428; captain in U. S. navy, vii. 293; commands "Constitution," ix. 74; his action with the "Cyane" and "Levant," 75, 77; escapes British squadron, 78.

Stockton, Richard, member of Con-

gress from New Jersey, threatens rebellion, viii. 277, 278.
Stoddert, Benjamin, i. 192, 219.
Stone, Senator David, of North Carolina, ii. 95, 157; iii. 139; re-elected senator from North Carolina, vii. 49; censured and resigns, 399; ix. 107.
Stony Creek, battle of, vii. 159, 160.
Story, Joseph, his description of Fulton's discouragements, i. 71; of Marshall, 193, 260; of Jefferson's dress, ii. 366; describes Giles, iv. 205; opinion on the constitutionality of the embargo, 270; elected a member of Congress from Massachusetts, 358; in opposition to Jefferson and the embargo, 358; letter describing the state of opinion at Washington, 370; determined to overthrow the embargo, 432, 455, 463; retires from Congress, v. 76; obnoxious to Jefferson, 359; Speaker of Massachusetts legislature, resigns to become Justice of Supreme Court, viii. 36; his opinion in the case of Martin against Hunter's lessee, ix. 190–192.
Stowell, Lord (see Sir William Scott).
Street, John Wood's colleague, iii. 273.
Street's Creek (see Chippawa).
Stricker, John, brigadier-general of Maryland militia, sent to meet Ross's army, viii. 169; his battle, 169, 170.
Strong, Caleb, re-elected governor of Massachusetts in April, 1805, iii. 9; again in April, 1806, 207; defeated in April, 1807, iv. 146; again in April, 1808, 212; re-elected governor of Massachusetts in April, 1812, vi. 204; his Fast Proclamation, 399; declines to obey call for militia, 400; calls out three companies, 400; re-elected in 1813, vii. 50; his speech to the legislature Jan. 12, 1814, viii. 2; places militia under a State major-general, 221; his address to the State legislature Oct. 5, 1814, 222, 223; his letter to Pickering on the British demands, 287, 288; ix. 45; approves report of Hartford Convention, viii. 301; his message of Jan. 18, 1815, announcing failure of loan, 302, 303; succeeded by Governor Brooks, ix. 133.
Strother (see Fort Strother).
Stuart, Gilbert, i. 127.
"Subaltern in America" (see Gleig), quoted, viii. 129, 140, 141, 143, 144.
Suffrage in Massachusetts and New York, vii. 50.
Sugar, stimulated production of, and subsequent glut in the West Indies, ii. 415; parliamentary report on, in 1807, iv. 67, 68; price of, in February, 1815, ix. 61.
Sullivan, James, governor of Massachusetts, iv. 146; receives Pickering's letter for the State legislature, 237; declines to convey it, 240; his reply, 241; re-elected, 242; replies to Jefferson's demand to stop importing provisions, 254; his death, 416.
Sullivan, William, iv. 411.
Sumter, Thomas, senator from South Carolina, iii. 139; appointed minister to Brazil, v. 11.
"Sun," London newspaper, on Madison, ix. 3.
Supreme Court, the, i. 274; sessions suspended for a year by Congress, ii. 143. (See Marshall, Chase, Impeachment.)
Sutcliffe, Robert, i. 34.
Swartwout, John, i. 109, 230; his duel with De Witt Clinton, 332; marshal of New York, iii. 189; removed from office, 208; Jeffer-

GENERAL INDEX. 355

son's reasons for removing him, 209.

Swartwout, Robert, quartermaster-general under Wilkinson, vii. 177; commands brigade, 184, 189.

Swartwout, Samuel, one of Burr's adventurers, iii. 252, 255, 263, 265; carries despatches to Wilkinson, 295; pursues General Wilkinson, 309; arrives at Natchitoches, and delivers Burr's letter to Wilkinson, 311; arrested at Fort Adams, 319, 460; discharged from custody, 340.

Sweden, Bernadotte, Prince of, v. 424; his rupture with Napoleon, 425, 426; Napoleon declares war on, vi. 251; mission to, declared inexpedient by the Senate, vii. 62-64.

Swedish Pomerania, v. 425.

Swift, Joseph Gardner, colonel of engineers, ix. 235.

"Syren," American 16-gun sloop-of-war, v. 378; captured July 12, 1814, viii. 193; at New Orleans, vii. 312.

TALISHATCHEE, Creek village, destroyed by Jackson, vii. 237.

Talladega, Creek village, relieved by Jackson, vii. 238.

Tallapoosa River, home of the Upper Creeks, vii. 217, 220, 240, 242; Jackson's first campaign to, 245-248; Jackson's second campaign to, 254-257.

Talleyrand, i. 335; his colonial schemes, 352 *et seq.*; becomes French minister of foreign affairs, 353; his negotiations with the American commissioners, 355; his instructions for Guillemardet, 355; his mistakes, 357; obliged by the X. Y. Z. affair to retire, 358; restored by Bonaparte, 359, 412; his letter with regard to Louisiana, 400; denies the retrocession of Louisiana, 409; his instructions to Bernadotte, ii. 11; opposes the cession of Louisiana, 25; proposes it to Livingston, 27; explanation of the sale of Louisiana, 55; assures Cevallos of Napoleon's opposition to the American claims, 293; his instructions to Turreau, 295; reassures Cevallos, 297; his attitude toward the United States, 309; report to the Emperor on Monroe's note, 310; answer to Monroe, 313; forbids discussion of Spanish spoliation claims, iii. 26, 30; rejects American claim to West Florida, 26, 54; his share in the Spanish negotiations, 34, 41; his jobbery, 41; writes to Armstrong the Emperor's demands concerning trade with St. Domingo, 90; sends an agent to Armstrong to suggest an arrangement between the United States and Spain, 103; informs Armstrong that the King of Spain refuses to alienate Florida, 377; prompts Armstrong to renew his request for the Floridas, 380; rebukes Vandeul for precipitancy in the Florida matter, 384; created Prince of Benevento, 385; removed from office, iv. 107; his letter of Dec. 21, 1804, on the boundaries of Louisiana, v. 321, 322.

Taney, Chief-Justice, opinion of, respecting governmental powers in the Louisiana case, ii. 126, 128.

Tariff of 1816, ix. 111-116.

"Tartarus," British 20-gun sloop of-war, with the "Avon" and "Castilian," viii. 189, 190, 192.

Taxes, abolition of, in 1801, i. 240, 270, 272.

Taxes, war, vi 157, 165, 166; postponed, 168, 204; reported June 26, 1812. 235; postponed by Congress, 235, 444; bill for, 447; bills passed

356   GENERAL INDEX.

in July and August, 1813, vii. 53–55, 67; receipts of, paid in Treasury notes or the notes of suspended banks, viii. 244, 245, 256, 257; doubled in 1814, 248, 255, 261; arrears of, in October, 1814, 255, 256; internal, shifted to customs in 1816, ix. 112.

Tayler, John, ii. 177.

Taylor, John, member of Congress from South Carolina, author of Macon's bill No. 2, v. 194; his speech, 195, 196; introduces Bank Charter, 208.

Taylor, John, of Caroline, i. 143, 146, 263, 338; ii. 94; his remarks on the Louisiana purchase, 105; his advice to Monroe, v. 369, 370; Monroe's letter to, June 13, 1812, vi. 66; his remarks on the presidential election of 1812, 414, 417; his "Inquiry," ix. 195–197.

Taylor, John W., member of Congress from New York, vii. 398.

Taylor, Josiah, lieutenant of Second Infantry, iii. 303.

Taylor, Peter, evidence of, concerning Blennerhassett's delusion, iii. 259; sent with a warning letter to Burr, 275.

Taylor, Robert, brigadier-general of Virginia militia at Norfolk, vii. 271.

Taylor, Zachary, captain in the Seventh U. S. Infantry, vii. 73.

Tazewell, Littleton, sent with a message to Captain Douglas, iv. 28; his political position, v. 161.

Tea, price of, in February, 1815, ix. 61.

Tecumthe, residence of, in 1805, iii. 15; his origin, vi. 78; his plan of Indian confederation, 78, 79; establishes himself at Tippecanoe, 79; character of his village, 80; joined by the Wyandots, 83; his conference with Harrison, Aug. 12, 1810, 85–88; seizes salt in June, 1811, 90; his talk at Vincennes, July 27, 1811, 91; starts for the Creek country, 92; his account of the affair at Tippecanoe, 105, 109; returns from the Creek country, 108; his reply to British complaints, 109; his speech of May 16, 1812, 111; joins the British at Malden, 329, 330; routs Ohio militia, 315; at the battle of Maguaga, 325; at the capture of Detroit, 332; absent at the River Raisin, vii. 94; at the siege of Fort Meigs, 104, 106; stops massacre, 107; reported to be moving against Harrison, 110, 111; protests against evacuation of Malden, 130; killed at the battle of the Thames, 140–143; his visit to the Creeks in October, 1811, 220; his speech to the Creeks, 221; effect of his visit to the Creeks, 222, 223; his intentions regarding the southern Indians, 232.

Temperance in United States in 1800, i. 47.

Tenallytown, near Washington, Winder's halt at, viii. 154.

"Tenedos," 46-gun British frigate. vii. 285, 286, 293; captures privateer "Enterprise," 329; chases "President," ix. 64, 67.

Tennessee, population of, in 1800, i. 2; militia, ordered into service, Dec. 10, 1812, vii. 207; dismissed, 209, 210; recalled into service, 235; claim discharge, 239; return home, 239, 240; sixty-day, join Jackson, 245; routed at Enotachopco Creek, 246–248; disciplined by Jackson, 252, 253; losses of, at the Horse-shoe, 256; the whole quota called out by Jackson, Aug. 27, 1814, viii. 320; march for Mobile, 328; ordered to New Orleans, 332, 333; reach New Orleans, 337; growth of population, ix. 155.

Terre aux Bœufs, encampment at, v. 171-175.

Terry, Eli, i. 181.

Texas, a part of the Louisiana purchase, ii. 7, 256, 294, 298, 300; boundary, iii. 33; Spanish definition of boundary, 34; included in the Louisiana purchase, 40; Spanish establishments in, to be dislodged, 69, 80; to be confirmed to Spain, and hypothecated to the United States, 78; to be purchased, 139; threatening military movements in, 310.

Thacher, Rev. Samuel Cooper, Unitarian clergyman, ix. 178, 179; editor of the "Anthology," 202.

Thames, Harrison's victory on the, vii. 128-143.

"Thanatopsis," ix. 207-209.

Theatre in New England in 1800, i. 49, 90.

Thiers, Louis Adolphe, on Napoleon, v. 225, 226, 236.

Thomas, John, major-general of Kentucky militia, ordered to New Orleans, viii. 336, 337; arrives at New Orleans, 368; unwell, 378.

Thompson, Smith, i. 108.

Thornton, Edward, his description of the inauguration of Jefferson, i. 198, 436, 440; letter to Hammond, ii. 342, 388; complains that desertion of seamen is encouraged, 345; Jefferson's confidential relations with, 347; proposals with regard to Monroe's mission, 351; on change of tone in 1804, 387, 388.

Thornton, Dr. William, i. 111; viii. 239.

Thornton, William, colonel of British Eighty-fifth Light Infantry, leads attack at Bladensburg, viii. 141; severely wounded, 144; leads the advance to New Orleans, 338, 342; his brigade, 344, 347; in the night battle of December 23, 1814, 348; ordered to cross the river, 371-373; crosses, 375; captures Patterson's battery, 377; wounded, 378; recalled, 381.

"Tiber," British frigate, captures privateer "Leo," viii. 196.

Ticknor, George, i. 63, 94; reports Eppes's remark to Gaston, viii. 262; reports John Adams's remark on George Cabot, 307, 308; reports Jefferson's remark on the British at New Orleans, 309; professor of Belles Lettres in Harvard College, ix. 206.

"Ticonderoga," 17-gun schooner, in Macdonough's fleet on Lake Champlain, viii. 105; in the battle of Plattsburg, 110.

Tiffin, Edward, governor of Ohio, iii. 282, 286, 289, 334, 335; senator from Ohio, moves an amendment to the Constitution, iv. 205.

Tilsit, treaty of, iv. 62, 105, 140.

"Times," the London, on the "Chesapeake" affair, iv. 44, 54, 132; viii. 201; on the Orders in Council, v. 62; on English apathy toward the United States, vi. 24; on an American war, 287; on the "Guerriere," vii. 5, 14; on the conduct of the war in 1812, 9, 357; on American privateers in the West Indies, 12; on the "Macedonian," 13; on the "Java," 16; on the Foreign Seamen Bill, 25; on President Madison, 357, 358; on the execution of British subjects taken in arms, 362; on the American cruisers, viii. 210, 211; on Madison, ix. 2, 3; on terms of peace, 4; on the defeat at Plattsburg, 35; on the Ghent correspondence, 43; on the Treaty, 55, 56.

Tin, price of, in February, 1815, ix. 61.

Tingey, Thomas, captain in U. S navy, commandant of Washing-

ton navy-yard, sets fire to vessels in the Eastern Branch, viii. 145.
Tippecanoe Creek, vi. 68, 79; Indian settlement at, 80; character of, 81; to be a large Indian resort, 91; to be broken up, 92, 94; Harrison's march on, 97; arrival at, 98; camp at, 101; battle of, 103; characterized by Tecumthe, 105, 109, 111; retreat from, 106; Harrison's estimate of effect of battle, 107, 108; charged upon England, 140, 143.
Tobacco, value of exported, in 1815, ix. 94; in 1816, 126.
Todd, Thomas, associate justice, vii. 74.
"Tom," Baltimore privateer captured, vii. 329.
"Tom Cringle's Log," vii. 321-323.
Tompkins, Daniel D., elected governor of New York in 1807, iv. 283; his attempts to enforce the embargo, 249, 259; his prevention of the Bank Charter, vi. 209; re-elected in May, 1813. vii. 50; viii. 12; candidate for the Presidency, vii. 403; offered the State Department, viii. 163; recommends a State army, 282; nominated as Vice-President, ix. 122, 123; elected Vice-President, 139.
Töplitz in Bohemia, the Czar's headquarters, vii. 351.
Toronto (see York).
Torpedo, Fulton's, v. 209.
Totten, Joseph G., captain of engineers, vi. 350, 352; major of engineers, constructs the fortifications of Plattsburg, viii. 108; ix. 236.
Town-meetings held in Massachusetts to resist the embargo, iv. 410; Jefferson's opinion of, 442; in January, 1814, viii. 5-7.
Towson, Nathan, captain of artillery, vi. 347; captain of artillery company in Hindman's battalion, viii. 37; attached to Scott's brigade at Chippawa, 43; at Lundy's Lane, 50-52, 53, 56; commands artillery on Snake Hill, 71, 72, 74.
Tracy, Uriah, senator from Connecticut, on the Louisiana treaty, ii. 107; believes disunion inevitable, 160, 162; votes against the impeachment of Chase, 238; his death, iv. 146.
Trafalgar, battle of, iii. 149, 370.
Travel in America, difficulties of, in 1800, i. 11 et seq.
Treason, Marshall's law of, iii. 443, 467; Giles's bill for the punishment of, iv. 205.
Treasury (see Gallatin, Jones, Campbell, Dallas).
Treasury Notes, five millions authorized in January, 1813, vi. 448; ten millions authorized in March, 1814, vii. 390; viii. 18; Campbell's only resource, 213, 242; discount on, Feb. 1, 1815, 214, 261; six millions as much as could easily be circulated, 242; no one willing to accept, 244; fifteen millions to be issued, 261; value of, affected by the peace, ix. 62; issues of, 90; Dallas's failure to fund, in 1815, 84, 98-103.
Treaties, with European powers, preliminary, between Great Britain, France, and Spain, Nov. 3, 1762. i. 353; ii. 7, 70; definitive, between the same, Feb. 10, 1763, i. 353; ii. 6; definitive, between Great Britain and Spain, Sept. 3, 1783, i. 353; definitive, between the United States and Great Britain, Sept. 3, 1783, ii. 90, 411; ix. 31, 44-49; Jay's, between the United States and Great Britain, Nov. 19, 1794, i. 348; ii. 316, 334, 339, 355, 421, 424; iii. 401; article xii. of, 410; of Basle, between Spain and France,

GENERAL INDEX. 359

July 22, 1795, i. 354; Pinckney's, between the United States and Spain, Oct. 27, 1795, 348, 349; ii. 246; iii. 38; between Toussaint and Maitland, June 13, 1799, i. 385; of Morfontaine, between the United States and France, Sept. 30, 1800, 362, 388; ii. 21, 42, 46, 47, 293, 296, 297, 383; of San Ildefonso (Berthier's), between Spain and France, retroceding Louisiana, Oct. 1, 1800, i. 370, 401, 403; ii. 43, 58, 70, 254; iii. 38; of Lunéville, between France and Austria, Feb. 9, 1801, i. 370; of Lucien Bonaparte, between Spain and France, March 21, 1801, 372, 406, 409; ii. 299; of Badajos, between Spain and Portugal, June 5, 1801, i. 372; preliminary, between Great Britain and France, Oct. 1, 1801, 374; ii. 344; settling British debts between Great Britain and the United States, Jan. 8, 1802, 358, 410; of Amiens, between Great Britain and France, March 25, 1802, 59. 290, 326, 347, 385, 414, 416; of claims between the United States and Spain, Aug. 11, 1802, 21, 250, 259, 278, 280, 293, 296, 297, 383; between France and the United States, ceding Louisiana and settling claims, 39-49, 51, 67, 85, 88, 92, 97, 100, 102, 105, 107, 108, 111, 245, 275, 289, 302, 308, 355, 399-401; between the United States and Great Britain for settling boundaries, May 12, 1803, 358, 383, 384, 391, 392, 410, 420, 424; between the United States and Tripoli, Nov. 4, 1796, i. 244; June 4, 1805, ii. 434, 436; of Pressburg, between France and Austria, Dec. 26, 1805, iii. 163, 370; with England, of Dec. 1, 1806 (Monroe's), iii. 409 et seq., 422, 429-436, 438; iv. 48-51, 129, 144, 154; ix. 33; of Tilsit, between France and Russia, July 7, 1807, iv. 62; of Fontainebleau, between France and Spain, Oct. 27, 1807, iv. 119; of Dec. 24, 1814, with Great Britain at Ghent, ix. 1-53; of Feb. 22, 1819, between the United States and Spain, ceding Florida, vi. 237.

—— Indian, of Greenville, Aug. 3, 1795, for the establishment of peace and boundaries with Wyandots, Delawares, Shawanese, Ottawas, Chippewas, Pottawatamies, Miamies, Eel Rivers, Weas, Kickapoos, Piankeshaws, and Kaskaskias, iii. 13; vi. 79; ix. 19, 20; of June 16, 1802, with the Creek nation, ceding land between the forks of the Oconee and Ocmulgee rivers in Georgia, vii. 220; of Aug. 13, 1803, with the Kaskaskia Indians, ceding lands, ii. 92; of Aug. 18, 1804, with the Delaware Indians ceding land, ii. 207; vi. 75; of Aug. 27, 1804, with the Piankeshaw Indians, ceding land, iii. 13; vi. 75, 77; of Nov. 3, 1804, with the Creek nation, ceding all the land between Oconee and Ocmulgee, vii. 220; of July 4, 1805, with Wyandots, Ottawas, Chippewas, Munsee and Delaware Shawanese, and Pottawatamies, ceding land to the hundred-and-twentieth mile due west of the west boundary of Pennsylvania, iii. 13; of July 23, 1805, with Chickasaws, ceding lands on the Tennessee and Duck rivers, iii. 14; of Aug. 21, 1805, with the Delawares, Pottawatamies, Miamies, Eel River, and Weas, at Grouseland near Vincennes, ceding land, vi. 75; of Oct. 25 and 27, 1805, with Cherokees, ceding land, iii. 14; of Nov. 14, 1805, with Creeks, ceding land, iii. 14; of Dec. 30, 1805, with Piankeshaws, ceding land, iii. 13; of Nov. 7, 1807, with the Ottawas, Chippe-

360 GENERAL INDEX.

was, **Wyandots,** and Pottawatamies, at Detroit, ceding lands, vi. 82; of Sept 30, 1809, with the Delawares, Pottawatamies, Miamies, and Eel River Miamies, at Fort Wayne, ceding lands, vi. 83, 85, 87; or capitulation of Aug. 9, 1814, with Creek chiefs, ceding lands, vii. 259-261; of peace, July 22, 1814, with Wyandots, Delawares, Shawanese, Senecas, and Miamies, vii. 261; ix. 32.

Treaty of June 30, 1815, between the United States and Algiers, of peace and amity, 105.

—— of July 3, 1815, between the United States and Great Britain, to regulate commerce, ix. 104.

Treaty-making power, defined by W. C. Nicholas, ii. 87, 88, 112; by Jefferson, 89, 90; by Gaylord Griswold, 96, 97; by Randolph, 98, 99; by Gouverneur Morris, 100 ; by Nicholson, 101; by Rodney, 102, 103; by Pickering, 105; by John Taylor of Caroline, 106, 107; by Tracy, 108; by Breckinridge, 109; by J. Q. Adams, 111; by Cocke, 113 ; summary of opinions on, 114, 115.

Trimble, W. H., major of Nineteenth U. S. Infantry, in Fort Erie, viii. 75; his account of the British assault, 76, 77; wounded in sortie, 88.

Tripoli, the war with, ii. 137, 426 *et seq.;* Pacha of, 430; peace with, 436; visited by Decatur in 1815, ix. 105.

Tristan d'Acunha, scene of "Hornet's" battle with "Penguin," ix. 71.

Troup, George McIntosh, member of Congress from Georgia, favors army, iv. 213; opposes war, 377; opposes Macon's bill, v. 185; on maintaining the army, 202; on admission of West Florida, 324; his war-speech, vi. 144, 145; votes for frigates, 164; his report on the defences of Washington, vii. 57; his bill for filling the ranks of the regular army, 381, 382-384; declares that no efficacious military measure could pass the House, 266, 267, 268; denounces Giles's bill, 273; his conference report rejected, 280; his bill for a peace establishment, ix. 84.

"True-Blooded Yankee," privateer, in British waters, vii 332.

Trumbull, John, i. 101; ix. 213.

Trumbull, Jonathan, governor of Connecticut, refuses to take part in carrying out the Enforcement Act, iv. 417, 455; calls the legislature to "interpose," 418.

Truxton, Commodore, sounded by Burr, iii. 239.

Tuckaubatchee, Creek town on the Tallapoosa, council at, vii. 220; Tecumthe's speech at, 221; councils at, 224, 225 ; chiefs escape from, 227.

Tucker, ———, British colonel of Forty-First Regiment, repulsed at Black Rock, viii. 69.

Tucker, Henry St. George, member of Congress from Virginia, ix. 107.

Tudor, William, ix. 202, 207, 208.

Tupper, Edward W., brigadier-general of Ohio militia, vii. 78.

Turner, Charles, member of Congress from Massachusetts. assaulted in Plymouth, vi. 400, 409.

Turner, J. M. W., ix. 213, 216.

Turnpikes, prejudice against, i. 64 *et seq.*

Turreau, Louis Marie, appointed minister to the United States by Napoleon, ii. 268; his domestic quarrels, 269; complains of the discredit of France, 271; embarrassments of,

GENERAL INDEX. 361

272; his description of Madison, 274; receives instructions from Talleyrand, 296, presented to Jefferson, 405; describes General Wilkinson, 403; his course with Madison in the Spanish business, iii. 81; his letter to Talleyrand on American policy and national character, 84; his abruptness, 86 *et seq.*; sends Talleyrand an account of Jefferson's conversation in December, 1805, 124; his part in the Madison-Yrujo matter, 188; acts as Yrujo's ally, 194; demands an explanation from Madison about Miranda, 195; reports to Talleyrand Jefferson's system for an alliance of nations, 204; writes concerning Jefferson's character and position, 205; writes to his government respecting Burr's schemes, 226; his comments on the embargo and war, 396; writes to his government respecting English relations, 424 *et seq.*; embarrassed by the Berlin Decree, 427; reports an interview with Jefferson after the "Chesapeake" affair, iv. 36; his letter describing the servile character of Americans, 140; alarmed by Jefferson's course in Rose's negotiation, 229; his letters to Champagny complaining of the embargo, etc., 220 *et seq.*, 297; his long conversations with Madison and Jefferson respecting a French alliance, 308; hopes, in January, 1809, that America will declare war, 396; his anger with the American government in the spring of 1809, v. 33-40; his report on the repeal of the embargo, 34; on the Non-importation Act, 35; on disunion, 36; on the Spanish colonies, 37; his advice on rupture with the United States, in June, 1809, 40; his report of Gallatin's remarks on renewal of intercourse with Great Britain, 74; his report of Robert Smith's remarks on Jefferson's weakness and indiscretions, 84; his note of June 14, 1809, remonstrating at the unfriendly conduct of the United States, 84; his recall ordered by Napoleon, 226; his successor arrives, 345. 346.

Tuskegee Warrior, murders white families on the Ohio, vii. 224; is put to death, 225.

UKASE, Imperial, of Dec. 19, 1810, v. 418, 419.

Ulm, capitulation of, iii. 370.

Union, used for nation in the language of the Constitution, ii. 85.

Union, dissolution of, as viewed by southern republicans in 1798, i. 142; attempted in New England in 1804, ii. 160-191; proposed by Burr to the British government in 1804, 395, 403; Burr's schemes of, iii. 219-244; prophesied by Randolph, 364; schemes for, renewed by New England in 1808, iv. 402-407; a delicate topic, v. 14; a cause of repealing the embargo, 34; discussed by Turreau, 36; discussed in New England, vi. 403, 409; affected by the seizure of Florida, vii. 213; "increasing harmony throughout the," 365, 366; jealousies in the, 402; Massachusetts federalists wish to resist the, viii. 4, 8-10, 13, 22; southern section of, suffers most by the war, 15; its duty of defence neglected, 222; practically dissolved, 223; amount of sentiment for and against, in 1814, 229; dissolution of, deprecated by Webster, 275; dissolution of, encouraged and avowed in Congress, 277; severance of, deprecated by Hartford Convention, 296; already dis-

GENERAL INDEX.

solved, 300, 301; alternative to dissolution of, 303; political effect of peace on, ix. 80, 92; difficulties of, overcome in 1816, 173, 194, 219, 220; its distinctive character, 226.

Unitarians in New England, i 89; ix 133; in Harvard College, 176, 177; churches in Boston, 178; opinions of, in Boston churches, 179, 180; literary influence of, 205, 207; optimism of, 239.

United States, banking capital of, in 1800, i. 26; credit and trade of, 27; monetary valuation of, in 1800, and distribution of wealth, 40; popular characteristics of the people of, in 1800, 41 *et seq.*; standard of comfort, 42; population in 1810, v. 280; population of, in 1817, ix. 154; growth of population and wealth in, 172, 173; character of people, 219-242.

"United States," 44-gun frigate, vi 363; first cruise of, in 1812, 366, 375; at Boston, 378; second cruise of, 381; captures the "Macedonian," 382, 383; blockaded at New London, vii. 278, 279, 287, 311.

Universalists, ix. 133; growth of church, 183, 184; significance of movement, 239.

University, Jefferson's recommendation of a national, iii. 346, 347; iv. 365; Madison's recommendation of, v. 319; recommended by Madison in 1815, ix. 105; again in 1816, 143.

Upham, Timothy, lieutenant-colonel commanding the Eleventh U. S. Infantry at Chrystler's Farm, vii. 189.

Urquijo, Don Mariano Luis de, i. 355, 365, 368.

Uti possidetis, claimed by England at Ghent, ix. 9, 17, 34; exceeded by British demands, 21; opposed to *status ante bellum*, 33, 34; rejected 37; abandoned, 41, 42.

Utica in 1800, i. 3.

VAN BUREN, MARTIN, his support of De Witt Clinton, vi. 409, 413; special judge advocate in Hull's trial, vii. 417; prevents Crawford's nomination to the Presidency, ix. 123.

Vanderbilt, Cornelius, i. 28.

Vandeul, M. de, French chargé at Madrid, confers with Godoy respecting the cession of West Florida, v. 380; rebuked by Talleyrand at Napoleon's order, 384.

Van Ness, William P., i. 109; author of pamphlet by "Aristides," ii. 73, 171; carries Burr's demand to Hamilton, 183.

Van Rensselaer, Solomon, colonel of New York militia, commands attack on Queenston, vi. 348.

Van Rensselaer, Stephen, major-general of New York militia, ordered to take command at Niagara, vi. 321; forwards letter to Hull, 324; his force, Aug. 19, 1812, 341; his alarming position, 342, 343; his force, Sept. 15, 344; expected to invade Canada with six thousand men, 345; his attack on Queenston, 346, 347-353; retires from command, 353; Monroe's opinion of, 396; Jefferson's comment on, 398.

Varnum, Joseph B., member of Congress from Massachusetts, ii. 123; candidate for Speaker of the Ninth Congress, iii. 128; chosen Speaker of the Tenth Congress, iv. 153; re-elected Speaker in the Eleventh Congress, v. 76; his rulings on the previous question, 353; elected senator, vi. 116; defeated candidate for governor, vii. 50; his speech on Giles's bill for drafting eighty thousand militia, viii. 269–270; votes against Giles's bill, 273; votes against internal improvements, ix. 150.

Vermilion River, Indian boundary, vi. 97, 98.

Vermont, militia recalled from national service, vii. 366; furnishes supplies to British army, vii. 146; viii. 93; militia not called out to defend Plattsburg, 222, refuses to attend the Hartford Convention, 227; chooses federalist Congressmen, 228; prosperous, ix. 160.

"Vesuvius," steamboat on the Mississippi, ix. 172.

Vice-Presidency, change in mode of election for, ii. 132–134.

Victor, Marshal, to command French forces in Louisiana, ii. 5.

Vienna, Napoleon's draft for a decree of, v. 143, 144, 150, 152, Congress of, ix. 24, 36.

Villeré plantation, at New Orleans, seized by British advance, viii. 337, 339.

Vimieiro, battle of, iv. 315, 340.

Vincennes, territorial capital of Indiana, vi. 68, 71, 79; the Shawnee prophet's talk at, 80; Tecumthe's talks at, 85, 91; citizens' meeting at, 92; Indian deputation at, 108; panic at, 110.

Vincent, Colonel, his account of Toussaint, i. 382.

Vincent, John, British brigadier-general, evacuates Fort George, vii. 157; attacks at Stony Creek, 159, 160; recaptures Fort George, 202.

Virginia in 1800, i. 32; farming in, 33, 131 et seq.; horse-racing, 51; Washington's views on the value of land in, 135; Church and State in, 136; adoption of the Constitution by, 139; Resolutions, 140 et seq.; law to prevent extradition, ii. 334, 345, 398; Madison's position in, ii. 217; iii. 120; iv. 226; hostility of, to cities and fortifications, iii. 352; opposed to Pennsylvania on the slave-trade bill, 356–369; effect of embargo on, iv. 265, 281; creates manufactures in New England, v. 19, 20; apathy of, toward the war, vi. 413, 414; exports of, affected by the blockade, vii. 264, 265; operations of war on the shores of, 265–277; militia, mortality of, viii. 219; her relative rank and obligations, 233; money furnished by, 234; men furnished by, 235; soldiers and sailors of, 236, 237; arrears of internal taxes in, 256; creates a State army, 283; effect of peace on, ix. 60, 61; congressional election in 1815, 93; increase of population, 1800–1816, 155; increase of wealth, 161–167; legislative reports on roads and banks, 165, 166; judicial decision of, in case of Martin against Hunter's lessee, 190–192; resolutions of 1798 obsolete in 1817, 194.

Virginians, i. 133 et seq; middle and lower classes of, 137; agriculture their resource, 138.

"Vixen," sloop-of-war, captured, vi. 386; vii 312, 313.

Volney describes the American habits of diet, i. 44.

Voltaire, i. 161.

WABASH, valley of, vi. 67, 68, 75, 77; Harrison's land purchase in, 83; war imminent in, 85.

Wadsworth, Decius, colonel commissary general of ordnance, detailed to erect fortifications at Bladensburg, viii. 132, 141; refuses to obey Monroe's orders, 158, 159.

Wadsworth, William, brigadier-general of New York militia, vi. 351; surrenders at Queenston, 352.

GENERAL INDEX.

Wagner, Jacob, chief clerk of the State Department, i. 236; ii. 267; editor of the "Federal Republican," vi. 406, 407.

Walbach, John B., adjutant-general to Wilkinson at Chrystler's Farm, vii. 189.

Wales, Prince of (see George, Prince of Wales).

Wales, R. W., captain of British sloop-of-war "Epervier," his report of action with the "Peacock," viii. 182, 183.

Walpole, Lord, British ambassador at St. Petersburg, his remarks on Roumanzoff, vii. 354.

War, Jefferson's recommendation of a fund for, iii. 3; cost of, 1812-1815, ix. 90, 91.

War with England, declared by Monroe to be nearly decided in November, 1811, vi. 130; recommended by House Committee of Foreign Relations, Nov. 29, 1811, 133-136; its objects explained by Peter B. Porter, 136; its probable effects discussed by Felix Grundy, 138, 141; Grundy's account of its causes, 139, 140; Macon's view of its object, 145; Monroe's remarks on, 190; Madison's message recommending, 221-226; expediency of, 223; Calhoun's report on causes, 226; Calhoun's bill for, adopted by the House, 228; by the Senate, 228, 229; and signed by the President, 229; criticisms on the conduct of, 392-399; opposition to, 398-403; apathy toward, 414; only attainable object of, 418; reasons of continuance, 430-432.

War Department (see Dearborn, Eustis, Armstrong, Monroe, Dallas).

War Power, ii. 100, 101, 105, 106, 108, 113; over the militia, vi. 159-161.

"War in Disguise," pamphlet by James Stephen, iii. 50.

Ward, Artemas, member of Congress from (Boston) Massachusetts, on defence of the Union, viii. 276.

Ward, Robert Plumer, vi. 279.

Ware, Henry, appointed Professor of Theology at Harvard College, i. 311; his Unitarianism, ix. 176, 182, 205.

Ware, Henry, the younger, ix. 206.

Ware, William, ix. 206.

Warren, John, iv. 411.

Warren, Admiral Sir John Borlase, his authority to suspend hostilities, vii. 4, ix. 33; his blockade of May 26, 1813, vii. 262; his operations in Chesapeake Bay, 265-277; his remarks on Broke's victory, 302.

Warren, Dr. J. C., his description of Boston customs in 1800, i. 91; professor of anatomy at Harvard College, ix. 206.

Warrington, Lewis, commander in U. S. Navy, commands "Peacock," viii. 181; captures "Epervier," 182, 184; sails from New York, ix. 63; fires into "Nautilus," 73.

"Warrior," privateer brig, her escape, vii. 326.

Warton, agent of Burr, iii. 238.

Washington city in 1800, i. 30; expense of living in, iv. 209; F. J. Jackson's impressions of, v. 116-119; threatened by British fleet in July, 1813, vii. 55, 277; fears for safety of, 56; declared to be adequately defended, 57; neglect of its defences, viii. 120; military district created to protect, 122; result of measures of defence, 123; British reasons for attacking. 121, 127, 130; measures of defence taken after August 18, 131, 132; Winder retreats to, 135, 136; natural defences of, 138; capture and burning of, 145-148; ix. 21; conduct of citizens of, viii. 158, 159, 160; militia system tested at, 218; report of investigating committee on capture of, 277; Ross's treatment of, approved by his government, 314, 315; defence of, compared with that of New Orleans, 340-342; news of capture received at Ghent, ix. 31, 42; Lord Liverpool on capture of, 38; news from New Orleans and Ghent received at, 57, 58; banks share in loan of 1815, 102; public buildings rebuilt, 142, 143.

Washington, (or Warburton) Fort (see Fort Washington).

Washington, President, opinion of American farming-lands, i. 35; his support of a national bank, 65; on emancipation in Pennsylvania and its effects, 135; establishes the precedent of addressing Congress in a speech, 247; his personal authority, 262, 320; denounced by Thomas Paine, 328; expenditures of his administration, v. 200, Jefferson's estimate of, viii. 232.

"Wasp," sloop-of-war, vi. 364, 378; her action with the "Frolic," 379, 380; vii. 310, 312.

"Wasp," new American 22-gun sloop-of-war built in 1813, viii. 184, 237; in the British Channel in June, 1814, 185; captures the "Reindeer," 186, 187; sinks the "Avon," 188-192; lost, 193; gunnery of, ix. 230.

Water communication in 1800, i. 8.

Waterhouse, Dr., i 93.

Waterloo, ix. 56.

Watmough, John G., lieutenant of artillery, in Fort Erie, viii. 76.

Watson, W. H., first lieutenant of the "Argus," vii. 306, 308

Watt, first lieutenant of the "Shannon," killed, vii. 296.

Wayne, Fort, vi. 294.

Wea Indians, vi. 71, 75, 87.

Weatherford, William, Creek half-breed, vii. 229, 244, 257.

Webster, Daniel, his Rockingham Resolutions, vi. 403; member of Congress from Massachusetts, vii. 53; his resolutions on the repeal of French decrees, 55, 58; his speech on repealing the restrictive system, 375, 376, 377; his speech on a defensive war, 382, 383; his speech on Dallas's bank scheme, viii. 258; his bank scheme adopted by Congress, 259, 260; deprecates disunion, 275; defeats conscription, 279; in the Fourteenth Congress, ix. 107, 108, 110; opposes protective duties, 115; opposes bank, 117, 118; favors Compensation Act, 120; his report on repeal of the Compensation Act, 144; becomes resident of Boston, 206; a type, 216.

Webster, Noah, i. 62, 105; presides at Amherst town-meeting, viii. 5.

Weld, Rev. Abijah, of Attleborough, i. 21.

Weld, Isaac, Jr., an Eng'ish traveller, describes condition of inns in America, i. 46, 52; describes Princeton College, 129; describes William and Mary College, 136; at Wilmington, 182.

Wellesley, Marquess, his character, v. 264, 265, 269; appointed ambassador to the Supreme Junta, 267; becomes Foreign Secretary, 268; his friendship with Pinkney, 270, 275; his promises, 271; his note on Jackson, 272; his remark on American hatred, 273; his procrastination, 277-280, 285; his contempt for his colleagues, 281, 282; resolves to retire, 285; his reply to Champagny's letter of August 5, 286; hopes for a Whig ministry in November, 1811, vi. 4; his controversy with Pinkney over the French decrees and the law of blockade, 5, 6, 9; abandons hope of a Whig ministry, 14; rejects Pinkney's demands, 14, 15, 18; appoints a minister to Washington, 16; his instructions of April 10, 1811, to the new minister (see Foster), 22, 23; criticises his colleagues for apathy toward America, 24; his instructions to Foster of Jan. 28, 1812, 191, 192; settles the "Chesapeake" affair, 121, 122, 270; urges his colleagues to choose a course, 267, 268; resigns from the Cabinet, Jan. 16, 1812, 271; on the American government, vii. 10.

Wellesley, Sir Arthur, Duke of Wellington, wins the battle of Vimieiro iv. 315; in India, v. 266; fights the battle of Talavera, 106; made a viscount, 264; general-in-chief, 267; retreats into Portugal, 268; fails in siege of Burgos, vii. 4, 9; invades France, 356; his remarks on Prevost's retreat from Plattsburg, viii. 113; his remarks on his troops sent to America, 113, 354; ix. 41; brother-in-law of Pakenham, viii. 353; on the negotiations at Ghent, ix. 40-42.

Wellesley, Henry, v. 264; envoy in Spain, 268; on Perceval's commercial policy, 283, 284.

Wells, Samuel, colonel of Seventeenth U. S. Infantry, vii. 89, 90-92, 95, 110.

Wells town-meeting in January, 1809, vi. 414.

West, Benjamin, i. 127.

West Indian Report, ii. 68.

West Indian trade, English policy toward, ii. 318; value of, to England, 331, 413, 415.

West Point Military Academy established, i. 301; school at, v. 319; value of, in the war, ix. 235, 236.

"Western World," the, iii. 273.

Westmoreland, Earl of, Lord Privy Seal, i. 282; his opinion on Spencer Perceval's proposed Order in Council, iv. 89.

Wewocau, Little Warrior of (see Little Warrior).

Wheat, value of export of, in 1815, ix. 94, 95.

Whiskey-tax, rejected, ii. 167.

Whitbread, Samuel, member of Parliament, i. 50; ii. 270; on the American war, vii. 11, 21, 24.

Whitby, Captain, of the "Leander," iii. 199.

White House, at Washington, burned by Ross, viii. 145, 146, 230, 231; rebuilt, ix. 143.

White, Samuel, senator from Delaware, iv. 146.

Whitney, Eli, i. 181.

Whittemore, Asa, i. 182.

Whitworth, Lord, British minister at Paris, Napoleon's announcement to, ii. 19.

Wickham, John, Burr's counsel; iii. 444; his opening speech in the Burr trial, 465.

Widgery, William, member of Congress from Massachusetts, vi. 400.

Wilberforce, William, member of Parliament, vi. 273, 280.

Wilde, Richard Henry, member of Congress from Georgia, on the decline of the House of Representatives, ix. 146.

Wilkinson, James, brigadier-general and governor of the Louisiana Territory, ii. 220; portrayed by Turreau, 406; his relations with Burr, 408; holds civil and military powers, iii. 176; his military force in 1806, 299; sends Lieutenant Pike to find the sources of the Mississippi, 213, and to New Mexico, 214; Burr's friend, 219 *et seq.*; joins Burr at Fort Massac, 222, author of Burr's projects against Mexico, 223, 234; discouraged, 227; opposed to attacking Spanish territory, 249; receives cipher despatch from Burr, 253; in communication with the Spanish authorities, 262, 263; Governor Mirò's agent, 269; denounced by Daveiss as a Spanish pensioner, 270; at New Orleans, 297; Laussat's opinion of, 298; ordered to Natchitoches, 310; receives Burr's letter at Natchitoches, and communicates its contents to Colonel Cushing, 312 *et seq.*; writes to Jefferson, 314; writes again to the President, 315, takes command in New Orleans, 317; tells Bollman his intention to oppose Burr's schemes, 318; demands of Claiborne the supreme command, 318; establishes a degree of martial law in New Orleans, 319; his letter to Clark, 321; his acts, 323; despatches including his version of Burr's cipher received by Jefferson, 336; assailed by Randolph and the Federalists, 341; in the receipt of a pension from the King of Spain, 342; arrives at the Burr trial, 454; deserted by Clark, 454; accused by Major Bruff, 454; supported by Jefferson, 456; escapes indictment for treason, 457; Randolph brings charges against, iv. 208; his movements, v. 37; Gallatin's remarks on his character, 38; military court of inquiry on, 169; his influence on the army, 169; ordered to New Orleans, 170; his encampment at Terre aux Bœufs, 171-175; summoned to Washington for investigation, 175; senior brigadier, vi. 291; appointed major-general, Feb. 27, 1813, vii. 37; ordered from New Orleans to Sackett's Harbor, March 10, 1813, 172, 215; causes of his transfer, 173, 216; arrives at Washington, July 31, 174; takes command of military district No. 9, 175, 176; his plan of campaign, 177, 178; goes to Niagara, 179; returns to Sackett's Harbor, October 2, 179; his relations with Armstrong, 180-182; his expedition down the St. Lawrence, 184-191; goes into winter quarters at French Mills, 199; throws blame on Armstrong and Hampton, 199; advises evacuation of Fort George, 201; his administration at New Orleans, 214; seizes Mobile, 215; viii. 322; on Armstrong, vii. 406; court-martialed, 407; on Jacob Brown, 408; at French Mills, viii. 24; demands a court martial, 25; attacks Lacolle Mill, 25, 26; relieved and court-martialed, 26 27.

William and Mary, college of, i. 136.

Williams, A. J., captain of artillery in Hindman's battalion, viii. 37; in Fort Erie, 71; killed, 76.

Williams, David R., member of Congress from South Carolina, iii. 358; iv. 213; his argument in favor of the embargo, 266, 378; declares that the embargo is the wish of the South, 421, 426; on the repeal of the embargo, 436, 439, 448, 450, 451; not a member of the Eleventh Congress, v. 76; in the Twelfth Congress, vi. 122; chairman of military committee, 124, 435.

Williams, John, colonel of Thirty-Ninth U. S. Infantry, ordered to join Jackson, vii 245, 251; arrives at Fort Strother, 252.

Williams, Samuel, iv. 167, Pickering gives Rose a letter to, 235.

GENERAL INDEX.

Williams, Timothy, iv. 117.
Williamson, Colonel, Burr's agent, iii. 219, 229, 234, 238.
Wilna, in Poland, Barlow's journey to, vi. 263, 264.
Wilson, Alexander, describes New England in 1808, i. 19; on North Carolina, 36, 57, 124.
Wilson, Judge, i. 127.
Winchester, James, brigadier-general, vi. 201; yields command to Harrison, vii. 75; commands left division at Fort Defiance, 77, 78, 79; hardships of his men, 80; by Harrison's orders moves to the Maumee Rapids, 84, 86; his force, 87; sends detachment to Frenchtown, 88; follows to Frenchtown, 90; his account of the position, 91, 92; defeated and captured, 96; effect of his defeat on the Creek Indians, 223, 226, 227; commands at Mobile, 383, 385.
Winder, Levin, governor of Maryland in 1814, viii. 122, 168.
Winder, William H., colonel of Fourteenth Infantry, vi. 357, 359; brigadier-general, vii. 156; takes part in capture of Fort George, 157; advances to Stony Creek, 159; captured, 160; appointed to command new military district at Washington, viii. 122; his physical activity, 123, 131, 132; takes command of forces at the Woodyard, 133; retreats to the Old Fields, 134; retreats to the navy-yard, 135, 136; his letter to the Secretary of War, August 24, 137; his supposed motives for occupying the navy-yard, 135-138; starts for Bladensburg. 139; rides about the field, 140; retreats to the capitol, 142; retreats to Georgetown. 153, 156; retreats to Rockville, 154; his fear of responsibility, 154, 155; goes to Baltimore, 156; yields command to Samuel Smith, 167; his measures compared with Jackson's, 340-343.
Windham, County of, in Vermont, sends delegate to the Hartford Convention, viii. 293.
Wirt, William, counsel for government, iii. 445; his eloquence in Burr's trial, 465; his opinion of Chief-Justice Marshall, 469; his description of Madison in October, 1814, viii. 230, 231.
Wistar, Dr. Caspar, i. 127.
Wolcott, Alexander, v. 359, 360.
Wolcott, Oliver, iii. 199; republican candidate for governor of Connecticut, ix. 133.
Wood, Eleazar Derby, major of engineers, constructs Fort Meigs, vii. 93, 99, 104; ix. 235; his comments on the affair at the River Raisin, vii. 93; with Brown on the Niagara, viii. 47; directs entrenchments at Fort Erie, 67; takes command of Twenty-first Infantry, 74; leads sortie from Fort Erie, 87; killed, 88, 89.
Wood, John, his career, iii. 272; made editor of the "Western World" by Marshall and Daveiss, 273.
Woodyard, the, Winder's army camps at, viii. 134.
Wool, John E., captain of Thirteenth Infantry, gains Queenston Heights, vi. 349, 350.
Woollen manufactures, v. 17; depressed by the peace, ix. 96; fabrics in the tariff of 1816, ix. 111, 113, 114.
Worcester, Dr. Samuel, his reply to Channing, ix. 180, 181.
Wordsworth, William, i. 94; his lines on America, 169, 172.
Workman, Judge, iii. 303, 319.
Wright, Robert, member of Congress

from Maryland, his motion on impressments, v. 3o1, 352; opposes Gallatin's taxes, vi. 167; his threats against opposition, 213; on the payment of taxes in suspended bank paper, viii. 256.
Wythe, George, i. 133.

X. Y. Z. affair, i. 355, 358, 359.

YALE COLLEGE, i. 106; remains orthodox, ix. 186.
Yarnall, John J., lieutenant in U. S. navy, Perry's first officer on the "Lawrence," vii. 123; his comment on Elliott, 125.
Yazoo Act, i. 304.
Yazoo bill, passage of, vii. 401, 402; Marshall's decision on claims, ix. 189, 190.
Yazoo Compromise, ii. 210; Madison's measure, 211; vote upon, 217; the test of parties, iii. 119, 350; bill for settling rejected, 177.
Yeo, Sir James Lucas, British commodore on Lake Ontario, vii. 160; his attack on Sackett's Harbor, 164, 169; reinforces Kingston, 180, 181; captures "Vixen," 313; attacks Oswego, 29, 30; brings charges against Prevost, 112.
York, or Toronto, capital of Upper Canada, vi. 316; captured by Dearborn, vii. 152, 154, 155; public buildings burned, 155.
York, Duke of, v. 57, 58, 105.

"Yorktown," privateer, captured, vii. 329.
"Young Wasp," privateer, viii. 196.
Yrujo, Don Carlos Martinez, Spanish minister at Washington, his intimate relations with Jefferson, i. 425; writes to Morales with respect to the right of deposit, 427; announces the restoration of the right of deposit, ii. 3; protests against the sale of Louisiana, 92, 252 *et seq.*; his anger, 258, 389; obtains from American lawyers an opinion, 259; attacks Madison, 260; his affair with Jackson, 265; visits Jefferson at Monticello, 266; publishes counter statement as to his affair with Jackson, 268; relations of, with White House, 362; indiscretion, 368; at the White House, 369; concerts reprisals with Merry, 373; to be sent away, iii. 73, 74, 79; criticises Jefferson's message, 184; arrives in Washington, 185; receives a letter from Madison asking for his withdrawal, 186; his reply and subsequent conduct, 187 *et seq.*; his remonstrances about Miranda, 194, named minister to Milan, 196; attacks Madison in the press, 209; receives a secret visit from Dayton, 233; his report to his government respecting Burr's proposal, 236 *et seq.*; writes to Cevallos of Burr's communications, 247; notifies his government of Burr's intentions, 261; Burr's message to him, 264 *et seq.*; letter on Wilkinson, 342.